N·F·S GRUNDTVIG

Tradition and Renewal

Edinburgh University Library

RETURN BY

04. APR 91

06. NOV 91

27. NOV

14. JUN

29. JUL

29. AUG

1 1 OCT 1994

13. 06

- 1 DEC 1996

FINES RATE:

1. 10p per volume per day for NORMAL loans (6 wks).
2. 50p per volume per day for RECALLED books.

N·F·S GRUNDTVIG
Tradition and Renewal

Grundtvig's Vision of Man and People,
Education and the Church,
in Relation to World Issues Today

edited by
Christian Thodberg and
Anders Pontoppidan Thyssen

translated from the Danish by
Edward Broadbridge

published by
DET DANSKE SELSKAB
The Danish Institute
Copenhagen
1983

This book has been published on the occasion of the
bicentenary of the birth of N.F.S. Grundtvig, with the
support of the following banks: *Andelsbanken, Den
danske Bank, Handelsbanken, Privatbanken, Den danske
Provinsbank;* the savings banks: *Sparekassen SDS,
Bikuben;* the building societies: *Jyllands Kreditforening,
Kreditforeningen Danmark, Forenede Kreditforeninger;*
the foundations: *Tuborg Fondet, Augustinus Fonden,
Kong Christian den Tiendes Fond, Carlsberg Mindelegat,
Brugsforeningsbevægelsens* (the Co-op Movement)
Støttefond; as well as *Tipsmidler* (the Danish Football
Pools, through the Ministry of Cultural Affairs).
The book is also available in a French and a German
edition.

Graphic design by Johannes Jørgensen
Cover by Erik Ellegaard Frederiksen, IDD
Copy-edited by Brigitte Nøsted
Printed in Denmark by Special-Trykkeriet Viborg a-s,
Viborg

ISBN 87-7429-045-2

Cover: N.F.S. Grundtvig in 1847 (contemporary drawing
by P.C. Skovgaard)

Contents

III. THE LATER YEARS AND GRUNDTVIGIANISM

Preface

The aim of this book is to illuminate the most important areas in Grundtvig's thought and field of activity through essays by scholars who are particularly involved in the subjects in question. For the sake of clarity the essays have been divided chronologically into three main sections, though without sharp dividing-lines between the periods. The third section also considers Grundtvig's importance and the influence he exerted, directly or indirectly, up to 1900.

The authors represent various interests and occasionally treat the same subject from different viewpoints. The editors believe that such diversity, which is characteristic for an evaluation of Grundtvig in the current cultural debate in Denmark, is a valuable guideline. Grundtvig's wide-ranging world of ideas allows for a variety of studies, interpretations and consequences, as will also appear from the final chapter on Grundtvig research.

To illustrate the continuity between the various areas a brief biography has been included, in addition to the three chapters under the title, Grundtvig's Ideas on the Church and the People, which together offer a continuous survey of Grundtvig's development and achievement.

Finally the editors wish to offer their thanks to the funds and institutions who have provided support for the publication of this book.

April 1983

Christian Thodberg
Anders Pontoppidan Thyssen

Translator's Note

The interpretation of Grundtvig's ideas and philosophy is a tough task. It is not without cause that despite his enormous influence on Denmark his works have found relatively few translators. He flourished in the golden age of Danish literature and language, and stretched both to the full, so that particularly in his hymns and mid-life sermons his conceptual world and poetic vocabulary confront the translator with a frustrating choice between approximations. The classic example of this is the Danish word *folkelig*, which means 'pertaining to the cultural tradition and the national identity of the people' – this must be borne in mind when talking, for example, of grundtvigianism as a *popular* movement.

The general principle behind the translation has been to attain unity from article to article amid the variety of criticism and application of Grundtvig's ideas. All the translations have been produced in co-operation with the authors; any mistakes that remain are mine. After poems and hymns mentioned in the text the original Danish title has been added. Italics in the essays by Anders Pontoppidan Thyssen are the author's own, and denote key names, events or concepts under discussion. The English versions of Grundtvig's hymns are primarily translations of meaning and rhythm, sometimes at the expense of rhyme. Biblical quotations are from the Authorized Version.

Finally, my thanks go to Niels Lyhne Jensen for guidance with the translation of Grundtvig's sermon included in the book, and to my wife, Hanna, for invaluable advice and assistance.

Edward Broadbridge

A Brief Biography

by ANDERS PONTOPPIDAN THYSSEN and CHRISTIAN THODBERG

Nikolaj Frederik Severin Grundtvig was born in Udby on September 8th 1783 and died in Copenhagen on September 2nd 1872 after major achievements as a poet, priest and theologian, as a Norse philologist and philosopher, and as a historian, politician and educationalist. His father, Johan Ottosen Grundtvig (1734-1813), was the rector of Udby, a village near the town of Præstø in south Zealand; he was a learned, quiet man, characterized by a conservative Lutheran theology. Grundtvig's mother, Cathrine Marie Bang Grundtvig (1748-1822), was a strong-willed woman from an old clerical family through which Grundtvig believed he could trace his ancestry back to the vikings. From the family's permanent maid, Malene, he gained an impression of the speech, beliefs and superstitions of the peasantry.

From the autumn of 1792 Grundtvig was coached for the grammar school by Pastor Laurits Feld in Thyregod in central Jutland, west of Vejle. Here he became acquainted with the journals, periodicals and booklets of the enlightenment. In September 1798 he was admitted to Aarhus Cathedral Grammar School. In his later battle against "the black school" he painted the two years at the Cathedral School in dark colours. In September 1800 he left with a good report and soon after he passed his school-leaving exam in Copenhagen. He then read theology at Copenhagen University, gaining a first-class degree in October 1803. In the spring of 1801 he had broken with the orthodox, pietistic Christianity of his home and adopted the rationalist belief in God, virtue and immortality.

In the first few years after graduation Grundtvig began to pursue his literary ambitions, but nothing was published. From March 1805 until April 1808 he worked as a tutor at the manor of Egeløkke on Langeland. Here he soon fell in love with the lady of the manor, Constance Steensen-Leth. In the writings that grew out of German idealism – first and foremost in the works of the romantic philosopher, F.W.J. Schelling – and in Norse mythology Grundtvig found an interpretation of life that enabled him to understand and control his own situation.

The outcome of this fascination with Norse literature was *Norse My-*

9

thology, published in 1808 after Grundtvig had left Langeland and again taken up residence in Copenhagen in May of that year. The work interprets mythology as a way of understanding existence and not, as was common at the time, as a primitive teaching about the gods or as an expression of natural phenomena; the work gained widespread recognition. A number of articles for periodicals from 1806-07 had also been well-received, and in Copenhagen he had a job at the nearby grammar-school, the Schouboe Institute, from November 1808. During these years he produced a textbook on world history, which remained in manuscript, and a lengthy poem on the Norse "heroic life" and its transition to Christianity, published in two volumes as *Scenes* in 1809 and 1811. He had a number of other literary plans and looked forward to a career as a writer.

He did not, therefore, take very kindly to his father's request for him to return as his curate to Udby. To fulfil one of the conditions of his ordination, however, Grundtvig preached an examination sermon, the so-called probationary sermon, in March 1810 and published it two months later under the title *Why has the Word of the Lord Disappeared from His House?* It was an attack on sermons of the time as "ostentatious words and ingenious speeches ... nothing but learning, which is merely human messages". The Copenhagen clergy complained to the chancellery over these unfavourable comments and at the beginning of 1811 Grundtvig had to face the university's governing body and receive a reprimand.

At the same time his application for a curacy was turned down by the bishop on the grounds of seniority. In the autumn of 1810 Grundtvig resumed his studies with renewed vigour and began to dream that he was called to reform the Danish Church. These reforming visions came to an abrupt end, however; early in December 1810 the persistent question as to how far he himself was a Christian assumed an overwhelming force. Grundtvig was cast into a violent spiritual crisis with the result that shortly before Christmas he had to travel home to Udby. Here he gradually regained his strength, and his father applied yet again to have his son as curate. This time the request was granted; in May 1811 Grundtvig was ordained and inducted.

During the two years or so at Udby he performed his duties with great zeal. He also found time for literary pursuits, making his greatest impact with *Brief Concept of World Chronicle in Context* 1812. Contemporary criticism of the work was directed mainly at its often sharp attacks on great men of the past and present. The book was a reworking of the textbook in world history that Grundtvig had produced earlier and it reflects "the strange metamorphosis" which as a result of the events of 1810-11 had altered his view of life. After the crisis he had returned spiritually to the orthodox, pietistic Christianity of his childhood home. On the basis of this biblical Christianity he had written out of the conviction that the Creation and Christ are the corner-stones of history, and that the overall control by God's Providence is the explanation of its course. At about the same time he wrote a long poem, *Roskilde Rhyme,* which was to be a national and poetic companion to the *World Chronicle.* In both works he sets out to describe "God's control and our forefathers' achievements" in order to revive both the Church and the people.

The publication of the *World Chronicle* gave rise to literary controversies with, among others, Christian Molbech, a friend since youth, and H.C. Ørsted, the physicist. The disagreement with Ørsted was mainly over their evaluation of Schelling, whom Grundtvig now accused of having harmonized in his philosophy of identity what are actually life's contradictions, including the contradiction between good and evil.

In January 1813 Grundtvig's father died and Grundtvig's position as curate automatically expired. He therefore moved back to Copenhagen, where he preached occasionally. Although he managed to publish two significant poetry collections, *Little Songs* and *Heimdall* in 1815, his situation grew steadily more isolated. Contributory causes to this were not only the above-mentioned literary feuds but also Grundtvig's provocative behaviour at the diocesan conventions. All the applications he made in the period 1813-20 were rejected.

In 1815 he decided to give up the ministry. He lacked support from his audience against the attacks of his contemporaries, who accused him of fanaticism. He preferred therefore to go indirectly to work. History itself must now contribute to a revelation of the truth concerning the meaning and purpose of life. The end of his biblical Christian period was marked by the publication of *Biblical Sermons* in 1816.

This new standpoint is the basis for his comprehensive historiography in the following years; mention must be made of his new world history *Prospect of the World Chronicle* from 1817, which concentrates its account on "the age of Luther". He later published major translations, of Saxo (I-III, 1818-22) and of Snorri (I-III, 1818-22). In addition he translated the Old English poem *Beowulf.* From 1816 to 1819 he published the periodical *Danevirke,* which contained poems such as *The Easter Lily,* a poetic drama (in Vol. I, 1816-17), and a number of weighty essays on philosophical and historical subjects. It is worth noting the clear strain of John Locke's empirical philosophy running through these essays. In this

11

period the foundations are laid of the major concepts of Grundtvig's later works, such as Danishness, the people, the spirit of the people, the living word, etc.

From 1818 Frederik VI supplied Grundtvig with an annual grant of 600 *rigsdaler,* thus enabling him to marry Lise Blicher. In February 1821 without applying for the post he was appointed to the living of Præstø and Skibbinge, and in the autumn of 1822 he fulfilled the long-cherished hope of acquiring a parish in Copenhagen when he was made curate of the Church of Our Saviour in Christianshavn.

The move to Copenhagen was at first a disappointment, partly because Grundtvig's literary efforts were not given the appreciation he had expected. At the turn of the year 1823-24, however, he took fresh courage. The best-known poetic results of this breakthrough in addition to *The Land of the Living* are *New Year's Morn,* a deeply symbolic poem of 312 stanzas, and the hymn *O Welcome Again,* written at Christmas 1824. In this respect it is important to note that in *New Year's Morn,* for example, Grundtvig demonstrates his own independent thinking on the relationship between form and content. In "the Word", the word as image, the content and the form are not, as is generally assumed, separated, but fused together.

During his ministry Grundtvig came to a deeper and deeper appreciation of the church service, and his antagonism towards the rationalist message of his age led him step by step to the conviction that God's *word* to man is not to be found first and foremost in the written, biblical word but in the word that is spoken at baptism and Holy Communion. Throughout history, he argues, the written word has been subjected to the divergent interpretations of theologians. The living word from the Lord Himself –, that is, the Creed, the words of personal address at baptism and the words of initiation at Holy Communion – have by contrast been heard and remained unchanged since the days of the early Church. Thus the Christian's firm foundation is not to be found in the Bible but wherever a congregation gathers around God's spoken word at baptism and Holy Communion.

There was a direct reason why Grundtvig came to the fore with his new view of life. In 1825 the young theology professor, H.N. Clausen, published a large volume on *The Church Constitution, Teaching and Ritual of Catholicism and Protestantism.* A fortnight later Grundtvig's response was ready – *The Church's Retort,* a counter-attack directed mainly at Clausen's view of the Church. Whereas Clausen had defined the Church in somewhat abstract terms as "a community for the promotion of general religiosity", Grundtvig maintains that the Church is a concrete fact with a historical origin. It is a community that has existed since the time of the apostles, and it is there that one must look for information as to what the Church is. This is the background for the charge of false teaching that Grundtvig levelled a Clausen, together with a demand that he resign his post as professor of theology. Clausen brought a libel case – and won it. Grundtvig was sentenced to lifelong censorship.

Whereas previously he had stood alone, Grundtvig now acquired a number of energetic and younger comrades-in-arms. Among those who joined him mention must be made of the highly-gifted Jacob Christian Lindberg (1797-1857), a master of arts, who continued the battle in a series of pamphlets. It was his historical achievement to establish a link between Grundtvig and the lay circles that were in the grip of the religious revival of the time. The basis was thus laid for the later movement within the Church known as grundtvigianism. Early in the movement's history we note that Grundtvig's view of the Church was gradually extended to include a special theory that the Creed concerning Jesus was imparted to the disciples in the 40 days between the resurrection and the ascension. The fundamental element of Grundtvig's view, however, was the unity created by the Holy Spirit between the risen Christ and the Word of Faith confessed by the Church.

In May 1826 Grundtvig resigned his post. There were several reasons, including the lawsuit and other setbacks. He also wished to resume writing. A year earlier he had joined a friend in publishing *Theological Monthly* (I-XIII, 1825-28), in which the double article from 1826-27 *On True Christianity* and *On the Truth of Christianity* are of theological importance. Partly for the use of his own children he produced the *Chronicle in Rhyme for Childhood Teaching* (1829). In 1827 *Nik. Fred. Sev. Grundtvig's Literary Testament* was published, induced by the censorship upon him; this was followed by *Christian Sermons or The Sunday Book* (I-III, 1827-31), which amplifies the preaching of previous years.

Between 1829 and 1831 Grundtvig was given official support to undertake three trips to England for the purpose of studying medieval English manuscripts. His plans to publish these resulted in English scholars also setting to work on the task. The most lasting benefit for Grundtvig himself was the confrontation with another way of life in England. It was the English realism and practicality together with their sense of spiritual and secular freedom that left the deepest impression on him.

A number of his publications in the 1830's are considered to be major works. This is particularly true of *Norse Mythology* (1832), in which he presents himself as the spokesman for a broad collaboration towards a new scholarship on the basis of the Norse cultural heritage. In Grundtvig's opinion this Norse tradition built on a deeper understanding of mankind and life than classical learning – not as clear concepts but as a wonderful mystery of divine forces that will only reveal itself in the course of history. The study of "the course of mankind" was therefore to be the main task of the new scholarship, with its centre in a civic academy, where all who were to be the leaders of society could study geography, history and the language of the country as well as working to develop practical skills. The positions adopted in *Norse Mythology* also form the basis for the description of the history of peoples and nations in *Handbook on World History* (I-III, 1833ff).

Other influential works of the 1830's are Grundtvig's educational writings, the first of which, *The Danish Four-Leaf Clover,* was published in 1836. In this and a number of later books and articles he presents his ideas for a free, living and natural popular education. The teaching was to be based not on books but primarily on the living, spoken word in the native language. "The school for life" could be realised through the interaction of conversation between teacher and pupil and among pupils themselves. Its content was to be found both in the present conditions of the people and in their history and literature (including their myths), which are the expression of their own particular nature. Education was to be realistic and at the same time "historical and poetic". Already in the 1840's and 1850's a number of folk high schools were founded whose aims and methods were greatly inspired by Grundtvig's ideas.

Equally significant was Grundtvig's work on the renewal of the hymnbook. He had taken up this task as early as 1811 but it was not completed until now. The first volume of his *Song-Work for the Danish Church,* published in 1837, contains about 400 of his own roughly 1,500 hymns. In addition to this original production the collection contains a large number of Grundtvig's adaptations of hymns from the Church tradition, not only from the Danish and the Lutheran but also from the Anglo-Saxon, the Roman Catholic and the Byzantine Greek Church liturgy. Grundtvig's hymn collection is thus universal in its design: it is the holy *Universal* Church that manifests itself here.

In 1837 Grundtvig was freed from censorship and was thus able to comply with the request from a number of young academics to give a series of public lectures on modern history. These lectures were given the title *Within Living Memory* and were held at Borch's College in the summer and autumn of 1838. They were an unqualified success, which was repeated in the winter of 1843-44 when he gave another series of public lectures at Borch's College on Greek and Norse myths.

From 1832 until 1839 Grundtvig worked as an unpaid preacher at evensong in Frederik's Church (now Christian's Church) in Christianshavn. Not until 1839 did he acquire a permanent post again, when he was appointed rector of Vartov Hospital Church, a modest living which he could manage alongside his studies and his literary pursuits. Grundtvig's steadily growing audience now had a gathering-place. The appointment also meant that for the last 30 years or so of his life he was free of financial worries. And his success with the public lectures inaugurated a new period in his life, characterized by a growing public acknowledgment of his importance. During the reign of Christian VIII and Caroline Amalie from 1840-48 he also enjoyed royal favour.

His educational theories gained a wider and wider hearing; they were put into practice especially in private folk high schools, teacher training colleges and free schools. The fact that he was a member of parliament (the *Rigsdag*) for most of the period 1848-58 can be seen as proof that he managed to win the confidence of the common man. As a politician he was an advocate of freedom in all areas, especially in school and Church matters; he also spoke out on behalf of the common man in general and the peasantry in particular. In Church matters grundtvigianism appeared in the course of the 1860's as a sort of Church party, not least at the so-called "friends' meetings". At the 50th anniversary celebration of his entering the Church he was placed alongside the Bishop of Zealand in recognition of his achievement in renewing the Danish Hymnbook.

Among Grundtvig's works from the later years there are a number of political booklets and poems occasioned by events of the time, such as the granting of the constitution in 1849, the Three Years War 1848-50, and Denmark's defeat by the Germans in 1864. The most detailed expression of his political ideas is to be found in the weekly journal *The Dane,* which he published from 1848-51. Then came a series of essays on the Church and Church politics. Posterity has been particularly interested in *Christian Childhood Teachings,* written originally for the journal *Church Collector* 1855-61 and first published in book-form in 1868. This work is still regarded by many as a major source for the study of Grundtvig's theology.

To his Christian didactic poetry belongs *The Pleiades of Christendom,* 800 or so stanzas first published in *Danish Church Times* 1854-55 and in book-form in 1860. Drawing on the inspiration of the visions in Revelation the poem interprets the history of the Christian Church as a development through six national Churches: the Hebraic, the Greek, the Roman, the English, the German and the Nordic. These ideas were elaborated in the lectures in Church history which were published in 1871 under the title *Church Mirror.*

Grundtvig's first wife was the daughter of a clergyman from Falster, Elisabeth (Lise) Christina Margaretha Blicher, born on September 28th 1787 and died on January 14th 1851. Their marriage took place on August 12th 1818. They had two sons: Johan (1822-1907) who became a historian, and Svend (1824-83) who became a Scandinavian philologist; and a daughter, Meta (1827-87, married Boisen). On October 24th 1851 Grundtvig married a widow, Marie Toft, who was born Ane Marie Elise Carlsen on August 4th 1813 at Old Køge Manor (*Gammel Køgegård*): her first husband had been H.P.N. Toft (1812-41) of Rønnebæksholm, who held a masters degree in law. Marie died on July 9th 1854 after bearing a son, Frederik Lange (1854-1903) later a folklorist and Danish clergyman in America. On April 6th 1858 Grundtvig was married for a third time, to Asta Reedtz, born Countess Asta Tugendreich Adelheid Krag-Juel-Vind-Frijs on March 12th 1826 at Vederslund. She had previously been married to a former Foreign Secretary, H.C. Reedtz of Palsgård (1800-57). With her Grundtvig had a daughter, Asta Marie Elisabeth Frijs (1860-1939, married Poulsen). Countess Asta died on October 5th 1890. She was buried near Grundtvig in a vault on Køge Ridge in the forest adjoining Old Køge Manor.

Grundtvig's importance for Denmark is hard to assess. As a poet, clergyman and educationalist, philosopher and politician his energies and achievements set up a chain reaction that not only encompassed the popular and Church movement that bears his name (grundtvigianism), but has also, for example, left its mark on the economic restructuring of Danish agriculture at the end of the 19th century and on the whole co-operative movement.

During the Second World War an intense interest in Grundtvig arose; among other things his songs for the people experienced a renaissance as an expression of the national character of the Danes. In 1947 the Grundtvig Society was founded, which has since been instrumental in publishing an extensive range of scholarly works. In developing countries too Grundtvig's ideas of national identity have been influential. In the last few years the youth protest movement, neo-marxism and its subsequent political movements have drawn inspiration from him. Recent Church movements have interpreted Grundtvig in a way that proves his ideas on the Church and the people are still far from being exhausted.

NOTE

The editors of this biography are grateful to *K.E. Bugge* for the use of his Grundtvig biography in *Dansk biografisk leksikon* (Danish Bibliographical Lexicon), 3rd ed., vol. V, p. 318ff. Copenhagen 1980. This "Brief Biography" differs, however, in several respects from K.E. Bugge's.

N.F.S. Grundtvig in 1820. Painting by C.F. Christensen, Frederiksborg Museum.

Udby Church, which Grundtvig attended as a child and where he later (1811-13) served as curate.

Udby Vicarage, where Grundtvig was born. The wing on the left was the curate's residence. (From A Hundred Years. A Memorial Volume, ed. F. Rønning, 1883).

I
THE YOUNGER GRUNDTVIG

Grundtvig and Romanticism

by Flemming Lundgreen-Nielsen

I

N. F. S. Grundtvig lived practically the whole of his active life as a writer in the age of romanticism. Danish literary histories regard him as one of the major figures in the golden age of Denmark, the period in which romanticism and neo-classicism united in a harmonious idealism. But was Grundtvig a romantic in the European sense of the word?

The question cannot be answered as easily as it is put. At least two possibilities come to mind. The first is concerned with Grundtvig's direct relationship to romanticism, above all to German romanticism, as it was moulded by poets and philosophers around 1800. This is dealt with in Sections II-VI. The second answer, in Sections VII-XI, considers which romantic ideas and structures Grundtvig admits into his imaginative world and his literary productions, especially in the later areas of his work.

II

In his early youth Grundtvig was, surprisingly enough, a supporter and pupil of 18th century intellectualism. Politically he was a radical – tolerant, and a champion of liberty after Voltaire's heart. His Danish models are the intellectual satirist, Ludvig Holberg, from the first half of the 18th century, and Holberg's bold and provocative disciples in the second half, the playwright and critic, P. A. Heiberg, and the versifier, T. C. Bruun.

Grundtvig's unpublished poetic efforts around 1800, the work of a schoolboy, student and fully-fledged theological graduate, imitate a number of late 18th century genres in Danish poetry, though not the hymn. In a historical novel in 1803, *Ulfhild,* Grundtvig writes a footnote in which he excuses his hero, Harald, for bursting out in poetry by explaining that in those days the poetic art was so respected that princes gained as much honour through poetry as through their warlike display. In his comedy *The Private Schoolmasters* from the previous year he ridicules a modern pedagogue called Fichte for his emotional and free-and-easy attitude to life by having him compose self-centred, lyrical, unrhymed verses. Grundtvig has no confidence in the romantic belief in the power of poetry and its prestige in the higher ranks of society.

This is not due to his ignorance of the main ideas of German romanticism. He had listened doggedly to, and taken random detailed notes from, the philosophical lectures and subsequent talks on Goethe that his cousin, the philosopher Henrich Steffens, had given in Copenhagen in 1802-03. But he had completely failed to understand the basic premises and had been content to note down the most paradoxical phrases so that he could use them, like another peasant student in Holberg, in order to excel in witty conversation – a social convention which by nature and upbringing he otherwise found difficult during his student days in Copenhagen.

Steffens had given an account of the German Jena-romanticism's view of learning in general, and of natural history, world history and the place of the individual in the overall unity in particular. According to the lectures that are preserved, however, he did not deal with romanticism's view of language, inherited from the monographs that J. G. Herder produced in his youth around 1770. Then, in the summer of 1804, in a period of intense self-tuition, Grundtvig learned Old Icelandic, and in a series of unpublished stories from the saga-material he transferred a number of Icelandic words to Danish and formed Danish phrases after the Icelandic. Without his knowing it, this practice was in accordance with the romantic philosophy of language: return to the source of language, to its original purity. This resulted in a breakthrough for his poetry in its concentration and power, while his prose remained dominated by the pedantic, intellectual style of argument that is characteristic of the late 18th century.

At the beginning of April 1805 Grundtvig arrived at Egeløkke Manor on the island of Langeland, where he was to work as tutor to a 7-year-old boy. He immediately fell violently and unhappily in love with the boy's mother, Constance Steensen-Leth. The pages of Grundtvig's diary that tell of his first six months on Langeland are lost: they have been torn out. Doubtless Constance handled her gauche, young tutor with the natural elegance and charm of the upper class, while Grundtvig, unaccustomed to society life and with precious little talent for it, let himself be blinded, enthralled, carried away. He read aloud to her while the boy played in the corner, and she played music to him or conversed with him spiritually. In the evening when he went up to his room, he sat down to work through all the dangerous impressions of the day. At this point romantic philosophy came to his aid. In his loneliness he tries to establish a picture of the world in which Constance does not rule; in his diary notes he recalls Steffens' lectures and now for the first time he understands them. As a further safeguard he decides to read in private romantics such as Fichte and Schelling.

In July 1805 he comments in his journal on a memorandum from his (now lost) 1802-diary concerning Addison's depreciation of music as an art form in *The Spectator*.[1] Grundtvig now believes that art – painting, sculpture, literature, music – can be defined as "poetic" in the romantic sense: it reflects a "higher existence only to be glimpsed". He introduces a terminological distinction between art and poetry. Art is the craft's form (in paint, stone, words, notes) and falls into randomly divided subjects. Poetry is constituted across the subject boundaries by a conception of life orientated towards a higher existence in eternity.

Immediately after his 22nd birthday in September 1805 Grundtvig joins the romantic school. That is the conclusion of a discussion that stretches over three days in his diary.[2] Its subject is the nature of poetry. Grundtvig rejects various definitions of poetry from the 18th century and discovers himself to be actually in agreement with Steffens in his 8th lecture: poetry is everything that bears the stamp of the eternal, and man has a means of sensing this in the pure, natural perception of the inner eye and ear. By natural perception Grundtvig understands an internal and innate ability to distinguish the higher meaning that lies beneath the surface that ordinary senses stop at.

However, Grundtvig also has objections to romanticism. For the time being he has no solution to the problem of how to express such a poetic totality in earthly form, for example in language. The perfect assimilation between the inner experience and the material medium can never be realised. A further problem for him is that a life striving towards the higher sphere of eternity will carry with it a painful discrepancy between the dull, everyday life and the higher but intangible existence. And thus the romantic poet suffers from a certain sickliness. He names Klopstock and Wieland as representatives of this type of romantic, but even more obviously he could have included Novalis and Hölderlin in Germany and the lyric poet, A. W. Schack Staffeldt, in Denmark.

Grundtvig ends by proposing a practical compromise to himself: he should also recognize as examples of the spirit's striving towards essential poetry lower and less perfect degrees of poetry than the absolute, which man in any case cannot achieve in this life. It is characteristic of Grundt-vig that he considers the poet's practical position in everyday life rather than turn his back on the world to plumb his own depths. It is even more characteristic that his conversion to romantic philosophy takes place rationally, tested for logic, not through the bursting of an emotional dam.

A book-list dated just before Christmas 1805 shows that Grundtvig now owns Fichte's *The Destination of Man* (1800), and Schelling's *Bruno* (1802). Both works would have confirmed him in his application of an overall view to existence in which the spirit is the motivating force in everything. This new widening of his perception, this new rethinking of his life from a horizontal plane onto a vertical one has a directly negative effect on his writing efforts. Whereas in previous years he had written freely in many different literary genres, he now writes nothing at all for the next six months.

His study of Schelling continues in the spring of 1806. In a diary which he writes in order to keep track of his pupil's progress, we can see how he has tried to teach the child "to place a deeper sense in reality without being repelled by its external effects", – in other words a practical application of the new-found poetic view of life.[3] At the same time Grundtvig tries to persuade himself to see Constance as an incidental expression – for him alone unhappy and painful – of a longing for eternity. She must be an instrument to turn his way of life towards the poetic, not the object of his desire. This is how peace of mind on earth is to be found: "the Ultimate must be purified of all the Confining, or it must coincide with its pure primordial vision. The inner vision must no longer be the enemy of perception (...)".[4] For the present Grundtvig cannot compose on this formula. A few love poems to Constance sent with a selection of flowers are allegories, and, being stylized on the pattern of Holberg's mock-heroic poem *Peder Paars*: "Of charming thoughts alone does poesie con-sist", they hardly amount to romantically transported self-expression.

Also Friedrich Schiller's aesthetic, historical and poetical works find a place on Grundtvig's writing-desk. Schiller's experiment in regenerating and renewing the Greek drama of fate in *The Bride from Messina* is discussed in some notes which in 1807 turn into a printed essay in the Copenhagen periodical *New Minerva*.[5] Grundtvig credits Schiller for the idealistic direction his poetry takes, but regrets that Schiller has engaged himself in an artificial, man-made harmonization of the eternal and the temporal. He maintains instead that the modern reader can only identify with heroes like Schiller's Karl Moor in *The Robbers,* Don Carlos, Joan of Arc and above all, Shakespeare's Hamlet. For they fought on the basis of their glimpse of the eternal in their miserable existence, just as their reader must do today. The unharmonious and incomplete element in them is the fact that their lives are not perfectly rounded off – there is a defect in art. But it is precisely this that at the same time is the signal for "a profusion of poetry", the longing for eternity. Here is where the modern reader can invest his feelings, be carried along in joy and tears. On the other hand Schiller's Sicilians, in classical style, submit calmly to the vicissitudes of life in their belief in a superhuman fate. For Grundtvig, only the absolute engagement in the poetic can free man from his detested earthly existence, and then only in flashes. In this amplification of his thought in the printed essay he shares romanticism's high estimation of literature as a path to the eternal. In a passage struck out of his private notes he has clarified his viewpoint: the reconciliation to existence of the classical Schiller – and also of Goethe – is an obvious illusion, in fact it is identical with Paul's category: man's service of vanity, in Romans 8:19-23, whilst the poetic form of life corresponds to the description in the same passage of the sighing of the creature longing for the glorious liberty of the children of God. In this rejected draft Grundtvig moves from self-centred romanticism to a subject that is greater than the self: Christianity. For various personal reasons he does not immediately draw the conclusions of this conviction. The years 1807-10 are the most romantic in his life as a writer.

For the rest of his long life Grundtvig prefers poetry – the right direction, to art – the polished form. Thus in painting he places Leonardo da Vinci's mere sketch of Christ's face in The Last Supper above Raphael's completed pictures (in a note from 1810).[6] Here perhaps is the reason why Grundtvig wrote so many fragmentary and half-finished poems, for which he has had to face much criticism from men of letters and literary historians.

III

In the years 1805-09 Denmark's principal romantic, Adam Oehlenschläger, was given royal support to live abroad in Germany, France and Italy in order to develop his poetic talent. In his absence Grundtvig appears before the Copenhagen public as a romantic.

On Langeland in 1806 he had acquired Oehlenschläger's *Poetical Writings* (1805). He was immediately seized with boundless admiration for *Vaulundur's Saga*, an Old Norse legend about the patiently striving artist which Oehlenschläger had re-written as an old-fashioned yet familiar-sounding prose tale. Characteristically for Grundtvig, he attached little or no importance to Oehlenschläger's programmed genie-drama *Aladdin and the Wonderful Lamp,* doubtless because at the end of it Aladdin trusts in his own strength in the battle against evil and fails to make use of the lamp, the God-given power.

Grundtvig's preference for Oehlenschläger's Norse saga rather than his oriental drama also had something to do with his own attempts after 1800 to utilize material from Norse antiquity. At Egeløkke one of his most effective safeguards against Constance's smile and glance had been his absorption in the Norse past. Grundtvig had a vague feeling – a romantic concept! – that there was more meaning in our forefathers' paganism than scholars of the 18th century could see.

At the same time as he was in raptures over *Vaulundur* his attention was drawn to a poem by the Copenhagen academic, Jens Møller, written in the contemptuous and deliberately anachronistic style of the previous decade on a poem, *Skirnir's Journey, (Skírnismál)* in the *Elder Edda.* In great haste (and indignation!) Grundtvig produced a retort to Møller's un-historical treatment of the material – *Brief Comment on the Songs of the Edda.* The article was published in *New Minerva* in September 1806. It is most noteworthy for containing the first sketch of an overall view of the Aesir-mythology. Its model is found in Steffens' 7th and 8th lectures where in fewer than 30 pages he surveyed the whole course of the history of the world.

Even more important, Jens Møller's verse narrative apparently prompted Grundtvig to attempt a rewriting of *Skírnismál* in a little Edda-like song: *Freyr's Love (Freis Kærlighed).*[7] This poem, which was first printed in 1808, is in several respects pure romanticism. The choice of subject, the nation's ancient religion, fulfils romanticism's search for the identity of the individual nation. The tendency to see the action around Freyr, his helper Skirnir, and the maiden Gerd as one episode amongst many leading to Ragnarok is a transference of romanticism's view of history as epic drama into mythology. In the actual poetic execution Grundtvig places great emphasis on burning love as a motive, in many metaphors of fire and flower, both of which were favourite areas of imagery for romantics such as Steffens and Staffeldt. In the long cursing-scene, extended even further by Grundtvig, the tremendous power of the word, i.e. poetry, is demonstrated romantically. And Grundtvig has very carefully adapted his style and content to a unique form. The motions of love are expressed in modern end-rhymed verse, whereas the rough action in the Old Norse story is worked out in short, chopping, partly alliterative lines.

Most arch-romantics are recognizable by their absorption in their own inner being and by their development of an imaginative world with only an airy connection to earthly existence. It is paradoxical that Grundtvig's way into literary romanticism is a flight *from* the self and sexuality into mythology, history and theology. The picture begins to flicker.

In the following years of his writing Grundtvig is now within the bounds of romanticism, now overstepping them from a direct or unspoken impulse in his view of Christianity. In an essay printed in 1807, *On Religion and Liturgy,* he rejects Schelling's philosophy of identity and any deification of literature in favour of the divine revelation. Another essay from the same year, *On Scholarship and its Encouragement,* romantically maintains not only that spirit controls and forms material reality, but also that the spiritual life presupposes the religious impulse. A more scholarly documented article from 1807, *On Norse Mythology,* presents an all-embracing interpretation of Norse mythology and by way of comparison describes Greek mythology as a work of art, while the Norse mythology through Ragnarok and the subsequent golden age is called truly poetic. Both judgements point back to Steffens' distinction between art and poetry.

In the summer of 1808 Grundtvig began bit by bit to interpret his own life so far. The draft of a poem *Journey in the Summer of 1807* (*Rejsen i Sommeren 1807*) is an early forerunner of his confessionary, symbolic poem, *The Hill by the Sea at Egeløkke* (1811) (*Strandbakken ved Egeløkke*). Here he describes his path away from Constance, from love and from his own narrow self towards an objective material, the pagan North, represented in the text by the friend of his youth, P. N. Skougaard. However, he still lacked the necessary distance to his Egeløkke feelings, nor had he developed his understanding of the coherence in Norse paganism in sufficient detail. The poem was not ready for printing until Grundtvig was on the other side of his human breakdown and Christian breakthrough around Christmas 1810.

In practice and in literature Grundtvig continued with romanticism. On his departure as chaplain to the Langeland militia he gave a sermon in November 1807 in which he urged the Langelanders to stand or fall in the battle, just like the Norse of old, if they should have to fight against Denmark's English enemies. In the booklet *The Masked Ball in Denmark* from March 1808 Grundtvig nurtures the romantic intention to exhort the present to serious action by referring to the heroic achievements of the past, heathen or Catholic, against the English. In its execution, however, this strange little story interspersed with songs – Grundtvig's first book –

is more a dry, intellectual allegory than what the sub-title promised: "a vision". In the confusion surrounding the death of Christian VII it quite escaped public attention.

Well-ensconced in Copenhagen in May 1808 Grundtvig set out to win over the general public and the educated reader to his form of romanticism. In a newspaper article in 1809 he recommended the preservation of the barrows that were scattered around the country, because only as monuments in their original positions did they have any meaning, whilst the unearthing of pots and bones would not increase the qualitative knowledge of the pagan past. He composed to order an inscription with an Old Norse ring to it for the monument to the naval hero, Peter Willemoes, and the other fallen in the battle against the English off Zealand Spit (*Sjællands Odde*) in March 1808, – probably some of Grundtvig's best-known lines. And in the summer of 1810, when the sudden death of the heir to the Swedish throne opened Grundtvig's eyes to the possibility of a united Scandinavia, he wrote a majestically authoritative elegy for the prince and followed it up with a pamphlet to the Swedish people. By pointing to Denmark-Norway's and Sweden's common language and religion he attempted to move the Swedish parliament into choosing Frederik VI of Denmark as the new heir to the Swedish throne. In this he failed, but he had placed himself before the Scandinavian peoples as a poet who delivered judgements and as a historian. Romanticism's very high estimation of the poet as, if not God's, then at least the Eternal's or history's mouthpiece, a worldly seer, breaks through here – just as it does in the meticulous composition and solemnly imposing style of the elegy and the prose-work.

Grundtvig's more traditionally literary initiatives were also strongly tinged with romanticism. The programme and confessionary poem from 1808 *Gunderslev Forest* (*Gunderslev Skov*) describes the self's intuitively motivated journey through a dark and enclosed forest to a large and ancient dolmen, which in a moment of inspiration he hails as an altar once used in honour of the Aesir. This apparent archaeological error of judgement has no serious consequences for the vitality of the poem. Its subject is the path, the direction of the spiritual endeavour, and passionate engagement as the driving-force. But the poem contains no mythological details, nor is there a proposal for the reawakening of belief in the Norse gods. In its form the content is adapted to the metre in verse-lines of different length with a variety of rhyme-schemes. The poem is a companion piece to the work that marks the breakthrough of Danish romanticism, Oehlenschläger's symbolic lyric poem, *The Gold Horns* (*Guldhornene*) from 1802.

Under the impact of the English bombardment of Copenhagen and the carrying off of the navy in the autumn of 1807, both Oehlenschläger and his older rival, Jens Baggesen, had published inspiring national ballads in the style of the old Danish popular ballad; Grundtvig joined in with poems in a Copenhagen newspaper, including in 1809 *Evening* (*Aftenen*) on the murder of Knud Lavard, which was followed historically by a regeneration of the race and the kingdom under Valdemar the Great; and the more personal *In Praise of Freyja* (*Freias Pris,*) where Grundtvig finds reconciliation with the nature of spring, which stimulates the senses far too much, by interpreting it in terms of Norse mythology. An elegiac romance on Peter Willemoes from 1810 *Come Hither, Little Girls!* (*Kommer hid, I Piger smaa!*) achieves a powerful effect by lauding the hero's posthumous reputation in the framework of a girl's song of mourning for his great deeds. The poem is reminiscent of the late 18th century historical everyday idyll by the dramatist, Thomas Thaarup.

A purer, and deliberately provocative, romanticism is to be found, also with imitations of Shakespeare and Oehlenschläger, in Grundtvig's most ambitious product of the decade: the plan to rewrite in numerous booklets of plays and prose a thousand years of Norse paganism from Odin's appearance to the end of the mythology in the fall of Palnatoke and Jomsburg. Apart from a few attempts at saga-like narratives Grundtvig only completed and published the first and last part of the whole project. *Scenes from the Decline of Heroic Life in the North* (1809), in deliberate competition with Oehlenschläger's tragedy *Hakon Earl the Mighty* (1807), describes the ending of pagan belief in Denmark. *Scenes from the Battle of Norns and Aesir* written in 1809-10, published in 1811, deals with the history of the Volsunga race with Sigurd and Brynhild as central figures; after his crisis around Christmas 1810 Grundtvig added characters and scenes with a Christian-didactic purpose in mind, even though they obviously conflicted with the purely pagan plot. Both of the *Scenes* are characterized by Grundtvig's vacillation between the aesthetically attractive pagan heroism and the steady advance of his biblical orthodoxy. Artistically the *Scenes* testify to Grundtvig's romanticism as regards both composition and language, with contrasts between the love idyll and scenes of brutal violence, with a certain aesthetic of ugliness in the dialogue's expression of strong passions, with unexpected changes from comedy to tragedy and vice versa, and above all with an old Norse and old Danish inventory of single words and set phrases that far exceeds what Oehlenschläger had offered his public. Grundtvig's pieces were also romantic in being closet drama (with stage instructions in the epic past tense) – not calculated for the Royal Theatre.

He was to persevere with his romantic philosophy of history and philology in 1810. At the start of the year he invited subscriptions both for as literal a translation as was possible of the *Elder Edda*, and for a journal (together with the philosopher F. C. Sibbern) to be called *Odin and Saga*, whose guiding principles were to be found in romanticism's overall view of history and poetry. But neither of the projects met with sufficient interest.

Privately he reached a high point of romantic symbolism as a poet with the poem he wrote on the occasion of his elderly father's 50th anniversary as a clergyman in December 1810. In one stanza at least he demonstrates his ability to develop and transform a number of in themselves ambiguous metaphors and to rivet them together in brief lines without padding and with rhyme that seems both natural and meritorious. This style, which is the best possible illustration of the justification of the high appreciation romanticism places on symbols, is to be found later in Grundtvig's writing in his most successful lyrical pieces – *The Easter Lily* (1817) (*Paaske-Lilien*) and *New Year's Morn* (1824) (*Nyaars-Morgen*).

However, already before the two *Scenes* (1809-11), with which his first period as a poet comes to an end, Grundtvig had broken decisively with the romantic view of life in favour of his former emphasis on the power of Christianity.

This happened in December 1808, when he published *Norse Mythology,* a major work in the literature of the decade. The book is the first attempt to create a comprehensive unity out of the heterogeneous sources of Norse mythology. Its principle of scholarship is precisely the same as romanticism's inner philosophy, "the deeper sense", and on this principle Grundtvig arranges the sources in accordance with their significance for the unity he senses. In his treatment of individual myths Grundtvig upholds a platonic dualism in his representation of love. Finally he presents a theory that the whole of Norse mythology has been created by an old and gifted poet, who wanted to put into order all the contradictory phenomena of life and therefore interpreted them into a colossal tragedy in five acts. So far the book's attitude is pure romanticism.

But towards the end of the work Grundtvig oversteps the borders he himself has set in a surprising manner. He resolutely declares that Ragnarok, which he depicts in detail on the basis of his guiding-star, the Edda poem, *The Sooth-saying of the Volva,* never came. There is reasonable evidence in the myths themselves for this, inasmuch as in the various medieval sources Ragnarok appears only in prophecies of the future. But that is not the reason Grundtvig gives for nullifying the Norse drama. He maintains that its progress was stopped when another son of the Norse Father of the Universe (*Alfader*) who was purer than Odin, namely Christ, descended to earth, dethroned the selfish Aesir, destroyed the wicked giants and blew fresh life into the dying divine spark. These heroic feats, which are not reported in the New Testament, triumph over the hypothetical pagan poet's explanation of the baffling conflicts of earthly life. They point forward to a time when with increasing power Grundtvig searches out the answer to all questions in the historical course of Christianity and ultimately in the Bible. And thus a direct clash with the self-validating overall visions of romanticism is unavoidable.

IV

After a deep spiritual crisis and several actual attacks of acute mental illness Grundtvig experienced a breakthrough in his Christian faith around Christmas 1810. Early in 1811 he began to search for new poetic assurance in the Bible and the history of the Church. He found it reassuring that poets such as David in the Old Testament, Johannes Ewald in the 18th century, and the Norwegian clergyman Jonas Rein in the present age had been able to use their poetic talents in God's service. In Paul's speech on the Areopagus (Acts 17:28) he found a New Testament argument for the justification of the poetic art, even pagan art, as a true relic of the image of God that was lost with the Fall. In 1811 it actually leads him to a kind of identification with the Old Testament prophets. The romantics' idea of poetic genius was derived from, amongst others, the Old Testament. Now Grundtvig returned to the biblical seers in a way. His retrospective poetry collection *Saga,* published in December 1811, carries a motto from the prophet Ezekiel (33:32): for they hear thy words, but they do them not. In the foreword to *Saga,* where the motto is given a detailed commentary, he even continues the quotation: then shall they know that a prophet hath been among them. In a draft of the foreword Grundtvig has worked on a Christian definition of the poet.[8] He sees two types of poet in his own age: the passive, who makes himself an unresisting tool for his own imagination and its impulses, presumably the romantic type; and the active, who strictly controls his imagination in the service of a particular goal, presumably the moralizing classicist. Alongside these he wishes to place a third type, which with a grammatical pun he calls the "deponent", a union of passive form and active meaning. The deponent poet regards the flight of his imagination intellectually in order to ascertain its direction before he gives himself up to it. Since in

1811 Grundtvig has for years been defining true poetry by its aiming for the eternal he can quickly conclude that deponent poets must be "religious or Christian".

Although Grundtvig omits this passage in the draft from the printed foreword in favour of a mosaic of biblical quotations, it looks as if in the following years he himself makes every effort to become such a deponent poet. It still leaves room for romantic elements on a lower level than the one that is concerned with an overall view of life.

For a brief period around the new year 1810-11 Grundtvig wrote some private lyric fragments in which his poetic style is ruthlessly ascetic, short on images and non-sensuous. But it is not long before he is again drawing on romanticism's emotional and ambiguous store of images in order to acknowledge and speak the unspeakable. The abundant use of metaphors for the "rose", the "source" and the "rune" in the long poem *Roskilde Rhyme* (1814), and the commentary on it in archaizing prose *Roskilde Saga* (1814), are clear evidence of his great need for and inspiration from a freely proliferating imagery that at times eludes rational understanding. Grundtvig actually had to give up a precise commentary on specific points in the Roskilde works as well as the later *New Year's Morn* (1824), because he watched his notes growing into an ever-thickening wilderness of associations that not even he himself could carve a path through for the reader. In 1811 Grundtvig had made a decision to speak directly without unnecessary circumlocutory images in his biblical Christian authorship. At Christmas 1815 he changed his mind. He had found that even gifted people were outraged by his truculence or completely misunderstood him, both when he spoke out directly about things and when he treated them in the poetic form he himself had found as natural as drawing breath. He then had to choose a means of communication that he felt he mastered best. This involved a deliberate resumption of the poetic technique from the romantic years of his youth, which in fact he had never really managed to discard in practice.

V

In the period before 1811 Grundtvig had gone beyond romanticism positively. He had made use of it as a lower-ranking philosophy of life which could lead on to the higher one of Christianity. After 1811 he regards romanticism for some years as one of the major enemies of the Christian faith and he directs furious attacks upon it.

Grundtvig's interest in world history was awakened in earnest while he was teaching from 1808-10 at the Schouboe Institute, a modern private school in Copenhagen. In a lecture there in 1809 or 1810 he named Goethe and Schiller as contemporary classics on a par with the ancient Greeks and Shakespeare. Manuscript corrections reveal that instead of Schiller he had originally written the names of two arch-romantics, Novalis and Tieck. Also these two, along with many others, came under fire in Grundtvig's culturally orientated *World Chronicles* of 1812 and 1817. In the 1812 volume romanticism is attacked for its pantheistic natural philosophy, lacking all distinction between good and evil, for its mythologizing of Christianity and for its delusion of the individual's ability to redeem himself. Writers like Novalis, Tieck and Werner are described in the same terms: at first their harps played glorious music, but then the poets got lost in their inner selves until only the sound of broken strings was heard. In 1817 he has harsh things to say about Fichte's arrogant self-worship, and about the unbelievable, illusionary trick of Novalis, Tieck and the Schlegel brothers: wanting to turn time into eternity, to immerse themselves in themselves and lose themselves in the world. In Denmark Grundtvig accuses Holberg, Baggesen and especially Oehlenschläger of similarly wishing to be controlled by a far too mundane and self-centred attitude.

Grundtvig's assault on Novalis is particularly enlightening. It is inserted into the middle of a pamphlet duel against H. C. Ørsted, a natural scientist from Copenhagen. Ørsted was a searcher for harmony who preferred calm inquiries within the framework of a speculative romantic system to Grundtvig's violent swings of faith and apparently haphazard subjectivism. In the controversial pamphlet, *Against the Little Accuser* (1815), Grundtvig portrayed Novalis as the typical representative of German romanticism and its errors.[9] Grundtvig translates a poetic fragment by Novalis, which according to Tieck was originally intended for the novel *Heinrich von Ofterdingen*. It describes how poetry's "secret words" will one day be able to unite all life's contradictions in song and play, whilst mathematics and other book-knowledge will be made superfluous. Grundtvig comments: "In brief, the *blue flower,* the forget-me-not of Paradise, that is what Novalis insists on finding and embracing, not as a weeping maiden but as the queen of life: then in a heavenly carriage he will float away with her over all worlds in poignant pleasure; light and dark, truth and lies will lovingly embrace each other in the night that is forever light". The words "weeping maiden" have been coined in Danish by Grundtvig to specify the servant relationship that the art of poetry has to religion. Grundtvig's portrait of Novalis continues: "A deep longing for rest and harmony, a deep look into the heart of nature, a burning love for

31

the great and the beautiful, these things were to be found in Novalis as in few others, but love developed into impure passion that infected his desires and confused his visions (...)".

Alongside this stern judgement on Novalis' wrong turning and subsequent impurity, infection and confusion to the point of madness, Grundtvig acknowledges that his poetry also includes moving moments in "certain deep and Christian notes". In the condemnatory *Chronicles* of the 1810's Grundtvig also admits that in the great battle between Christianity and materialism (the latter being particularly apparent in the French philosophy of enlightenment) German romanticism has a role to play as a viable spiritual ferment.

Grundtvig's last direct clash with literary romanticism takes place in October, November and December 1818, when he throws himself into the so-called Twelve Controversy, a literary feud between on the one side Oehlenschläger (represented by twelve admirers and many others among the young Copenhagen academics) and on the other side Oehlenschläger's old rival, Jens Baggesen, who as a critic had been attacking Oehlenschläger since 1813 – not without some justification – for the falling curve in his career as poet and cultural personality. Grundtvig supported Baggesen because he regarded him as more spiritual than the young supporters of Oehlenschläger. He was now standing face to face with Danish romanticism's second and third generation, people like Carsten Hauch and Poul Martin Møller, who had not yet published works bearing their own individual hallmark. The line of argument against them is therefore directed more towards their immaturity as critics and their rebellious contempt for historical tradition and order. Only in his demonstration of the unspiritual sensuality for which the young blindly worship Oehlenschläger does Grundtvig return to the bitter line of thought with which he attacked Novalis in 1815.

By the end of the decade Grundtvig is no longer a literary figure. He becomes a vicar and for a number of years he transfers his interest to theology and church politics. At any rate he no longer takes part in literary campaigns and does not seem to keep up very well with modern literature either. In the 1830's, when he returns after a number of quiet years to writing for a wider public, it is not in the capacity of an old member of romanticism's first generation, but simply as Grundtvig. At about the same time the literary critics stopped reviewing his works as "ordinary" literature and accepted that being Grundtvig, a legend in his own lifetime, he must be read on his own premises.

The Lady of Egeløkke,
Constance Steensen-Leth.

Egeløkke Manor on the island of Langeland, where Grundtvig was engaged as a private
tutor (1805-07). (From a contemporary painting, Royal Library, Copenhagen).

Heinrich Steffens (1773-1845), Grundtvig's great inspiration.
(Royal Library, Copenhagen).

VI

To summarize: in a great many ways Grundtvig came close to romanticism in the first two decades of his writing career, but he never became a proper romantic. This is primarily due to his changing yet steadily growing sympathy for evangelical Christianity – and secondly (though not dealt with here) his respect for scholarly hard work and learning, an inheritance from the polyhistory of the 18th century.

VII

Romantic ideas, patterns and concepts are to be found in many places in the last fifty years of Grundtvig's writing, right up until his death in 1872, the year after Georg Brandes introduced modernism. Several of Grundtvig's principal ideas are derived from the romantics, though their origin is sometimes difficult to trace, since the romantics and their predecessors, the pre-romantic philosophers, occasionally borrowed them from Christian or ecclesiastical thought and reshaped them secularly. And because already at an early stage in his life Grundtvig was extremely well-read, a study of sources is required in every single instance before a line of thought in its first manifestation can be revealed as Christian or romantic.

What is most important is that Grundtvig takes seriously the romantics' *high estimation of the creative process of literary composition*. He uses words as tools to a degree that no other Danish golden age writer does, in poetry and prose, in speech and in writing, in his private as well as his public life. The majority of his titles are written for the occasion, sometimes in a great hurry, with the aim of intervening in and changing some situation or other whose possible consequences he compares with his interpretation of the meaning of the course of history and the world. That is why he takes a strong line without respect of persons when other poets such as Baggesen and Oehlenschläger engage in frivolous games with their muse. His own major poem *New Year's Morn* (1824) is a perfect example of romanticism's obscurely prophetic poetry, centred around the typical and the universal in his personal life so far and leading into a grand prophecy and hopes for the future.

Grundtvig's *view of nature* is romantic. Nature is depicted not for its own sake but is lit up, given a spiritual light, "transfigured", just as it is in Oehlenschläger's boldest poem of his youth, *The Life of Jesus Christ*

Repeated in the Annual Cycle of Nature (1805). This is also and in particular true in poems where a modern reader feels the apparently realistic details to have been convincingly depicted. Nature becomes transcendent, and Grundtvig can read it like a book – his own expression in 1808 to his friend, Christian Molbech. In such poems Grundtvig is a good romantic writer in his preservation of the ambiguity between what is real and what is invisibly spiritual in his metaphors from nature.

Also in more limited areas, for example in his *enthusiasm for Norway* as the birthplace of heroes, and in his *love of the old popular ballads* Grundtvig continues the lines that marked the breakthrough of romanticism into Denmark in 1802.

In his *writing of history* in the 1810's, 1830's and 1840's Grundtvig has demonstrated a supremely comprehensive view of history. He has a tendency to structure the events into vast patterns of artistic composition which in the end form universal unities. He calls this ability to find meaning in the course of events a "hawk's eye" (in 1818 in connection with Baggesen's concept of spirit). In his only work on contemporary history, *Within Living Memory,* lectures given in 1838 and published posthumously in 1877, Grundtvig suggests that the reader should regard the French Revolution in 1789 from the meeting of the Assembly to the execution of the King as a Shakespearean tragedy. In general, throughout his life he prefers to use accounts of older history – antiquity, the Middle Ages, the Reformation – for the purposes of a national and Christian revival.

In Grundtvig's use of *myths and mythology,* both the existing (from antiquity or the Old Norse) and the self-made (often lifted out of the Bible, Saxo or the Old Danish Rhymed Chronicle) we can observe the same ambiguity as in his descriptions of nature. In the course of a few words the language becomes heavy with associations, rich in details and yet unbelievably far-reaching. The development of subtle details is guided by an overall vision, in perfect accordance with the methodology of the romantics' research into myths. And the myths are not merely to be illuminated, but to be used themselves in order to illuminate. The age of a myth is most reliably decided by the sympathetic reader's living feeling, and at this point scholars should submit to poets. For as Grundtvig sees it, the myth-forgers employed a romantic-poetic principle: they denoted the invisible through the visible. Nor were they in any way learned empiricists, consciously transforming the phenomena of visible nature into invisible allegorical events – a dig from Grundtvig's side at the rational myth-interpreters in both the 18th and 19th century who had attempted to read myths as disguised lessons in meteorology and geology.

Grundtvig's plan for a *folk high school* and for *adult education* is coloured extensively by romantic ideas. "The living word", in the sense of the spoken native language employed in spontaneous interaction between teacher and pupils had been demonstrated to Grundtvig in his youth by Steffens. He never lost faith in its ability to ignite. In the folk high school that he hoped to set up at Sorø in mid-Zealand as a national counterweight to the Latin-dominated university in Copenhagen, his priorities were lessons in the native language, in folk-song, in the history of the country and in the nation's literature – a continuation of ideas on national upbringing and education from both German pre-romantics and German romanticism. His so-called historical and poetic method of teaching makes use of the "hawk's eye" from romanticism's philosophy of history, in contrast to the mechanical passing on of the compilatory chaos of the common, dry textbooks. He wishes to ensure a knowledge of the native language by amongst other things including dialects and proverbs in the teaching – areas that romanticism had rediscovered and given status to. In his commemorative poem for Steffens in 1845 he dreams of having the philosopher's ashes buried in the middle of Sorø High School in recognition of the fact that it was Steffens who gave him the first impulse for a Danish high school.

In the latter half of the 18th century J. G. Herder had published his essays on the philosophy of history, in which he maintained that a nation's soul and identity are to be found in its language, its literature and its culture. He proclaimed that genius is always national, and he laid down a pattern of organic development over the history of the world. His work began a new epoch. Until 1750 it had still been possible, despite differences in language and temperament, to maintain the feeling of a common European culture that was established from the Latin Middle Ages. Now the European history of ideas was split into a number of national histories, internally quite different from one another. In Denmark it is none other than Grundtvig who mediates Herder's ideas and changes them into genuine politics of culture. Under the influence of Napoleon's demise he saw in the years 1814-15 with increasing clarity that God's chosen people in recent times are the Danes, with their unequalled feeling for truth and love. On this basis Grundtvig develops a concept of *Danishness,* not in the sense of a random nation with a random language, but as a call, a God-given gift, an ability to see true Christianity in the earthly phenomena and give it room, – in other words, a Christian version of Steffens' definition of Poetry. This concept of Danishness is ready for use in Grundtvig's active role as encourager and comforter in the two Schleswig wars of 1848-50 and 1864. In literature it finds expression in his self-produced journal *Danevirke* (1816-19) and in his wartime magazine *The Dane* (1848-51) – both titles intended as trumpet fanfares.

Danishness is also the driving-force behind Grundtvig's *national philology* in the great translation projects of the 1810's. He produces a Danish version of Saxo's Latin Chronicle of the Kingdom of Denmark, *Gesta Danorum,* and Snorri Sturluson's Old Icelandic companion work on Norway *Heimskringla,* both from around 1220. Grundtvig chooses to translate them into the simple, oral style of a Zealand peasant – a style that corresponds neither to the Latin original's embellished rhetoric nor to the Old Icelandic's terse saga diction. Grundtvig's own compass under the laborious translation work is once again romanticism: a feeling for what the text conceals. In his defence in 1816 against a pedantic philologist's criticism, he exclaims in enthusiasm for Signe's song in death that he better than the scholars can capture "what inflames the song, what penetrates all barriers and plays under the open sky like a sounding flame", – also or especially where the text does not contain direct utterances.[10]

To Saxo and Snorri Grundtvig added in 1820 a verse rendition of the Anglo-Saxon poem *Beowulf,* a project financed by a patron. The text itself had not been published until 1815 in a Copenhagen edition, with a rather misleading parallel text in Latin. In the foreword to his version Grundtvig maintains the same intuitive method of translating into Danish: his rewriting is in every respect precise, "historically faithful, so I have never deliberately altered or inserted anything, and poetically faithful, so I have endeavoured with all my might to render into living speech what I saw in the poem."[11]

The Saxo and Snorri translations whetted Grundtvig's appetite for a major, practical project: nothing less than a national subscription to finance the publication of these national historians, in which people should give what they could and take what they needed. The impoverished should be able to buy copies at cost-price or less, and Grundtvig declined a translation fee and never covered his costs incurred in the considerable administration connected with distribution. It was a major aim to circumvent the commercial bookseller. In this idealistic project he abandons his scholarly study and goes out, so to speak, to compose romantically with the nation itself as his material. But the poverty especially of the self-governing farms in the wake of the financial ordinance of 1813 had the effect of more or less quietly killing off the project when all six volumes were finally ready in 1823. Grundtvig had been too early on the market with his idea for a public co-operative publishing company.

Grundtvig's lifelong attempt to delineate *Danish* as a concept that was Christian, national, geographical, linguistic and cultural is perhaps the boldest of its kind in European romanticism. As a result of Denmark's decline as a military and political power in Europe in the course of Grundtvig's lifetime his ideal of Danishness as an attitude to life did not have the same catastrophic consequences in the following century as the Germans' simultaneous development of German ideology had in the empire and the Third Reich. On the contrary, his linking of the life of the people to Christianity and to the native language, as expressed in his long didactic poem, *The Pleiades of Christendom* (1860),[12] has had a tangible effect on Danish culture right up until today.

Along with the idea of Danishness we find in Grundtvig – from the 1830's onwards – a belief in the Danes' unequalled popular spirit (*folkelighed*). In the public debate on the advisory assemblies in the 1830's, which prepared the ground for the Constitution in 1849, and in his capacity as a member of parliament Grundtvig attempted, though largely without success, to turn the popular spirit into a political programme. It proved a better bet to turn it into a cultural programme at the high schools.

Finally, the *theology* that Grundtvig arrived at in his maturity and old age also clearly includes romantic elements. The idea of organic growth inherited from the romantic philosophy of history is transferred to an optimistic Christian faith, where it can be illustrated in the biblical words of an "illumination" of all mysteries in the fullness of time (Eph. 1:8,10) and of growth only on God's conditions (I.Cor. 3:7). In *The Pleiades of Christendom* Grundtvig actually reproaches Luther for having placed too much emphasis on Jesus' suffering and too little on the spiritual rebirth in man and the consequent growth in God.[13]

Earlier Lutheran poets in Denmark, from Hans Christensen Sthen at the end of the 16th century through Thomas Kingo a hundred years later to H. A. Brorson and Johannes Ewald in the 18th century's pietism and pre-romanticism, glorified God by confessing their own sin and wretchedness. Grundtvig regards his own existence as a sign of a (coming) Christian renewal; he sees himself in images of an Easter lily (in the poem of the same name from 1817), one of the heralds of spring in the Danish countryside. He becomes a summoning and prophetic watchman on a par with the Old Testament prophet, for example in the poem *Commemorative Song at the Ancestors' Grave* (1815) (*Mindesang paa Fædres Gravhøi*). He mirrors himself in Henrich Steffens' work as a light-bringing and awakening blaze of fire, an Easter angel for the living, crucified, dead, buried and resurrected word (in the obituary poem on the writer in 1845). In volume III of his world history handbook from 1843 Grundtvig defines Martin Luther as a prophet of a particularly modern kind: he carries a whole age within him and develops it out of himself, manifesting in himself, so to speak, what he prophesies.[14] This is a Christian adaptation into a practical and world-historical use of the teaching of romanticism concerning the omnipotence of artistic genius.

VIII

There are areas of romanticism that Grundtvig definitely rejects; for example, the romantics' favourite idea of *the artist as creator,* "a Prometheus sub Jove" (Shaftesbury), in nature like God, albeit in miniature – and the consequent idea of the work of art as a microcosm, akin to the universe. Admittedly he never wrote the theory of literature that he busied himself with in the 1810's, a theory that was in opposition to the 17th century's interpretation of Aristotle, the 18th century's aesthetic of imagination and harmony in Shaftesbury, Christian Wolff and Edward Young, and the 19th century's classicism of Goethe and Schiller and romanticism of Novalis and Jean Paul. But in fragmentary writings he keeps a safe distance from romanticism's self-creating genius.

In some manuscripts for a series of lectures on the conditions of man from October 1813[15] Grundtvig thus emphasizes that even in its highest expression the power of imagination is unable to create out of nothing. It is always dependent on something it can imagine and relate to, and since it is impossible to imagine a nothing, the phrase "freely creating" activity becomes meaningless. This is, he notes, the cosmological evidence of God derived from the nature of imaginative power instead of building as is usual on the existence of external, tangible realities. For Grundtvig, both the material, phenomenal world and the inner world of man affirm the idea of "the invisible Creator, in whom we live and move and have our being", – a quotation from Paul (Acts 17:28).

In a draft for an article in *Danevirke* four years later, *On Revelation, Art and Knowledge,*[16] Grundtvig traces true poetry back to the ancient Hebrew prophets with their incomplete or rough visions. At the same time he distrusts sensuous perfection or beauty in a work of art, because these qualities are often merely "empty ting-a-lings" or "savoury sausages". In the article as published the main weight is transferred from these attacks to a positive view of true poetry as conditioned solely by God's intervention. It is Christian art, he says, coming to the world for our benefit through an incomprehensible wonder that alone can complete the work, which is to say "transform and transfigure the sensuous which through the Fall became subject to death and corruption". Grundtvig's Christian poetics presuppose the dogmas of the Fall and the Atonement through the power of a supernatural revelation. There is no question of a romantic self-redemption.

Nor can Grundtvig accept another of the romantics' favourite ideas, *the originality of the artist*. As a writer he is himself the type who reacts spiritedly to his surroundings, through reading the works of earlier periods or in an interaction with contemporary writers. With his very wide reading he had a less naive relationship to the age's ideal of originality than, say, Oehlenschläger. In an article in his youth *On Oehlenschläger's Balder the Good* (1808) he had written off his own ability to reproduce his inner visions in poetry. In the verse "Foreword" to the epic poem *Ragnarok* (1817) (*Ragna-Roke*) he prefers a simple, purposeful poetic activity in continuation of the historical chronicle tradition, pouring scorn on slogans about the self-validation of art and the artist's originality.

Also in the writings that fall outside his fictional authorship Grundtvig opposes in theory and practice the demand for originality. He feels it to be an unreasonable narrowing down to the subjective and the specific – that is, a devaluation of what the romantics found most valuable: the mirroring of the endless inner wealth of a distinctive personality.

This is especially true when he regards the whole genre of hymns. In his essay *An Impartial View of the Danish State Church* (1834) he regrets that he himself and other modern hymn-writers have "far less feeling for the essential and ordinary, and a far greater *preference* for our '*individual*' way of seeing and for 'our own eggs' than the old writers".[17] The endeavour to join the historical tradition and to lose the reprehensible predilection for individuality is the motivation behind Grundtvig's many translations and adaptations of older and newer hymn material. The expectation by modern art theorists of a sharpening artistic individualism is detrimental to the general understanding, validity and use of the texts. To counter this he employs a more or less gentle modernization of dead and living predecessors. Doubtless his age regarded his work as more successful than posterity would grant. Seen at the end of the 20th century, in which literary forms are so decisively different from romanticism's, Grundtvig appears rather to have grundtvigianized Luther, Kingo, Brorson, Ingemann and others. Such is the irony of history.

IX

Christianity and romanticism have a common basis in the belief that the individual's existence as well as the world in general is driven by an invisible but incontrovertibly real, spiritual power. In faith man puts himself into a relationship with God. The romantic puts himself first and foremost into a relationship with himself, his mysterious, enticing inner self. The difference for the believer is insuperable so long as Christianity remains the only meaning of life. The romantic on the other hand absorbs the religious element without great difficulty and finds an undogmatically conceived God in his fertile inner chaos.

In the midst of his furious battle against Schelling's philosophy of identity, Grundtvig believed, as mentioned, that German romanticism in spite of everything had been a useful ferment in turbulent times.

When Grundtvig separated the human from the Christian in *Norse Mythology* (1832) and declared the first to be a necessary condition for the second, he was also reconciling himself with the romantics. He made peace and an alliance with those he characterized as "Naturalists", people who like the Greeks of antiquity and the ancient Norse were conscious of man's spiritual source and nature.

In his much-quoted introduction to *Norse Mythology* – the *Rhymed Letter to the Norse Kinsfolk* (*Rim-Brev til Nordiske Paarørende*) – Grundtvig uses the war-god Thor with his hammer to denote the power of all spiritual freedom, and the poetry-god Bragi to stand for the force of the wingéd word, while the giants and their ally, Fenrir, represent the massive bestial materialism. But Loki, the father of the wolf, half-Aesir, half-giant is deliberately allowed the freedom to act, for with his wit and his intelligence he awakens the truly divine to spiritual battle. In Grundtvig's eyes it is of course only the truly divine that can win in the confrontation with a spiritual opposition of inescapably lower rank. Loki is a dialectic figure, kindred to the Greeks' chained Prometheus – partly an expression of reason's ingenious rebellion against the divine, partly the father of materialism (his son Fenrir swallows Odin, the leader of the Aesir, at Ragnarok), of spiritual impotence (his daughter Hel rules in the kingdom of death) and of falseness. Grundtvig regards Loki's negative capabilities as the necessary consequences of self-conceit and the worship of reason. On the positive side a Loki provokes the spiritual battle and thus benefits the highest form of spirituality, the religious, which he had hoped to tear down.

A similar though more sympathetically formulated view of the intellectual worker with no clear faith is outlined in a commemorative poem Grundtvig wrote in 1844 (published in 1848) on the famous sculptor, Bertel Thorvaldsen.

X

After a spiritual adolescence approaching romanticism Grundtvig breaks with romanticism's radical individualism. In place of the individual and unique formation and development of personality he sets as his ultimate goal the incorporation of the individual into a greater community – linguistically into the community of the native language, nationally into the community of history, socially into the community of society, ecclesiastically into the community of the congregation and religiously into the community of evangelical Christianity. In the perspective of the history of ideas Grundtvig begins in Jena-romanticism with universal-historical interpretations of Norse mythology and ancient history in the years 1806-08, moving on from there to a parallel with the Heidelberg school in the national and Christian works from 1809-1824, and finally more or less sliding backwards to romanticism's pre-conditions, Herder's philosophy of the organism. However, in the 1830's, following his three trips to England, Grundtvig linked these thoughts of Herder in an original manner to the political and economic liberalism of England. He summoned all spiritual forces to battle and competition, thus setting the late, autocratic Denmark in motion towards popular education and popular government, in a faster tempo in fact than he himself actually believed was reasonable for the beginning of a movement.

Faced with the visions of the great communities romanticism's cultivation of the individual begins to pale in his world of ideas. The scrupulous observer, however, will soon note the romantic individualism in spite of everything in Grundtvig's authorship. In his 7th Lecture in 1802 Steffens had worked at the problem of uniting a concept of programmed necessity in history with the freedom of the individual. In his preparations for this Steffens offered a formula for the placing in his age of the great and unusual human being, a formula that could be applied to Grundtvig: the consciousness of the man of significance is "a larger or smaller, more or less all-embracing encapsulation of the past, individualised by his special character". The past is here the historic tradition of the above-mentioned communities. The specific character is to a large degree in Grundtvig's

41

case an inheritance from romanticism. This manifests itself most clearly in his poetic work.

Where Grundtvig's poetry is artistically at its best, it rests on the aesthetic principles of romanticism: the ambiguity and multiplicity of symbols and images, the fertile growth of associations, the leaps across different levels of meaning, the rapid change of overall atmosphere, the informed use of mythology and history – all these are characteristic elements.

Even in Grundtvig's last poem from 1872 the romantic features of his imagery and combinations of images form largely unevangelical myth. The recognition "Old enough I have become" (*Gammel nok jeg nu er blevet*) is an echo of Norna-Gest's last words in Olaf Tryggvason's Saga. The voyage across the stormy sea to destruction or the safe haven, here to the kingdom of the dead or Paradise, is well-known as an aria metaphor in the 18th century. *The Owl's Song* in the kingdom of the dead may be Minerva's, that is human reason's, helplessness, but in Ewald's heroic ballad opera *The Fishermen* (1779) the owl's song with its howling u-vowel expresses exactly in music the danger of shipwreck and destruction. *Soul-Ferry-Prow* is Grundtvig's positive adaptation of Charon's boat. Not until the two final stanzas, where the haven of heaven opens before him, does the poet turn to Christian expressions.

XI

In the most dramatic years of his youth, 1805-10, Grundtvig was inspired and influenced by romanticism in a decisive manner, without his forgetting that its world of ideas was to be placed on a lower level than Christianity. From 1810 he fought romanticism for twenty years or so, first in literature then in theology. After 1832 he became reconciled to it again in the recognition of its unquestionably spiritual nature, though more as a general current in the culture than as a grouping together of particular authors or particular books.

In Grundtvig's own works the imagery of mystery, which will in the fullness of time be "transfigured", is a major artistic category. The mysteries are presented out of his own sub-consciousness or consciousness, out of his age, out of history. Their elucidation is the prerogative of God. Perhaps Grundtvig's literary philosophy should be called a christened romanticism.

NOTES

1. *N. F. S. Grundtvig's Diaries & Journals, ed. Gustav Albeck, I, 1979 p. 241-44.* N. F. S. Grundtvigs Dag- og Udtogsbøger, ved Gustav Albeck, I, 1979 s. 241-44.
2. *Ibid. p. 218-26.*
3. *Ibid. p. 330.*
4. *Ibid. p. 370.*
5. *Ibid. p. 385-90, and in New Minerva June 1807 p. 225-48.*
6. *Grundtvig Archives, The Royal Library, File 213.1 1v.* Grundtvig-arkivet, Det kongelige Bibliotek, Fasc. 213.1 1v.
7. *N. F. S. Grundtvig's Selected Writings, ed. Holger Begtrup, I, 1904, s. 295-317.* Nik. Fred. Sev. Grundtvigs Udvalgte Skrifter, ved Holger Begtrup, I, 1904. s. 295-317.
8. *Gustav Albeck: On Grundtvig's Poetry Collections, 1955, p. 102-04.* Gustav Albeck: Omkring Grundtvigs Digtsamlinger, 1955, s. 102-04.
9. *N. F. S. Grundtvig: Against the Little Accuser, 1815, p. 191-201.* N. F. S. Grundtvig: Imod den lille Anklager, 1815, s. 191-201.
10. N. F. S. Grundtvig: *The Evaluation in The 'Literary Times' of my Specimen Translations of Saxo and Snorri. 1816, p. 20* N. F. S. Grundtvig: Literaturtidendes Skudsmaal i Henseende til Prøverne af Saxo og Snorro, 1816, s. 20.
11. *Beowulf, ed. N. F. S. Grundtvig, 1820, p. XXXIV.* Bjowulfs Drape, ved Nik. Fred. Sev. Grundtvig, 1820, s. XXXIV.
12. *N. F. S. Grundtvig: The Pleiades of Christendom, 1860, The Nordic Church, stanzas 62-86.* N. F. S. Grundtvig: Christenhedens Syvstjerne, 1860, Den nordiske Menighed, str. 62-86.
13. *Ibid, The German Church, stanzas 85-89.*
14. *Selected Writings VII, 1908, p. 541.*
15. *Selections from the Works of N. F. S. Grundtvig, ed. Georg Christensen and Hal Koch, II, 1941, p. 241-70.* N. F. S. Grundtvigs Værker i Udvalg, ved Georg Christensen og Hal Koch, II, 1941, s. 241-70.
16. *Grundtvig Archives File 161.1 and Danevirke III 1817 p. 293.*
17. *Selected Writings VIII, 1909, p. 84.*

Grundtvig's Christian Breakthrough 1810-12

– the Strange Metamorphosis in Grundtvig's Life

by WILLIAM MICHELSEN

Grundtvig's parents decided at his birth that he 'was to be a clergyman, like his elder brothers; but his own immediate interest from early childhood lay in reading history. It therefore suited him extremely well that having torn himself away from Constance Leth and Egeløkke he found not only rooms in Valkendorf's College in Copenhagen close to the university and the libraries but also a job as history teacher at a modern grammar school, Schouboe's Institute, beginning in the spring of 1808. He made his name as a scholar and poet with *Norse Mythology* and *Scenes* from the Lives of the Norse Heroes; he became a close friend of young poets and scholars, including the philosopher Sibbern, the historian Christian Molbech, and Norwegian historians and theologians living at Valkendorf's College. He produced *Textbook in World History* for his pupils, which he transmitted to them in lecture form. He kept up with the latest literature and studied written sources of history for all he was worth: this had always been his heart's desire – and continued to be so until the day he died.

In these circumstances it came as a disappointment to receive a letter around March 1st 1810 from his father, the rector of Udby, who needed a curate if he was to retain his post. This was an absolute necessity as he had nothing else to live on. He wished his son to apply for the post and thus make use of his training for the priesthood, which his parents had both intended him for and paid for. Grundtvig replied on March 5th that he would not "shirk from his holy duty to support a venerable father in his old age", but he added that it was not his intention "immediately to take over a post which would force him to change course" – a somewhat contradictory reply. On March 11th his father demanded that he should "come to a swift decision and leave immediately"; Grundtvig replied on March 16th that he neither would nor could – out of regard for his pupils. In the meantime he gave his examination sermon – the "probationary sermon" – for which he was given the highest possible marks, even though he had "tried to answer the question: Why has the Word of the Lord Disappeared from His House? and was therefore forced to say things that did not sound too well in the ears of my revered adjudicator," as he wrote in a letter to his father on March 19th. At the beginning of May he published the sermon with an introduction, dated April 10th, in which he declared in a metaphorical expression that he was incapable of acknowledging God from an intellectual viewpoint, as the leading philosopher of his day, Schelling, demanded; and he urged the clergy not to lead the congregation down this dubious path to true faith:

"Do we really have a chain in our hands which we ourselves have used to make fast the suns in the high firmament? Let he who has it pity me! I freely confess: I have it not".

With this declaration and with a confession of faith in "the Word of the Lord" Grundtvig abandoned the view he had expressed in 1806, that "the religion of Jesus" can "solve the riddle of existence ... by showing what none till now could manage – that the identity of poetry and philosophy, by being linked to the Eternal, can be religion's representative in the Ultimate". Obscure words, which must mean that since modern man no longer has any religion, an idealistic philosophy and a poetry based on this can take the place of religion here on earth – a standpoint characteristic of the epoch 1800-1870, which was Grundtvig's age and which has been called the golden age of Danish literature. One might perhaps call this standpoint today "the ideology of the golden age".

How decisive a step Grundtvig had thus taken away from the prevailing direction of his age he himself did not yet realise. His letters to his parents show that he considered it possible to keep his new principle standpoint – the Bible must take the place of philosophy – out of his private life. But the Copenhagen clergy were deeply offended at the sermon's title: "Why has the Word of the Lord Disappeared from His House?" – as if they did not preach the Word of God in accordance with their oath of office! They sent a complaint to the university over Grundtvig's publication of his probationary sermon. This resulted only in a newspaper controversy and Grundtvig receiving a reprimand (in January 1811) for publishing. But he was now in practice excluded from any incumbency in Copenhagen.

Nor did Grundtvig apply for one, but only for a minor post as stipendiary curate (capellan pro persona) in Udby. And he knew even before he applied that he would not get the job: there were far too many other theological graduates applying. To give the post to the elderly Rector Grundtvig's son would be an extreme case of preferential treatment. But that was precisely what his father wanted – and that his son should contrive it by applying *directly to the King himself.* In a letter dated April 20th Grundtvig writes that he would only do so if his father applied for retirement "on a decent pension". His mother replied in a letter known only from Grundtvig's answer on April 30th. She reproached him for his "ingratitude, fickleness and the cowardly frame of mind that put pleasure before duty". To which Grundtvig retorted, "Personal advantage is not my idol, I take no part in any worldly pleasures ... And so, dear mother, I cannot change my decision, even though the whole world agreed to blame me: for I have not taken it on grounds of vanity."

On May 7th Grundtvig sent his parents two copies of his probationary sermon with a dedicatory poem to his father, ending with the wish that he should pray to God that his son might vigorously preach the Word of God and not be mastered by "sin and pride" ... "that my tongue shall not shame my deed". Grundtvig sent these words to his parents only a few days after he had refused outright to follow their wish that he should go directly to the King with his father's application to have his son as personal curate! It is strange proof of the degree to which Grundtvig believed in the spring of 1810 that he could keep his personal attitude to the ministry and his parents separate from his reference to the Word of God in the Bible – without being a hypocrite. Nor, later on, did he value his probationary sermon very highly. In 1815 he wrote that it "is not much more than a declaration that I believed I ought to make at some point about what I myself believed in and what ought to be preached". (*Selected Works* I, p. 99).

In mid-September 1810 Grundtvig's father sent him his retirement application, expressing the hope that his son would be his successor. However, on September 21st Grundtvig replied that there was no chance of that happening; so far nobody had managed to succeed their father. He continued, "Furthermore I have no wish at all to be the rector of Udby, even if I could be". At the same time, however. Grundtvig applied for a position in the nearby market town of Præstø, "a call which I have both higher hopes of gaining and which suits me better". This presumably is the letter that reveals the gap between Grundtvig's words and deeds most sharply.

In the autumn of 1810 all Grundtvig's energy was gathered into his history teaching and history reading. He had concentrated on a number of new works on the crusades, which he read in quick succession and which completely altered his view of medieval history. This led to him suddenly breaking off work on his handwritten textbook on history. Among the works Grundtvig read was the first volume of August von Kotzebue's *The Early History of Prussia* (Preussens ältere Geschichte, Riga 1808), which he was reading at the beginning of October 1810. The crusade against the pagan Prussians was represented with a provocative sympathy for paganism and contempt for the missionaries ("the Cross-madness"). The Prussians held out, even though the rulers of Poland also attempted to spread the new faith and the dried-up cross was closing in on the Prussians' holy tree – the green oak. It is not surprising that the young Grundtvig felt the challenge of these words. Now it was his turn to be a crusader! A number of poems on the subject from these months have been preserved. Some of them were published in the new year collection of poems *Idun* (December 29th 1810).

From October-November 1810 there is also a manuscript on the *Book of Revelation* containing strange biographical information about Grundt-vig's inner life during this year. It was found lying scattered amongst Grundtvig's papers and had never been published because his state of mind changed so much soon after he had written it. But read in collected form it offers a vivid impression of his mood at the time – that of an inspired religious revivalist or prophet. The letter to the seven Churches in Revelation 2 and 3 is here regarded as a prophecy of seven reformers in the history of the Church at roughly 300-year intervals; Martin Luther is the most recent with Johan Huss as his forerunner, while the seventh has yet to appear. Grundtvig writes that he regards himself as a forerun-ner for the last reformer! As mentioned, these papers were found scat-tered around and have only recently been identified as an unbroken account. It is not until in a sermon, which he probably never preached but which he published in vol. III of his *Sunday Book*, that Grundtvig discusses his interpretation of the *Book of Revelation*, though only of the two letters to the Church in Sardis – the "Lutheran" Church and to the Church in Philadelphia which is identified with the contemporary Danish Church. And not until 1854-60 did he develop this thought – in the poem *The Pleiades of Christendom*, in which the reformers have retired to the back of the stage, and the seven Churches are characterized as the He-brew (the founding Church), the Greek, the Roman, the Anglo-Saxon, the German and the Danish, whilst the seventh and last is still unknown. The salient point is, that at this stage of his Christian breakthrough Grundtvig has spotted a coherence in the history of the Church that he had not seen before, but which adds to the coherence of the history of the individual nations that he had discovered the year before; their power rose and fell with their religiousness, whether Christian or not. To this was added the idea, taken from Henrich Steffens, that the Roman conquest represented the lowest subjugation of the lives of the nations; and only with the aid of Christianity could the Nordic peoples liberate themselves from it.

Of course Grundtvig pondered the fact that he was born 300 years after Luther, and that as a result of the biblical criticism of the rationalists Christianity had lost the foundation that Luther had given it through his translation of the Bible into the vernacular. In the following years Grundtvig regarded it as his task to restore to the Bible its character of being a holy book – a real revelation of a truth from above – by comparing it with the history of the Church, of the world and of the nations – all at once. Not until 1825 did he realise that the Church is older than the Bible, and that the oral tradition is stronger than the written. He had not come so far in October 1810 when he wrote in his interpretation of the *Book of Revelation*, "I was reading Kotzebue's History of Prussia, which really angered me. Then, on October 9th, I was wonderfully, indescribably seized; from that moment all fear left me and it is as if a mist has passed from my eyes. Now I saw that, as in the North, Christianity everywhere characterizes the life of the nations, and its decline, their death; and I have realised that only history could give Christianity rebirth." (The text quoted here is from *Grundtvig-Studies 1956;* the ending was found and published in the same journal in 1959).

Grundtvig never relinquished this view of history; but he was gradually forced to realise that the idea that he could thereby convince his age of the truth of Christianity was a misconception; people cannot be forced to believe – not even in the face of what one regards oneself as "indisputable evidence". But the *attempt* to convince his age lies behind his three *World Chronicles* from 1812, 1814 and 1817. The first came into being, as he himself wrote in 1833, through "a strange metamorphosis" of his *Textbook in World History,* which he had begun to dictate to his pupils in 1808. This metamorphosis, he says, "belongs to my biography, since my writings have always been a poorly corrected, yet precisely for that reason a truer picture, of my life." A pertinent comment on the whole of Grundtvig's authorship.

Now, however, in October 1810, Grundtvig had to throw himself back into the Bible, the revelatory nature of which he had discovered at a stroke. He read the New Testament in Greek, but he was not so good at Hebrew, so for the Old Testament he settled for the Danish Bible which Constance Leth had presented to him: it was therefore "doubly sacred" to him, as he wrote on the flyleaf. It contains underlinings in red and black, especially in the prophetic books. During this re-reading of the Bible the words struck home time and again – like "stones on my heart", he wrote in his old age in the book *Church Mirror*. Only now did he ask himself seriously: "Are you a Christian?" "Have your sins been forgiven?" he writes. Only now did Grundtvig realise how poorly word corresponded with deed in his personal life.

The first thing he did (as far as we know) was to write a congratulatory poem to his father on the occasion of his 50th year in the ministry, celebrated on December 5th – and then in the new year to withdraw into himself. This poem introduces his little poetry collection *New Year's Eve* (*Nytaarsnat*) – published on December 29th 1810 and has a quite different character from the dedicatory poem to his probationary sermon. There is another poem that carries the stamp of his new frame of mind, *Lovely is the Clear Blue Night* (*Dejlig er den himmel blå*), the story of the three kings told for children in simple verse, which to this day belongs to his most-loved Christmas carols. But after this he ran out of energy. On the same pieces of paper there are verse fragments of the confession of a crushed man, stanzas broken off and with no coherence. One morning he remained in his bed and would not get up. His friends at the College called his uncle, a chief physician and professor of medicine, who realised that it would be necessary for Grundtvig to return home to Udby and that he could not travel alone. His friend, F. C. Sibbern, promised to accompany him. They had to spend the night en route at an inn. There Sibbern was awakened by Grundtvig on his knees praying aloud to God. The next morning he told Sibbern he had felt the Devil like a snake twisting his body. When Sibbern told Grundtvig's father what he knew of Grundtvig's condition the old rector answered, "My son is troubled in spirit". He realised that these troubles were not merely a morbid depression but were necessary for the peace of his soul. It is clear from Grundtvig's letters to his friends that he himself realised this too – above all in a letter to Sibbern dated December 24th 1810. The way Sibbern stood before him in Vindbyholt Inn is the way he will always stand in his soul, he says. For another six months Grundtvig writes now and then of morbid obsessions which he has difficulty in "shooting away", and it could also be seen on him when he again returned to Copenhagen and was together with his friends (we have a description of him in a letter from the Norwegian clergyman, Fr. Schmidt, who visited Copenhagen in the early months of 1811); no one must shake Grundtvig's newly-won Christian faith!

Most important of all, Grundtvig now fulfilled his parents' wish and went to the King with his application to become a curate in Udby. This was already in January 1811 – and his request was granted. He did not speak to the King himself, however, and was not ordained and inducted until six months later. His father lived for another two years, after which Grundtvig could not remain in the position any longer, but during these years he carried out his duties with a zeal that people he had confirmed could remember even in their old age. He also took an active part in the clergy conventions, giving lectures and a reading of a lengthy poem about Roskilde Cathedral which takes the shape of a description of the history of the Danish Church as a contrast to the moral and religious decay of the present-day, with a powerful and urgent plea to the bishop and the clergy to regenerate the Christianity of the people. The poem was published in a revised and greatly expanded version in 1814 under the title *Roskilde Rhyme* with a commentary on it called *Roskilde Saga*.

Grundtvig's writings in these years changed his status in Danish literature completely. He became an extremely controversial man. One of his closest friends, the historian Molbech, publicly repudiated him; the physicist, H. C. Ørsted, attacked in particular Grundtvig's judgement on the natural philosopher, Schelling, in the book *Brief View of World Chronicle* (1812). Others found it outrageous that he dared to attack persons still alive in a "World Chronicle"!

Grundtvig's *World Chronicle* (1812) was a piece of confessionary writing but it became a cause célèbre. Yet the book is something else besides; it is the first expression in Grundtvig's authorship of his biblical view of history. For Grundtvig, as for St. Paul, history was a realisation of God's purpose with mankind. The history of the Jewish people and the Christian Church comprise, so to speak, the framework for the history of the whole world and give it cohesion. The history of the world is the history of the salvation of mankind, and the pattern for this view is the Old Testament account of Israel's history. The whole of history becomes God's guidance and education of His people through the good and evil vicissitudes of life – as in Judges chapters 2-3: God is the lord of history, He intervenes when He wishes and leads the nations according to His plan, and even against their will. He educates them by punishing them, but also by showing them love – from the creation of the world, despite the fall, through salvation in Jesus Christ to the everlasting life.

Grundtvig also wrote the history of the world from another viewpoint, which he calls the "Greek". This he did in his *Handbook on World History I-III* (1833-43), on the grounds that at the time it was the most suitable "for school use", i.e. *scholarly*. But he says at the same time that the "Mosaic-Christian view of life in all its directions and all its utterances now as ever" was "the only true and everlasting one" *for him*. This is precisely the biblical view of history that he had reached in 1810.

The period from 1810 to 1832 in Grundtvig's writing was characterised by a Christian cultural programme that encompassed both scholarship, politics and religion: "the Church, the State and the School", as he puts it. He insisted at all costs on a unified culture which was truly Christian and not merely a Christian-tinged idealism. His duty as a clergyman bound him to this view, as did his Christian faith.

In 1832 this cultural programme was altered considerably – but without any change in either his faith or his view of life, which remained the biblical view of history, "the Mosaic-Christian view of life". The change was in his attitude to his own day and age: now he would no longer thrust his faith at, or force it on, his contemporaries. In the introduction to his *Handbook on World History* he writes:

"I have gradually learnt to make a sharp distinction between Church and School, faith and knowledge, temporal and eternal, and I now realise quite clearly that just as the Christian Church must powerfully reject every attempt by the State and the School to reform it as they please, so is the Church equally unjustified in forcing the State or the School into a Church mould."

In these words lies a *new cultural programme;* and it was through this that Grundtvig left his mark on his age and its successors. Without *freedom* the Christian faith is not a true faith. Religion, like scholarship, cannot do without freedom. So one must be allowed to be a non-Christian, to be a pagan! And that was exactly what our forefathers were, before they became Christians.

Naturally this discovery of the necessity of freedom for faith, as for scholarship, was a major discovery both in Grundtvig's life and in Danish intellectual thought. But it nevertheless presupposes the discovery that Grundtvig had made at his Christian breakthrough in 1810. It taught him to distinguish clearly between *Christianity and paganism.* Without this clear division it was impossible for Grundtvig to recognize the contemporary demand for a distinction between faith and knowledge.

Grundtvig the Historian

by Sigurd Aage Aarnes

A General View of Grundtvig's Historical Writings

Placed as they are in the middle of the positivist 19th century, Grundtvig's historical writings are a strangely antiquated phenomenon. Grundtvig was first and foremost a philosophical historian and narrator of history, to a lesser degree a source critic. In his relationship to the main line of positivism in 19th century historical scholarship Grundtvig, with his markedly subjective and emotive attitude to history, was throughout his life an outsider. He was a contemporary of the pioneers of positivist history research, men such as Ranke and Niebuhr, but he represents – at least in his point of departure – an old-fashioned theological tradition of history with roots as far back as Augustine's *De civitate Dei* and the orthodox Lutheran view of history.

What is original about Grundtvig's historical thought is that he combines these old-fashioned elements with impulses from contemporary German romanticism to form a very distinctive alloy. It says much for the power of his personality that in the grundtvigian communities and in the folk high school of which he became the ideologist, he created a sustained renaissance for ways of thinking that are otherwise far from typical of his age.

Grundtvig's ideological development moves from an evangelical Lutheranism to his famous thesis, "First a man, then a Christian". For the young, orthodox, Lutheran minister, writing history was a purely theological business, a "secondary theology". He was not much interested in history, "as it really was" (*wie es eigentlich gewesen*), to use Ranke's well-known phrase, but set out history's testimony to the truth of Christianity to strengthen the faith of his fellow-Christians and educate them in the fundamental conditions of human existence, "the conditions of man". Only slowly – in his middle age does Grundtvig's philosophy of history undergo a certain secularization as he moves in his major historical work

Handbook on World History from spiritual history to political history. Whereas his *World Chronicles* are books of Christian edification which show how God forms the course of history, this view recedes into the background in *Handbook on World History* in favour of a presentation, full of references and ideologically more detached, of political events in history.

It is well-known that Grundtvig's ideological development is of a dramatic nature, characterized by a series of "breakthroughs", which on the whole he himself has set in motion following his many reviews of his life. Two at least of these "breakthroughs" are indisputable: his acceptance of contemporary German romanticism while he was house-tutor on Langeland in 1805-06, and his conversion to an orthodox Lutheranism in December 1810. Grundtvig's first historical works – the three *World Chronicles* of 1812, 1814 and 1817 – are increasingly marked by a co-ordination of "the human" (romanticism) and "the Christian" (Lutheranism).

From this co-ordination there is a clear path to his moderately secular political history in the *Handbook* from the 1830's. And here I hint at the main thesis of this article. I shall attempt to show how the first shoots of a moderate, secularized view of history are already present in the co-ordination between "the Christian" and "the romantic" in the *Chronicles,* and how the tension that despite everything else lay *in* that co-ordination is later slackened in the *Handbook* as Grundtvig learns to distinguish more sharply between the three areas of life he defines as the Church, the State and the School.

In the following I shall limit my attentions to the *Chronicles* and the *Handbook* both because I believe that Grundtvig's view of history finds its clearest expression in his presentation of "world history" and because his collected historical works are too numerous to deal with in such an article. Nevertheless, we must not forget that in his more than 60 years as a history writer Grundtvig cultivated many other historical genres than "world history". Two of his particular genres are versified history (on the medieval model) and the historical talk. The major works in these genres are respectively: the history of Denmark in *Roskilde Rhyme* written in 1812 and published in 1814, and *Chronicle in Rhyme for Living School Usage* from 1829; Church history in *The Pleiades of Christendom* from the 1850's; and talks on history with the ladies of Amalienborg Palace from 1839 to 1844, together with the talks on contemporary history *Within Living Memory* from 1838.

Grundtvig's most significant achievement as a source critic is with the Anglo-Saxon poem *Beowulf.* He both translated the poem into Danish in

1820 (revised edition 1865) and published the Anglo-Saxon text in 1861. In addition he translated into "servant Danish" the Norwegian royal sagas, written in Old Norse by the Icelander, Snorri Sturlason, and the history of Denmark written in Latin by Saxo. Then comes his major work in Church history, *Church Mirror,* from the 1850's, and various unpublished historical writings which have yet to be researched – for example, the hundred-plus talks he gave to the "Danish Society" from 1839 onwards and the lectures in world history for "The Danish Association" in 1855. And this imposing list is incomplete!

General Introduction to the World Chronicles

Even for Grundtvig with his incredible work capacity the *World Chronicles* of 1812, 1814 and 1817 are an outstanding achievement. Three times in the course of five years the young Lutheran minister sets out to give a unified presentation of European history (at that time regarded as "world" history). The continuity from book to book is emphasized by giving the volumes almost identical titles – *Brief View of World Chronicle in Context* (1812), *Brief View of World Chronicle Considered in its Context* (1814) and *Prospect of World Chronicle Especially in the Age of Luther* (1817). "Chronicle" is defined in *Dictionary of the Danish Language* (vol. 11, Copenhagen 1929, p. 680) as

> a presentation (especially in the Middle Ages) of historical events in their chronological order without attempting to show their connection or their developing context.

Grundtvig presumably uses the "chronicle" designation in all three titles in order to underline the ideological continuity with an older Christian tradition – the rhymed chronicle of the Middle Ages – represented on Danish soil by *The Danish Rhymed Chronicle* from the 14th century, which so absorbed Grundtvig.

This Christian tradition is also emphasized by the pious mottos on the title-pages, such as the words from the Lord's Prayer – "Thine be the Kingdom, the power and the glory, for ever and ever" – in the 1812 volume, and from Psalm 111 in the 1814 volume – "He hath made his wonderful works to be remembered: the Lord is gracious and full of compassion." The 1817 *Chronicle* is distinguished by a temporal motto – the proverb "What is truth, Time will show" – and a quotation in Greek from Pindar's first Olympic ode, taken from a passage where the comforting, conjuring and convincing power of poetry is praised. This alone is a symptom of Grundtvig's less rigid orthodox Lutheran attitude in the 1817 *Chronicle*.

For the young Grundtvig history is *Geistesgeschichte* – spiritual history and the history of ideas. Social and economic approaches to history were always alien to him. As the Danish scholar, Flemming Lundgreen-Nielsen, puts it in his doctorate *The Operative Word: N. F. S. Grundtvig's Poetry, Literary Criticism and Poetics 1798-1819* (Copenhagen 1981) Grundtvig "places poets and philosophers as signposts in his comprehensive reading of history and scans their works to discover the symptoms of their times".

This suggests that in all three *World Chronicles* it is the written word – literature in the broadest sense – that is the central subject. Lundgreen-Nielsen has also pointed out (vol. 2, p. 558) that the *Chronicles* are in fact literary histories. In the preface to his *Handbook* Grundtvig also characterizes the 1817 *Chronicle* as "Studies Especially in German Literary History" (*N. F. S. Grundtvig's Selected Writings* abridged, edited by Holger Begtrup, vol. 6, Copenhagen 1907, p. 11). In the writing of Danish literary history, says Lundgreen-Nielsen, the *Chronicles* constitute a major step in the direction of the organic presentation of literary history that N. M. Petersen established 40 years later and which Peter Hansen and Vilhelm Andersen continued.

Of the three *Chronicles* those from 1812 and 1817 are the closest linked. The first third of the 1817 *Chronicle* (to p. 191 in the original) is, with a few alterations, a reprinting of the 1812 *Chronicle*. Both presentations balance on Luther and the Reformation as their central axis. The structural consequence of this is that the final chapter on the Reformation and the age of Luther in both books is expanded out of all proportion to the treatment of the pre-Reformation period. In the original edition of the 1812 *Chronicle* this chapter takes up 311 of the book's 422 pages, in the 1817 *Chronicle* 540 out of 675. In both works there is a striking contrast between the concise first part in a popular, simple style – as in *A Little Bible Chronicle for Children and the General Reader* 1814 – and the analytical, critical second part. In both *Chronicles* Grundtvig has set out to give a critical presentation of the history of the Lutheran cultural community under the impulse of the approaching 300th anniversary of Luther's theses in 1517.

Whereas the 1812 and 1817 *Chronicles* are carried right up to Grundtvig's own time, his most daring and most ambitious project in these world chronicle years – the 1814 *Chronicle* – remains a torso. As a result of "pressure of work and weakness of body", he explains in the preface

(XIII), this very broad account ended after 552 octavo pages at the Jewish captivity in Babylon. Grundtvig dismisses the 1814 *Chronicle* somewhat unjustly in his preface to the *Handbook* as "an attempt to produce a handbook in political history which turned out to be a total failure and which for many years robbed me of the courage to try another one" (*Selected Writings* vol. 6, p. 11). Grundtvig thus links the 1814 *Chronicle* with the *Handbook* as an attempt to write in the genre of source-critical political history.

In its incomplete state the 1814 *Chronicle* appears as a broadly-based Old Testament Bible-story with paragraphs inserted on Israel's neighbours and with digressions on various and (for us) somewhat curious subjects: the location of Eden, man's abode after the Fall, the "kyriological" nature of the original language, the origin of idol worship, the specific character of poetry and "the origin of writing" – to name but a few. However, the digressions on language and literary theory are central texts for an understanding of Grundtvig's romantic-Christian poetics. I would think that a number of these passages will prove to be of considerable interest in the history of learning, because they have a bearing on the position, anno 1800, of a number of Middle Eastern subjects. The 1814 *Chronicle* also contains 9 poems – verse adaptations of Old Testament texts (listed in Steen Johansen's *Bibliography of N. F. S. Grundtvig's Writings,* vol. 1, Copenhagen 1948, p. 95-6).

Ideologically and stylistically, the *Chronicles* and the contemporary essays in his self-produced journal *Danevirke* 1816-19, show Grundtvig in rapid development towards his own mature, individual character. This is clearly visible if, for example, one compares his analysis of German idealism in the 1812 *Chronicle* with that in the 1817 *Chronicle*. A number of concepts central to Grundtvig, "spirit", "poetry", "power" are being marked out to be given their later content in Grundtvig's own language. One of his contemporaries, Christian Flor, Professor of Danish at Kiel University, could already speak of his language and style as

> consisting not only of a large number of powerful and striking images, but also of a knowledge of the materials of the language and a sort of sculptor's ability to create his own linguistic concepts.
> (*Bragi and Idun, a Nordic Quarterly,* vol. 1, Copenhagen 1839, p. 230).

Lundgreen-Nielsen says (op.cit. vol. 2, p. 562) that in the *Chronicles* we find "a highly imaginative world of imagery illustrating the movement and development of history". Grundtvig employs a sort of emblematic symbolism which may seem strange to a modern reader, but which one gradually becomes familiar with when one has spent some time on his writings. Lundgreen-Nielsen has studied Grundtvig's use of the "shadow" symbol in *World Chronicle* 1817. Another example is Grundtvig's use of the appropriately heraldic symbol of the "eagle" for the alleged German tendency to speculative thought and the construction of concepts (*World Chronicle* 1817, p. 379 et. al.). The idea behind this seems to be that just as the eagle soars up with its prey into endless space, so German idealistic philosophy constructs an "airy" concept of truth that has nothing to do with historical reality. Becoming acquainted with Grundtvig's conceptual world is to a large extent the same as becoming acquainted with a specific symbolism that is being moulded by Grundtvig precisely in the years when he is writing the *Chronicles*. Not least as a way into his poetry a command of this symbolism is of course absolutely necessary.

The 1812 *Chronicle* ends with an open, ideological criticism of prominent people in Danish society, mentioned by name, which must naturally have seemed particularly provocative. The 450 copies of the first printing were snapped up very quickly. A press controversy followed with Professor Jens Møller and the historian and philologist, Christian Molbech, which prompted Grundtvig to write a whole book in his defence, *The Chronicle's Retort* (1813). Socially, this is a crucial event in Grundtvig's life. His "outsider" status as a historian in relation to the official historiography at Copenhagen University begins with the 1812 *Chronicle*. Already in 1815 and 1817 he had to pay dearly for the cause célèbre when he applied for a professorship in history at Copenhagen University; nor did anything come of the attempts by his Norwegian friends to get him appointed professor of history at the newly-established University of Oslo. In spite of the fact that he had toned down his most provocative comments on his contemporaries in the 1817 *Chronicle,* in that year the nomination committee at Copenhagen University criticized Grundtvig's latest world history as follows:

> As well as revealing an ignorance of and indifference to every art of history and genuine scientific treatment, it contains so many warped judgements and ignoble expressions that it must be regarded as fortunate for the fatherland that the person from whose hand such products come is not allowed to present himself as a public teacher at any scientific institute. (quoted from *The Origin of Grundtvig's View of History* by William Michelsen, Copenhagen 1954, p. 28)

The 1814 and 1817 *Chronicles* were more or less killed off by a stony silence, and even 50 years later the limited impression of the 1817 *Chronicle* had not sold out.

The Ideology of the World Chronicles

It is natural to regard the *Chronicles* as the central body of Grundtvig's writing in the years 1810-20, because it is here that he argues forthrightly for what he calls his "historical view". Grouped around the *Chronicles* we find a number of essays – first and foremost in *Danevirke* – in which he systematically analyses the same basic anthropological questions that he had dealt with historically in the *Chronicles*.

A key concept both in the *Chronicles* and in *Danevirke* is "the conditions of man". This is the background for Grundtvig's major project in this decade, namely, the establishment of a Christian anthropology to fight the unhistorical systematization of thought in 18th century rationalism and in contemporary German idealistic philosophy. Against the *lack* of a transcendental perspective on man – found in 18th century rationalism – and against the *presence* of an overbearing, intransigent, transcendental perspective on man – found in German idealism – Grundtvig insists on the Christian idea of creation: how can man, created by God, exist outside a spiritual relationship to his creator and sustainer? I believe that not even in the introduction to *Norse Mythology* (1832) does Grundtvig reach greater heights in his criticism of ideology than in his profound analyses of the "intellectual view of life" in its two latest versions – French rationalism and German idealism – in the last chapter of the 1817 *Chronicle* and in the *Danevirke* essays.

The attack from Grundtvig's side is motivated by his conviction that European man is trying to forget the transcendental perspective on himself and his existence. This consciousness of the present crisis dominates the whole of Grundtvig's work in the years during which the *Chronicles* are being written, and it helps to explain the pressure he is working under. (In the crisis year of 1814 he publishes no fewer than 7 books!). All that remains of "the rose" (Christianity) is a "bud in autumn", he sings in *Roskilde Rhyme* (1814). And as the 300th anniversary of the Reformation approaches, Grundtvig writes that the fate of Christianity is to be decided in the North:

> Can the rose bloom so late here,
> Planted in our Northern clime?
> I know not, and now I fear
> How great the danger, short the time;
> If in the North it cannot bloom,
> Its time on earth is surely doomed.
>
> (*Selected Writings* vol. 2, p. 578)

In the midst of this crisis Grundtvig has endeavoured to present the historical testimony to the truth of Christianity as the Church's only means of regeneration. In the *Chronicle* years he sees his task as a historian in a clearly defined Church context. He writes history in order to answer the call he feels God has given him within the Danish Church in a particular historical situation towards the end of the Napoleonic wars. The historical testimony to the truth of Christianity – *that* is the literary programme that dawns on Grundtvig during his crisis in 1810, and which he has fulfilled in his *Chronicles*. The programme is formulated in the grandiose style he was employing at the time, in the preface to the strange little piece *New Year's Eve or A Brief Glance at Christianity and History* from December 1810:

> On the edge of the bottomless abyss towards which this age is rushing, there I will stand, I will lay out its own picture before it, and by its side I will place two blazing torches: the Word of the Lord and the testimony of the past. Call and warn in the name of the Lord, that is my task so long as He lends me strength and lets me lift up my voice; for His is the glory and the power for ever and ever.
>
> (*Selected Writings* vol. 2, p. 53)

The type of historical writing that the *Chronicles* represent can best be described in theological terms. In this description I shall draw considerably on my book *The Writing of History and the View of Life in Grundtvig. An examination of the two-world motif in the World Chronicles*, (Bergen-Oslo 1961), which I refer to once and for all here.

Grundtvig distinguishes between a truth for salvation, which God's revelation in the Bible alone is the bearer of, and a truth for "the transfiguration of life" which history gives us access to. The first is for Grundtvig the area of pure theology, the second of natural theology. To write history thus becomes for the young Grundtvig the pursuit of natural theology within the natural revelation of God in history.

Many years later, in the preface to his *Handbook* Grundtvig names his theological model for this type of historiography. It was a brief history of the world in Latin from the time of the Reformation, Johannes Carion's *Chronicles from the Beginning of the World to Emperor Charles V,* translated into Danish in 1595. In the preface to the 1812 *Chronicle* Grundtvig lists a number of contemporary, mostly German-speaking philosophers and historians as his masters: Steffens, Schiller, Heeren, Johannes Müller, Creuzer and Sismondi. In *The Origin of Grundtvig's View of History* (see above) and *The Strange Metamorphosis in Grundtvig's Life,* (Copenhagen 1956), the Danish scholar, William Michelsen has collected all the available information on Grundtvig's historical reading (cf. *Udby Garden*). He has researched the sources and in a well-documented, comparative examination explained the influences, the lines of contact and the parallels with these and a number of other historians, theologians and philosophers. Michelsen summarises the position of the *Chronicles* in a European context as follows:

> Grundtvig's *World Chronicles* belong to a series of writings in defence of Christianity, especially those that take the form of universal history. From this angle they appear on the scene remarkably late. The effect on their contemporaries was of a voice from the past, as the continuation of a line in spiritual life that seemed broken off long before, and as the resumption of a genre that was hopelessly out-of-date.
>
> (*The Origin of Grundtvig's View of History*, p. 37)

"Deus transfert et stabilit Regna. The Lord our God hands on the Kingdom and changes the government in a strange way" wrote the Danish-Norwegian translator of Carion's book in his introduction to the Danish edition in 1595. It is in order to prove the same thesis: "the necessity of Christianity for the History of the Nations", that Grundtvig tells the story of Europe in the 1812 and 1817 *Chronicles* with the major emphasis on the time after the Reformation and concentrating on the Lutheran countries. Grundtvig formulates his aims in the 1812 *Chronicle* thus:

> [If it is] true that not only all true virtue in these countries throughout eighteen centuries springs from faith in Him who was crucified, but that the Spirit died and awoke, the power was wasted and renewed, states fell and rose again with this faith, then it ought to be said loudly and clearly, so as to shame the madness of the people who dare to say that one can be a heathen, the enemy even of Christ and the Cross, and still be the faithful friend of virtue and learning, of one's neighbour and one's country.
>
> (*Selected Writings*, vol. 2, p. 179)

In the preface to the 1817 *Chronicle* he expresses his belief in the necessary connection between Christianity and "power", inasmuch as he will

> point out how power and virtue and all that at least on paper was supposed to be the nobility of the nation, withered and died in step with the disappearance of the ancient Christianity which rested on the Bible and was felt in the heart.
>
> (p. IX)

To Grundtvig's age this must have seemed a highly conventional theological project. The original element in Grundtvig's historical account in the *Chronicles* lies, as mentioned, in his combination of the orthodox Lutheran thesis that "deus transfert et stabilit regna" with impulses from contemporary German romanticism to form his own alloy. The special character of the *Chronicles* lies in particular in this alloy. Christianity and German romanticism – the two ideologies which colour the whole of Grundtvig's thought – have in common a "historical view", as he puts it. Christianity teaches that God became man in history. It follows from this that Christianity is composed of a series of historical events. Christianity is a historical religion. On the other side German romanticism insists that man can be understood purely historically, "because man develops in time and can only be comprehended in time" – says Grundtvig in one of his *Danevirke* essays. It sounds like Marx, yet the aim is not a communist society but man's total recognition of the truth about God and himself.

It is *this* "historical view" that Grundtvig builds up in the *Chronicles* and *Danevirke* against all forms of speculative systematic philosophy – what he calls the "intellectual view". The major question for Grundtvig is this: does the truth about man lie within him – in his brain – or must it be found outside him, coming from a divine revelation given to him and from history? Whilst the "intellectual view" isolates the individual through its insufficient intellect outside the historical life-course, the "historical view" makes a powerful contact with all the great men and works of the past – in the final instance with the "power from on high" which works through and in it all. Because the "intellectual view" is always the work of a single person, it is for Grundtvig fragmentary and haphazard, whereas the "historical view" offers contact with the collective, ongoing, cognitive process which fulfils itself in the history of mankind. Luther is presented as the main representative of this "historical view" in the 1812 and 1817 *Chronicles,* whilst the intellectual "villain" in both works is Voltaire and French rationalism.

In spite of the aggressive Lutheran orthodoxy in the *Chronicles* there is in the "historical view" an opening that leads out of the confessional ghetto, and one which was to have wide-ranging consequences for the mature Grundtvig. A close reading of the 1812 *Chronicle* will reveal that in it Grundtvig is speaking not only the language of the Lutheran orthodoxy but also the language of the German romantics. In long passages in the text his value judgements are defined by orthodox criteria such as Christian/non-Christian, Lutheran/non-Lutheran, orthodox Lutheran/unorthodox Lutheran. But then suddenly a value judgement appears that does not fit into this system. Grundtvig makes much of art and scholarship – phenomena that did not concern the Lutheran orthodoxy much when compared with "the one thing necessary". In fact in

Grundtvig's account the individual nations are contrasted not only on the basis of their creed but also of their attitude to poetry and scholarship: not just the Roman-Catholic Europe against the German-Lutheran, but also the "earth-minded" and "sensuous" Frenchmen against the "spiritual" and "poetic" Germans and Danes. The nations are evaluated not only on their creeds but also on such romantic criteria as: is prose or poetry dominant in their literature, theology and history or the natural sciences in their scholarship?

We find the same double criteria when we come to Luther, the central figure in both the 1812 *Chronicle* and the 1817 *Chronicle*. Why does Grundtvig place Luther above Calvin and Zwingli? The answer is as one would expect from an orthodox Lutheran: because Luther's theology is considered to be a more genuine interpretation of the Bible than the other reformers'. But here too another criterion breaks in. Grundtvig sets Luther above Zwingli also because the German reformer was more "poetic" than his Swiss colleague. Luther developed the "historical hymn" and read the Bible with "a poet's eye", while Zwingli with his "cold sensibleness" "lacked nearly all poetry". It should therefore not come as a surprise that the "most intense", "most historical" Germans gathered around Luther whereas the "acrid" Germans supported Calvin!

These examples could be supplemented by others from practically every page of the three *Chronicles*. They prove how inadequate it is to characterize the books as Christian or Lutheran history pure and simple. They are that, of course, but a confession-based history such as could blossom in its meeting with German romanticism. A Lutheran-orthodox and a romantic-idealistic evaluative norm go hand in hand. The high prestige that the orthodox Grundtvig attributes to the concepts of "poetry", "spirit", and "history" both here and throughout his later works can hardly be explained without reference to another background in the German romanticism that Grundtvig opened his heart to on Langeland in 1805-07. As I said at the start of this article (p. 53), it is my thesis that there is a connection between the romantic-idealistic element in the *Chronicles* and the moderate secularization of Grundtvig's historiography in the *Handbook*.

Handbook on World History

In the preface to *Chronicle in Rhyme for Living School Usage* 1829 reprinted in the 3rd edition, Copenhagen 1875, p. XIII-XXXVI we find the first synopsis of the account of European history which Grundtvig was later to publish in the *Handbook*. In the same place he also announces the plans for his major historical work. It is his

> intention to work out a prose survey of universal history, of roughly the same size as Johannes Müller's well-known twenty-four books in the three volumes, where as far as possible nothing is mentioned unless it is narrated directly from its source, so that children know what it is they are reading about.
>
> (op.cit. XXXVI)

Handbook on World History. According to the Best Sources. An Attempt by Nik. Fred. Sv. Grundtvig, Minister of Religion, was published in three thick volumes between 1833 and 1843. In the most available edition today – (Holger Begtrup's *Nik. Fred. Sev. Grundtvig's Selected Writings,* Copenhagen 1904-09), the *Handbook* fills about 1,400 pages. Both in its volume and in its work-load the *Handbook* is far and away Grundtvig's most ambitious historical work. It has also passed into the Danish tradition as his major historical work, has been republished several times, and in contrast to the *Chronicles* was used extensively and for a long time in the folk high schools.

Since the *Handbook* stands so centrally in the Grundtvig tradition, it is regrettable that scholars have so far neglected the work. I would think it has something to do with the fact that most Grundtvig studies are chronologically arranged, beginning with his first written exercises and following their hero up to the mature man. Few of them have reached the 1830's and the *Handbook*. And perhaps the sheer bulk of the *Handbook* has scared them off. For it demands an almost disproportionately great effort to become really acquainted with the three weighty volumes. Whilst I have so far been able to build on the research of others as well as my own, I have now precious little to hold on to. I shall therefore confine myself to a summary characterization of the *Handbook* with regard to genre and ideology, based first and foremost on the four prefaces – the collected preface to the whole work and the individual prefaces to each of the three volumes. At the same time I wish to emphasize that in the *Handbook* there are a number of areas of research for Grundtvig scholars to examine.

Like *World Chronicle* (1817) the *Handbook* contains a "secular" motto on the title-pages of all three volumes, a quotation from the Swiss historian, Johannes Müller (1752-1809), whom Grundtvig and his Danish contemporaries were very interested in: "Where there is most life, there is the victory". The *Handbook* is conventionally set out: the first volume covers antiquity, the second the Middle Ages and the third modern times. The first edition of the *Handbook* stopped at 1715. In the second edition, published between 1862 and 1869, Grundtvig added a brief supplement of some 10 pages on the period from 1715 to 1866.

Of the three volumes it is the second, on the Middle Ages, which has enjoyed the greatest respect. Holger Begtrup, an excellent representative of the first generation of Grundtvig scholars, calls it "in some ways his greatest work of genius" (*Selected Writings*, vol. 6, p. 532) and has found room for the entire work in his ten-volume selected writings of Grundtvig.

The crux of Grundtvig's account of the Middle Ages is the Anglo-Saxons as intermediaries between the older nations grouped around the Mediterranean and the new ones around the Baltic. The Anglo-Saxons were "the founding fathers of the new Christanity" because they took possession of the gospel and the mother-tongue "linking them to their strange way of thinking and the whole folk character" (*Chronicle in Rhyme*, 3rd Edition, p. lx1). Thus for Grundtvig the Anglo-Saxons were in high degree the bearers of the universal-historical continuity from antiquity to the Middle Ages. This is precisely the element that Holger Begtrup emphasizes as being a decisive new step in the *Handbook*, adding that "it has since passed into the general consciousness" (*The History of the Danish People in the Nineteenth Century* vol. 2, Copenhagen 1910-11, p. 153). The American, Kemp Malone, makes the same point in an article on *Grundtvig's Philosophy of History* in *Journal of the History of Ideas*, vol. 1, New York and Lancaster Pa, 1940, s. 281-298. And the Danish scholar Helge Toldberg writes in *Grundtvig Studies* 1948:

> The lasting service of both Grundtvig's work and Malone's evaluation is the re-appraisal of Gibbon with Boniface and his English mission as the centre of events.

All in all Grundtvig's positive assessment of the Middle Ages as "the new Creation" (*Selected Writings* vol. 6, p. 511) has a peculiarly modern ring to it. Today historians place great emphasis on the unbroken continuity between Roman imperialism in its last phase and the feudal society of the Middle Ages. A recent scholarly account of European history in the Middle Ages, by the Norwegian Johan Schreiner, is called aptly enough from this point of view *A Thousand Years of Growth*, Oslo 1953.

Whereas in the *Chronicles* Grundtvig addressed himself generally to the middle-class reading public of his time, the *Handbook* is an educational book, intended for use in a school context. In the preface he sees the *Handbook* as a continuation of his educational works such as *Chron-*

The monument to the fallen at the Battle of Zealand Spit (*Sjællands Odde*) bears Grundt-vig's inscription and the following sonorous verse:

One eve at sea the ships met,
The air began to burn.
They played all over the open grave,
And waves to red were turned.

Here am I placed as a monolith,
A witness to each Northern race:
Danes they were whose mouldering bones
Crumbled lie beneath this place,
Danes in speech, in blood, in deed,
Posterity shall call them thus,
Our forefathers' worthy sons.

(Poetical Writings I, p. 160, 1809. Photo by Inga Aistrup).

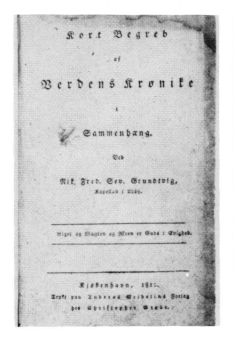

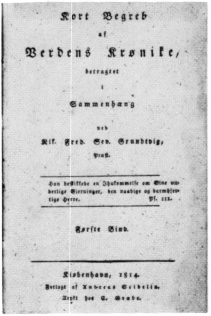

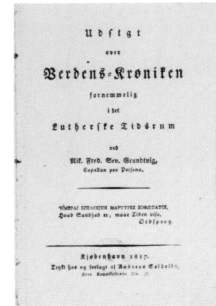

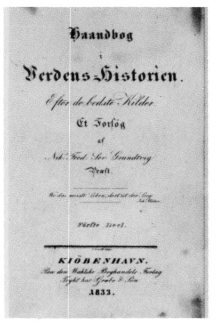

Title pages of the three "World Chronicle" of 1812, 1814 and 1817, as well as of the "Handbook on World History", 1833. (Royal Library, Copenhagen)

icle in Rhyme and the introduction to this, published separately, *Historical Teachings for Children*. With the genre designation, "handbook", which he uses in a book-title only this once, he signals that the work is

> not a textbook and not an encyclopedia, but a reading-book, in which
> those who know *Historical Childhood Teachings* and the *Chronicle in
> Rhyme* will find clear outlines of the most important facts of political
> history and references to the main sources, so that a competent teacher can
> easily examine their authority and acquire or refresh his knowledge for the
> oral communication that alone bears fruit.
>
> *(Selected Writings* vol. 6, p. 14-15)

The *Handbook* was written at a time when, under the influence of German national romanticism, great efforts were being made to secure and arrange source material for historical research. This material was often published in excerpts, much as Grundtvig does in the *Handbook,* only with the difference that he does not print his sources but refers to them and retells them. His principle as regards method is that the older the source used and the less one adds later evaluations of the source, the closer one comes to the historical events. Grundtvig summarizes his reflections on the use of source-material in the introduction to the first volume of the *Handbook:*

> When, after the sacred history of the Jews and the Christians, we wish to
> give information about antiquity, then we must of course give it as we find
> it, otherwise we shall be falsifying it and committing the awful anachronism
> of passing on history as the thoughts of a bookworm from the eighteenth or
> nineteenth century A.D. as being an account of the contemporaries of
> Christ or of Moses and others who lived many centuries before. We must
> be allowed to add our own view, if we so wish, but we must pass on the
> information as it came into our hands, otherwise we confuse instead of
> enlightening, and prevent the reader as far as we can from making a proper
> judgement both of the information and of our view.
>
> *(Selected Writings* vol. 6, p. 23-24)

In accordance with this Grundtvig makes a distinction throughout the *Handbook* between facts based on source-material and his own or others' "added view". The great majority of the *Handbook* is devoted to source references, while the "added view" plays a far more withdrawn role than in the *Chronicles.* And here I would suggest two different approaches to the work. On the one hand we can examine Grundtvig's relationship to his sources. How well does he know the sources that were available in his day and how does he use them? And on the other hand: what sort of "philosophy of history" is built up by all the statements in the text where Grundtvig gives his "added view"? How does he link the events he is narrating into a meaningful unity?

It goes without saying that there is only room for the latter approach in this essay – his "philosophy of history" or the ideology of the *Handbook*. One of the first problems must of course be the relationship between the *Chronicles* and the *Handbook*. Are we dealing with a break or a continuity? In a central and much-quoted comment on his development as a historian Grundtvig himself, in the collected preface to the *Handbook*, emphasized the break. He writes that the two works

> are related to one another about as much as the Hebrew and Greek view of human life and history are related, but I must add that I now prefer the Greek for educational purposes, not because it is for me the highest or the most correct but because it is the best one, at our present stage, to be scientifically based and produced. The Mosaic-Christian view of life, in all its directions and all its forms of expression is still for me the only divinely true and eternally valid one, but I have gradually learned to make a sharp distinction between Church and School, faith and knowledge, temporal and eternal, and I now realise quite clearly that just as the Christian Church must powerfully reject every attempt by the State and the School to reform it as they please, so is the Church equally unjustified in forcing the State or the School into a Church mould.
>
> (*Selected Writings* vol. 6, p. 11-12f)

Between the *Chronicles* and the *Handbook* there is a process of human liberation going on in Grundtvig that frees him from the orthodox Lutheranism of the *Chronicles* and carries him towards the more relaxed attitude noticeable in the *Handbook*. It is my thesis in this article that the moderate secularization of Grundtvig's historiography which this liberation carried with it into the *Handbook* is already under preparation in his high estimation of the non-Christian spiritual life, particularly in the 1817 *Chronicle*. It is thus characteristic that even the distinction between Church, State and School which Grundtvig makes in the passage quoted above can be traced back to the *Chronicle* years. It is to be found, already fully-formed in an essay in *Danevirke*, in 1819, *On the Church, the State and the School:*

> The Church gives expression to man's relationship to the Godhead, the State his relationship to the human race, and the School his relationship to himself. The Church denotes his imagination, the State his emotions and the School his sense.
>
> (*Danevirke* vol. 4, p. 20-21)

It was especially the Dane, Kaj Thaning, who in his major work *First a Man – Grundtvig's Struggle With Himself* (Copenhagen 1963) directed our attention to the process of liberation in the middle-aged Grundtvig. Thaning's thesis is that, particularly in the drafts for the preface of *Norse Mythology* 1832, Grundtvig writes his way into a life-long awareness of the crucial distinction between "what is Christian" and "what is human" (op.cit.).

To support his thesis Thaning writes a 44-page chapter and 4 pages of notes (vol. 2, p. 293-341) on the consequences of the secularization in the *Handbook* – the most comprehensive account of the work available. In spite of the kernel of truth in Thaning's idea, the major weakness in the chapter is that he throws the baby out with the bathwater, so to speak. Thaning will not give full weight to Grundtvig's clear statement, quoted above, that "the Mosaic-Christian view" is quite simply "the only divinely true and eternally valid one" for him, and he is therefore unable to see how limited and moderate the secularization of Grundtvig's presentation of history really is. William Michelsen hits the mark exactly when he says in *The Origin of Grundtvig's View of History* (p. 41-42) that Grundtvig's view of history is the same in 1833 as in the *Chronicle* years, "but his opinion as to how far it could be scientifically realised has changed from book to book".

How secularized is the presentation of history in the *Handbook* in fact? It is true that Grundtvig time and again stops himself when he has got on to events in Church history and the history of ideas. In contrast to the *World Chronicles* it is now political history he wishes to write, and he is determined to stick to the point. Nor will he any longer urge his Christianity on others, especially when he finds himself on State or School, though not Church, territory. A closer look will reveal that the account is perhaps not so secularized as it seemed at first glance.

A central concept in the *Handbook* is "major peoples". In antiquity these are the Jews, the Greeks and the Romans; in the Middle Ages, Western Christendom – especially the Anglo-Saxons; and in modern times, Protestant especially Lutheran Europe (cf. *Selected Writings* vol. 7, p. 445). Grundtvig's aim in the *Handbook,* according to his own comment, is to outline the "universal-historical link from Palestine through Greece to us" (*Selected Writings,* vol. 6, p. 41). However, as the Danish scholar, A. Pontoppidan Thyssen, has pointed out in *Church History Collections* (row 7, vol. 5, Copenhagen 1965, p. 589) this is precisely the path that the biblical revelation has taken from Israel to the grundtvigian Denmark! I agree with Pontoppidan Thyssen's argument (p. 590) that this cannot be called a secularized view of history:

The scholarly naivete that characterizes the introduction to World History
is, however, far from typical of the educated circles of the time;
Grundtvig's view of the Bible and history are far more ecclesiastical and
conservative than, for example, H. N. Clausen's.

There are four ideas which in particular help to structure the view of
history put forward in the *Handbook:*

1. "Universal history" posits a collective human life which moves
through the same stages as the individual human life: youth, manhood
and old age, corresponding to antiquity, the Middle Ages and modern
times.

2. Grundtvig links these three stages to the psychological framework of
imagination, feeling and intellect. The youth of the human race – antiquity – is the age of imagination. The manhood – the Middle Ages – is the
age of feeling. And the old age – modern times – is the age of intellect.

3. Grundtvig couples the same psychological framework to the three
co-ordinate areas of life: Church (imagination), State (feeling) and
School (intellect). The Church (imagination) expresses man's relationship to God; the State (feeling) expresses man's relationship to others;
and School (the intellect) man's relationship to himself – on the basis that
in antiquity the Hebrews are "the Church people", the Greeks are "the
State people" and the Romans are "the School people" (*Selected Writings,*
vol. 6, p. 344).

4. The universal-historical "major peoples" and "major events" manifest "the world-history side of human life" (*Selected Writings* vol. 7, p.
445). When one is presenting universal history, one must of course "distinguish between the events that had a perceptible influence on everything and those that only affected the individual race" (*Selected Writings*
vol. 6, p. 534). This of course makes it easy for Grundtvig – in accordance
with the practice of the time – to keep the Middle East and the Third
World out of consideration, for

> world history has nothing to do really with those countries where human
> life does not visibly stir itself or express itself.
>
> (*Selected Writings* vol. 7, p. 416)

Historical Effects

I cannot conclude this article without touching on the major subject, hard
as it is to define, of the long-term effects of Grundtvig's historiography. I

shall limit my remarks for the most part to Denmark and the rest of Scandinavia.

Of Grundtvig's historical works it seems that the *Chronicles* were the first to be forgotten. Only the 1812 *Chronicle* was reprinted later in its entirety – in the second volume of Begtrup's *Selected Writings* (1905). A German translation of the *1817 Chronicle* was published in Nuremberg in 1837 under the title *Grundtvig's Prospect of World Chronicle especially in the Age of Luther* by a certain Dr. Volkmann and with a preface by Grundtvig's friend, the theologian A. G. Rudelbach. The adverse judgement on Grundtvig the historian which Danish historians passed in his youth was based on the *World Chronicles*. It must be said to have been withdrawn later in the official accounts of historiography in Denmark, such as Johannes Steenstrup's *Historiography in Denmark in the 19th Century*, (Copenhagen 1889), and Ellen Jørgensen's *The Study of History in Denmark in the 19th Century*, (Copenhagen 1943). In both books Grundtvig is given serious treatment on a par with his contemporary scientific historians. It seems as if it was not least the prestige that the *Handbook* enjoyed for its wide range of sources and its faithfulness to them that helped to alter the official judgement on Grundtvig the historian. Summarizing the period 1800-40, Ellen Jørgensen maintains (p. 64) that the *Handbook in World History* is the Danish history book

> that covered the most ground, immense in its design and deeply personal, a source from which his disciples over the years drew knowledge and strength and constant renewal in their efforts to educate the people.

In the Danish folk high school, of which Grundtvig became the ideologist, history was a major subject. In fact for many grundtvigians the folk high school actually was "the historical high school", a feeling that was borne out by the fact that history teaching occupied a stronger position at the markedly grundtvigian folk high schools compared to other schools (Roar Skovmand: *The Folk High School in Denmark 1841-92*, Copenhagen 1944, p. 259). In history lessons at the folk high schools the *Handbook*, together with *Norse Mythology* (1832), was for a long time the most important written source for the teachers' "living words". We know that the *Handbook* was the most cherished and most used book of Christen Kold's, who along with Grundtvig was the great founder of the folk high school, and that he made an abridgement of it for his own teaching purposes (op.cit. p. 73-74). Including the printing in Begtrup's *Selected Writings vol. 6-7* the large and expensive *Handbook* went through three editions.

At any rate up to the end of the 19th century the *Handbook* and Grundtvig's historical sketch *The River of Time or Outline of Universal History* from 1829 were amongst the most important teaching aids available to history teachers in the Danish folk high schools. (op.cit. p. 64, 66, 100, 261). As late as 1907 Begtrup can inform us (*Selected Writings* vol. 6, p. 6) that the *Handbook* still

> after the passage of 70 years... is widely used by many folk high school teachers and speakers at meetings as an indispensable guide to the presentation of the course of the race in a spiritual light.

Some of Grundtvig's elementary textbooks in history also enjoyed a relatively wide circulation and remained in use for a long time. For example, *A Little Bible Chronicle for Children and the General Reader* (1814) ran to three editions in Denmark and Sweden and one in Norway and Finland in the course of the 19th century. Grundtvig's little *Elementary History for Children,* originally written as an introduction to *Chronicle in Rhyme* (1829), ran to no fewer than nine editions between 1829 and 1890 and was translated in the 1880's into Finnish. As late as 1916 the sketch of history, *The River of Time*, reached its sixth Danish edition, etc.

However, none of Grundtvig's historical works became a popular book in the sense that Grundtvig had dreamt of. And the work which has probably lasted longest is his Saxo translation into a popular "servant's hall Danish" (1819-22). It ran to four editions in the 19th century and has since been reprinted in 1924, 1941 (two different editions) and finally in 1962 as the first of Grundtvig's historical works to be published as a modern pocket edition (in the series by Hasselbach). In *The Study of History in Denmark in the 19th Century* (p. 37), Ellen Jørgensen says of Grundtvig's Saxo translation:

> Again and again we find in biographical sketches and letters down the century evidence of how powerfully it has affected fresh, young minds.

But the effect of Grundtvig's historical authorship cannot just be measured by adding up editions and numbers printed – that is not even the way to begin. We must never forget that Grundtvig the historian in so many ways was an inspiring and motivating force in Denmark. He was to influence a whole series of popular historiographers – we can even speak of a grundtvigian historical school in Denmark. This is true of men like Ludvig Christian Müller, Frederik Hammerich, Ludvig Helweg, Frederik

Barfod, Ludvig Schrøder, Holger Begtrup and Anders Nørregaard, to name but a few of the well-known historians. We must also point to the impulse that Grundtvig gave to the foundation of such organisations as the "Danish Society" (1849), the "Society for Denmark's Church History" (1849) and the "Society for the Translation of Foreign Sources into the Mother-Tongue" (1875).

Writing of Luther in the *Handbook* Grundtvig says that he

> was obviously a prophet, albeit of the kind that usher in a new year, since they carry a completely new age within them and seem to develop it out of themselves; in a way they themselves bring about what they predict.
>
> *(Selected Writings* vol. 7, p. 541)

Such a prophet was Grundtvig the historian in his own age and in the age that followed in Denmark and Scandinavia.

Grundtvig and the Old Norse Cultural Heritage

by ANDREAS HAARDER

I

Such a title is something of a challenge. It is so obviously right; for a Dane "Grundtvig" and "the Old Norse cultural heritage" are so inseparable that one cannot really talk about the one without mentioning the other. On the other hand the title embraces so much that to meet its challenge it is necessary to isolate themes, adopt lines of approach, form the material. The aim of this article is to contribute in some degree to an understanding of how in his work on the Old Norse material Grundtvig was able to exert so powerful an influence on his age and on posterity.

Starting with a modern evaluation of Grundtvig as a textual critic in an international context we shall define his distinctive character and special status (II), after which we shall treat and comment on the writings of Grundtvig that may be considered representative and important for an understanding of his line of thought and his contribution in the field of Old Norse literature (III). In particular we shall look at *Norse Mythology* (1808), the three translations: *Beowulf* (1820), *Saxo's Chronicle of Denmark I-III* (1818-22), and Snorri's *Chronicle of the Kings of Norway* (1818-22), and finally at *Norse Mythology or the Language of Myth* (1832).

We shall not distinguish in the article between the Anglo-Saxon or Old English poems on the one hand and the old Norse poetry on the other, since Grundtvig himself to an increasing extent takes it as a matter of course that the two areas form a synthesis. In fact we shall see how the Old English poem *Beowulf* takes up the key position for an understanding of the Old Norse context in general.

II

It is often either suggested or asserted that Grundtvig was so many things: poet, priest, leader of a folk-culture revival, educationalist, politician, historian etc., and it is always a temptation to take out a patent on him for one or two of these many things or shrug one's shoulders at him, call him a unique muddle, and leave him in peace.

When one experiences him in not just a Danish but also a foreign perspective, his apparent complexity manifests itself in a special way. Within the area of international research into Old English poetry he has been recognized as one of the great names for approximately the last 150 years. Many of his textual readings as well as his contributions to the dating of texts are still valid.

If, for example, one picks up a recent volume of *Anglo-Saxon England,*[1] the leading journal of its kind in England (and perhaps in the world), a journal whose strength and limitation lies in its emphasis on historico-philological research, one will find Grundtvig discussed in a scholarly context and with the greatest respect. Doubtless this would have surprised and confused him a good deal if he could see it – for he never once thought he enjoyed such respect among the scholars of his day, and thus contemptuously had to reject the need for it.

The Oxford professor, Eric Stanley, in an article that deals with the very broad lines of pioneer scholarship, points to Grundtvig's quite amazing contribution to *Beowulf* research ("astonishing brilliance"). Grundtvig's observations, he says, came to be included in the generally accepted understanding of the great heroic poem (p. 246). In another article, by an equally respected scholar, the American, John Collins Pope, Grundtvig is given special mention for his work on the manuscript collection *The Exeter Book,* containing among many other poems *The Phoenix,* which he was the first to edit and translate into a modern language, namely Danish.[2] Pope calls him "distinguished Danish scholar" (p. 140). And it is Grundtvig the scholar these writers are appreciating, a scholar who in their eyes has produced excellent research. To scholars the rest of Grundtvig's work, all the marginal matter, used to seem – and to some extent still seems – somewhat obscure. In a lengthy footnote Stanley lists the books and articles on Grundtvig's research achievements. He also refers to P. G. Lindhardt's English introduction to Grundtvig from 1951 and his book on Grundtvig in Gad's Biography Series (Copenhagen 1964), which, however, he has not seen himself. He then concludes: "Clearly

Grundtvig's importance has not remained unrecognized" (p. 246, p. 89), perhaps with the implication that the subject has now been pretty well covered. In the world of English and American research Grundtvig is a scholar who was actually more than that – but first and foremost a scholar.

In Denmark on the other hand, encouraged by Grundtvig himself and not less by grundtvigians, the idea – cultivated by his supporters and sneered at by his detractors – has gained the most amazing circulation that Grundtvig was anything but a research scholar, that he rejected learnedness outright, the dusty world of books, the black school etc.

These two attitudes, the foreign and the Danish, are of course far too categorically outlined. Grundtvig is becoming known abroad as more than the *Beowulf* scholar. Thus there is a new tone in Stanley's article when he argues that people like Grundtvig and the Grimm brothers have an irrational influence on the reader. One would "rather be wrong with them than right with other scholars" (p. 246). And in Denmark there has long been an awareness, at least among Grundtvig scholars, that his attitude to research and scholarship was rather ambivalent. Nonetheless the two attitudes are there, or perhaps we should say the two impressions of Grundtvig – the pioneer and research scholar on the one hand, the poet and preacher attacking scholarship and learnedness on the other. It is this characteristic duality that we must concentrate on to begin with, at the same time rejecting the two attitudes because they cut straight down the middle what actually manifests itself uniquely in one person. The vision gives a grasp of detail, and the interest in and commitment to detail give meaning because they spring from an overall view.

In this context an expression such as *living scholarship* has a meaning above and beyond the simple ascertainment that a number of Grundtvig's textual conclusions still hold true. It underlines the fact, first and foremost, that with Grundtvig – the man who debated with himself so much but on whom we must now offer an opinion, the man who somehow in his life turned his existential experience into a dialogue – an either-or is transformed into a tension-based and dynamic both-and.

Grundtvig himself touches on the inevitable duality in *Norse Mythology* (1832), for example in his myth-bound comment on the possibilities of poetry in recent times where he says,

> For it is truly a condition for a genuine art-poetry that what is left of
> inspiration unites with diligence and scholarly research –

and where he points to

> This great and important truth, that poetry must be scholarly so that
> scholarship can be poetic –

(p. 622)

It is Grundtvig's ability to greet the preserved, dusty, well-nigh inaccessible text as poetry – the scald's work, narrative and message – that makes him a better textual critic than his contemporaries. He has imagination when he researches. He has imagination to do research with.

On this basis he belongs to a very modern company of scholars and critics who have been widely influenced by J. R. R. Tolkien, the scholar and author of, inter alia, the three-volume novel *The Lord of the Rings* (1954-55). They have reacted against a centuries old tradition of dealing with texts like *Beowulf* as everything but a poem; of treating the ancient text as a storehouse for everybody else except the person who is interested in the poetic unity. Not until almost half-way into this century do we witness a coming together in *Beowulf* research of philology and literary interpretation. Grundtvig was odd and out of place in the company of 19th century philologists and historians, obsessed as they were with details. But he was a hundred years before his time. He is relevant now, and for this reason many of his writings deserve to be translated into other languages.

In the attempt to define what it is that gives Grundtvig his special position – and his modernity – in textual research, we must finally consider the area where as a man of the spirit and an interpreter of myths he reaches out a hand to the modern folklorist.

One theory that has played a major role over the last three or four decades in the study of ancient texts, Greek as well as West European, has been the theory of oral composition, ascertainable through an analysis of the formulaic character of the version handed down to us. The pioneers here are two American scholars, Milman Parry and A. B. Lord, who at the beginning of the 1930's followed up their idea of comparing their work on texts of Homer with a study in Yugoslavia of living oral poetry. On the basis of the poetry material collected from singers who could neither read nor write, they acquired techniques for analysing the ancient texts. In contrast to previous discussions of oral poetry, as we know them for instance in biblical and saga research, the discussion in connection with the results of Parry and Lord was based on concrete facts. There are definite form criteria, and if the text meets these criteria, then it should be oral, i.e. a written copy of the poet's oral performance.

With regard to Homer the formulaic character is such that it points in the direction of oral composition. *Beowulf* appears to be somewhat similar, even though the material for comparison in this tradition is thinner.

There has been a long and heated debate on the oral theory which it would be out of place to relate here. What can be adduced, however, is the fact that the oral theory points to something in literature that in our culture, marked as it is by the written word, has been far too often completely ignored. Even the word "literature" is misleading, inasmuch as it signifies something made with letters. In reality – and the idea of oral composition reminds us of this – it is the living, communicative situation that is central to the making of poem and tale. This communicative situation, the narrative situation, the interaction between the poet and his public, is ancient as the hills and forever new.

Whether or not we can call it directly oral composition, our own oldest poetry is close to its starting-point; a poetry that lives through and is conditioned by the interplay between the poet and all around him. There is thus with the oral theory an indication of a perspective which has actually always been of importance. It is a perspective that Grundtvig – and here once more he is a hundred years before his time – feels forced to point out again and again. In *Norse Mythology* he tells the reader:

> However, there is … no point in my forcing the reader to admit that the oral word is both the first and the most natural, and that even the *Iliad* was *heard* long before it was *read*. For if he has no living conception of the unparalleled power and glory of the inspired word as it swings through the heavens on the wings of a voice rather than being written on to paper like a shadow, then perhaps I can be of use to him another time. For here I cannot help him, and he might just as well close the book at the start as at the end, since he does not understand a single word of it.
>
> (p. 49)

Even the *Iliad* was heard long before it was read. For Grundtvig the same was of course true of Old Norse poetry. What matters – and it is not just imagery but springs from a plain and honest establishment of a fact – what matters and what must be given priority is the living word. And this conviction has wide-ranging consequences. The Danish folk high school could be built on it. In the following, much later verse, the demarcation of the central idea is so sharp that passions over it have run very high among folk high school teachers of successive generations:

Only words that pass in story and song
from mouth to mouth where people throng
sustain the life of the people;
Only in their own and ancient words
is education to be found
given by the spirit of the people.[3]

Grundtvig had visions that were to stimulate as well as integrate research. It is fascinating to experience the meeting at the crossroads between him and the 100-year younger folklorist and social anthropologist doing fieldwork with his notepad and portable gramophone. In spite of all the differences they greet one another.

In his duality, his inclusiveness, we find part of the explanation for Grundtvig's impact as an interpreter of the Old Norse cultural heritage. Another part has to do with his view of "the Old Norse life", which reveals itself as the demonstrable result of the above-mentioned attempt to combine the sharpness of detail with the broadness of vision. We must therefore make a closer examination of the way Grundtvig deals with the Old Norse literature.

III

When a poet has lived and written for many years, literary historians traditionally divide him into "stages". This is also what we have to do with Grundtvig, if we are to keep a hold on him. Yet just as the division of history into periods is an abstraction designed to help those working on them, so are stages something we impose upon Grundtvig. For it is not as if a person wakes up one day, looks out of the window and ascertains that now it is no longer the Middle Ages, now it is the present; nor does Grundtvig return from his trips to England (1829-31) without the earlier Grundtvig – or the earlier stages – with him. As he himself confirms in the preface to *Norse Mythology:*

> And since I now felt that after twenty-five years I regarded the Norse myths with the same eyes as when they first inspired me, and since I was constantly discovering more and more of the hidden glories that in my youth I had glimpsed and briskly assumed in the beloved, then it could not but strike me that I was actually one of the few happy suitors of the bride of scholarship.
>
> (p. xv)

Similarly there is an indissoluble connection between the Grundtvig who in a footnote in *Norse Mythology* (1808, p. 130) expresses his heartfelt desire to see *Beowulf* published (so that "a glorious light will dawn" on the relationship between the peoples) and the Grundtvig who publishes a new edition of the poem himself in 1861 and his second version of the translation in 1865.[4] And this is perfectly natural. Put another way, when an attitude that is romantic, characterized by imaginative assumptions and an insistent striving for unity, finds expression in 1808, to be followed by a period of increased effort and study, it reflects two attitudes to Old Norse literature which in Grundtvig are both considered to be right. And with the second edition of *Norse Mythology* in 1832 he has found and can use his voice partly to tone down the infatuation that cannot distinguish between man's world and God's world, and partly, being the scholar he is, to establish that historical and literary scholarship is something different from the mythical world, where he wishes to wander about freely as interpreter and advocate and let people and events be reflected.

What needs to be particularly emphasized is that the stage from 1815 to 1823, Grundtvig's "winter stay in the study" is and must be included in the area embraced by the two mythologies. After the stocktaking quoted above he explains about the interval in his own way:

> It is true that peculiar circumstances in my own middle age had, with regard to *Scholarship,* parted me from the beloved of my youth, but I had remained faithful to her *poetically* and *historically*. And I now felt when we met again that our scholarly separation on the whole means no more than the physical separation resulting from a trip abroad or some such hindrance, which, far from disturbing a happy marriage, actually by making it freer makes it happier and, so to speak, rejuvenates both bride and suitor.
>
> (pp. xv–xvi)

At the beginning of this article mention was made of the tendency to split Grundtvig up. The problem is also connected with the division into stages. Just as there is no point in the philologist refusing to concern himself with everything else that Grundtvig stood for, so it does not help for the theologian or the folk high school teacher to reject philology, when as is the case, philology receives no less attention in Grundtvig for the sake of life as well as for his own sake, than other areas of his experience. If we skip the stage from 1815 to 1823 – and the suggestions of similar stages at other times – we can receive Grundtvig's confirmation that they were tough times which, thank God, are now over. But that does not mean they were of no importance. On the contrary, they are key areas to an understanding of Grundtvig's special nature. The various stages are in a dialogue with one another.

So a knowledge of the period he spent in his study, immersed in learning, is in itself of crucial importance if we are to understand how committed Grundtvig is to his material, which is really what provides the basis for his powerful grip on Old Norse literature.

In *Norse Mythology* (1832, p. 139) there is a paragraph in which he presents a kind of overview of the impulses he initially received in his work on the ancient literature. He mentions a number of works which play a part in building up his knowledge before and in the direction of *Norse Mythology* (1808). In addition he draws attention to his great debt to Henrich Steffens and Adam Oehlenschläger. In 1806 comes his *Brief Comment on the Songs of the Edda*,[5] "my first literary exercise on the Norse gods" (ibid.). It is a well-written and relevant piece of work from his youth. In the nature of an attack on the wrong way to treat an ancient text, as seen in Jens Møller's rendering of the Edda poem, *The Journey of Skirnir*,[6] the essay anticipates the clash with the editor of *Beowulf*, G. J. Thorkelin, nine years later. It thus includes Grundtvig's considerations on the proper way to present the ancient texts to a modern audience, which connects with his later and comprehensive translation work. Last but not least, we experience how he attempts to include each little glimpse of the past, each relic, each poem, in a unified outlook, as it is so powerfully expressed in *Norse Mythology* (1808). The journey of Skirnir is part of the movement towards Ragnarok. The mythical poetry of the North constitutes a vast drama, in which man, as a historical being, plays his part. As Grundtvig points out, full of awe, in his pioneer work, *Norse Mythology* (1808):

> ... our inner sense is fulfilled and the historical pattern to be sought in the world of myth is found when we look to *Norse mythology*, which in five great acts unfolds the most wonderful victory drama that was created or ever *could* be created by a mortal poet.
>
> (VIII)

It is on the basis of a desire to give dramatic reality to the historical life of man that we must judge the great plan that resulted in the poetic works *Scenes from the Decline of Heroic Life in the North* (1809) and *Scenes from the Battle of Norns and Aesir* (1811).

It is 1815, however, that really heralds a renewed and reinvigorated scholarly immersion in the literature of the past, and the spur is an obligation – not to create – but to *translate* three central historical texts.

In *Latest Pictures of Copenhagen* (1815) he directs a vehement and on

79

the whole deserved attack on Thorkelin's long-awaited edition of *Beowulf,* the first in the world, with a Latin translation appended – and at the same time he commits himself to making a better job of it. And it is as if this obligation, thrown into relief by the scepticism of the scholarly world over what it called his flights of fancy, never lets go of him. A whole range of writings on the subject, published and unpublished, from his long life as a writer are a clear testimony to this. By 1815 he has also come so far as to publish *Specimens from the Chronicles of Snorri and Saxo* in a new translation, which, in spite of the fact that Grundtvig had much to say about its reception, was received all in all better than his specimens from *Beowulf* in *Latest Pictures.* The difference is simply that in his work on *Beowulf* he is a pioneer and had to pay the going price for daring to make imaginative leaps over chasms, whilst ordinary scholarship preferred to remain on the side where it was already standing.

Translation means several things. Every single element in the linking together of a large body of material has to be treated. It is relatively easy to read a text if one has a reasonable command of the language, but to deal with every single element, control it, and find a fitting garment for it, is a laborious journey. And the area Grundtvig had to traverse was gigantic. But the translator must also deliver the text as a whole, in a language that can be received and understood. In this particular instance the originals are in Old English, Old Icelandic and Medieval Latin, respectively, and it is the common man whom Grundtvig is addressing.

There are literary historians and writers on Grundtvig who pass by this mammoth task too quickly. Some mention only the two texts, Snorri and Saxo; others note that as a result of his work on these texts Grundtvig starts on *Beowulf* etc. Swift and somewhat misleading comments on a work process that was anything but swift, and where the words "well done" mean done well and not just done with, thank God, even though this is what Grundtvig sometimes says himself.

What then was the result of all this? Two translations into prose, with occasional verses as in the original texts and a translation of *Beowulf* into verse. But the distance between the translations is really greater than in the distance between prose and poetry. As a whole Grundtvig's translation of *Beowulf* is a peculiar construction; its aim is partly to tell a good and amusing story fit for children as much as adults, partly to inform contemporary readers of the poem's background, context, meaning, etc., and partly with the aid of notes and other paraphernalia to secure for the work an acknowledged status in the scholarly world of medieval research. On top of all this the whole work is introduced with a poem in Old English (in addition to the usual one in Danish), with kind Old English

Rolf and his Warriors. The tale, found in Saxo amongst others, was the inspiration for the poem *The Sun is up* or *The Echo of Biarka-speech* (Danevirke III, 1817). (Drawing by Lorenz Frølich, 1852, reproduced here from *Danish Heroic Legends* by Axel Olrik, 1900).

Nordens Mythologi

eller

Sindbilled – Sprog

historisk-poetisk udviklet og oplyst

af

Nik. Fred. Sev. Grundtvig,

Præst.

Vildae Valfödr
vel fyrtelia
forn–spjöll fira
þau ec fremst of nam.

Völospa.

Anden omarbeidede Udgave.

Kiöbenhavn.

Forlagt af *J. H. Schubothes* Boghandling,

Trykt i *Thieles* Bogtrykkerie.

1 8 3 2.

Title page of the 1832 edition of Grundtvig's work "Norse Mythology" with the characteristically grundtvigian subtitle "The Language of Symbols Historico-Poetically Developed and Illuminated". (Royal Library, Copenhagen).

words for both his patron, Johan Bülow and for King Frederik VI, which they must have enjoyed! The translation is in varied but always end-rhymed metres, alternating between a more continuous verse structure – at the start a harmonized imitation of the half-line of the original with two accents – and several more singable poems, more or less ballad-like, of which at least one example, with the refrain "Thus joy will come after sorrow", found its way into the *Folk High School Song Book,* only to find its way out again later.[7]

The prose translations of Snorri and Saxo are different. In the prefaces we can feel Grundtvig's closer fellow-feeling with Saxo, which is also due to the recent separation of Denmark and Norway. But for both works it remains true that the scholarly apparatus has all but disappeared. Here we find the Chronicles of Norway and Denmark ready and waiting, in an orally-flavoured "homespun language" or "servant's hall Danish", a style characterized first and foremost by Grundtvig's desire to pass the story on as vividly as possible, in a way which he himself had found best suited for coming into contact with the general public. It can be clearly seen from, inter alia, *Grundtvig's Literary Testament* (1827) that the Chronicles have their own place as part of a special cultural campaign. In answer to his critics he speaks as follows about the content, the aim and the consideration of prospective readers:

> ... was it perhaps foolish fancy when I regarded it as a great joy for the North to have a glorious folk-life from the shadows of antiquity, in which all generations and all peoples are fused together, and to have it depicted in the Middle Ages by scribes whom the same dim feeling inspired with enthusiasm for the folk heroes and folk exploits! Or was it ... foolish fancy that I dreaded the abyss that even in the North had been dug by the pen between the ear and the tongue, between the people and their scald, between the forest and the bird; for there was no hope of renewal and of the continuation of folk-life in the spirit unless the pen was cut according to folk-speech so that the written word became at least for the liveliest people a fiery utterance of the ancient folk-spirit, whose peculiarities one must get used to for the sake of the content. And was it stupid of me to withdraw from the world, from my ordinary reading-public in order if possible to make a good start on the great deed of love...
>
> (pp. 24-25)

So what are these translations like? Their appeal? Their effect? In *The Poets of Denmark* Hans Brix says briefly of the Chronicles – he does not appear to have looked at *Beowulf* – that their language "has a highly individual smell – like that of a hundred warm, brown loaves". He continues, "When one is talking about Grundtvig one dares to use such a simile."[8] It is not perhaps quite clear what he means by this. What *can* be established is that all three translations bear the clear stamp of the age they were produced in, and so it must be. They actually came to play a role in the education of the Danish people, Snorri probably less than the two others. Nor should it surprise us that the language in this, *their* chronicle of the past, should seem particularly foreign to Norwegians. Today the translations ought perhaps to be read as much for Grundtvig's sake as for the sake of Saxo, Snorri, or the Beowulf-poet, and perhaps the reworking of the Old English text seems the least accessible. There is nothing strange in the fact that the translations should be characterized thus in 1983. Grundtvig himself would have been the first to acknowledge it. In fact he actually points it out, when he sits with Anders Sørensen Vedel's translation of Saxo, which had last been published more than two hundred years earlier, which Grundtvig himself had read in his early youth, and which he himself is to write about now in the preface to his own new translation of Saxo:

> If anyone ... asks why, with all the praise I can heap on Vedel's translation, I have nevertheless kept my distance from it, and not attempted to follow it and improve it either, then my answer, like Frodi's, is that mending is always patchwork, and that we should be ashamed of ourselves if after the better part of two and a half centuries we cannot apply the pen to the mother-tongue more keenly and simply, especially in prose, than the best writers of those days! It is the same with old books as it is with old vats of gold and silver; if you want to improve them, they must be *melted down,* to rise again like a Phoenix from the ashes. Only then can the proper likeness be achieved, only then can the books become what as expressions of different ages they should become: separated by the letter, but united in the spirit!
>
> (p. XXXII)

United in the spirit. That is where the emphasis must lie. If we who live at the end of the 20th century are to follow Grundtvig's instructions, we must attend to the *idea,* formed through the cultivation of the poetry of antiquity, as it comes to permeate his greatest work on the Old Norse cultural heritage: *Norse Mythology* from 1832.

Although this book is called the "Second Revised Edition" and is thus linked to *Norse Mythology* (1808), we are now dealing with a heavy-weight, many times the size. As will already have appeared from the quotations it is written in an exalted language. Here is clarification. Here is freedom with regard to the reusing and renewing of the ancient cultural material. A rejuvenated suitor and a rejuvenated bride. All of which has something to do with the fact that his colossal knowledge of the past has now gathered itself together in a historico-poetic unity of vision, which partly is presented in the long introduction, and partly forms the basis for the subsequent interpretation of the myths which constitutes the main part of the book.

Man exists as an individual, as the member of a family and as part of a nation. With his three stages of childhood, youth and old age, or the ages of imagination, feeling and intellect, his very existence is drawn into the great battle between what is alive and what is dead. From a historical viewpoint this triad has sufficient resilience also to incorporate the history of the peoples or the whole universal history with antiquity, the middle ages and the present-day and with three nations or "national spirits" – the Greeks, the Jews and the Norsemen – to carry it through to the age of rebirth.

Our age is an age of make or break. It is in our time that it will happen. And in the awakening of the heroic spirit of the North through the release of the power that lies hidden in the imagery of the ancient myths, old and new, imagination and intellect will finally ride together in a gold wedding carriage.

Again one must be wary of overlooking the scholar in Grundtvig in favour of the prophet. His conviction of the coherence of the Norse past, which must now be summoned up, is something he has worked towards. The working material has been *Beowulf* first and foremost:

> ... as soon as we lend an ear to *Beowulf,* we can feel it is the voice of the spirit, which desires that all the peoples it moved over shall make *spiritual* peace, and faithfully stretch out a heroic hand over the Sea and the Sound, as foster-brothers in the Norse spirit, who already in the cradle mixed their blood, to stand like a wall against the power of the giants and the cleverness of the trolls, whose only aim is to bury Mjollnir fifteen miles under the earth and to place Idun in chains, so that the gods grow old, Asgard is destroyed and Valhalla crumbles in ruins and the Ash withers, before the victory is won and the course is run.
>
> (pp. 194-95)

It is the prophecy that captures the attention; but the fact is there too: *Beowulf* stretches over precisely those peoples Grundtvig mentions. It is a factual remark when he says:

> *Beowulf,* which is not just the laurel-wreath with which Asa-Bragi went to rest, but which weaves the Gjallarhorn into it ... had to come to light before we could discover the coherence of the Old Norse life and with insight endeavour to continue it and illuminate it.
>
> (p. 193)

In other words he had to know precisely that text before he could write his mythology.

The "Anglo-Danish" (*anguldanske*) is applied to the Angles and the Danes *before* the emigration west, and with Grundtvig this is the closest we get to antiquity in Old Norse poetry – the antiquity or the age of imagination, which unfolds itself in the world of Greek myths. But the Angles leave Denmark for England, just as the Goths moved south out of Sweden, and just as the Normans were to set out for the west and the north. We then have an age of "Biarka-speech" (age of feeling) instead of the earlier age of "Asa-speech" (age of imagination), and the age of "Biarka-speech" is the actual period of the Norse poetry of the past, the period to which also *Beowulf* primarily belongs. Finally, and again it is of course the Grundtvig triad – though here in a special Norse context – comes the age of "crow's speech" or the age of intellect, the age of art-poetry with a kind of beginning in the scaldic poetry of the Icelanders, which Grundtvig was not so keen on. But there has been a spate of crow's speech ever since.

Everything hangs together and can be stretched out in a long historical sequence, or it can be made into a concentrated power behind the interpretation of the individual myth, which will then lend a value of experience to what would otherwise not stretch very far.

One thing is surprising: presumably first and foremost because the Anglo-Saxon (Old English) transmission is so early – which of course is the main reason for its central position – Grundtvig considers the Elder Edda and Snorri's Edda to be by and large translations from the Anglo-Saxon. There are perhaps other early scholars who entertain theories of this type, but they are also different. What is surprising is that the idea of the living word, on which he lays such stress and which he himself uses to such effect, first in his writings and then later as a speaker and lecturer,[9] does not lead him to think of the scald who sings about the same themes whether he finds himself on his travels in one land or the other. "Widsith" or "Long Journey", the main character in the Old English poem of the same name, has – as Grundtvig well knew – broken all the limits of space and time in order to, and by being able to, narrate.

But translation from one language to another or not, more letters or fewer, for the sake of scholarship or prophecy – whatever the case, a feeling for bringing alive the past and the present is always there in Grundtvig. In the union of spirit and dust, in the union of history and the moment, he administers the Old Norse cultural heritage so that it can be felt to this day. The key word is coherence. Whatever does not rhyme cannot be carried. Let the following stanza from one of his numerous, still singable poems stand as one among a thousand, in which his engagement with the past has come to leave its organic, image-making mark:

> Birds fly like wind on the wing
> Lightly over the wild sea,
> Poets fly as the rhymes ring,
> Smoothly over the graves of generations!
> Therefore we bear the flame with joy![10]

IV

As evidence of the radical demand that was made on Grundtvig in his work on the crumbling Old Norse material, consider the following reflection on *Beowulf* from the time of his "winter stay in the study" (in *Danevirke* II, 1817):

> ... indeed, is not the whole poem a brand seized from the fire, a gold harp from heathen times, whose strings broke, and whose tuning-pegs melted in the fire!
>
> (pp. 270-71)

Not so long ago, after a laborious effort, archaeologists succeeded in putting together some fragments, almost impossibly small and almost hopelessly unrecognizable, which had been unearthed shortly after the Second World War at Sutton Hoo in Suffolk. The result can be seen in the British Museum: the harp, the instrument of the scald. Long before then, long before anybody else, Grundtvig, the thinker, had touched its strings.

NOTES

1. *Anglo-Saxon England* 9. Cambridge Univ. Press 1981.
2. *The Phoenix, an Anglo-Saxon Poem*, Copenhagen 1840.
3. *Tidings in the High North*, Copenhagen 1864, v. 54.
4. *Beowulf's Barrow or The Heroic Deeds of Beowulf*, Copenhagen 1861. *The Heroic Deeds of Beowulf, an Old Norse Heroic Poem*, Copenhagen 1865.
5. *New Minerva*, Monthly Journal, Copenhagen, Sept. 1806, pp. 270-99. Grundtvig does not mention that already in the following year the essay had a sequel, *On Norse Mythology, New Minerva*, May 1807, pp. 156-88.
6. Ibid. May 1806, pp. 212-31.

7. The first line of the song was "I no longer recall with sorrow," and it was included in the *Folk High School Song Book* as recently as the 15th edition (no. 346.).

8. *The Poets of Denmark* Third Enlarged Edition, Copenhagen 1951, p. 208.

9. cf. *Within Living Memory. Lectures on the history of the past fifty years, given in 1838.* Published by Svend Grundtvig, Copenhagen 1877, and in connection with this article see not least *Braga Talks on Greek and Norse Myths and Ancient Legends for Ladies and Gentlemen* (lectures held in the winter of 1843-44, Copenhagen 1844).

10. "Autumn" (1847), v. 5, *The Dane* II, No. 51, Copenhagen 1849.

Grundtvig's Ideas on the Church and the People up to 1824

by ANDERS PONTOPPIDAN THYSSEN

The Background

The Church and the People were major concepts in Grundtvig's world of ideas throughout every stage of his life, but they always existed in an interacting relationship as the focus of an ellipse. Many different areas of thought were linked to these concepts, and Grundtvig's understanding of them changed gradually along with the ebb and flow of his own intellectual development as a whole. In the first section here, up to 1824, we shall see how they came into being through the young Grundtvig's struggle to understand himself and his age.

His point of departure was a time of unrest, a tension between the old and the new in Denmark around 1800, that is, in Grundtvig's childhood and early youth. This was to a degree true at that time of the whole of the Danish-Norwegian-German "United Monarchy", which was Grundtvig's national and cultural horizon; in addition to Denmark proper it embraced the kingdom of Norway (until 1814) and the officially German-speaking duchies of Schleswig and Holstein (until 1864).

Since the 1770's public debate had been dominated by the ideals of the age of enlightenment, which found expression in numerous periodicals and pamphlets, societies and clubs, especially in Copenhagen, the cultural centre of the United Monarchy. Around these ideals there gathered a new, self-assured, middle-class intelligentsia, who were critical of the feudal ways of the authorities as well as the Church orthodoxy, in fact of any kind of "powers-that-be"; instead they were eager for reform in the Church, in cultural life and in popular education, in agriculture, city trade and social conditions. Their efforts were encouraged to a certain extent by the Government, and it was not without some justification that the men of this enlightenment regarded their age as one of outstanding progress. The most significant results were the introduction of common schooling with public schools available for every child, and agricultural reforms that freed the Danish peasantry from their heavy dependence on the landowners.

But in spite of a favourable wind the broad movement still ran into opposition and trouble, particularly as a result of the reformers' interest in the Church and the schools as the channels through which enlightenment was to be spread. The clergy were to function as "teachers of the people" for the benefit of the whole nation, in particular through teaching in the schools; religion would encourage industry and civic virtue, a worthwhile effort for the common good with a view to a reward in the afterlife. This implied an understanding of Christianity that was moralizing and rationally simplified, and it received official recognition through a new textbook in religious studies for young people (1791) and a new hymnbook (1798). Powerful forces were working for a similar reform of the Church service, and a radical reform of the liturgy was actually achieved in Schleswig and Holstein (1796).

However, the expected religious renewal failed to materialise; on the contrary, the decades after 1800 are years of decline in the life of the Church. For the most part the peasantry remained "unenlightened" and in Church matters more or less conservative; the reform of the liturgy in the duchies provoked an atmosphere approaching rebellion in the Danish-speaking area of North Schleswig, and the new textbook gave rise to similar protests in east Jutland, where laymen began to hold religious assemblies on the basis of evangelical and orthodox Lutheran prayer-books. There was also opposition to enlightenment theology among many of the older clergy, and in 1800 an anti-rationalist society was formed "for the spreading of the gospel" by clergy and laymen on Funen and in south Jutland which was linked to the Moravian brethren in Christiansfeld. Several bishops refused to introduce the new hymnbook in their dioceses and the wide-reaching plans for partial secularization of the educational system were held up after 1800 by Church opposition, first and foremost by N. E. Balle, Bishop of Zealand, who in the 1790's had made a stand against the radical enlightenment. The criticism also left its mark on the Government, who found it necessary to tighten the reins by limiting the freedom of the press (1799).

Furthermore, the "enlightenment" was overtaken on the blind side, so to speak, by a new literary movement. It originated in two lecture courses given in Copenhagen in 1802-03 by Henrich Steffens, who was both a natural scientist and a philosopher, and, with his Danish, Holstein and Norwegian background, a typical child of the United Monarchy. But it was German romanticism and in particular Schelling's "natural philosophy" that he presented: the philosophy of an all-embracing unity that can be *sensed* between nature and spirit, between poetry, religion and science and in the course of history. This "sensing", which finds its deeper meaning behind all "forms", breaks through most powerfully in the artistic genius, but it is to be found as a sense of poetry in everyone and is also the driving-force behind all scientific research. History regards it as an unbroken line rising and falling, but mostly the latter: this is the "fall" from an original mythopoetical golden age, at its lowest in the Roman Empire, rising again under the influence of Christianity but falling anew especially in the age of enlightenment with the French revolution at its centre. Now the renewal had begun in Germany; and a sense of the significance of past ages can conjure up "the most glorious ages in the most deeply fallen".

These lectures turned everything upside-down. They were strictly against the enlightenment belief in progress and they stirred up considerable resentment; Steffens was regarded as a dangerous man, even an atheist. But they were presented with great eloquence as a programme for cultural renewal and they were an inspiration to many young people, who were tired of the utilitarianism of the time. This was particularly true of the young poet, Adam Oehlenschläger. He began to write in the spirit of Steffens on "The rays of the divinity/in suns, in violets/ in the smallest, in the greatest", and in his choice of subjects he preferred the Norse Age as the time "when heaven was on earth". Oehlenschläger's early poems (1802-05) were a real literary event. They immediately secured him a leading position in poetry and they initiated a new epoch in Danish literature.

All these upheavals had a decisive effect on the young Grundtvig. They entered into his personal experience as stages in his childhood and youth, and the problems they presented occupied him for the rest of his life.

On both his father's and his mother's side Grundtvig came from clerical families of long standing. His father was a poor country rector in the "spirit of Martin Luther and days of old" (Grundtvig – 1815). He was not unaffected by evangelism and stressed, for example, the importance of conversion and "the exercise of piety"; and his ideas for a special kind of natural theology and natural moral law were coloured by enlightenment theology. But in the main it was orthodox Lutheranism that Grundtvig grew up with at home, and the same is true of the years 1792-98, when he was coached for the grammar school by Laurits Feld, the vicar of an out-of-the-way Jutland parish that was marked by old Church practices. On the other hand, Grundtvig made an early acquaintance with the ideas of the enlightenment. His teacher during his childhood was an out-and-out "jacobin", an enthusiastic supporter of the French revolution; and although Pastor Feld was orthodox, Grundtvig was given access to numerous radical writings that were being published in the 1790's. He read them without much sympathy, though; this was reserved for a counter-attack in the periodical published by Bishop Balle in the same years – *The Bible Defends Itself*. Balle was Grundtvig's uncle on his mother's side, and Grundtvig vowed to himself that he would offer his support one day as champion of the faith.

But during his student years in Copenhagen – after two boring years at grammar school in Aarhus – he adopted wholeheartedly the ideas of the enlightenment. This is clear from his diaries, especially in a lengthy retrospect from 1804. Politically he joined in the radical writers' criticism of the aristocrats, the "peasant-bullying" landowners, and of the Danish kings, who according to his diary had not excelled in intelligence. In religion he explicitly declared himself a heretic and poked ironic fun at the stupidity and superstition of the orthodox. He now regretted the time he had been forced to spend on the "soul-destroying" rigmarole of the catechism. Even though he now wished he could have taken up some other subject, he had become a theologian; but he had begun studying with no prejudice, he assures us. The pious children of God who mourned the Devil's victory over him could take comfort from the fact that he had since denied him all form of supremacy. He had also given up the doctrine of the Trinity, "that concoction of stupidity and rigorism, that caricature of arithmetic and antipode of all common sense". To regard Jesus as God is against reason; rather must He be seen as the perfect man; and the doctrine of the Atonement, in particular the dogma on salvation through the merits of Christ, must be left to the Catholics, who by rattling off a prayer can get even the worst scoundrel into heaven. Had he not become a theologian, he writes, he would most likely have been a bible-mocker, to the detriment of "those who cannot distinguish what is essential from what is incidental", the weak souls who only dare to hope for eternity through the merits of another and only perceive the authority of the teaching on obedience through the orders of the Holy Spirit.

This last statement suggests that in spite of everything he was thinking along the lines of a future clergyman. He had preserved "the essential", a sensible, purified Christianity that was not just of use in the pulpit – and a theology student was expected to preach now and then – but also formed the basis of a personal relationship with "the supreme good", with morality and conscience and "Jesus' wonderful teaching". Apparently, however, it did not play a large part in his life: his great interest was reading and writing. Since childhood he had been an out-and-out bookworm, ploughing through large historical volumes; as a student he had read anything and everything, in particular early Danish and Norse history, and he continued in this vein after graduating in the autumn of 1803, turning his reading into a serious study of the Old Norse chronicles. At the same time the pile of manuscripts he himself had written continued to grow until he hardly had room for them: all sorts of rhymes, plays, stories and tales, particularly on Old Norse subjects. They lacked originality, however, and were never published.

But the cool, earthbound attitude that had so far characterized him was completely overshadowed in the spring of 1805 when as a tutor on Langeland he fell hopelessly in love with the lady of the manor, Constance Steensen-Leth, and was simultaneously overwhelmed by the new romantic philosophy and poetry.

The first period was a happy one. "The days flew by in cheerful amusement and that glorious exchange of loving glances and intoxicating handsqueezes". The nights were even lovelier: "the hand that I had kissed warm by day embraced in dreams my bowed head and fastened my beating breast to the swelling bosom that by day entranced my gaze". His former plans of a career in the Church or the university and of being a famous writer faded; what was my greatest triumph, he wrote in his diary, weighed against "a gentle press from her hand ... a heaven of bliss seemed to pour itself out of her very fingertips into my open, embracing heart".

But his love soon became a ravaging, tortuous passion that he could only forget by immersing himself in his studies, firstly of the new romantic literature – sent to him via a reading society – and later of the Old Norse. And precisely by being aware of the "sanctity of love" his eye was sharpened "to view the wonders of poetry and antiquity, these original forms in time". "I read Fichte's book on the destiny of man, Schiller's marvellous plays and deep speculations. I left behind this life with Schelling in his Bruno." His nearest source of inspiration, however, was Oehlenschläger's poems and Steffens' lectures. He had a personal impression of Steffens; he was Grundtvig's cousin, and Grundtvig had followed the lectures – a series of which were published in 1803. But it was not until now that he understood them, and it was Steffens' ideas in particular that he discussed in his diaries.

His reflections centred first and foremost, in September 1805, on Steffens' definition of poetry. Grundtvig had understood poetry to be everything that bore the stamp of the eternal, while prose has merely a finite tendency. Thus a gap arose between poetry and "existence", everyday life, a gap that Grundtvig would not deny; the everyday life of man in "the morass of the finite" seemed meaningless to him, and his own existence had become a daily torture. But he found it necessary first of all to distinguish between the poetic vision itself, which "senses" the higher meaning of things, and its artistic expression. This distinction, which actually he could find in Steffens too, became of great importance to him later. Secondly he rejected the limitation of poetry to a higher sphere which the poet morbidly loses himself in, with no interest in life in general. Such a higher existence, which is poetry throughout, he found completely impossible. In his opinion the poet should "lend the finite the stamp of the infinite", and there must exist lower levels of poetry that through "viewing visible nature" could stir the "half-educated". Grundtvig's educational ideas as a tutor pursued this aim: he set out to teach his pupil "to raise himself above all earthly things, to the eternal Highest, without allowing himself to be disgusted by life", "give a deeper sense to reality without being offended by the external", (for further treatment of these points see Lundgreen-Nielsen's essay, p. 22).

Doubtless these views were linked to the fact that Grundtvig's horizon, despite his poetic dream, was still determined by his role as a "teacher of religion", a "teacher of the people". These were the terms of the enlightenment for the call to the ministry, emphasizing their responsibility and their importance for "the people". Grundtvig's own reasons are that he took a *practical* view of poetry: "according to the influence it has and can have on mankind as the cheerer of hearts, the arouser of good feelings and above all one of the vehicles of morality". A simple natural poetry is necessary "to raise the mass up from the morass in which they cannot see at all" – where they find happiness only in the finite and regard poetry as merely a flight of fancy. This, according to Steffens, was proof positive that deep in each man there lies the desire for a better existence. Poetry "cannot help but conjure up a happier existence than the one in which they move, but equally it must be regarded from a finite standpoint, it must be an ascending chain, in which the first and crucial link lies within the limits of experience". Otherwise it loses its purpose.

Grundtvig was undoubtedly thinking of "religion" here: it belongs to poetry. In the same context he stresses that "every subject connected with the Christian religion bears the stamp of the eternal", even in protestantism "the most unpoetic form of Christ's teaching" – at least in the old hymns. His personal religious notes made on Langeland reveal a greater warmth. On New Year's Eve 1805 he thinks about death and prays to the Supreme Goodness for strength in his struggle against all temptations and for wisdom to educate his pupil, to "ennoble his heart and instil a warm love for you and for his fellow man!" Then Grundtvig would be able to die cheerfully in the conviction that here on earth he had worked "to spread your kingdom of truth and virtue". This mode of expression belongs to the enlightenment, and his sermons on Langeland dealt mainly with virtues and vices; but there is no doubt that his "new life", as he calls it, has also given him a new access to the religious and the Christian world.

His falling in love was the first link in his "ascending chain". Love and life must be one, he writes already in 1805; it is the highest that we can comprehend on earth, "a spark of the divine fire that burns steadily on the other side of what we call death". Now for the first time he understands Paul: "when all is past, faith, hope and charity abide". Later he emphasizes the difference between the object of love and the higher element that it points to; the finite must be purified or collapse with "its pure primeval image" (May 1806). But also in his retrospect in September 1806 the first days of falling in love are like "a song of praise to the Father of Love", and he again quotes Paul: even had he learned to speak in all tongues, it could not outweigh "the loss of the only thing in life worth saying, love". These reflections proved to be of great importance; for the rest of his life love became the centre for his understanding of Christianity.

One of the next links in the chain was Norse mythology, to which we shall return. He was much occupied with it in the summer of 1806. But after that he took up in his diary the crucial task of trying to unite "the first theologians" and "the message of the Bible" with "the true ideas about human destiny" which he had learned from the German philosophers. In particular the teaching on eternal damnation and hell had been a problem for him. Here he sought help from the new speculative philosophy, notably Schelling's, which made room for far more religious concepts than the theology of the enlightenment. Briefly, his line of reasoning was that the existence of God also presupposes the existence of the world and of man, and with man's freedom follows the possibility of a fall, that is, the pursuit of a finite goal. What God was able to do then was to "send down" the true image of His nature as the way to reunion with the infinite. The "definite opponents" of this thereby cut themselves off comprehensively from the infinite. This is a necessity of logic! For the time being Grundtvig was satisfied with this; he ends up, "thus I reached agreement with myself on a matter that had long been a cause of concern".

A Criticism of Contemporary Culture through Religion and Mythology (1806-10)

Hardly had Grundtvig more or less reached agreement with himself before he began to go into print. This took the form of long or short essays and poems with which he hoped to establish a reputation as a writer. But they did have in general a religious and cultural purpose. At the same time as he was clarifying and substantiating his own views he took up the cudgels against what he saw as the demoralising forces in contemporary society, especially the philosophy of the enlightenment, which had by now become his chief opponent.

His first major essay, *On Religion and Liturgy*, was written in the autumn of 1806, apparently as a continuation of the ideas in his diary mentioned above. They were, he wrote ten years later, "thoughts on the wisdom of the time, my own inner soul, my destiny as a teacher of the people, my task as educator and preacher". He manages better than in his diary to combine his Christianity with his impressions from romanticism into a coherent philosophy of life.

He founded this on his own fundamental experience on Langeland: "the wonderful riddle of life", the inexplicable desire that transcends the finite. It distinguishes man definitively "from the other animals"; if he wishes to be "a clever animal" who is satisfied with the pleasure of the moment, then he must continually flee from himself, from his conscience, as he would from a pursuing demon whose attack grows stronger with the years. As an image, human existence can be compared with life in a valley, limited by a boundless sea; we sense that on the other side there must be a land of more beautiful trees and plants and of purer air, and it draws us to it as our original home. But we are separated from it. Neither poetry nor philosophy can help us. Admittedly poetry can construct a higher existence, but it cannot offer everlasting life in it; philosophy can lead to a consciousness of "life's conflict" but not solve the problem. Only religion can unite the finite with the eternal; it is "the golden chain in Jupiter's hand that is to lift earth to heaven".

This was Grundtvig's point of departure when he began, as he said, "to add my voice". It is characteristic of him that he now clearly gives priority to religion; and, no less, that he agrees with Steffens in finding the way from religion to Christianity through a historical and mythological philosophy: the religions lose themselves in a golden age when the heavenly and earthly merged together. The meaning of the mythologies is clearly expressed in the Bible's talk of an original state of innocence

94

with an eternal life which man lost by eating of the tree of knowledge, that is, by devoting himself to acquiring knowledge of the earthly existence. Thus religion lost its meaning of communion with the eternal; all that was left was a striving for poetry, and all the ancient religions were poetry. But with Jesus religion once again came down to earth; the idea of His two natures, the divine and the human, is an expression of his uniting the eternal and the finite. The doctrine of Atonement means that He reconciled the eternal and the finite, man and God. This is the religion of Jesus, "God's secret wisdom". But we can only approach this on earth through symbols, and this leads Grundtvig on to the liturgy, which achieves its importance precisely through its Christian symbolism.

All this is presented, however, in a running polemic that fills at least half of the essay. It was directed first and foremost at the contemporary debate on the liturgy and the demand for radical reforms without clarifying the concepts of religion and Christianity and without regard to "the great revolution" that these concepts had undergone in the previous ten years. Since the reform proposals were typical products of the rationalism of enlightenment theology and Grundtvig himself had problems with the new philosophy, his aim is extended to a general attack on the intellectualism of the time. Principally it is directed against the cultivation of knowledge, of which philosophy is an expression: and it is pursued all the way back to the snake in Paradise. When it came to the "critical philosophy" inspired by Kant, the latest fashionable trend in Danish enlightenment theology, Grundtvig was merciless. It reduced the religion of Jesus to philosophy, inasmuch as it determined mankind's nature on the basis of an inherent moral law which nevertheless could not eliminate all excesses; so we are promised a continuation of life in "a kind of eternity". But here there is actually "no connection between earth and heaven without the chain of morality which will itself ascend from the depths upwards". Grundtvig admitted that he himself had shared this view, intoxicated "with the hope of being able to stand as a free creature of reason on the firm earth", with a religion that was purified of "all the unreasonable things that Jesus and his apostles had taught". But he would soon have to shiver at the sight "of the naked skeleton that stood before us with no strength or backbone".

At the same time Grundtvig is leading a widespread campaign against the religious practice of the enlightenment. It was based, according to him, on a view of religion as mere "knowledge of the transcendental", which is why schools were to be the places for religious knowledge, while the churches would become superfluous. "But what nonsense!" It contributed on the contrary to "the contempt for religion that has infected

95

mankind like a plague for the last ten years". The highest was turned into a child's pursuit, even though a "glimpse of the eternal" is still only sleeping in the child. Under this heading Grundtvig also followed the enlightenment educationalists in rejecting the orthodox teaching of the catechism that he himself had been forced to suffer; as a contemporary manuscript shows, the school was not to teach Christianity at all, especially not as learning by rote, but was to attempt to guide pupils "to an awareness of man's highest goal". Yet Church practice under the enlightenment was no better. The sermons of the clergy were sleep-inducing: the dogmatic interpreted the system without understanding it themselves, and the moral gave instruction in agriculture and the like, or moralized with no sense of the religious; the rituals were recited in a hurry, even with "harmful boredom"; collects, prayers and hymns lacked poetic life, and church buildings were being neglected, and were even falling down.

There was not much left to be said after this attack. However, Grundtvig had to give a special position to the romantic-idealistic understanding of poetry and philosophy by which he himself was greatly inspired. But he apparently sought to distance himself from this with the development of the reflections from 1805 on the disparity between poetry, ideas and reality. Even Schelling, whose system he praises as "a marvellous new creation", came under fire here: "What use is the strictest logic when the first link is floating in air...?".

Grundtvig's next published essay, *On Scholarship and its Encouragement*, from the beginning of 1807 was a parallel essay on the higher cultural level. It had the same structure: a new definition of the task, the main point of view, and then on the basis of this a powerful attack on existing conditions. Scholarship is defined from an idealistic, romantic point of view, especially with ideas from Schiller and Goethe, as a harmonious development of the human spirit in branches of knowledge and in poetry; metaphorically, as a figure with both feet on the ground and a head in the stars, whose arms embrace nature, and to whose eyes the past and the present and heaven itself are transparent. Scholarship therefore presupposes "a truly religious frame of mind, an unshakable belief in the heavenly, and a sense of its glory", and Grundtvig now confesses himself a Lutheran Christian, albeit with a reservation concerning the Augsburg Confession. The positive religions, to be sure, will not allow any path to heaven, but "the genius will always be able to reduce two paths to one"!

Since the French revolution, however, "the eye of enlightened Europe" has moved "from heaven to earth, in order to observe a new heaven on earth". The branches of knowledge have become "mere vehicles for the enjoyment of life", narrowed down to the earthly life and put to the

N.F.S. Grundtvig in 1831. (Painting by C.A. Jensen, New Carlsberg Glyptothek, Copenhagen).

Facsimile of page from original manuscript, 1837, of Grundtvig's "Song-Work for the Danish Church", showing the hymn *Blomstre som en Rosengaard* (Blossom like a rose garden). In a supplement to the Danish Hymn Book published in 1843, Bishop Mynster included only one hymn by Grundtvig. Grundtvig commented: "It was chosen at random from my collection of hymns and ominously set to the melody of *Herre, jeg har handlet ilde* (Lord, I have sinned) and edited with pedestrian fingers." (Royal Library, Copenhagen).

service of politics, the social life. Also in Denmark-Norway we are standing at a point that bodes destruction for both scholarship and literature.
"People are becoming such sensible and industrious earth-citizens", the
"falsely enlightened" settle down in their irreligious morass, feeding themselves on worms and insects, and the students fix their eyes on their
examinations and their daily bread without the least feeling for history,
philosophy and poetry; and after their examinations and their appointments they exercise themselves vigorously with "dancing, riding, hunting
and ombre" etc., and as clergymen they are more likely to be found in the
field and the stable than in the study.

Grundtvig, however, had many reform proposals and great expectations of a release from the imprisonment of the branches of knowledge.
They were to be diffused by the "brilliant geniuses" of the nation and,
from the university via the clergy to the country. The peasant's eyes were
to be opened to the burial mounds of his forefathers and the importance
of nature which was to follow him to "the Lord's temple", and through
hymnsinging and the service of the Word "all the strings of his soul should
be tuned to the one note, ascending to heaven, hallelujah!"

From April 1807 Grundtvig began to concentrate all this efforts on a
study of Old Norse history, in particular the mythology of the Edda
poems. This was an old interest he was reviving; but this time the ancient
gods and heroes had acquired a deeper significance through his acquaintance with Steffens' lectures and Oehlenschläger's Norse poems. In the
summer of 1806 Grundtvig had sharply criticized a recently-published
adaptation of an Edda poem on the god, Freyr, who had sacrificed his
sword for his love for a giantess. It annoyed Grundtvig greatly that this
episode had been treated humorously with no feeling for its significance
as a link in a larger drama. Grundtvig himself knew from bitter experience what falling in love could involve, but *he* could not sacrifice his
"sword", and he "turned to the glorious days of the heroes to forget myself
and my bleeding heart" (c. April 1807).

However, mythology became more than merely a subject of scholarly
study for him; it became an obsession, a question of existence. Grundtvig
had a vague notion that behind its many episodes, mostly battles between
Aesir and giants, there must be a unifying view, more poetic and express-
ive than his own in *On Religion and Liturgy*. "Day and night my soul
struggled, and I lived among the Aesir" (May 1807). He found the key in
the Aesir's alliance with the cunning Loki, the symbol of the giant-race's
ingenuity. This "fall" became for Grundtvig the turning-point in the
mythology, just as the biblical Fall is in *On Religion and Liturgy*.

The most important result of this was the essay *On Norse Mythology*

(1807), an introductory outline, and the detailed treatment in the book *Norse Mythology* (1808). The main line of thought is the understanding of the mythology as a composite poetic work whose core was precisely the same problem as Grundtvig's own, "life's conflict". Through his "divine spark" the unknown poet had lifted himself up to eternity – just as Grundtvig's love had lifted him up to see, "an image of the eternal". But when the poet sought "the image of harmonious glory" in reality, he saw only conflict. "The growling bear and the hour of the wolf mingled with the howl of the storm and the dashing of the waves... In the unremitting battle against the earth, against the animals and against one another, he saw mankind standing victorious and beaten." His nature shrank, his spirit was close to despair – just like Grundtvig's. But then a light was lit in the poet's soul. Life's conflict was a *necessary* struggle, a struggle that embraces the whole of history, in fact the whole course of this world.

At first he saw the Father of the Universe ruling supreme. But when "the wild, formless mass" develops into independent life in the giant race, the Father must let his power be felt through the Aesir, led by Odin and Thor. They, however, seek their independence in a pact with Loki, cleverness, and through a peace treaty with the giants. In the next "act" the Father intervenes again through the Norns, fate; the Aesir must go to war against the giants and they create men to help them; after many episodes the long conflict between "power and mass" ends in the last great battle, Ragnarok, in which they all die. The earth is then renewed, "the eternal day" begins; the Father of the Universe has achieved his goal.

This is the skeleton, and there is not room here to do justice to the dramatic, eventful myths. They were a great inspiration to Grundtvig, also as a poet reworking the Edda poems. The mythology became a kind of parallel to the Christian "myths", which apparently could not inspire him in the same way. Indirectly his Aesir-ideas rested naturally on Christianity, and in *Norse Mythology* he introduced Christ directly into the mythical drama as a purer son of the Father of the Universe who deprives the giants of their "poisonous sting" and prevents Ragnarok. The dependence on Steffens and especially Schelling is also clear (as has been proved by C. J. Scharling), but the use of Norse material is new and distinctive. It is important to note that the major concept of *power,* which in Schelling is mainly impersonal and pantheist, is defined by Grundtvig as mainly "fighting quality", that is, basically a human power that manifests itself in action. In this form it was of great importance for Grundtvig's later interpretation of history and Christianity.

It was thus a new Grundtvig who came on to the scene. The essays on religion and liturgy and scholarship followed more or less the current academic norms; but now Grundtvig reveals his soul and implores his readers to grasp the significance of his great discovery. *On Norse Mythology* begins immediately in a highly-charged Old Norse style: with obscure talk of the indescribable pain he himself has lived through and of the "light that shone" in his dark night through the twinkling stars of the North, "whose glory alone helps me to bear the burden of life"; now he expects to die soon, called by Odin "to a higher struggle", but before that he will offer up his life "as a sacrifice to the North". The actual method of presentation also takes the form of a message from the dying giant, who, "marked by the spearhead", stands at the side of the grave. *Norse Mythology* is a much more learned account, but presented with life and inspiration and as a personal confession: "Belief in the great significance of the Aesir myth has merged together with my nature." Odin is the father of poetry, through which he has given mankind a link between heaven and earth; poetry is the Aesir's "imprint on earth", a spring "whose strong waters alone can revive the dying race and again conjure up flowers on the parched earth".

This quotation hints at the connection with Grundtvig's criticism of contemporary society in the essays on religion and liturgy and on scholarship. His fear of the final destruction had increased, especially after the English bombardment of Copenhagen in the autumn of 1807, which led to war with England until 1814. He experienced the events at close quarters as an army chaplain on Langeland, and from the autumn of 1808 as a student in the shattered capital, where he was given a room in Valkendorf's College. In the essay on scholarship he had described himself as a cosmopolitan, in Schiller's sense of the word, but the Aesir myth had made him a Norseman, eager to revive the old Norse spirit, "for it is the most glorious form in which any *man* has presented the eternal and its modification in time"; and "only the strong Norseman ... could conceive the giant idea of sacrificing the whole of time (history) to the struggle for harmony". Through the disasters of war he had also become a committed Danish-Norwegian patriot: his personal fear of final destruction, the impression of cultural decline and the threat to the fatherland fused into one; now more than ever the Old Norse spirit needed to be reawakened in the fight against rationalism's giant-cleverness, materialism and the enemies of the fatherland.

This line of thought was powerfully expressed in *The Masked Ball in Denmark,* from the spring of 1808 – a national, mythological judgement-day sermon, at once poetry and drama. Despite the war, he begins, crowds are gathering from all the assemblies "to dance and have fun at the edge of Denmark's grave". But the ball is interrupted by a pale and trembling old man with the name of Denmark on his breast. He raises burial-mounds, reminds them of the heroic deeds of the past, and cautions seriousness: "I call my sons out. Alas! Few are they who hear..." They see me ill but still wallow in "the lap of leisure"; they scorn the king of heaven and will not repent their sins, so "the temples of the Lord" stand empty.

> O rise up now, ye wasted fallen race,
> To heaven from indulgence's foul couch
> Recall your birth as heroes of the North
> For action, not for southern mawkish lust.

But the dancers will not listen; the wild fear continues until soon the old man dies and the whole company march off to "Hel" (Hell). Then "two groups of ancient Norse heroes" enter, a heathen and a Christian, who together hold a ceremonial cremation of the dead; the fire is lit in the sign of the cross and of Thor's hammer, for both Christ and Odin are sons of the Father of the Universe and both loved Denmark, "our father".

Also in 1808 Grundtvig sent out a subscription plan for a series of *Scenes from the Decline of Heroic Life in the North,* which was to continue the line from Norse mythology through the era of legends down to the introduction of Christianity. He did not attempt to hide his motive: in direct contradiction of "those who praise our age" he declared it to be "one of the great disasters in which time, so to speak, has been knocked off course". The question was whether it would lose itself in "a long silent sleep of death" or could be aroused to "life-enchancing, powerful effort" on the pattern of their forefathers in the North, "the earthly fatherland of serious life and unshakeable power!" Through dialogues in verse saga-form Grundtvig presents the battle between "the two forces, the Aesir and the giants, in their earthly kinsmen," until they are replaced by Christianity as "a third force from the south". The two volumes he published, *On the Decline of Heroic Life* (1809), and *On the Battle of Norns and Aesir,* printing of which was delayed until 1811, are Grundtvig's largest collected poetic work. He dedicated the former to Oehlenschläger, who was not entirely enthusiastic; he regarded Grundtvig as one-sided and chasing shadows but he had to acknowledge "the fire and power in the language and familiarity with the ancient myths" that distinguish the book (cf. p. 27).

From 1808 Grundtvig also began on a *study of history* that marked a new departure (dealt with in particular by W. Michelsen, see p. 410). Partly he produced a lengthy manuscript on world history for use in his teaching at the private school to which he had been appointed, a manuscript that by 1810 had reached the Middle Ages. Partly he studied Danish-Norwegian history on the basis of the two most important medieval chronicles, by Saxo and Snorri. They raised the question for Grundtvig of the meaning of Christianity for the history of the nations, which was at least equal to the influence of the Aesir myths in the legendary ages. Typical of his thoughts is the solemn appeal to his fellow-countrymen which he drafted at the New Year 1810. Here he develops the connection between the Christian faith of their forefathers and their powerful deeds, especially in the period of national greatness around 1200; on the basis of this he warns against the consequences of the unbelief of his age which he now links to their scorn for the Bible.

He developed this idea of the importance of biblical faith with even greater force in March 1810, when he gave his probationary sermon. It was in fact only a test sermon, a condition of ordination, but Grundtvig published it under the title, *Why has the Word of the Lord Disappeared from His House?* This provocative question is answered with particular reference to the development of learning within both the natural sciences and philosophy, but with a stinging attack on romantic, speculative thought which believed it could solve the riddle of existence through "human ingenuity". Especially "the Word of the Lord" should be preached again, in particular for the sake of unstable, simple Christians – but how it was to be done was never really explained.

The climax came in the autumn of 1810 when Grundtvig threw himself into medieval history in order to make a closer examination of the importance of Christianity. In October he achieved full clarity on the subject: "Now I saw that, as in the North, Christianity everywhere characterizes the life of the people, and its decline their death" – and he could substantiate this historically! Through this discovery Grundtvig felt himself called to be a reformer. He had to "put a brake on the wheel of time" and "turn it back to the ancient paths". Or as he wrote later in December 1810: attempt to stop his age "on the edge of the bottomless abyss" that it was hastening towards by laying out its own picture and by its side placing "two blazing torches: the Word of the Lord and the testimony of the past" (Preface to *New Year's Eve*, cf. p. 49).

The whole period 1806-10 was characterized by an increasing and finally a feverish intensity. In addition to the works mentioned Grundtvig wrote numerous minor essays and poems and also made a name for himself as a literary critic. His style was often unpolished, but always self-aware and self-confident. In his appearance in general – tall and well-built, serious and rugged – he resembled the old Norse warriors as he admired and presented them. After 1808, despite his awkward nature he gained friends of his own age and admission to the leading literary circles. This was a proof of his growing reputation that he undoubtedly appreciated. But ambition was only one of his driving-forces; more important was his passion for man's greatest questions, which for him were the major questions of his age. It was these that he attempted to solve through his comprehensive reading and strenuous thought in his search for a healthier and truer basis for religion and culture.

The Cultural Battle for the Bible and Christianity (1811-15)

The year 1810 ended for Grundtvig in a nervous breakdown. The immediate causes were physical strain and a painful clash with his parents, who wanted him to come home and be his father's curate. This conflicted with Grundtvig's literary plans; on the other hand his father was so weak that he needed help – and he *had* paid for Grundtvig's education (cf. p. 44).

But behind this lay many years of doubt for Grundtvig about Christianity; he could confess the religion, but only use it in a philosophical, poetic or mythological disguise, at least outwardly. In fact he shared the animosity of his age against blind acceptance of orthodox doctrine and therefore wished as far as possible to make Christianity understandable. His probationary sermon was more an observation of the age than it was a sermon; its effect was provocative, with its title and its vaguely orthodox tendency. His ideas for reform were based less on inspiration from Christianity than on its importance as a cultural factor. But as he later says, they caused him for the first time since his childhood to get down to reading the Bible and the old hymns of Luther and Kingo seriously. The impressions he thus gained did not harmonize too well with his ideas of a triumphant Christianity as the foundation for national greatness. He was forced to ask whether he himself was at heart a Christian. A few days before the sermon planned for December 21st, the first after his probationary sermon, he broke down and travelled home in a confused state of mind.

Shortly before, he had hinted at the path he must take in *Lovely is the Clear Blue Night*. The starting-point of the hymn is the night sky, full of golden stars drawing his gaze upwards – the stars of mythology, poetry and history. But on Christmas night they are outshone by a new star, bright as a blazing sun, and heralding the birth of a unique king. The "wise men" from the East set out to look for a king's son but sought in vain in "the palace of the king"; the star led them to a poor hovel:

> There they found no royal throne.
> Only a poor woman sat,
> Rocked the baby in her lap.

Grundtvig's new standpoint was his childhood Christianity, built on the stories, pictures and "myths" of the Bible, understood as literal truths. He thus made a completely conscious break with the learning of his time, both the rationalist and the romantically inspired, and he gave up his own great plans in order to become his father's curate.

Theologically he doubtless believed that he was thus returning to orthodox Lutheranism: with a faith in the "clear revelation of God" in the Bible, in salvation alone through the merits of Christ, in the doctrine of the Atonement and in the Trinity. But what his letters speak of in the course of the crisis resembles more "a revival" – his own term – which so many experienced in the days of pietism and in the 19th century. It was a conversion which he immediately proclaimed in writings published around the New Year 1811 and in the period following; and he added to his sketches of *The Battle of Norns and Aesir* (published 1811) "Christian conclusions", in which the ancient heroes are converted to Christianity. He also sought to persuade his friends to be converted, and even sent serious exhortations to distant acquaintances such as Bishop P. O. Boisen and the respected clergyman, J. P. Mynster, who were not particularly sympathetic. Thus he attempted to catch up on what had been lacking before his conversion: "Concern for the soul and its eternal bliss" (*Little Songs* 1815). It was this concern that characterized both his activity as a curate from 1811 to 1813 and then the sermons that he gave occasionally in Copenhagen after moving back in 1813. The sermon collection that he published in 1816, *Biblical Sermons,* was first and foremost revivalist preaching.

But Grundtvig differed from pietism and from Luther in the great importance he continued to attach to culture and learning, the state and the people. At least from the end of 1811 he firmly held that all things are sanctified by God in Christ, both history, philosophy and poetry, when they are used to the glory of God, and he maintained this particularly against the pious, who were only interested in hearing "one unchanging note" (preface to *Saga*). But when he saw unbelievers ruling in his day and age he resumed his cultural criticism of 1806-10, only much more sharply since he now felt himself on safe ground. The most important weapons were the same two "blazing torches" from the autumn of 1810:

103

the Bible and history. They filled his thoughts just as mythology had done earlier; in 1813 he thus read the New Testament through five times.

His efforts were directed first of all to history as the basis for a battle with the enemies of Christianity. It now became "universal history", guided by God's Providence, as was Israel's history in the Old Testament historiography – and it thus replaced his mythological drama that had been controlled by the Norns. The idea of a connection between the Christian faith and the life of the people was now treated from the point of view of God's housekeeping through the ages. The result was his first *World Chronicle,* which was published in the autumn of 1812.

In a new adaptation it develops, especially in the preface, Grundtvig's main ideas since the meeting with Steffens: faith is the power-source of history; faith in something eternal, in something spiritual above us, is the condition for self-conquering love, that is, for the formation of the social spirit and for "spiritual pursuits", learning and art. Without faith society dissolves into selfishness and materialism. This is true in general; "every nation's achievements" depend on the degree and the quality of its faith, and faith in this context is closely associated with poetry: the ability to see and feel dependence on the creator. But since Christianity regards man as a creature in God's image and shows that God is love, it must especially create love, courage and strength, learning, national culture and "the great achievements of a nation".

God's control of history unfolds itself in front of this background with the Bible as the guideline from the Creation and the Fall through Israel's history to the dark days of the Roman Empire and thence through the history of the Church to the Reformation. In the main section on the time since the Reformation the book changes character into an increasingly bitter attack on all tendencies towards decay, which in addition denote defection from the Church. Against these Grundtvig applies a cutting edge as the guardian of biblical faith: with hasty judgements on nations and Churches, with an attack on rationalism and the German idealistic philosophy and terse, as a rule condemnatory, characterizations of the great names of recent times, especially in Germany and Denmark-Norway and including names from Grundtvig's own age.

The book created a great stir and involved Grundtvig in furious debates right up until 1815. The criticism came in particular from the dominant literary circle around Oehlenschläger, who now represented a vaguely romantic neo-humanism, searching for harmony and well-disposed towards religion and Christianity. From this group came Grundtvig's opponents: the friend of his youth, Christian Molbech, who publicly renounced their friendship, and the famous physicist, H. C. Ørsted. They were incensed by Grundtvig's harsh judgements on the great men of the age, they emphasized their merits and leapt to the defence of especially Schelling and the natural philosophers; Grundtvig's attack derived solely from his delusions and fanaticism. In his written replies, Grundtvig acknowledged his debt to natural philosophy, but he sharpened his criticism; by uniting all contradictions natural philosophy removes the difference between truth and lying, bad and good, God and the Devil; the identification of God with the principle of development in life is not just pantheism but a denial of God; God only receives a personality through mankind, whose reason becomes the highest element in life.

Elsewhere in his writings Grundtvig continued his cultural attack after the *World Chronicle*. In spite of everything it had ended with a hope for Denmark-Norway: from here a Christian rebirth was to spread "to the south and the west". Immediately after the *World Chronicle* he therefore began on a history of the Danish-Norwegian fatherland. This turned into a lengthy historical poem called *Roskilde* (the old cathedral city on Zealand), adapted in 1813 for publication as *Roskilde Rhyme* and published in 1814. It underlines the significance of Christianity and the Christian kings until Christian IV around 1600, and it prophesies in apocalyptic colours the destruction of Europe as an infidel Babel, whose kings and merchants will "scream in horror". But in the North the Christian spirit of the forefathers will be renewed, the Christian faith will blossom like a rose – and "If in the North it cannot bloom, its time on earth is surely doomed!" He advanced the same ideas in an almost political essay, *To the Fatherland* (July 1813): the Danish-Norwegian people had reached a crucial point at which it was to be decided whether they would be wiped out or reborn and shine like a light amongst the heathen. But the condition was "serious conversion".

The background to this was the unfortunate war, now against both England and Sweden, who wished to annex Norway. But Grundtvig had pinned his faith particularly on Norway as the starting-point for the Christian rebirth – like Philadelphia, the sixth Church in Revelation 2 and 3, which influenced him so strongly. With the aid of his Norwegian friends he himself also hoped to become a professor in Oslo. When King Frederik VI had to cede Norway to Sweden in January 1814, he exhorted his friends at the university in Oslo to resist and to gather together the Norwegian constitutional ideas on the regeneration of the Church. He even sent them a proclamation on it to the Norwegian people and it was a great disappointment to him that it was never published. For a while he continued his efforts for Norwegian resistance, at least "up in the mountains", where he himself was willing to aid the battle and the victory and to "sing with you the great hallelujah on Dovre"! But in the end, to Grundtvig's grief, the Norwegian parliament "betrayed Norway" to Sweden.

However, Grundtvig was also politically active in Denmark. In January 1814 he worked for a voluntary student body, but he accepted only members who expressed on oath their Christian attitude to life. In February 1814 he published the piece, *A Strange Prophecy,* according to which Napoleon, Denmark's ally, would become more powerful than ever; the question was only one of whether he would now serve God! In the early summer he wrote a supplement to the *Roskilde Rhyme* called *Roskilde Saga,* marked by the situation of national defeat but with the same tendency as before: the King and the people should build on the Church; "if it is built up in the heart, the fields will blossom", otherwise Denmark would be ripped to shreds. In July 1814 he prophesied with surprising optimism that it was in Denmark that Christianity would be reborn. That was the meaning of the great hardships she was suffering. The Danish people were unique in Europe and were "the heart of the North"; Norway had "failed them", now Denmark was to become Philadelphia, the sixth Church, with the key of David to history's proof of the truth of Christianity – *On the Prospects for Christ's Church.* Around the same time he wrote a solemn appeal to the King to proclaim that the preaching of "God's revealed word" should now be resumed, and to make it clear that the salvation of the country was to be found solely in true conversion.

He apparently had the vague idea, as he himself later stated, that the King and the leading men of the state should take it upon themselves to restore the Lutheran State Church in an acknowledgement of the socially disintegrating effects of unbelief. He himself did what he could with continual fulminations against the unbelief of the clergy partly in his writings, partly in a series of lectures at diocesan convents. Most powerfully of all, in the last of these convent speeches, *On Polemics and Tolerance,* in October 1814: the Church's teaching was now mostly "lies and vanity"; "if the Danish clergy does not rise and fight for the faith, then there will be no Christian Church any longer in Denmark, then its altar will be broken down and its choir desecrated by heathen crowds..." In *Roskilde Rhyme,* published in the same year, he even reprimanded the Zealand bishop, Frederik Münter, whom he urged to put on "the leading strings of the cross" and to find "the sword with the keen edge", which was to protect the Church; for midnight was brooding over the earth, and the people were asleep, poisoned by the "trolls" of time.

The violent fighting spirit and the prophetic self-awareness which

106

characterized Grundtvig's actions in these years still astonishes today. It can, however, be explained largely as a consequence of his ideas on the importance of faith for the state and the people. His Danish-Norwegian fatherland was in the greatest danger and in Grundtvig's opinion could only be saved by a reawakening of the Christian faith. But his many attacks and various prophesies only seemed to damage himself and the cause he was fighting for. Still more people regarded him as arrogant and overwrought, even insane. The literary circles wrote him off after the debate on the *Chronicle,* and when he applied to the King for a professorship in 1815, the University of Copenhagen stated that he was no good either as a historian or as a university reader. He had already infuriated the Copenhagen clergy with his probationary sermon, which led to an official reprimand; and after his convent speech in October 1814 his bishop, Frederik Münter, sent him a letter of serious disapproval of his "storming polemic" and "unkind condemnation". Fewer and fewer clergy urged him to preach, and after preaching on St. Stephen's Day 1815 he declared that he would no longer stand up in a pulpit in the capital unless he was called upon as a minister of God. As a reason for this he referred to the fact that he was still being maligned as a dreamer, fanatic and a seducer of the people, without any of his listeners publicly defending him.

Grundtvig's Historical View (1815-20)

In 1815 all roads seemed to be closed to Grundtvig. He would prefer to be a parish priest and he sent off one application after another even though they were for the poorest livings, but with no result for six years. He had to make his name known in Copenhagen as a "beggar-like scholar", mostly through private support from various sides. But for his writing it meant a new chapter and a very different one from the previous period. The change was both conscious and deliberate. When he wrote the preface to his collection of sermons, *Biblical Sermons,* in April 1816, he declared that he had now been preaching his faith for five years without anyone taking note of him; he would therefore keep his place as a clergyman and instead "let the poet and the scholar speak", especially about the past. A contemporary letter shows that he considered it to be "a necessary detour" in order to disprove the opinion which had spread that his sharp words were dreams, fanaticism and natural hot temper.

Another letter, from July 1818, dates the decision back to the autumn of 1815; but already from the beginning of 1815 he was working on his new plans, first and foremost the translation of Saxo's and Snorri's chronicles from Latin and Icelandic into reading for the common man. In August 1815 he started up a little publishing company which was to be responsible for subscriptions or contributions; the idea was that the books should be sold as cheaply as possible, with no profit for Grundtvig.

Outside the Copenhagen literary circles Grundtvig expected to find an interest in the project and the group supporting him actually came to include the whole country, particular government officials and relatively simple folk. The work, which also involved the Anglo-Saxon poem, *Beowulf,* confined Grundtvig to quiet philological studies and in the end took seven years.

Grundtvig limited his participation in the contemporary debate largely to the periodical *Danevirke,* which he himself published and wrote for the first four years, 1816-19. The name refers to the ancient earthworks on the southern border of Schleswig, but Grundtvig took it as a spiritual rampart against alien forces, especially rationalism and romantic philosophy, which were encroaching from the south It contained poems, translations of the Old Norse texts, historical, philosophical and topical articles illuminating Grundtvig's view of man; he hoped thereby to find out, as he wrote in 1817, "whether the eye is just as blind to man, his conditions and his needs as it is for man's saviour". His new attitude is characterized formally by a much more controlled, "light-hearted", broad and simple style.

In addition to this he published a third and larger work, *World Chronicle* (1817). This was a reworked version of the first *Chronicle,* but now Grundtvig wished to appear solely as a historian, not as a clergyman. Faith should be people's own business; Grundtvig wanted only to pass on what "saga and sense" have to tell us. In fact in many cases he also softens "the hard expressions that only the zeal of the priest found authorised by the scriptures". The book is drawn up along the same fronts, however, and follows in the main the same line as the first *Chronicle,* though with the main emphasis on the history of ideas and with a particularly thorough treatment of the tendencies to decay in German culture after the Reformation.

These writings contained an important new departure in Grundtvig's ideas on the Church and the people. It became clear in this period that his *view of history* contained much more than his tough judgements and constant demands for conversion had led one to suppose. True it was based on the Bible, but not exclusively; and his use of the Bible was far from being bound to the traditional Lutheran biblical orthodoxy.

One of his major points is already hinted at in the poem, *Odin and*

Saga, from the autumn of 1810 (published in *Idun*). As in *On Religion and Liturgy,* man is seen as metaphorically bound to a strange country from which he longs to escape. Here it is not the sea but the mist that closes around us, the mist of the past and the future. But through the country there runs a stream which "comes from our fatherland". It is the stream of history, in which the past is reflected; and when one has drunk of it, songs about men and their feats are sung cheerfully and the times unfold themselves in the saga-writings:

> The mist is lifted more and more
> Many a glimpse the eye will catch
> From home they seem to come.

This view of history cannot be immediately identified with the biblical one. On the other hand it does point to a general sense of the "men and deeds" of history which *also* characterizes Grundtvig's account of history. Particularly in the *World Chronicle* of 1817 and throughout the *Danevirke* period it becomes clear that history is not just proof of the importance of the Christian faith. History is full of strange occurrences, people and ages of progress which unexpectedly overcome great difficulties. They must be understood as a manifestation of spiritual power, just as outbreaks of rebellion and periods of decay are due to impotency or wilful dissociation from the invisible world which is the source of man's power. The great historical examples for the Church are Christ's advent in a remote corner of the Roman Empire, then the victory by the fragile orthodox Church over the Roman state, followed by the reformers' renewal of the Church – which had such importance for the enlightenment of the people and learning. But the power of the spirit and the faith also expressed itself amongst the heathen as it did with the advance of the mohammedans and in the great age of the Old Norse, which coincided with the flourishing of the age of mythology.

Nonetheless the view of history in *Odin and Saga* is collated in a strange way with the biblical one. That is apparently what he sets out to achieve in the preface to the first *Chronicle,* but it is very much the case in the 1814 *World Chronicle*, a strange torso, which begins with the Creation and Fall and only reaches the early history of Israel. But the book is also an account, influenced by Steffens and Schelling, of the meaning of history which is traced all the way back to the Creation. The creation of man in God's image made him not only a picture of God but also involved a task: his idea of God was to be illuminated in the course of time by "seeing through a glass" (using Paul's expression in Corinthians) until in the end it fused together with God. At the Fall the image of God in man is corrupted, but not completely; man still has the same destiny, which is also the goal of history. The words of primitive languages were images of the creative word, which was forgotten after the Fall. However, remnants of this image-language stayed alive for a time among the ancient peoples and religions, particularly in Israel, and this can still be "glimpsed" by an inspired poet. For in fact everything reflects its first pattern in Paradise, but we are surrounded by mist, which makes it hard to see. Furthermore God is reflected in a special way by history, understood as God's action and control of development. This is true symbolically of the history of ancient Israel as the chosen people, who – as the Bible shows – were particularly well-endowed poetically and historically and who time and again after a deep fall were recreated in a mysterious way.

The book contains in addition a number of other ideas that are basic to Grundtvig, such as the nature of man, the variety of languages and the different characteristics of the nations. His view of man is also treated in contemporary philosophical thought (under the title *On the Conditions of Man*), which was continued in *Danevirke*. The ideas on the different languages and nations find topical expression in the essay, *Europe, France and Napoleon*, from 1815, in which Grundtvig seeks new hope for his country after the national defeat. He maintains that most European nations are driven by a craving for power, in politics, the natural sciences and in philosophy, and thus they actually serve the Devil in a continuation of the clash with God at the Fall. The historical model is the Romans, who suppressed one nation after the other; the Roman power-craving was taken up especially by the French with the French revolution and Napoleon as its latest expression. But the Danish people were never suppressed and therefore preserved their "folk-heart"; that is why Christianity can unite with the Danish "people of the heart" and it is Grundtvig's hope that "the spirit of Rome will fall before the angel of Denmark"!

This was the background for Grundtvig's new-found enthusiasm for *the Danish people*, which began in 1814 (see p. 35), but which is particularly characteristic of the period 1815-20. This was not due merely to ordinary national sentiment; it is Grundtvig's long historical perspective that gives Denmark a special position corresponding to that of ancient Israel. Christian and national rebirth are fused together; the rebuilding of the old Danevirke will turn Denmark into "a fenced Church field", and Grundtvig can nourish this hope, in spite of the people's unbelief on the basis of the accounts in the history of Israel of God's intervention and help in the darkest periods of the Jewish people.

This line of thought is a continuation of the main ideas in the period

1811-15, but it now has a much *greater breadth*. The emphasis on the heart of the Danish people rests on their natural warmth, which has manifested itself in their feel for poetry and history, just as in ancient Israel. Grundtvig discovers this feel in the old hymns and in a number of older and more recent historians with a Christian background, while at the same time quite naturally underlining the people's Christian fore-fathers as a model for the present age. However, the main evidence is Saxo's history of Denmark, which contains for the most part legends and poems from the pagan period. In a presentation of his translations from 1815 Grundtvig praises not least this older part of Saxo's work as a testimony to the kind heart of the people, who must continue to "tune their mind to love and truthfulness". This natural love has its root in God, whose love purifies everything and destroys nothing that is of God. And "where not even natural love is to be found, there to be sure is God's love even less to be found". In his articles in *Danevirke* Grundtvig also shows an interest in folk-memories of every kind, folksongs, folkstories, proverbs, dialects and graces of the past.

Grundtvig's philosophical observations also led him on to a general *philosophical elucidation* of human existence which far exceeded the orthodox Lutheran dogmatics and was stamped throughout with a great originality. These considerations began, as mentioned, around the time of the *World Chronicle* in 1814, but were voiced in particular in *Dane-virke*, in unpublished articles and also in the *World Chronicle* of 1817. They do not constitute a system, nor do they build on a consistent and uniform conceptual idea. On the contrary, Grundtvig rejects categori-cally the philosophers' artifice; he wishes to couch his thought in the everyday language of the common man, and to appeal to the general common sense. This point of view was partly inspired by English empiri-cism; but otherwise his observations are an attack on the whole of 18th century philosophy from Christian Wolff to Schelling. The argument is directed not least against Schelling's natural philosophy and the "intellec-tual view" that claims directly and of its own accord to be able to apprehend the reason and aim of existence. Against this Grundtvig sets what he calls "the historical view". Every closed philosophical system is a great lie, says Grundtvig, since it demands that the philosopher himself stands outside time. A thorough understanding of existence can only be of a historical nature, but the 18th century philosophers lacked precisely that sense of history, which they neglected and despised.

Only three major points of view will be stressed here. Firstly, Grundt-vig clearly rejects the division that rationalist and idealist philosophy makes between *the spiritual and the corporal*. We must assume that the

111

senses do not function of their own accord but really do receive impulses from external sources, to which they respond. The word "sensing" has something to do with truth,[1] according to Grundtvig; to sense is to see what is true. The link between the external and the internal goes much further than this, however. The three main senses – sight, touch and hearing – are only the external end of the corresponding inner senses. Sight corresponds to the power of fancy or imaginative ability; touch and feeling correspond to inner touch; hearing to the intellect or the ability to receive concepts, and understand them, which again links up with reason; and reason comprises both imaginative thoughts, feelings and concepts, and evaluates them.

But both the intellect and reason are secondary and more limited than the first two inner senses, which bear on reality in its most comprehensive meaning. Through the power of the imagination we can receive and recall impressions of distant things: "foreign countries, men long dead, unseen events, the invisible conditions of things, everything invisible". The highest expression is poetry, the poet's vision, seeing things in their spiritual context as images of a higher, eternal truth. The inner feeling, which is assigned to the heart, is the ability above all to receive impressions and thereby the foundation for the other outer and inner senses and for all manifestations of life. It reaches its highest in its sensing of or anticipation of spirit, that is, the power that works on and through us, in fact through everything.

In brief: man is nothing in himself, but encircled by and dependent on not just a visible world but on an invisible reality that ranges much wider. But since we ourselves have a consciousness, this invisible reality that we and the human race have been dependent on from the beginning of time must also be conscious of itself. "Serious, sober man" must already with this consciousness of his dependence feel himself driven to an idea of an invisible creator of the world. Nor can he be far away from us, for in him we live and move and have our being (Acts; 17,28).

The second point I would emphasize is this: that man is perceived at one and the same time as an *apprehending and active* creature, in contrast to philosophy's distinction between theoretical apprehension and "practical reason", ethical ideas and moral activity. The power of imagination is not content with "seeing" the invisible, but can be inspired by it and thus give expression to it in words. This happens especially for the poet, but in fact every person has a relationship to the spiritual power in the invisible that reveals itself in words. The "word" is therefore the highest expression

1. Grundtvig is here playing on the words *sans* meaning sense, and *sand* meaning true.

Professor H.N. Clausen (1793-1887), left, and Bishop J.P. Mynster (1775-1854), right, Grundtvig's two most formidable opponents. (Royal Library, Copenhagen).

Grundtvig talking to a predominantly female audience at Borch's College, Copenhagen, on Greek and Norse mythology (1843). (Drawing by J.Th. Lundbye).

N.F.S. Grundtvig in 1847. Drawing by P.C. Skovgaard.

of human life, the link between the spirit and the body; if the human race was dumb, it would be without progressive development, without achievements and history. For the word is the medium of all genuine human activity in the world. It is the word of poetry and religion that has created all ideas of spiritual greatness, and those for whom "it penetrated the heart endeavoured to express it in life and work..."

Thus the heart, touch, is drawn in, which also unites "life" and "light": "Just as man is outwardly dead when his heart stops beating, so is he inwardly dead when his heart does not beat for anything, when nothing is dear to him; and it is impossible for a man who loves nothing to be able to take the trouble to understand anything." Whatever a man loves, that is what he will be occupied with, and what he loves most sets its stamp on the whole of his activity and creates his way of looking at life. But what sort of purpose should a man have with his life as a whole? One might justifiably say the purpose is to go on living – survival; but precisely because life itself is the condition for every expression of it, including the purpose of survival, man's highest purpose must be to understand his own life.

What that involves is illustrated by the third point: that both apprehension of life and activity are limited to *time and place*. The individual's understanding of life is already dependent on time, that is, on the experiences that he has as time passes throughout his life, childhood, youth, manhood and old age. The same must be true of any understanding whatsoever of the riddle of man: it must be linked to the history of the human race, "the great life of man". Here the individual must acknowledge his insignificance, that he is in fact only a single link in the whole human race, soon to become invisible. Added to this, every man is bound to his closest context, to his nation, which has its own particular way of thinking, and to the group of concepts that he at any one time embraces. But even so there is a spiritual kinship that is evident from the community of language, and the individual relates to the whole human race as the individual to his nation. This is the reason why we can build on the experiences of previous generations and seek to understand the conditions of man on the basis of the development of history up to our time. And if we accept that there has been a development, then we must also accept a purpose, namely, that man will little by little come to understand himself.

Thus the task of history is, to use a clear image, the rebirth of time gone by. Thus the historian needs his reason but also his imagination, so that he can see spiritual forces in history, "the spirit as it moved, clad in dust". Furthermore, he must be gifted "with a living feeling for the days gone by, with a historical heart, into which the spirit of the past can be taken with love so as to emerge in vivid memories". Thus history can produce new achievements, creating life in a continuation of former generations.

With these historical and philosophical reflections the basis was laid for all Grundtvig's later ideas on man and on nations, on history and enlightenment of the people. Outwardly in this period he had acquired a new and calmer face as well as contact with new circles, especially students and many more or less educated people who shared his interest for the old Norse period. He had succeeded in collecting the necessary money for publication of his translations from contributors throughout the country and partly from Norway. Even though their powerful, popular language was criticized, the translations were nonetheless an achievement that also gained royal recognition. From 1818 onwards Grundtvig received a modest annual grant from the King, so that he could at last get married – after a seven-year engagement.

For himself personally these were in general difficult years. As mentioned (p. 107), he had from the start regarded the "temporal" tasks he had assigned himself in 1815 as a detour to the priesthood, which was his real calling. In a letter dated July 1818, however, he took a more positive view of his work on history as actually a "devout work" of great importance, a safeguard for the Church in the coming "attack from the Devil"; but he did not hide the fact that every day he longed for the pulpit. In October 1819 he went so far as to offer his services as unpaid curate to an elderly Copenhagen vicar. Nothing came of this, but now – following the demise of *Danevirke* – he felt his great translation task to be more and more like being buried alive. "Even physically I felt I was close to the grave, when the hour struck" that at last called him to the priesthood.

The Historical Church (1821-24)

In February 1821 without his applying Grundtvig was appointed rector of the Zealand town of Præstø, and a year and a half later he was moved to a curacy at the Church of Our Saviour in Copenhagen. This gave him fresh courage; once again he was back on "the battlefield of the gospel". But his sermons, which are the most important sources in these years, are quieter than those he had previously given in Copenhagen, which were actually a message for his age. The form is in general more straightforward; for example, he addresses his listeners as "my friends" or "Christian friends", not as before with the solemn "beloved". We can feel that he now belongs to a particular congregation and is pursuing a practical calling.

In addition his first years in the priesthood were of considerable importance for his *understanding of the Church*. Until now the Church had been an undefined concept which he employed in various ways. Either it was equated with the Lutheran State Church or it was the orthodox Lutheran Church; in 1818 he goes so far as to define it on the lines of enlightenment theology as the community of faith that arises wherever many people believe the same thing. Or it was a very broad concept to be equated with Christianity or truth, or above all an expression of "man's relationship to God" (1818). True his understanding of the Church was historically orientated, but in the broad sense that the history of the Church was one and the same as the history of the spirit of man. Now, however, the Church increasingly becomes the historical Church in which he himself serves. This is already hinted at in his induction sermon, which in both Præstø Church and the Church of Our Saviour took as its text Psalm 118: This is the day that the Lord hath made; let us rejoice in it and be glad! This is how he understood the day of Jesus Christ (in history), He whose name is transmitted from generation to generation and who became the corner-stone in this house of God, He who has defied the storms of the ages and will continue to do so in the future. He it was whom Grundtvig was now to serve, and doubtless he hoped that also the coming age would be a "day of the Lord".

Other characteristics are the richness of imagery in the sermons and a core of evangelical narrative, linked especially to Christmas, as was the case in December 1810 (see p. 102). His Christmas sermon in 1822, for example, stresses that the ancient narrative Christmas carol, *A Child is Born in Bethlehem*, is the greeting from former generations on this day – corresponding to the emphasis in the *Danevirke* period on the old hymns and the ancient "Christian fathers"; this particular hymn he had rewritten in 1820, making it even more a narrative hymn. But he also underlines that occurrences in days gone by must be relived as if we were present; only then does the word come alive, the story a real picture of the occurrence and not merely a shadow. We must therefore place ourselves alongside the lowly shepherds, with "the poor, simple, but devout and humble shepherds", whose hope and doubt as to the coming of Messiah is then described by Grundtvig. For, as the hymn says at the end, this is how our forefathers sat among the sheep, and this is how children sit when we tell them the Christmas story. And if Christianity is to be alive amongst us then also in this regard the children's heart must be turned to their fathers and the heart of the fathers to the children. For the light of the Lord "always shines in the child's eye, his glory shines only round the shepherds".

The central *content* of his preaching was fixed, and could be briefly expressed in the angels' message to the shepherds at Bethlehem; but it could also be expressed in many other central Christian teachings. It was the gospel of Jesus Christ as our Saviour and Redeemer, who died for our sins and was resurrected for our justification, the gospel of the community of Christ's suffering and the power of His resurrection, which Paul in particular preached. This could be expressed freely as God's revelation in the Scripture as Father, Son and Holy Spirit, or especially in the Third and Fourth Articles of Faith; but as in Præstø shortly after his induction Grundtvig could refer to all three Articles of Faith as the main cornerstone in the Church of Christ. He dwells particularly often on John 3, 16; For God so loved the world that he gave his only begotten Son...; These words contained the core of Christianity, according to Grundtvig, enabling it to be passed on from generation to generation even if the New Testament was destroyed or hidden. It has joined millions of widely differing people into one congregation, one spiritual body, he says in the sermon for Whit Monday 1823.

Even though Grundtvig continued to insist on the Bible's unconditional credibility as the basis of Christianity, he now distinguished between the important and the less important. His view of the Bible has become freer; for example, he can separate the divine from the human and admit minor discrepancies between the books. It is the content he emphasizes, the central message, which stands out so clearly for him and is beyond question.

On the other hand Grundtvig's preaching also resumed the battle against his former *opponents,* in particular the rationalist and philosophizing form of Christianity. Already in his induction sermon in Copenhagen he maintains that it is a fairy-tale when people say that the world no longer leans to the Devil and is willing to receive the truth in Christ. Such people come only in the name of their own wisdom and piety, which the world gladly receives. Time after time Grundtvig turns against wordly wisdom that will only believe what reason can grasp. It rejects the Trinity in favour of its own airy philosophical constructions, as though these castles in the air could contain the omnipresent, the almighty and the incomprehensible. It must not be faith in Christ but good deeds that save; this is the interpretation put upon Jesus' teaching by innumerable people who are considered to be well-informed Christians. In contrast to former times, Christ's enemies are now flattering Him and misusing his words, so it is important that we separate our cause

116

from the world's cause as clearly as possible. For the Jesus they praise is but a shadow of human reason. Such fine, camouflaged idolatry: to worship under the guise of God's and Christ's name the creatures of our own heart is far more dangerous than the grossest idolatry of heathen and papistic times. It is the great plague of the Church that the unbelievers carry the name of Christ on their lips and do not say out loud that they will have nothing to do with Him.

In this connection the sermons also contain expressions of a darker, *despondent mood,* especially in 1823, late into the autumn. Christians too can have their doubts, he says for example on Easter Monday of that year; the World seems cold and dead to us, and our enemies deride us and say: where is your God now? In recent times all Christians have known dark hours, when the enemy triumphed and they hardly dared to open their mouths. And if they sought out a moment in private with the Bible, they closed it for the most part with a sigh. There is a regular emphasis on Christians being somehow surrounded by the world and being dangerously connected to it; they are infected by it, he says on Prayer Day 1823, by the spiritual sleeping sickness that is the plague of the age. We find a similar view expressed in the preface to the printed sermon on "daily bread difficulties" on the 7th Sunday after Trinity, and three Sundays later Grundtvig even maintains that it is doubtful whether there have ever been so many unbelievers since the days of the apostles, so many are shocked and seduced.

This despondency is confirmed by a series of autobiographical statements, not least the preface to the major poem *New Year's Morn* a year later. Grundtvig had had great expectations of the calling in Copenhagen; it was the centre of unbelief, but he had great faith in the effect of his preaching and hoped in particular to start a dialogue with the young students. Since 1814-15 he had convinced himself that the Danish people were a specially chosen people, and in his New Year sermon 1823 he was still expressing his hope for a rebuilding both of the Church and of the nation, which corresponded to his major idea up to this point that there is a link between the renewal of the Church and the renewal of the nation: Christmas and the New Year belong together, a blessed new year is dawning for us all when Christ is born for us as our Saviour in a true and living faith. But apart from having large congregations Grundtvig did not notice any change; on the contrary, as his sermons prove, he had a strong feeling that it was his opponents who were dominating Church life. His lengthy translations, which were completed shortly after he moved to Copenhagen, were also received with indifference. He thus felt that his high hopes had been dashed; and when in the autumn of 1823 he began on a major apology for Christianity to "stir up the Dead Sea a bit", he could not get going. This period was perhaps, as he himself writes, "the hardest trial I have faced so far".

But approaching *Advent 1823* a change sets in that is of crucial importance for Grundtvig's understanding of the Church. It is felt in his sermons through a more powerful insistence on the Church as the people of God and the congregation of Christ. As late as the 16th Sunday after Trinity the house of the Lord is only a place of eternal dwellings (from Psalm 84), but on the following Sunday it has become a visible Church in which wonderful things are spoken (from Psalm 87), in connection with Christ's invisible congregation, built of living stones, gathered by the Spirit from all corners of the earth in the course of time. The believer can feel himself fused together with the whole congregation as the body of Christ with one Lord, one faith, one baptism, one God and Father of all. Grundtvig is referring in particular here to the faith of the early Church fathers, doubtless on the basis of his study of Irenaeus that autumn; yet he looks in vain for a contemporary gathering that will acknowledge this faith. However, the few who join the Lord and His Church can rest assured in His promise to be present wherever two or three gathered together in His name, and in His words: Fear not, little flock; for it is your Father's good pleasure to give you the kingdom.

On the 18th Sunday after Trinity Grundtvig refers amongst others to the great deeds Christ has wrought in His Church, and the singular power of His words which have sustained it. On the 19th Sunday he speaks to the confirmation candidates as members of the Church of Jesus Christ through the baptismal covenant by which God has given us His spirit; on the 20th Sunday he talks of the need for an awakening, when the Spirit shouts to the sleeping Church: rise up from the dead and let Christ shine for you. An open struggle against those who have deceitfully assumed the name of Christian is a necessity – a decision for or against the Church of Christ. On the 22nd Sunday Grundtvig stresses that the Holy Spirit is our only comfort in the dark hours from evening to morn, when Christ is born through faith in our hearts, and on the 25th Sunday he speaks of the hope of Christians that seems to grow like the seed in the earth of its own accord. It is changed to a clarity above all clarity, when to our wonderment we are lit by the rays of the Scripture so that we see Him who rose like a morning-star for the shepherds of Bethlehem and arose for His grieving disciples like the breaking through of a golden sun.

On the following Sunday, Advent Sunday, the culmination is reached when Grundtvig could proclaim: the night is past and the day is approaching. Darkness had covered and was still covering the earth, but on the stroke of midnight the light descended to us as it did to the shepherds at Bethlehem; the day comes from the Lord in a wondrous way, so that when it comes His Church will always sing: This is the day that the Lord hath made; this is come from the Lord and it is wonderful to our eyes. In the preface to *New Year's Morn* Grundtvig has stressed this line of thought as a personal experience which "struck like lightning" at the beginning of the Church Year; he felt that he himself had come alive again and he now hoped to see the same wonder of God striking many thousands of others in the North. This has been seen as a psychological upturn, but it has an objective explanation in the main idea of the sermon: the Church will always be like a light in darkness, and when it feels only darkness itself and is longing for the day of the Lord, it comes when least expected. The illumination is the work of the Holy Spirit alone. He had previously preached on this text (in 1814) but it was not until now that he realised it applied to his own work as a clergyman, both as a reservation and as a comfort.

This meant that Grundtvig's great concern over a rebirth of the Church was taken from him. The Church of Christ was a reality, whatever its numbers, purely on the strength of the working of the Holy Spirit down the ages. His sermons now began to concentrate on the elements that bore up the life of the Church itself and secured the transmission of that life. On the 4th Sunday in Advent, for example, he preached on the Second Article of Faith, which he repeated in its entirety, on Christmas Day on the old Christmas hymns, from which he quoted numerous verses, and on the Sunday after New Year 1824 he again preached on the Christmas story as words which at one and the same time embrace the past, the present and the future. On Septuagesima he stressed that the central biblical texts were easily understood even by the simplest, without the scholars' interpretation "with Roman intellect and German reason". On the First Sunday in Lent he spoke of baptism as the most wonderful thing a person can experience and the guiding spirit of the Church from the beginning to the end of the world. On Easter Day and the Monday in Easter Week he again quoted numerous verses, this time from the old Easter hymns as a testimony to the "living ideas" among former generations. On the 6th Sunday after Easter the subject was the reflection that in spite of all enemies our Christian faith is protected by the shield of God's love. On Whit Sunday he preached on the three great festivals, Christmas, Easter and Whitsun, and on Trinity Sunday he spoke on the whole Church Year.

There is much more of a similar nature that could be considered. His sermons were now on the whole concentrated on the Church, though no less biblical for that. In the summer of 1824 he himself discussed from the pulpit the change that had come about in him: his listeners had doubtless noticed that the light shone more brightly for him now: he could now place himself under the Lord's guidance with more confidence, and with the hope that his ministry was not in vain, that the night was past and the day approaching. He had shuddered at the thought that the heart of the people had become hardened, he had believed, doubted, hoped, feared and grumbled until he found comfort in the knowledge that the change was in the hands of God, and depended solely on whether He would send out His Holy Spirit (5th Sunday after Trinity).

At about the same time he returned afresh to poetry in *The Land of the Living* and the much longer poem *New Year's Morn* (cf. p. 12), which, like its preface, is a retrospect on the whole of his development so far, a sure sign that he was aware of the sudden change that had taken place. He also looked forward, though not to new battles against the general indifference, "the plague of the times", which had so far been his own plague. Now he only looked forward to working together with a little circle who, like him, "trusted in the Lord" and in spite of everything held fast to the hope of a national Christian revival in Denmark. This "unreasonable" hope was now linked to his new conviction that – as he wrote in the preface – "Death will never get the better of the Lord's Church." The sermons also demonstrate this, not least the last-mentioned above. The connection between the Church and the people was no longer a matter of course. The Church itself was a people, far more comprehensive than the Danish nation, and in Denmark it could consist of a mere handful. It had its own history over two thousand years, with the same word of God since the angels' message at Bethlehem, which the Spirit still quickened in the Christian Church. That was Grundtvig's personal experience since the autumn of 1823.

This had become and continued to be the guiding spirit in Grundtvig's understanding of the Church. The basic idea in his later view of the Church was in fact anticipated in these sermons from the first years of his ministry, especially after the breakthrough in the autumn of 1823.

II
GRUNDTVIG'S BASIC IDEAS
ON THE CHURCH AND EDUCATION

Grundtvig the Preacher

– the Poet in the Pulpit

by CHRISTIAN THODBERG

In the Grundtvig archives there are between 60 og 70 files. In addition there are Grundtvig's own publications: *Biblical Sermons* (1816) and *The Sunday Book*, three volumes from the late 1820's and early 1830's which differ considerably from the sermons as they were actually *preached*. The third volume of *The Sunday Book* also contains original sermons, i.e. with no preliminary draft to the sermons as preached.

Grundtvig preached occasionally during his period on Langeland (p. 9). His probational sermon in 1810 is a turning-point (p. 10). But the first stage of his preaching ministry is actually the period in Udby, from the 1st Sunday after Trinity 1811 (June 16th) to the 9th Sunday after Trinity 1813, that is, a little over two years.

Following this, Grundtvig preached the occasional sermon in Copenhagen. After his major sermon in Frederiksberg Church on St. Stephen's Day 1815 he gave up the cloth – or so it seemed. For it was only in Copenhagen that he stopped preaching; in the following years he preached occasional sermons here and there on Zealand.

The second stage of Grundtvig's preaching is his ministry as rector of Præstø from Palm Sunday 1821 to the 25th Sunday after Trinity 1822, a year and a half in all. This was a preparation for the third stage, when Grundtvig was curate at the Church of Our Saviour in Copenhagen from the 1st Sunday in Advent 1822 to his famous resignation on the 6th Sunday after Easter 1826, that is, for about three and a half years.

He then stopped preaching for a time, but as mentioned above he wrote *The Sunday Book,* which with the exception of the last half of volume three, which is new, represents a reworking of sermons preached in the Church of Our Saviour. This may be regarded as a fourth stage, though I shall be concentrating here on the sermons Grundtvig actually *preached.*

A fifth stage began on Septuagesima 1832 in a rented room, and continued with the help of a dispensation at Evensong in what was then Frederik's Church in Christianshavn, Copenhagen. A sixth stage began in 1839 on Grundtvig's appointment as rector of Vartov Hospital Foundation; he was again given permission to celebrate baptism, Holy Communion and confirmation. This sixth stage lasted until his death in September 1872. Thus, with occasional breaks Grundtvig preached over a period of nearly 60 years.

This means that in the sermons we are faced with the largest genre in Grundtvig's works, and it is regrettable that it has yet to be treated as a collected unity. What follows is no more than a survey, and a survey from a particular point of view at that, concentrating on the first stages and ending in 1839, by which time Grundtvig's sermons had assumed the form they were to retain for the rest of his life. I am concerned here expressly with the sermons as a *genre;* that is, I will deal first with the style of the sermon and then on the basis of this, attempt to evaluate the content.

I

The Udby Sermons

In their structure Grundtvig's sermons are no different from those of his contemporaries. They are in three parts: 1) a development of the text for the day, leading into 2) an emphasis on a theme, preferably of a doctrinal nature, which 3) is then expounded. Take, for example, the 7th Sunday after Trinity 1811, on the feeding of the four thousand in the desert. 1. Grundtvig defends the miracle of the bread somewhat half-heartedly: Jesus "made the bread go round"; 2. the theme is: "That when we follow God, there is no need to renounce either bodily or spiritual need". This is followed by 3. an apologetic exposition demonstrating with examples especially from the Old Testament the way in which God tests people.

For the most part the sermons are passionately moral. The Bible is used first and foremost as a lever for the moral passion that ranges from threats to persuasion, for Grundtvig is a child of his time. There is not so great a difference between him and his contemporary preachers. This means that the classic dogma do not figure so strongly in the content of these sermons as they do later.

Even so there is a clear reworking of the language, particularly in the first part of the sermons – the retelling of the gospel. For example, the introduction to the sermon for the 23rd Sunday after Trinity 1811 on the tribute money: "The holy gospel of the day is easy to understand. We hear how the Pharisees and supporters of King Herod, who were otherwise the bitterest of enemies, united in order to tempt Jesus. The Pharisees' wickedness becomes even more apparent when we consider the means they used to tempt him. They asked him whether it was permitted to pay tax to Caesar or not? The shameless hypocrites! It was the Emperor of Rome they meant; he ruled over the Jews at that time, and when the Emperor demanded taxes nobody was more furious about it than the Pharisees. On other occasions it was these very Pharisees who urged the people to refuse and to start a revolt. So were they asking Jesus in order to gain his support? Oh no! purely to see if they could get Jesus into trouble. It was cleverly done, to the Devil's way of thinking. If Jesus said no, they had the Herodians there, who would immediately inform the King that Jesus was out to make the people revolt. On the other hand, if He said yes, they thought that the people, who would rather not pay the tax, would get angry with Jesus and stone Him, or at least not take His side." Here we see Grundtvig using more or less idiomatic speech, the like of which is certainly not to be found amongst his contemporaries and which is evidence of his linguistic awareness.

So Grundtvig employs the same main structure in his sermons as his contemporaries but differs from them in his use of language.

With regard to this use of language it is vital to read the Udby sermons meticulously and with one particular guideline in mind, namely the fragment from about 1813 on sermons as a genre, to be found in File 72. Here Grundtvig says about the language of sermons: "It is clear that the language becomes metaphorical, as it does in the speeches of Jesus and Paul, since as long as the heavenly can only be seen in a mirror it must be seen as an image, and without imagination mankind could not possibly have any idea of the invisible,..." In other words, the *speeches* of Jesus and Paul are presented as an example. Grundtvig then moves on to talk in general terms about euphony, first and foremost as he finds it in *poetry:* "No one doubts that poetry must have the greatest euphony of all and the reason is easy to see, for what else is poetry but a form in which we weld together words, conjure up an image of the indivisible word, whose metaphor the word originally is." By the "indivisible word" Grundtvig means Christ, as at the beginning of John's Gospel: *In the beginning was the Word.* A similar interpretation is to be found in another fragment, *On the Word and the Mother-Tongue* from the *Danevirke* period.[1] The crucial point is made in File 72: "Broadly speaking speech becomes more

1. From 1816 to 1819 Grundtvig edited his own journal, *Danevirke.*

euphonious the closer it approaches poetry, and in euphonious prose metre always lies hidden, as can easily be seen in amongst others both the Lutheran Bible and the Catechism".

It is that sentence: "in euphonious prose metre always lies hidden" that I wish to take as a starting-point for a brief survey of the Udby sermons and their successors.

The poetic tone breaks through powerfully on the 3rd Sunday after Trinity, June 30th 1811, on the parables of the lost sheep and the lost coin (Luke 15:1-10): "Oh what lovely, what comforting images of God's mercy these are," says Grundtvig. They are a mirror that has become "so clear", so "that we only need to lift up our gaze to see in it *the brightness of God's glory and the true image of His person*" – the italicized words are a quotation from Hebrews 1:3, which from this point onwards becomes the main written source for the use of imagery and poetry in the sermons – the biblical legitimation, so to speak. The break in style in the sermon before us is quite clear.

There is a lift in feeling in the sermon for September 8th 1811, Grundtvig's birthday, which falls on the 13th Sunday after Trinity, when the gospel of the day is: "Blessed are the eyes which see the things that ye see" (Luke 10:23ff), a text that never fails to move Grundtvig. There is no need to search for the poetic sermons: there are, as I hope to show, certain fixed points.

The sermons in Advent 1811 are important as background for the *World Chronicle* (1812). The mirror motif returns with great force in the Christmas Day sermon, in which *nature,* in the shape of the birds, is also included – on a licence from the Bible itself. Behind this lie Jesus' words in Matthew 6: *Behold the fowls of the air: for they sow not, neither do they reap, nor gather into barns; yet your heavenly Father feedeth them. Are ye not much better than they?* (6:26), *Consider the lilies of the field, how they grow; they toil not, neither do they spin* (6:28) etc. (cf. the hymn p. 164ff).

In the Church Year 1811-12 not much happens at first, but from the Annunciation of Mary, March 15th 1812, an enthusiasm for Kingo[2] makes its mark amid great excitement. The key words are *strange, special, wonderful, joyful.* The high spirits culminate oddly enough on Good Friday, March 27th, and the following extract from the sermon for that day can be written out as a prose-poem:

> Every time we think seriously
> about someone's death,

---

2. Thomas Kingo (1634-1703) Bishop of Odense.

we are faced with our own.
One day we too,
in only a few hours and days,
must put off our raiment,
our eye too must close,
our bodies too be food for worms
and become dust,
from which they were made.
On that day neither money nor prayer will avail,
neither riches nor rank,
neither health nor strength.
We must leave when the call comes,
and it can just as well come
today as tomorrow,
just as soon in the midnight hour
as at noon.

This exclamation is clearly stamped by the many Kingo verses on the subject and by Kingo's treatment of vanity in such hymns *O, World, Goodbye* (Far, verden, farvel, DHB 525) and *Sorrow and Joy* (Sorrig og glæde, DHB 41). As in the other prose-poems we note here how the form is intensified towards the end through alliteration and vowel rhyme.

The poetic element returns on Ascension Day, May 7th 1812. The text *Blessed are the eyes* is again the subject, in which the ascension is made contemporary. This is in keeping with Grundtvig's theological interest in the great events of Christ's life. The following prose-poem deals precisely with this point:

We must believe
that none has ascended into heaven
without His descent from heaven
the Son of Man
who was in heaven
when He was on earth
who is with us all
until the end of the world
even though He ascended
and a cloud took Him away
from our eyes
He was on earth
and He was in heaven,

He is in heaven
and He is on earth,
the man Jesus Christ
who was crucified,
died and was buried.

Theologically it is of great interest that Christ's works are advanced precisely in their poetic context and quite without the Lutheran evangelical conditions which Grundtvig would otherwise prefer to demand. It is a proclamation of faith. The unconditional nature is expressed in the phrase:

He is in heaven
and He is on earth,

In other words, the image of the earth as a vale of tears is brushed aside and the lines from 1824 spring to mind:

My country, says life, is heaven and earth,
where love has its home!
The Land of the Living, (De levendes Land, see p. 168)

It is characteristic of Grundtvig that the "poem" is followed by a commentary in the normal style of sermons on how blessed it is to see "the brightness of God's glory in Jesus and the express image of His person", i.e. Hebrews 1:3, which we have previously seen to be the biblical key to the prose-poems. In other words Grundtvig regards even the preceding context as an "image", a piece of poetry or "euphonious prose" with "a hidden metre". Here as elsewhere, the poetry is clearly taken from the Bible, nearly all the prose-poem being a biblical mosaic and culminating in the hymn from Philippians 2, to which Grundtvig returned as a favourite text for the rest of his life.

The inspiration of Luther while Grundtvig was at work on *Why Are We Called Lutherans?* and the publication of the *World Chronicle* in December 1812 (see p. 10) have undoubtedly influenced the amazing sermon for the 1st Sunday in Advent 1812, which is from first to last a major exposition of Revelation 3:14-22, i.e. the message to Laodicea, and in particular v. 20.: "Behold, I stand at the door and knock: if any man hear my voice, and open the door, I will come into him, and will sup with him, and he with me."

In most of the sermon it is *I,* that is, Jesus, who is speaking. It is nearly all a prose-poem: for the first time this style is completely dominant. Here is the first line in ordinary sermon-style, followed by the introduction to the prose-poem:

"He comes to us in humble form, but even so he says

> Let me in,
> show me honour,
> for I am your Saviour
> and your King!
> Let me in
> so that I and my Father
> may have a room in your home,
> until your hour-glass has run out,
> then you will be free
> to go home with us
> and stay with me
> in the Father's house forever.
> ...
> but is it right
> that you will let the enemy live in the house
> that I have built
> and have even repurchased,
> not with silver or gold
> but with my holy and precious blood.
> Is this the thanks I am to have,
> I who, being in the form of God
> humbled myself
> and took upon me the form of a servant
> and became obedient unto death,
> even the death of the cross.

The whole sermon is reminiscent of the Roman Church's *improperia* in the Good Friday Liturgy, in which Christ reproachfully holds out His arms to His people. Such a consistent use of the first-person in a sermon in the style of a prose-poem is quite unique and extremely convincing evidence of Grundtvig's self-awareness. It is after all Grundtvig himself who says "I" from the pulpit!

The first-person style is equally pronounced on the 2nd Sunday in Advent, December 6th, and on the 3rd Sunday in Advent, December 13th. In the latter he even says: "Here I am again, I followed you through the Church Year" – after which the story of salvation is again unfolded.

Three Sundays running Grundtvig breaks every imaginable rule and convention for the form of a sermon. He had already put into practice the breaking of conventions that he had discussed in his essay on the sermon as a genre in 1813, in the same File 72 mentioned above.

This powerful expression of self-awareness may well explain some significant contemporary events: the important letters to J. P. Mynster (later Bishop Mynster) on December 1st and to the writer, Molbech, on December 2nd 1812, in which Grundtvig calls their Christianity to account. Is it not likely that it is the Grundtvig of these sermons, full of self-awareness, that determines the timing of these crucial letters?

The sermon on Christmas Day 1812 ends with a little prose-poem:

> They had seen with their own eyes
> that there were ladders
> between heaven and earth
> with angels moving upon them,
> they had seen the Lord of Heaven
> as a Son of Man
> and thus they knew
> that He would take them as brothers
> with Him into heaven.
>
> *(end of sermon)*

Here we see a preliminary working of the contents of O *Welcome again, God's Angels Small* (Velkommen igen, Guds engle små) from 1824, in particular the ladder motif (see p. 169).

The beginning of the Church Year 1812-13 is without poetic elements, with the exception of Whit Monday, June 7th 1813. The sermon for that day contains 8 pages of an imposing prose-poem, which begins as follows:

> The sun shines
> so softly on high,
> the flower and corn
> growing from earth
> for food and delight,
> the forest is green
> and the birds sing,
> praising the heavenly Father
> who gives them food,
> though they themselves
> neither sow nor reap.

Yea, beloved,
truly the shining sun
the fertile fields
the blossoming meadows
are in the eyes of the believer
living pictures
of the light of the world,
the brightness of God's glory –
whom the Father sent to the world,
of the sacred growth of the Word
and its blossoming in the believers' hearts.
Dark and cold
as in winter-time
was the heart of the people,
they knew not God,
the heathen had no hope
in affliction and in death,
they knew not
what would befall them,
when they sighed in the grave,
they had not that love of God
without which He can never be known
without which we cannot do His will
and enter His community
and find salvation in beholding His face.
But God so loved the world
that He gave His only-begotten Son,
in Him was life
and the life was the light of man.
He is the true light
that lighteth every man
that cometh into the world.

II

However, the crucial development in Grundtvig's poetic sermons and imagery can be traced first and foremost in the Præstø sermons of 1821-22, sermons that have been seriously neglected by researchers.

The first outpouring comes, strangely enough, on the 2nd Sunday after Easter 1821 in the gospel of the good shepherd (John 10). We know beforehand from *World Chronicle* (1814) that Grundtvig has raised the shepherds, and amongst them of course Abraham, Isaac and Jacob, to the status of the most poetic people in history – at a time when poetry was simply the language of which *we* can only see a faint afterglow. The shepherds' life and language become for Grundtvig an image of paradise then and paradise at the end of time: "If we have ever felt how uplifting it can still be when we manage for a moment to forget our many alien pursuits and worldly sorrows, to wander under God's clear heaven through blossoming meadows and May-green woods where flocks graze and birds sing; if we have felt that, my friends, then we can understand that for modest hearts under the soft, heavenly regions no pursuit could be as delightful as walking in the light from the cradle to the grave together with everything that breathes and grows and refreshes at the wave of our Maker's gentle, invisible hand, which reveals itself every day with a blessing to satisfy all that lives."

It is this paradise-life that Christ renews as the good shepherd, and Grundtvig concludes with a little prose-poem which deftly links the shepherd-image with Christmas night and the Christmas gospel:

> O see, my friends!
> from amongst this shepherd-nation
> the seed of the shepherds, Abraham and David,
> God raised the Saviour and Lord
> whom he worship,
> the Lord Jesus Christ,
> who says in the gospel of the day:
> I am the good shepherd;
> so, who was it for
> that God's angels in heavenly host
> proclaimed with exultation
> that the Saviour was born in the city of David,
> who was it for but the shepherds at Bethlehem,
> keeping watch over their flock by night,
> fulfilling God's will that it should be
> from the lips of shepherds
> that the first song of praise on earth
> for the Saviour should ring from choirs of angels.

The sermon ends characteristically: "So, my friends, Jesus Christ is the good shepherd, and everything that a shepherd's life only vaguely signified in the eyes of holy men and in their way of life was fulfilled, brilliant with heaven's brightness, in Him who is the root and branch of David, the seed of Abraham who was before Him. He is the true image of God's being...".

Again we note the final words, the same quotation from Hebrews 1:3 that we have already singled out. The biblical image, as it is presented in the prose-poem, is the means of interpretation that by the very force of its imagery reveals Christ, the Christ who became human like each of us and who can therefore make Himself known to those who are created in the image of God. It is precisely this image or this poetry that is the link – or the communication – between heaven and earth: "It is a question of whether we can again recapture the mind of a child, the holy, modest heart, the heavenly eye to see God's work and His image in ourselves and His gifts in everything which the god-fearing shepherds of old had ... And this, my friends, can happen when with a whole heart we return to the Shepherd and Bishop of our souls..."

Both the biblical imagery and the imagery of what is highest in the created world reflect God's person and action among mankind. For Grundtvig it is still an *indirect* revelation and so the contemplation of it is to a great extent romantically inspired; the images and the poetry are an expression of an aspiration towards the highest. The fact that this receives a Christian signature from Grundtvig does not conceal the romantic inspiration.

Thus Grundtvig is not a fundamentalist in the traditional sense of the word. The biblical word is no longer a vehicle for the revelation. He fastens on to the important narratives and parables in the Bible. And we must – as he says – walk in the spirit with the people out of the city, when we hear the gospel about the widow of Nain's son. We must become contemporaries with the image, and thereby see Christ's glory.

As an example of Grundtvig's style of preaching at this time we can look at the sermon for All Saints Day 1821, which initiates a lengthy series of highly passionate sermons. The key word in the great opening prayer is *light*. God Himself will "shine through" us,

> so that we behold the brightness of the Godhead
> in Jesus Christ, the countenance of Thy image

probably yet another hidden quotation from Hebrews 1:3. We must

> behold it now,
> as in a mirror
> but then with an enlightened eye.

133

The question is thus raised: whereabouts in the sermon do we find the "image" which is to shine through us? Or in other words: where is the imagery actually at work? I think it is to be found in the emotionally-charged central section of the sermon, which can be rewritten as a prose-poem. Grundtvig takes as his starting-point David's last words in II Sam. 23 and depicts in the following how David's prophecy was fulfilled for the people of that time and for us now.

> Now these be the last words of David. David the son of Jesse said, and the man who was raised up on high, the anointed of the God of Jacob, and the sweet psalmist of Israel, said, The spirit of the Lord spake to me, and his word was in my tongue. The God of Israel said, the Rock of Israel spake to me, He that ruleth over men must be just, ruling in the fear of God. And he shall be as the light of the morning, when the sun riseth, even a morning without clouds; as the tender grass springing out of the earth by clear shining after rain.

It happened as he said,
for the righteous one came
to justify many
and ascend again into heaven
to rule with the sceptre of righteousness
over the children of man,
He was the light of the morning
when the sun rises
when there is no cloud in the sky
and the grass in the meadow glistens after rain
as thus it was written:
the sunrise from on high
that visited us in Christ Jesus
and created for our souls a blessed morning-hour
when the sun of grace
pierced the thunder-clouds of God's wrath
and a new paradise blossomed
through the heavenly dew in the believers' heart
...
He came, the bright living truth
the Word which was in the beginning
He came and revealed again
God's paradise to the children of man,
He revealed for Sinners
a way to it beneath the cross,

134

and accompanies
with His Spirit, the Holy Spirit,
all that believe in Him
to God's holy mount and His mansions
to the house of the Father,
where He Himself has prepared rooms for them
to the high altar before the throne of the Eternal,
where with a joy
that none can steal
and nothing destroy,
they thank with harps the God of their salvation,
whom the holy John heard in the spirit,
and saw them with the palms of eternity before the throne,
and heard the heavenly song of praise:
Amen, blessing, glory and wisdom
thanks and honour,
power and strength
be unto our God,
for ever and ever, Amen!

The prose-poem is a christological creed, which includes the contents of the Second Article of Faith with an emphasis on its fulfilment. The christological creed is still in the past: it is something which happened in those days and which we must try to appropriate. The image places, so to speak, a distance between us now and salvation hereafter. We glimpse it only in a mirror but we are ourselves links in a chain that is moving towards transfiguration.

The sermon for All Saints Day is perhaps the best poetic example of Grundtvig's *evangelical* preaching. Here the longing for heaven is expressed in words of apocalypse. It reminds us almost of Brorson.[3]

By focussing on Grundtvig's use of images and imagery we can also approach Grundtvig's recurrent problem: the question of Christ's *presence*. He comes closest to Christ through imagery. The image is transparent. Through it we see Christ in the distance – transfigured.

Finding the imagery in Grundtvig's prose-poems aggravates the problem. For the image is not only a historical picture to whose time we must return and whose future realisation we are awaiting. Already in the Præstø period the imagery is close to becoming an expression of the here and now.

3. Hans Adolf Brorson (1694-1764) Bishop of Ribe.

This development can be followed in a succession of highly impassioned Advent and Christmas sermons; perhaps the best of these is the sermon for New Year's Day 1822, which summarizes the Christian message as a present-day fact. Note that the poem is written in the *present* tense:

Let us on this day
as on every New Year's Day
recollect with heartfelt gratitude
that we who are called by the new name
after the Lord Jesus Christ in David's city
live in a holy and blessed new year,
in the year of God's grace,
where the light shines brightly,
when the brightness of God's glory
streams through the world
in the days of peace and goodwill
and blessedness,
when, wherever the Word is spoken,
God is speaking peace to His people
and giving blissful comfort
to mourning hearts,
so that in truth
we can say with the Patriarch:
This place shall be called Bethel;
for here is the house of the Lord
and the gate of heaven,
here we see in spirit
the high, firm and glorious ladder
stretching from earth to heaven,
where God's angels ascend and descend with their
Glory be to God in the highest
for peace on earth
and God's goodwill
to the children of mankind,
where they ascend and descend
bearing up Christian souls
into the bosom of Abraham,
all this through the testimony of the Spirit
on the great new year's day of life!
Blessed are the dead

who die in the Lord hereafter!
In truth, Christians,
wherever we wander with this blessed name
stamped on our hearts,
there is God's house,
wherever we stand or kneel
in prayer in Jesus' name,
there heaven is open and the ladder raised up:
the holy ladder of *faith* and *hope*
to the land of *love*
beyond the heaven of heavens.

The Word goes out, speaks peace, and comforts *now,* but note that it is the human heart that is its object. The heart is Bethel, the heart with Jesus' name is God's house. In particular the prayer in Jesus' name links earth and heaven. The expression "to the land of love beyond the heaven of heavens" points forward to the solution to Grundtvig's problem in *The Land of the Living* (p. 168).

In the sermon for Epiphany 1821 there is a "homiletic note" that Grundtvig has added, a thought which he has amplified in the pulpit: "The application of Our Saviour's birth by the faith within us." Here perhaps for the first time is a hint of the thought which will later become so well-known, namely that the Christian is now one with the infant Jesus. Christ is at hand in the weak, unsure faith. It is a question of becoming a child with the infant Jesus. Or in other words, it is a child-like expectation and faith that can seize hold of Christ. The child has such a living memory of paradise that it comes closest to God's likeness and can therefore be fused together with Christ. Thus in nature and in biblical imagery the child looks more directly at God Himself. We shall return to this point. Before that, however, it is necessary to point out that in the following sermons we meet a significant exposition of biblical imagery as well as seeing the imagery at work, particularly around Easter and Whitsun and in the very important sermon for the 2nd Sunday after Trinity 1822.

We now move on to Grundtvig's Friday sermon for June 17th 1822 over the words: "Who is the greatest in heaven?" It is worth noting that this sermon comes immediately after the important sermon on imagery for the 2nd Sunday after Trinity. Here the idea of the child's direct relationship with the Creator is developed, so that this text becomes an interpretation of the first three verses of *The Land of the Living* (p. 168):

"In our own eyes we were always small, and all of us carry in our hearts only a more or less living recollection and memory of childhood innocence and freedom from care. Yet who does not at times look back with delight and longing to days long past that are like a life-giving early morn, when, as it were, we clap our hands at life's rising sun, and find in every stalk that hursts into leaf on our path a smiling flower, a morning-hour when life's day floats before us like an image of eternity, when sorrow is brief and hope fresh, when what is past is forgotten and the future is a copy of our desires painted in the loveliest and brightest colours.

This is the question we must ask, my friends! For it is surely unnatural never to recall with joy the days when only fleetingly fear and sorrow broke the sway of happiness and hope in our hearts; it is surely unnatural never with a sigh to desire their return.

The only objection that could be made with a grain of justification would perhaps be the question of whether it is not vain to wish for childhood days again, and whether it is not therefore bad to dwell too long on recollections and arouse longings that cannot be satisfied, whether in fact it is not all a glorious self-deception, inasmuch as we forget the many hardships of childhood and stare only at its advantages, regarding it only from its light and smiling side?

This is the question that might be raised, and in fact it often has been, and the attempt has thus been made to obscure the memory of childhood and, as it is said, to take comfort from its demise. Nor have the strength of manhood and the wisdom of old age been forgotten, the benefits of industry, freedom and independence which are the appointed lot of the happiness of childhood, which seems only to be built on disappointment and foolishness, like the joy of the child in a coloured bubble that shines and bursts into nothing.

But, my friends, be as it may with all these wise words, it nonetheless remains a fact throughout all time that as Christians we cannot agree with or applaud this; as disciples and supporters of Jesus Christ we must always look back on the age of childhood as a picture of the true humanity – of nobility and joy. For He says, "Except ye repent and be as children ye shall in no wise enter into the Kingdom of Heaven; and here it is the greatest of all who humbles Himself as this child – It is impossible for us to be like children again, we ask in our heart with Nicodemus."

I shall end this survey of the Præstø sermons by pointing out that I have deliberately called attention to the sermons that have mythopoetic elements. I am well aware that I have ignored a whole series of sermons that are more ordinary in their content, with exhortations and apologetics. On the other hand I would claim that I have selected the most significant sermons as regards both content and importance for Grundtvig's later development.

The Præstø sermons are so significant because it is in them that biblical imagery and imagery from the natural world make their decisive breakthrough. We find in them not only prose-poems but important explanations of the meaning of the imagery that presage the third stage of Grundtvig's preaching – namely in the Church of Our Saviour, Copenhagen from 1822 to 1826.

III

The Church of Our Saviour 1822-26

Grundtvig began his ministry in Copenhagen with a number of noteworthy sermons following a set pattern. Only gradually does he take up the mythopoetic thread from the Præstø period. This happens for the first time on Quinquagesima Sunday 1823 in a powerful prose-poem on the two great men at the River Jordan – John the Baptist and Jesus. At the baptism of Jesus it is the voice from heaven that is the crucial factor:

> Then the voice was heard over Jordan,
> ringing through time and eternity,
> the voice and testimony of God the Father:
> This is my son, the beloved
> in whom I am well-pleased ...

is how the prose-poem begins. From then on it is referred to as a "vision". We shall also

> ... descend and arise with Him
> see heaven open before us,
> receive the Holy Spirit
> and take possession of the Father's testimony
> this is my beloved son
> in whom I am well-pleased,
> take possession of it
> because the Spirit testifies with our Spirit
> that we are God's children in Christ Jesus.

We note that the image at the centre of the prose-poem is the voice from heaven, God's words to Jesus. They are words that "ring through time and

139

eternity", i.e. words that are for the present, words in fact that ring for everyone of us who is baptised, even though we are then told that we must *take possession* of them. That is, the words are not yet directly and personally addressed.

On Ascension Day 1824, for example, he says that on this day we "... according to our circumstances and time's convenience will uplift our eyes and behold where the Lord ascends. listen and hear what the angels testify for *us* (*my italics*) Galileans..." (p. 5) After a lengthy prose-poem on the 15th Sunday after Trinity 1824 Grundtvig says that "... the scriptures must be opened for us, so that they become a living image of the Word for us, as it was in the beginning, became flesh and dwelt amongst us..." The image is thus a major thread in the preaching.

It is furthermore important for the imagery at the beginning of the 1820's that it lives through a growing correlation between God and the created. The most common scriptural passage used in this period is without doubt John 3:16, and it carries such weight because it corresponds to the human experience in nature and in inter-personal relationships. That God is love is, so to speak, already known by his creatures – see the sermon for the 1st Sunday after Trinity 1823 (1 John: 16b-21).

What is love,
without the life-warmth itself,
where it is aware of itself,
is in full vigour
and is one with the light.
What does it denote,
what does it mean,
summer-life in its glory
what else do the leaves whisper of
in the May-green forest
what else does the lily smell of
in her bridal clothes,
what is the birdsong in the grove for,
why does it cheer us
why does it delight us so,
except that it speaks
with warmth to our heart
of life and happiness,
that is, of love;
of the life-giving summer sun
its wonders in the spiritual,

140

in the inner, invisible world.
And what else could He be
He with whom our life's spirit dwells,
from whom all life
the inner and the outer,
the spiritual and the physical,
the visible and invisible flowed out,
what could He be but love,
what could He be in truth
but that which is the unfailing source of life itself,
the source that never began to be
but only began to reveal itself
in the innumerable streams
that flow like blood
in the veins of the living.
And if God is love
how should He be served,
with whom should He be compared
but with the very same thing,
What does love cherish
what can reflect it
except itself.

In this poem the first step has been taken on the road to the great poem of 1824 – *The Land of the Living* (p. 168).

The next advance comes around the 16th Sunday after Trinity 1823. The whole sermon for this Sunday is like an anthem, as will appear from the lay-out of the sermon below. This is, so to speak, the second stage on the road to *The Land of the Living*. One can reflect on vv. 4-6 in the original poem – on the dream that deceives – as one reads the section of the sermon beginning with the words, "But, O Man!..." (p. 145f).

Sermon for the 16th Sunday after Trinity 1823 (Luke 7:11-17)

One thing have I desired of the Lord,
that will I seek after;
that I may dwell in the house of the Lord
all the days of my life,
to behold the beauty of the Lord
and to enquire in his temple.

Thus sings David,
the man with the sweet psalm-tongue in Israel,
and the song of the sons of Korah answers loud and clear:
My soul longeth, yea, even fainteth
for the courts of the Lord:
For a day in thy courts is better than a thousand
I had rather be a doorkeeper in the house of my God
than to dwell in the tents of wickedness!

When we listen reverently to such tones
the heart cannot help but ask
what sort of house is this,
where is it to be found,
cannot the gate to these courts
cannot the door to these rooms
be opened for me too,
so that I may learn to feel
the blessed joy the psalms breathe.
Then the heart sighs
and beseeches with the psalmist:
O God, send out thy light and thy truth:
that they may lead me,
let them bring me
unto thy holy hill, and to thy tabernacles.
Then will I go in unto God,
my exceeding joy:
yea, upon the harp will I praise thee,
O God my God!

Truly, my friends!
Once the heart has learnt
to ask and then to sigh
in the deep realisation
that in none of the dwelling-places
that men build
is there constancy,
is there peace and happiness
without fear and without loss;
and that in all of them, even the brighest,
there are gloomy corners
where the night-owl lives

and spreads the terror of the night;
and that all are of the dust,
and all turn to dust again,
as the best of all visible dwelling-places,
the Eternal's earthly work,
the works of His hands in the dust,
this wonderful human body
in His image
in which the living invisible lives
as we call ourselves,
which finds expression in the Word
that passes across our lips,
and treads its invisible, wonderful path,
flying as a thought-bird
from spirit to spirit,
from heart to heart.

Truly, once the heart has become
acquainted with its desires,
its deep desires for a quiet habitation,
that shall not be taken down,
whose stakes shall never be removed,
and whose cords shall never be broken,
once the heart has become
acquainted with these desires,
which may for a time be strange to us,
but which slumber in the chamber of every heart,
and will awake one day, if not before
then on the day this habitation is broken down by death,
and we are alone with ourselves,
with the invisible
that seeks and sorrows and sighs,
that is afflicted in its tabernacle
and will awake, if not before
then one day – like the rich man in the gospel
when in pain he lifted up his eyes,
and saw the yawning gulf between himself
and the house of rest in Abraham's bosom –
Once the heart has become acquainted with the desires,
then the sigh mounts up,
as deep as the desire,

then it mounts up to Him
who dwells in the hidden light
in the glory from which all dust is barred,
whose rays we behold everywhere,
wherever the eye turns,
whose warmth we feel in our innermost being
whose flame lights up our breast
and lifts up our eyes to heaven
leads us in every thought to the eternal,
in every longing and in every sigh.

O Man, do you know what this means?
Has your ear understood it
and have you heard its echo in your heart?
Do you know the house
that is sung about in Israel
whose praises are so loudly extolled
in Zion's hymn of praise?
Do you know the House of the Lord
that hovered before David's eyes,
that aroused in his soul those deep desires,
and whose beauty he cannot praise enough,
wishing for an eternity
to gaze upon and see beyond it,
whose loveliness flowed through his heart
and poured out of his lips
in the sweet and blissful tones.

Yes or no –
how shall I answer for you, my friends?
Yes or no –
your lives will answer for you
though your lips be still,
and, consider this, they will tell the truth
though your tongue lie
and your heart deceive itself,
they will tell the truth
and He who sees in secret
He shall hear it and He shall judge –
If your eyes are nailed to this earth

by worldly pleasures,
if it is here you seek
your heaven for your rest
your peace, your joy,
if with your spirit and your hand
you pile dust upon dust
to build yourself a house
that can glitter and sparkle
houses that can stand,
houses that can hold and increase your happiness
if it is your life's work
if it be your greatest pleasure
then you do not know the desire
that tuned David's harp
nor the house,
up to whose balcony its notes soar.

But, O Man!
If you know nothing of this
what do you know at all?
What else do you know
apart from what is today
and perishes tomorrow?
What do you know
of all that you saw
of all that hovered before you
within and without?
What do you know other
than the outer garment,
the ephemeral, passing form?
What is your life's achievement,
what is your day's work,
what have you wrought and thought?
What is it but childishness,
ridiculous beyond belief
when it is taken seriously,
when the prime of life
when the course of all your days
is taken up with it
What do you build on
except a house of cards

which the breath of Time
overturns in the next moment?
What are you fighting against
except your own shadow,
which you deceive yourself
into thinking you can beat
when it passes behind you,
whence comes your joy
but from the shining bubbles that burst in the air
before you can even fix your eyes upon them?
What is your whole life
but smoke, a vapour, that vanishes?
What are you, with your greatest gifts
in your finest splendour
with your health and strength
with honour and power
with riches and wisdom
with all this what are you
but a flower,
a strange flower,
planted by an unseen hand on this earth
only to disappear in a little while
and to confirm by your fall
that all the dust is man's kinsman?
What is your pleasure and your pain,
your rest and your unrest,
your joy and your sorrow,
when all that you build upon must fall,
when all that you love must die,
when all that you think is vanity,
when the finest house you know
is the wonderful but frail tabernacle
in which you found yourself,
in which you dwell and move,
in which you think and speak,
you, the invisible, the intangible
living human soul?
What are you then
if this body,
this tabernacle,
is the highest, the best, the loveliest

the sweetest house you know?
What are you
when it is destroyed,
and you know that it must be destroyed,
perhaps today, perhaps tomorrow,
and even in the longest life
still one of the days that soon can be numbered,
in one of the years that children name
as they sit on your lap and count to a hundred?
You know that of that building
there shall not be left here
one stone upon another,
one bone with another,
that shall not be thrown down.
These limbs shall have no joints left
but shall be parted, dissolved and crumbled to dust.

And what then,
you may protest,
What then?
Believing that this building
this my body's tabernacle,
the loveliest, the happiest house I know
probably also is the most glorious,
the loveliest house to be found –
or rather, which I can find,
what use is it that I delude myself
that there is a better house, a loftier,
brighter, more permanent house, an everlasting house,
and tortured myself desiring it?
And even destroyed the grain of joy
that had come my way
growing more and more bitter
in the span of days
allotted to me?

Fools, lying fools!
What are you trying to say?
Why must you lie against the truth?
For you know very well,
you must know,

that the desire for the house
that is eternal and has an everlasting loveliness,
the desire for a quiet tabernacle
that shall not be taken down,
whose stakes shall never be removed,
and whose cords shall never be broken,
you know very well
that this desire dwells in your breast
even when it makes no sound!
you know very well
where it lies sleeping
in the gloomy chamber of the heart,
and every time you quite rightly
rejoiced over life
and found a dwelling-place
where you wanted to build,
then you yourself awakened it with your wish
that this building might never be destroyed,
that this happiness might last for ever;
you awakened it and could not do otherwise,
even though you learned each time
that you thereby called forth more torment for yourself,
called forth the worm that smote your gourd
and bit the flower of your happiness
so that it withered and died.
Therefore never speak of avoiding these desires,
the deep desires for a house,
built without hands,
built on the eternal heights,
secure against flood and storm,
and which possesses and everlasting loveliness!
Never speak of it!
Never deny that you know them
nor deny that they torment you
embittering your days
and destroying your happiness
for as a long as you fail
to find the abode of your desires,
the permanent tabernacle,
and see the door ajar,
see it open for you too.

Never deny it!
For God knows you are lying,
and so do all those of us
who have learnt from your word
that in this house of flesh and bone that we behold
there lives an invisible one, as it lives in us,
a living soul that is created like ours
and in whom our Word finds an echo.
Never deny it,
O Man, whoever you may be!
And if you would take the only useful advice,
then do not hate this desire
for the everlasting, for the eternal,
however much it torments you;
learn rather to love it and believe
that that which is the highest and deepest in you
can only be the best.
Open your eyes
and see what is so crystal clear –
that this desire that tormented you,
which you hated, fought against
and could never conquer,
– see that it is not of your own doing.
It must have been planted in you by a hand
against which you tried your strength in vain,
the invisible hand of the Creator
that made you as the clay,
that forms and crushes everything according to His will.
What is the point
of confining your deepest desires to the tabernacle
until it falls
so that you desire nothing eternal
except what you know to be impossible
– eternal life in this tabernacle,
which day by day approaches its irrevocable fall?
And can it help you
when you feel that at the same time
you are deceiving your heart?
– when you feel at the same time
that what the Word testifies is true,
namely that when the tabernacle has fallen

without you seeking and finding
a better dwelling-place
and when you are dead and buried,
then you will take up like the rich man,
homeless and in torment,
and you will see, on the other side of the gulf
in the bosom of Abraham,
the quiet habitation
that you would not appreciate
and would not win.

O, Man!
Do rather what is better
and listen with devotion to the psalmist
when he sings:
One thing have I desired of the Lord,
that will I seek after;
that I may dwell in the house of the Lord
all the days of my life,
to behold the beauty of the Lord
and to enquire in his temple.
Indeed, my Lord
I shall dwell for ever in thy tabernacle.
Listen to the prophet who cries:
Look upon Zion, the city of our solemnities:
thine eyes shall see Jerusalem,
a quiet habitation,
a tabernacle that shall not be taken down,
whose stakes shall never be removed
and whose cords shall never be broken,
and no inhabitant shall say, I am sick:
for the people that dwell therein
have been forgiven their iniquity.
Learn then to pray,
to raise a song to your Maker:
O God, send out thy light and thy truth:
that they may lead me,
let them bring me
unto thy holy hill, and to thy tabernacles.
Then will I go in unto God,
my exceeding joy:

yea, upon the harp will I praise thee,
O God my God!
For if you but lift your eyes from the dust
to seek the eternal dwelling-place,
if you but sigh with your heart for it,
sigh that also your eyes may glimpse Zion,
that also for you the gate and the door will be opened
to the court of Heaven
and the sanctuary of the Lord,
then He is standing beside you in Spirit,
the blessed one,
whose countenance is as the dawn of eternity
the words of whose lips are as dew upon plants
as life out of death.
For you know him well enough,
it is He who looks down
from the lovely rooms at the Father's right hand
and testifies:
Ask and it shall be given you
Seek and ye shall find
Knock and it shall be opened unto you.
Come unto me,
Come unto me, all ye that labour and are heavy laden,
and I will give you rest,
Ye shall find rest unto your souls,
For in my Father's house are many mansions,
and where I am there shall my servant also be.
You know him well, O Man,
you who were baptized through His word
and in His name.
And if you do not know Him
or have forgotten Him,
then get to know Him,
remember then your Lord,
your Master, your friend and Saviour.
Go to Him and be not afraid
when your eye looks for the house of the Lord,
when your heart seeks eternal comfort.
Be not afraid that He will reject you,
for He has vowed
that whoever comes to Him

will never be rejected.
Say not, who shall ascend into heaven
to bring Him down to me,
Say not, where shall we find Him,
for truly He is not far from any of us,
He is as near to us as the word
in our mouth and in our heart,
the Word of Faith that we preach,
and He has said:
I dwell in the high and holy place,
with him also that is of a contrite and humble spirit,
to revive the spirit of the humble
and to revive the heart of the contrite ones.
Search for Him then in the Word alone,
there you will find Him.
Search for Him then in today's text,
there you will find Him by the bier,
by the body of a mother's only-begotten son,
where with a human heart and a spirit divine
He pities and comforts,
says to the widow, Weep not,
says to the dead, Arise,
and is obeyed and praised.
Go to him, you whose longing
makes you a sorrowing widow
whose only son,
whose hope, they carry to the grave.
Go to Him and hear
whether He does not say
Woman, weep not,
and to your hope, Arise,
and see if it does not raise itself up living,
and sink into the bosom of your longing
and bear forth the praise of Jesus Christ on your tongue.
– Feel then if, through faith in Him,
it does not open up
the everlasting dwelling-place of your gaze.

It is a peculiarity of this sermon that having depicted the deceitful world and the fall and morality of mankind it should turn to the gospel of the day on the Widow's son in Nain, whose crucial words are now interpreted as being directly addressed to human longing and hope: "Go to Him, you whose longing...", that is, the image or the prose-poem paves the way for the direct address.

Often the prose-poems also become brief, confessionary formulations. Particularly noteworthy in this context is the sermon for the 4th Sunday in Advent 1823, where the Second Article of Faith appears in the prose-poem.

"... And we all know that the word about what happened in Bethabara was merely the herald of good news; it went out into the world only as an enlightening introduction and annotation to

> The word about
> what happened in Bethlehem,
> and in Gethsemane,
> on Golgotha,
> on the road to Emmaus
> and in Jerusalem,
> the word about Jesus the Christ,
> who was God's only-begotten Son,
> conceived by the Holy Spirit,
> born of the Virgin Mary,
> crucified, dead and buried,
> descended into hell
> on the third day rose again from the dead,
> ascended into heaven,
> sitting at God's right hand,
> from where He shall come
> to judge the living and the dead.

This has given me occasion to present the hypothesis that Grundtvig is not quite so unprepared for the "unparalleled discovery" that comes much later – in the summer of 1825 – because he has shown a predilection in the previous years for summarizing the contents of the sermon in a type of confessionary prose-poem, one of which is the Creed – or at least its Second Article.

There is good reason to mention the powerfully euphoric sermons for the 4th and 5th Sundays after Epiphany, which form the third stage towards *The Land of the Living;* and finally the fourth and last stage in June/July 1824.

Here I will confine myself to concentrating on the great prose-poem in the Whitsun sermon for June 6th 1824, where the second chapter of the

Letter to the Philippians is used to draw a parallel between Jesus humbling himself and the natural humility of the child.

What reminds us as Christians
more lovingly and more vividly
of the Saviour born in the City of David,
of the child laid in a manger
who sustains the world with His power,
of Him who was humble of heart
in whose mouth was no guile
who, when He took on the form of God
thought it not robbery
to be equal with God
but made Himself of no reputation
and took upon him the form of a servant,
He who smiled heavenly peace on the earth,
what reminds us of Him, Christians,
so kind and so alive,
Him and His happy birth,
so much as the child in the cradle,
the christened, blessed child,
who resting in the Saviour's embrace
is with Him in the form of God,
but does not think it robbery
to be equal with God,
rests with the heavenly peace of innocence,
smiles peace on us as an angel of light,
is much better, much greater than us
but never thinks himself so,
is always submissive to us
looks humbly up at us
receives with gratitude quite undeserved
the least or greatest proof
of our goodness and love,
as though we were doing great and wonderful things
when we love the blessed children
who love us and are our happiness!
What reminds us more vividly
of God's Son on earth
than the children whom He blessed
whom He represented to us as our pattern

> as the lords of heaven
> and gave us the testimony
> that their angel always sees the Father's face
> which is in heaven.

I submit that this is one of the most central passages to an understanding of Grundtvig's development. We find here – as early as 1824 – the core of Grundtvig's view of mankind and the theology of baptism which he later developed. The likeness of God is to be found in the child, or rather, in the adult who must become a child again. The childlike can glimpse paradise. The childlike can directly comprehend God.

In addition to this the prose-poem becomes, as far as I can see, the main basis for *The Land of the Living*. For now the elements have been gathered. We met the first three verses of the poem – about the child's dream – for the first time in the Friday sermon for June 17th 1822. The next three verses – about the vanity and deception of the world – appeared in amongst others the great hymn-like sermon for the 16th Sunday after Trinity 1823. And we find the background for the recaptured child-dream in Christ, at the poem's climax, in the powerful prose-poems about love as the interpretative medium between heaven and earth, God and mankind, and finally in the prose-poem for Whit Sunday about the childlike and the child's likeness to the humility of Jesus. Thus the problem for Grundtvig of God's presence is solved for the time being (p. 158).

Finally, we must emphasize that the mythopoetic features in the sermons form a direct transition to the hymns. In this context *The Land of the Living* is an obvious example. Other preliminary drafts for hymns of this period could be mentioned but I shall concentrate here on the hymn-like sermon for Christmas Day 1824, which leads directly into *O Welcome again, God's Angels Small* (p. 169), in which the individual motifs are thoroughly treated in the sermons of 1823 and 1824.

> Sing unto the Lord a new song
> sing unto the Lord; all the earth
> sings for the Lord
> praising His name,
> announcing His blessedness
> from day to day,
> preaching His glory
> amongst the heathen,
> His wondrous works

amongst all people.
The heavens are glad
and the earth rejoices,
the sea and its abundance roars,
the field rejoices
and all that grows within it,
all the trees of the forest
sing with joy,
for the Lord is come
salvation is revealed,
peace proclaimed
the light has dawned
fear retreats
hope rises
high above all the stars
high above all times
and their vicissitudes
to the maker of stars
in the heavenly mansion,
to the fullness of time
in the land of eternity.

Contemporary witnesses confirm that on this Christmas morning Grundt-vig spoke of "a new song the Lord had given him". Nor is it without interest that the first tune specified for *O Welcome again* (1832) was *With Joy We Greet the Blessed Day* (Den signede dag, p. 169). The carol was so to speak a day-song before the real carol appeared in 1826 (p. 172). Grundtvig's hymnwriting is now making rapid progress.

IV

The hymn collection is closely connected with the sermons (p. 169). I have already mentioned that the "unparalleled discovery" has its formal back-ground in the many confessionary prose-poems of 1823-24, and that the Creed appears in this context as early as 1823. It is curious, however, that the "unparalleled discovery" does not play a greater role in the sermons given in 1825-26.

The Creed is given a new significance. From 1824 onwards and espe-cially in *The Sunday Book* Grundtvig's interest increases in the words of command in the gospels, that is, words like *Weep not, Rise up,* (see 16th

Sunday after Trinity) etc. The Word comes alive most in the imperative. In addition to the imperatives, the *proclamations of the gospel,* of which we have met a great deal, have almost the same character. But the proclamations of the gospel and the imperatives in the gospels are not directed at "us", but at people of that day and age. Alongside Grundtvig's developing view of the Church and the Holy Spirit we see this concern increasing for the actual words of the service, which have the same character of questions and imperatives in the rituals of baptism and Holy Communion. The pattern of interpretation that is developed in the 1830's is as follows:

Preaching Proclamations
John 1:16
Phil. 2:6ff
John 1:1-14
etc.

Preaching Imperatives
a) *Worldly*
   God's peace!
   Happy Christmas!
   Happy New Year!
b) *Biblical*
   Become!
   Be light!
   Fear not!
   Weep not!
   Arise!
   Come over!
   Go!
   Come!
   Go out!
   Open (effata)!
   Pray and Knock!
   etc.

Baptism
Receive the sign of the Holy Cross
The laying on of hands
Our Father, in Jesus name

157

Do you renounce the devil...?
Do you believe in...?
I baptise you...
Peace be with you.

Holy Communion
Take this...
Eat...
Drink ye all of it
Do this...

Service
The Lord be with you

In the ritual words of direct address Christ is present in His Church. On any Sunday they are our Weep Not and Arise.

This development in the sermons culminates, I believe, in the spring of 1837, where Grundtvig amongst other things challenges the orthodox Lutheran view that places the Lord's presence in the bread and wine. He himself finds the Lord's presence in the living word, that is, in the ritual words of personal address, including the the questioning in the Creed, and thus the Creed is at last integrated into the proclamation of the gospel – one might add "again" – for it also appeared as the proclamation of the gospel in the sermons of the 1820's.

Thus the Church service gradually becomes the hall of interpretation for God's Word. God's Word is an address, and an address demands an answer. The answer is the Creed, prayer, and last but not least, the song of praise. The hymns become the absolutely indispensable answer to the address, and the ladder between heaven and earth becomes the address and the answer. In the interchange heaven is on earth.

What becomes then of the mythopoetic? The answer is, it makes only slow progress. From 1832 onwards Grundtvig was moving into his penultimate stage as a preacher, and the language of the sermons partly changes character, especially at the beginning of this period. The language becomes more colloquial and straightforward. It is superfluous to give specific examples here. These sermons are succeeded in 1836-37 by Grundtvig's own hymns. In this six-month period he naturally takes up the hymns he has just written, in fact in the sermons for this year we often meet the hymns from the *Song-Work* before they are printed. From now on they quite consistently take the place of the prose-poems.

I have deliberately emphasized the development in Grundtvig's early

158

stages as a preacher. Here the mythopoetic element is first a romantically-inspired attempt to defeat empty fundamentalism by introducing the imagery we meet in the prose-poems. But with regard to content and function the imagery is not romantic. It transmits in a consistent way the Bible's own expressions. For Grundtvig it becomes, in addition, a means of interpretation that clarifies his own ideas about divine imagery in preaching. The imagery from created life and from the Bible is a mirror through which God and the final revelation are to be seen. Poetry is a divine mode of recognition and a testimony to mankind's divine nobility.

In the 1820's the imagery or the prose-poems take on an increased significance, for the central content of the preaching is concentrated in the prose-poems. They open the way for a discovery of the Creed as a sort of metaphor. But at the same time the imagery or the prose-poems become the framework within which the biblical words of address can unfold. God is so close in the imagery that He can speak directly to the Church. From this point the emphasis is transferred from the imagery to the direct words of address in the rituals, through which the "unparalleled discovery" begins to have a decisive influence on the sermons. But the imagery remains as the medium through which the later hymns find their expression.

NOTE
With acknowledgement to the Grundtvig Society and Centrum Publishers for permission to reprint the sermon for the 16th Sunday after Trinity (pp. 140-52) from their publication »A Grundtvig Anthology« (1983).

Grundtvig the Hymnwriter

by CHRISTIAN THODBERG

The Danish Hymn Book from 1953 (abbreviated to DHB) contains 754 hymns, of which Grundtvig wrote 272, (171 original hymns and 101 adaptations or translations). It is first and foremost through the Hymn Book that Grundtvig is known to the Danish people. Verses and single lines are part of the folk heritage. It is doubtful whether there is any other Church in the world where a 19th century hymnwriter has made such an impact on a modern hymn book.

I

There is a strong tradition of hymnsinging in Denmark. When Martin Luther transformed the Roman mass into a service of hymns in his *German Mass 1526,* so that most of the liturgical prose texts were turned into rhymed verses over folk-tunes, other Lutheran Churches followed the tradition; but none has remained so faithful to it as the Danish Church. The reason why attempts to renew the liturgy in the 20th century have met with such little success is the powerful hold that hymns in general have on the Danish Church, and Grundtvig's hymns in particular. For tó a great extent Grundtvig's hymns already are "liturgical"; partly he adapted the classical liturgical texts with great energy, and partly he wrote original hymns, in particular centring on baptism and Holy Communion.

An outline of the historical background begins in the century following the Reformation, with the broadening of the Danish hymn tradition through translations of German hymns – especially Luther's – and through new Danish hymns. This culminated in the 17th century with the great baroque poet, Thomas Kingo, whose hymnbook from 1699 appointed certain hymns for every Sunday and holy day in accordance with the contemporary demand for uniformity within the Church. This major contribution of hymns was supplanted in the 18th century by Hans

Adolph Brorson, a pietist and probably the best ecclesiastical poet in Denmark.

The ponderous system of learning by rote the texts of the Church Year in the form of hymns referring to the epistles and gospels broke down at the end of the 18th century. First came a 'sensitive' hymnbook in the spirit of Klopstock (1778) and soon afterwards came a relatively small hymnbook called *Evangelical Christian Hymnbook* (1798), although according to its critics it was neither evangelical nor Christian! For with this hymnbook rationalism made its breakthrough into the service, but only, be it noted, into the hymnbook, which was no longer arranged according to each Sunday, but according to "the teachings of the faith", and the choosing of hymns now passed into the hands of the clergyman, as is still the case today. However, the rest of the service (the rituals, the readings, the prayers) remained faithful to the classical Lutheran model despite many attempts to introduce radical liturgical changes in keeping with the spirit of the time.

Furthermore, Kingo's hymns did not disappear completely; well into this century certain congregations in Jutland ("the strong-in-faith Jutlanders") have used the 1699 hymnbook, which was to be of such importance for Grundtvig.

II

This then was the service that forms the background for Grundtvig's hymnwriting. On the whole he was happy in his youth with the 1798 hymnbook, even though it was "more moralizing than poetic", and "only poetry with its heightened feeling can serve morality", he says in 1806. Not until he had been writing poetry for a number of years did Grundtvig turn to specifically Christian poetry. Poetry above all was his idiom, and played a part in his Christian revival in 1810-11 (see p. 10). It is characteristic of Grundtvig that he uses the *first*-person in his hymns, e.g.

> When others to church have departed,
> Out here in my nook I remain,
> They sing with such great inspiration,
> But I must not hark to their strain;
> My song is to sigh and lament,
> And my holy days are all spent
> Like weekdays in anguish and pain.

(DHB 377,5)

The model for both the form and the content of these first attempts was taken from Kingo's Hymnbook, which was used in his childhood home on Zealand and at his school in Jutland (p. 9): "Thomas Kingo writes the hymns/For the Danish Church's Choir", he later sang, and in the next 20 years the inspiration of Kingo was dominant. As was typical of poetry in the baroque age, Kingo depicted the great events in Christ's life (in particular His birth and resurrection) with powerfully dramatic imagery and with an emphasis on the "repetition" or reenactment of those events in the service here and now. This view became Grundtvig's yardstick, when he emphasized that Christianity is a story which is reenacted for the congregation today.

We see this in Grundtvig's first original, Christian poem, the Christmas hymn *Lovely is the Clear Blue Night* (Dejlig er den himmel blå) (1810, DHB 113) which draws on Matt. 2:1-12 and the star that the Wise Men from the East followed to Bethlehem. It appears to be a Christmas carol for children, but the poem is ambiguous: the three Wise Men become in Grundtvig's hands a king, his son and an astrologer – corresponding to Nebuchadnezzar, Balthazar and the astrologers in the Book of Daniel, and the "childlike" song thus also tells how contemporary "wise men" and the contemporary "Babel" must return to Christianity to find the truth. In one way it is a highly personal hymn, since it reflects Grundtvig's own situation in 1810-11, when he returned to the Christianity of his fore-fathers and came home to Udby to become curate for his aging father.

Compared with Kingo the novel feature of the hymn is the use of the folksong form. Most important of all, the hymn has a progression. It seeks to lead the singer on to realising Jesus' words: "Except ye be con-verted, and become as little children, ye shall not enter into the Kingdom of heaven" (Matt. 18:3). In 1811 when Grundtvig published the song or hymn he presented it as an ideal type of hymn: "... the historical hymn is like a running stream, and the dogmatic or moral hymn by contrast is much more like still waters", and he compares "the historic-Christian hymn" with the old myths and folksongs: "... most Church songs ought to be living images of *Jesus'* life and the lives of the saints; and bygone times learnt that such songs speak loudly to the heart and lend the soul wings to fly high above earthly things." (*Poetical Writings* p. 299-300).

"Song" was thus given the acknowledged status of "hymn". It is peculiar to Grundtvig that it is precisely in a poetic context that he seizes intuitively on insights which he only later reasons out into theology; here, that the heart of Christianity is "to become as a child again". The same view is incorporated into his adaptation in 1820 of the Danish reformed edition of the classical hymn, *Puer natus in Bethlehem* or *A Child is Born in Bethlehem* (Et barn er født i Bethlehem, DHB 85), where the ending in particular is changed radically: the Christmas message means that we become God's children again. This is described in an eschatological vision:

> God's children we become again,
> Our Christmas is in heaven's domain.
> Hallelujah!
>
> On starry carpets azure-blue,
> We gladly come to worship you.
> Hallelujah!
>
> God's angels teach us with delight
> To sing like them on Christmas night,
> Hallelujah!
>
> (DHB 85, 6-8)

Already here we can glimpse the contours of Grundtvig's later, more distinctive hymnwriting: the hymn draws its strength from and finds its purpose in the heavenly song of praise. Hymnsinging is in itself clear evidence that mankind is on its way to its heavenly fatherland. The hymnsinging Church is part of a historical progression.

Prior to this Grundtvig had taken a very independent line with a Danish translation of Luther's *Vom Himmel hoch* in his *The Christmas Bells are Ringing now* (Det kimer nu til julefest, DHB 76). In the same year he made a draft of an original Easter hymn in his imposing drama, *Easter Lily*. Here the despised country flower becomes the symbol of Christ, the resurrection of nature, of history *and* of the poet himself. This very personal poem was to become one of the most popular Easter hymns (DHB 206).

This drama was published in *Danevirke* (1816-19), a journal Grundtvig himself edited and wrote. Here we also find a serious consideration of song as the highest art-form, mediating the divine revelation in its original language, imagery: "In the revealed or prophetic word, revealed inasmuch as it enounces something hidden, and prophetic inasmuch as the secret will be discovered in due course, in this word we find both what art must form and especially what it must form it in; but *where* then is the art? To find it we must not just look at, but *also listen to* the imagery, and hear it *singing*. Song, as the bird tells us, is the most natural of all arts, that is, art in its own nature: the expression of *true* sensuality, the winged sound of the Creator flying to heaven and with melting voice calling upon the Word from which it is separated. Every time the bird sings above our heads it is as if it feels, and wants to remind us, that in mankind the great meeting has been effected and that there the holy re-union takes place. (*Danevirke* III 266ff).

Song reveals the divine origin and destiny of mankind. Even though we are dealing here with poetry in general the comment nonetheless has a theological signature. The bird that through nature reminds mankind of its divine roots is not chosen by accident. Behind it lie Jesus' words: "Behold the fowls of the air: for they sow not, neither do they reap, nor gather into barns; yet your heavenly Father feedeth them. Are ye not much better than they?" (Matt. 6:26).

III

The bird as an image of mankind's origin and destination is one of the most important themes in Grundtvig's hymns. For the poet a bird is the clearest symbol of mankind's advantages: man can speak and sing. He says in one place that if man had neither mouth nor speech, a beak would grow out of his breast, for man's highest task is to listen to and talk with God and his fellow-man.

Much later – in 1851 – Grundtvig wrote his major hymn from this viewpoint: *All Creatures that were Given Wings* (Alt hvad som fuglevinger fik, DHB 10). It treats the bird as the bearer of creation's original power and becomes a hymn about *hymns:*

> All creatures that were given wings,
> All creatures that like birds draw breath
> The sound of song to follow,
> Sing praise to God, for He is good,
> Who in His mercy will redeem
> All mortal grief and sorrow!

In addition to the birds Grundtvig is here thinking of man, who resembles a bird. The birds, unceasingly praising God with their song, must make man pause for thought, for he can both think and believe, speak and sing. In the hymn man therefore says to himself:

> My soul, of all that is on earth
> In thought and in your speech you have

> The best of wings God-given,
> And freest is your spirit's range
> Whene'er so deep in song you breathe
> That heaven's vault is riven.

In the very act of singing man feels a relaxation and a naturalness that shows a glimpse of his destiny. He must always be thinking and praising God:

> What other creature on this earth
> Compares with you in needing
> God's mercy and compassion?
> It was for you His mercy sought
> When with our Lord to earth it came
> In most mysterious fashion.

This is the central verse of the hymn. The bird needs only food , but there is no created being that has more need of God's mercy than man, because he can think and because he has imagination enough to picture himself life's risks and death. By virtue of his created nature he is in need of God's mercy. God has provided for the birds in His own way. But He meets man's deepest need with His unconditional love, His mercy in Christ.

The crucial truth about man has been established in verse 3. In verses 1 and 2 man was persuaded to realise that his reality was the same as that of the birds. Now he must take his destiny in his own hands:

> Awake my soul, break out in songs
> Of praise and glorify your God,
> Your Maker and your Saviour
> Who in His mercy looked on you,
> And through the Comforter pours out
> His loving care and favour.

In other words we must put on the feathers that suit us far better than any other creature. The birds reminded us for a brief second that that is how *we* should be, but now we have been allowed to be like the birds for ever, for God has not just created us; He has also redeemed us through Christ, by whom He has made us His children. We are told this by the *Comforter* or Paraclete (from John's Gospel), that is, the Holy Spirit, which is God's

165

spokesman on earth. We are worth far more than the birds, and therefore the whole hymn is turned upside down in the last verse.

> And say to every bird on earth,
> And say to every angel choir,
> Whose blissful song rejoices;
> That you will try to rival them,
> In praising God eternally,
> For souls and wings and voices.

Before, it was man who had to learn from the birds how to thank God. Now the roles are reversed: we have learned that we can sing and fly far better than the birds. Both angels and birds will lose in the contest to sing best.

The hymn thus has a progression: something happens to the singer. During the song he learns why he should praise God. Man experiences on his own body what the creation and the redemption are. The hymn becomes a salvation story in microcosm, and is deservedly one of the most popular hymns in the present Danish tradition.

IV

In studying this hymn we have anticipated a later stage in the poet's life, but only in order to emphasize that good hymnsinging was for Grundtvig a determining factor in the function of the service. He maintained this forcefully from the beginning of and throughout his ministry as rector of the Church of Our Saviour in Copenhagen from the 1st Sunday in Advent 1822. Even though he was forced to use the appointed 1798 Hymnbook he spoke continually of the rewakening of hymnsinging. The outpourings of prose poetry in the sermons (p. 139ff) cannot be considered separately from this; to the degree that the preaching of the gospel was brought alive and made poetic, hymnsinging would also awaken us "... since sound is the life of the Word and tone is the power of the sound which reveals the Spirit (Christmas Day 1822). Grundtvig was reminded time and again of the Kingo song of his youth: "The story goes that when groups of people met on Christmas morning, they competed as to who could shout Happy Christmas the loudest, and then every face lit up as the words were repeated, as the notes grew in force and tuned every heart to a loud hallelujah! It is even more certain that past generations shout a Happy Christmas to us with a living tone in their Christmas carols and hymns about the child born in Bethlehem bringing joy to Jerusalem (cf. *Puer natus in Bethlehem*, p. 163). But to hear this greeting from the past, to feel how sweetly it reverberates in the heart is a lesson we learn only late in life if it has not echoed within us in the days when the heart is tuned. And if it has not, then all is well, provided we miss what we have lost; the sleeping notes will awaken again and burst into life with such a tone that it will be heard in our greeting how the heart takes a living part in the Happy Christmas we proclaim..." (*ibid*). The Christmas song will spread the Christmas joy; this is especially true of the angels' song of praise, Luke 2:14, *Gloria in excelsis deo*, which is both a proclamation and a hymn. The living gospel message calls forth the loud song of praise in answer. On Whit Sunday 1823 it is said, "... that we barbarians have learned to recognize the power of the sound and to give birth to the word again in the language we are born with; that we heathens, who went after dumb idols and heard the voice of God as it rings out in Israel's song of praise were added to the people of whom David sings: '... Blessed is the people that know the joyful sound: They shall walk, O Lord, in the light of Thy countenance'." (cf. Ps. 89:15); Grundtvig later used this as the basis for one of his great hymns (DHB 335).

In the most important Church Year of his ministry, 1823-24, a positive ecstasy of hymnwriting comes over him. It is above all else the *hymn* which testifies to the life of Christianity. Thus we find in the spirited sermon for Christmas Day 1823: "... as long as there is a trace or a remnant of this happy faith of the Christians on earth, just so long will the echo of the angel-voice inevitably be heard, the echo in the Christmas hymns, in the song of praise to the heavenly Father who let a Saviour be born, who gave us light and life and peace through Jesus Christ". This is more of a programme than a reality for Grundtvig; he knows that hymn-singing has almost dropped to a whisper in the Church of this day, but the nadir of hymnsinging becomes a prophecy of its rebirth: "The notes of the song of praise may rise and fall as times change; for the intensely moved, the burning hearts, they swing boldly up to heaven; for the luke-warm and the cold they sink to the earth; but they cannot be silenced completely while there is still faith in Him who when He was in the shape of God debased Himself and took upon Him the form of a servant".

Just as hymnsinging is the life of Christianity so is it in the last resort a testimony of Christ's own presence, and the almost-silenced song is in consequence a repetition of Christ's humbling Himself (cf. Phil. 2:5-11), but at the same time also a promise of "resurrection": "...He that speaketh of the earth is of the earth. And if we look up to heaven then we see light, then the consoling hope is born and nourished that the notes of the song

167

of praise will come falling on the air to us, to the true of heart, as angels rise up to whence they came, for it is also true here that no man hath ascended up to heaven, but He that came down from heaven". The link between heaven and earth is often depicted as a double ladder down which God's Word climbs and up which the song of praise climbs as a resounding echo – a movement that repeats the incarnation and the ascension. In this lies the comfort for a hymnless age: "... From days of old it has been the Lord's good habit to reveal His hidden wisdom, His wonderful glory, when His servants are spreading the seed with sighs and tears, then the desert can be glad, the wilderness rejoice, for then it will bloom, bloom like the rose, the glory of Lebanon; for when we sow tears, we reap the song of praise!" This quotation from Psalm 126:5-6 often appears in the sermons, and Isaiah ch. 35 became the model for one of Grundtvig's most popular hymns, *Like the Roses in Full Bloom* (Blomstre som en rosengård, DHB 60) in 1837, an Advent hymn about the rebirth of the song of praise.

In the following period of this exciting Church Year the inspiration of Kingo is dominant, especially of his great hymns about the delusions of this world in contrast to the heavenly salvation: *O, World, Goodbye* (Far, verden, farvel, DHB 525), built on the account of the rich man and Lazarus (Luke 16: 19-31). Grundtvig uses the metre of this Kingo hymn for perhaps his greatest hymn *The Land of The Living* (De levendes land, cf. DHB 279 and 649). Grundtvig's point of departure is the same as Kingo's: the delusion and vanity of the world, which for Grundtvig, however, is the rationalism and romantic philosophy of his age. The contents of the poem have been examined in detail alongside the contemporary sermons of 1824 (p. 137, 140, 154). The linguistic wealth of nuances is so great that no translation can do it justice. The main theme is that Christianity involves becoming a child again (cf. the Christmas hymns p, 163 and 169), but now with a firmer foundation: the childhood dream of life as an everlasting paradise is confirmed by Christianity's basic word of God's unconditional love: "For God so loved the world, that He gave His only begotten Son, that whosoever believeth in Him should not perish but have everlasting life." (John 3:16). This love finds its expression in Jesus' sharing of the child's destiny in baptism. This gives man an equality with Christ ("a likeness to Christ", cf. the prose poem for Whit Sunday, p. 154) and unites life in heaven with life on earth. As the last stanza of the original poem runs:

O likeness to Christ!
You give to our hearts what the world does not know.

> What we only glimpse whilst our eyes are alive,
> And yet it lives in us and in us it thrives
> My country, says life, is heaven and earth,
> Where love has its home!

(DHB 279,1)

At almost the same time in 1824 and as an expression of the same exhilaration Grundtvig writes his greatest and strangest poem, *New Year's Morn* (312 stanzas). In this context too, he laments the dearth of hymns. From now on his criticism of the statutory 1798 hymnbook becomes sharper: "It is an important matter, Christians! for it is a matter of life, life in our hymns, in our sermons, in all that serves to uplift us" (Easter Monday 1824). The imagery of the Bible, which his age despises, is the only medium that can renew the song of praise. That is how it was for Kingo, his much-admired model, and that is how it was for Grundtvig: "...if the Lord is willing to be called a lamb then surely we ought not to mind being called sheep" (2nd Sunday after Easter 1824). With these words Grundtvig also formulated the programme for his later efforts as a hymnwriter; the world of biblical motifs became his most important source of inspiration together with the Danish countryside.

Alongside *The Land of The Living* we find the Christmas hymn that Grundtvig read out on Christmas morning 1824 on the subject of "singing the Lord a new song" (see p. 155). Luke 2:14 is "the great Christmas hymn of the angels". Grundtvig's own hymn makes its singers contemporarize with Jesus' birth: now it is *our* lowly cottage the angels visit in spite of its meanness. We sing of the children who "sweetly dream of Bethlehem", and it becomes clear that it is in fact the adults who must renew their childhood dream of Paradise by becoming children again with the child Jesus, cf. the "likeness to Christ" above, p. 168. Then the song of praise awakens and is depicted characteristically enough with the help of the ladder-image described above (p. 130).

> God's angels then wander up and down
> The carol's tonal ladder,
> Our Saviour Himself enjoins God's peace
> To those desirous of it,
> The heavenly gateway opens wide
> Then truly comes God's kingdom!

(DHB 81,7)

It is the angels' song of praise that goes down and up like a joyful echo sung by the redeemed. Several central biblical references appear in the stanza: 1) the greeting of peace (Peace be with you (John: 20:19 & 26), which is part of the Lutheran baptism ritual) – and more obscurely 2) Matt: 18:3: "Except ye become as children", the gate to the Kingdom of God will not open – and 3) Genesis 28: 18-19: Jacob's dream where he actually saw the ladder, awoke, discovered the stone and said, "This is none other but the house of God, and this is the gate of heaven" ... "and I knew it not". From now on this Genesis text becomes for Grundtvig an image of the baptism that the adult has forgotten, but which he awakes to recognize as the place of salvation.

Like the two other Christmas hymns considered here (p. 162 and 163) this one also moves on two levels: the purely narrative and the theologically meditative. The hymn also has a sequence: the singer relives Jesus' birth as his own rebirth in baptism. It thus becomes a sacramental hymn, but in a childlike and popular form.

V

The view of the Church which Grundtvig developed in the course of the 1820's (see p. 226ff) was reflected in his view of the song of praise or hymn. Grundtvig could agree with the Confessio Augustana (art. VII) that the Church is where the gospel is preached purely and the sacraments are administered properly. The Word of God can be heard. But it becomes increasingly clear to Grundtvig that the Church or the congregation ought to, in fact must, be heard too. This does not make the Church more *visible,* for everything depends on the hearts of the singers.

Grundtvig wanted hymns that would strengthen the self-awareness of the congregation as the bearer of the power of the resurrected and ascended Lord. He thus moved slowly away from the theology of Kingo's hymns, which deal in particular with what the Christian is freed and saved *from.* The hymns Grundtvig wanted would express positively what man is saved *for.* The congregation are living on what Christ has *won.* This view received powerful encouragement from John 3:16, which to an extraordinary degree is the dominant NT text in the sermons of 1824 (p. 140). The so-called "unparalleled discovery" of 1825, that the Creed is the indisputable foundation of Christianity (see p. 153), strengthened this consideration theologically, but in practice in 1825 it is first and foremost baptism and Holy Communion that became the exponents of Christ's presence in the Church as the resurrected and ascended Saviour.

In the middle of the battle within the Danish Church in 1825 (p. 13) Grundtvig wrote his first hymns about the *Church,* amongst others *Zion's Song* (Sions Sang), in which he draws on Psalm 137:1-9 to convert Israel's exile in Babylon, the return to Jerusalem and the rebuilding of the Temple into an image of the renewal of the Church of his own day and age based on a new foundation, namely, the Creed, baptism and Holy Communion, which for Grundtvig means Christ Himself. Through this, man comes back to his destiny, which he had only had as a "childhood dream" (p. 137f), a parallel with the Jews' all-but-vanished memory of Jerusalem:

> Who is there who dare remember now
> The heart's sweet morning dream.
>
> (DHB 306, 1)

It is only with tears in her voice that "Zion" dares to strike up her old song, but in the new "temple" the cornerstone (Christ) is set fast; no enemy can touch it. Even when the actual Church is derided as a poorhouse, *God's* Church, the invisible Church is full of glory, for

> Only the creator's hand can
> Build the house with lofty rooms,
> Only God the Father's Spirit
> Can from heaven descend to dust;
> Here from trunks of tender beechwood
> Under songs of nightingales
> We are building but a guest-room
> For a heavenly Eucharist.
>
> (DHB 306, 6)

Here Grundtvig uses an image from the Danish countryside: the beech forest with its high, straight trees in the twilight with the nightingale, whose song reflects the as yet frail but nonetheless everlasting song of praise. From the pulpit Grundtvig looks down on the congregation, so to speak, a crowd of people standing up and resembling a forest. This is the real "God's house"! The living congregation forms with its own body a "guest-room", a provisional room for the communal meal which will be completed with God in heaven – at the table together with Abraham, Isaac and Jacob. The secret is that Christ Himself is present in the "cottage"; it will grow strong together with Him:

Wise and valiant men of this world
May our cottage well despise
Yet the greatest still will hold
Communion in the poorest nook;
Early he has curled up meekly,
Happy in his mother's lap
He who once lay in a manger
In the cottage will break bread.

(DHB 306, 7)

At Whitsun 1826 Grundtvig's position as a hymnwriter became a political problem for the Church in connection with the one-thousandth anniversary of the arrival of Christianity in Denmark. He was under the misguided impression that on that day the clergy could choose hymns from other than the statutory 1798 Hymnbook, and he therefore published a little booklet with 3 hymns for use at his service on the anniversary. The Church authorites forbade this and Grundtvig demonstratively resigned his post the Sunday before Whitsun (p. 13).

The first article in the booklet was Grundtvig's revision of the old Reformation hymn (from the 1569 hymnbook). Here he praises "the blessed day" with the image of the sunrise and the spreading light. It was for him a metaphor for the arrival of Christianity in Denmark in the past and of the renewal of Christianity in the present:

We joyfully greet the blesséd day
Ascending from the ocean;
It lightens the heavens and inspires
To joyfulness and devotion!
As children of light 'tis seen on us
The shadows of night are in motion.

(DHB 367,1)

The renewal of Christianity is described in powerful images of spring and summer growth. It is fitting that almost every Danish Church festival service begins with this hymn, which ironically was banned at the festival service it was written for!

VI

In the following years Grundtvig was regularly urged to return to hymnwriting. In particular Gunni Busck[1] kept on at Grundtvig, for example in a letter from 1832: "Dear brother! Help us now, by letting God help you, so that we can come together to sing in our forefathers' ancient, faithful tones about our Saviour so that we can believe and sing and rise up singing to Heaven! Amen!" A few days later (on Easter Saturday) Grundtvig replies: "...I must send you a new song the Lord gave me, for although I don't know whether it will be sung aloud, "Like the golden sun arising" (Kingo's Easter hymn), or how it will sound in the congregation's ears, yet in yours it will probably sound more or less as it does in mine, that is, not unpleasantly."

In the hymn Grundtvig sent Busck, the *Easter* hymn (following the Christmas hymn) comes powerfully to the fore:

> Take the black cross from the graveside!
> Plant a lily in its place!
> As we walk in death's own garden,
> Seeds are shooting up apace!
> Angel wings upon our grave
> The broken pilgrim's staff replace!
> The palm-bird flees the jar of ashes!
> Songs of joy all sighs erase!

(DHB 207,1)

Grundtvig linked this to the account of Mary Magdalene at Jesus' grave (John: 20:11-18); but the scene becomes in addition a present-day churchyard, where Grundtvig replaces the well-known symbols on the grave monuments with symbols of life: the Phoenix (palm-bird) instead of the urn (jar of ashes) etc., for Christianity must not dwell with death but bear and be borne by life itself.

In this hymn Grundtvig completes the break with Kingo's theology that had begun in the 1820's (p. 170). For Grundtvig the real clash in our existence was between life and death (as he formulated it to the German theologian, Marheineke). At about the same time he defined his new view of hymns: "As long as our hymns fail to express the living feeling that we have already passed over from death into life, that we have found the everlasting life in God's love and have drunk from the chalice of His salvation, but express only the memory of God's great and wonderful works among the children of man and the hope of redemption from the chains of vanity, then they remain flat and weak compared with what the

---

1. Gunni Busck (1798-1869) rector at Stiftsbjergby near Holbæk.

173

song of God's servant Moses, and the psalms of David and Asaph[2] meant
to Israel's people who believed." (4th Sunday in Advent 1832). Already
in 1828 he had distanced himself from Kingo and defined his programme
for the "new hymns": "It is remarkable that our old hymnbooks contain
hardly any *clear* hymns to express the *clear* truths about people's *natural*
relationship to God, to each other and to temporal conditions..." For
already through the fact that he himself is created, man has an idea of his
destiny (p. 164), and Christianity as life is first and foremost a renewal of
the original, natural life which was allotted to everyone.

Here the first notes are sounded of Grundtvig's real determination as a
hymnwriter. So far it had just been an approach. From the 1830's
onwards more and more of Grundtvig's hymns were published in private
collections, and what is more, people began to sing them – not at church
but at home. A number of Grundtvig's greatest hymns saw the light of
day in the first half of this decade, amongst them the great Ascension
hymn with its originally very *Danish* beginning that refers to the *flag* (the
white cross on a red background) which can look like a banner of the
cross, and which Jesus is often depicted as holding (on the resurrection
scenes of altarpieces):

> Fly the cross above the ocean,
> Roll now, waves of azure-blue!

The power of the ascending Lord is described as follows:

> All the peoples, all shall feel it,
> Yes and amen are God's words,
> Earth is lifted up to heaven,
> Heaven descended to the earth,
> Raised to angels is the ladder
> While the dust sings out in praise:
> Our songs climb the tonal ladder
> Mingling with the seraphs' praise.

> (DHB 220, 1 & 3)

Once again Grundtvig uses the ladder-image (p. 130 and 169), but now the
union between heaven and earth is complete, for the Lord penetrates
into the whole universe and is a living presence through the Word.

---

2. Asaph – musical composer and leader of David's choir. Psalms 50 and 73 to 83 are
   ascribed to him.

VII

The renewal of the hymnbook as a collected work still awaited Grundtvig. Characteristically, it became a work done to order. Busck wrote in
1835: "...I pray to God that if it be His will that you will carry out this
task, that He will in fact guide and strengthen you for it and every day
bless your task for His mercy's sake, and I offer you before God and in
the name of our Lord 1000 *rigsdaler* in the hope that it will be sufficient,
and more if it is not." But not until 1836 did Grundtvig set to work. On
October 30th he inserted the announcement: "Pastor N. F. Grundtvig has
published *Song-Work for the Danish Church,* 1st Booklet, containing the
"overture" to *New Year's Morn* 1824, and 30 living hymns, partly new and
original, partly older and reborn hymns; and the whole booklet, which
consists of 6 sheets is on sale at Wahl's Bookshop for 1 *rigsmark*".

The date was no coincidence; the booklet came out at the same time as
the celebration of the introduction of the Reformation in 1536. Nor was
the title a coincidence; during the English bombardment of Copenhagen
in 1807 the spire of Copenhagen's main church, the Church of Our Lady,
was hit, and the "song-work" (the famous peal of bells that played the old
hymn-tunes) was destroyed. The church lay in ruins for a number of years
and became for Grundtvig a symbol of both national and Church decay.
The "Song-Work" was the rebuilding of "the Church".

The first booklet is marked by the Reformation anniversary and therefore contains many hymns about the Church. It is true in general of all
the first booklets in the collection that in very many of the hymns Grundtvig establishes his view of the Church and its constituent elements, baptism and Holy Communion.

Otherwise the framework of the collection is the seven congregations
(cf. Revelation 1:20 to 3:22), which he has already identified as 1) the
Hebrew, 2) the Greek, 3) the Roman, 4) the English, 5) the German, 6)
the Danish congregation. Who it was that represented the seventh national congregation was the object of Grundtvig's speculation for many years.
Grundtvig thus drew on Old Testament material (especially the prophets
and the psalms), Greek and Latin hymns (which he had learned among
other things during his visits to England), and Danish hymns from the
Reformation century up to and including his own.

This framework is repeated throughout the book in the form of a series
of sequences, most especially in connection with Christmas, Easter and
Whitsun. Thus the *Song-Work* is founded on Church history, with

Grundtvig himself in the centre, but there is a theological purpose behind this: hymnsinging must comprise the holy, Universal Church's song of praise on its way to consummation in the heavenly song of praise: "What especially pleases me about it is the fusion of sounds from all the major denominations in the Universal Church which during preparation reached my ear and touched my heart; and although I am aware that the various notes have lost many of their distinctive features by having to go through me, I make bold to hope nonetheless that traces remain that will gladden believing souls as a herald pointing forward to the new song in which all nations and tongues shall praise Him by whom, through whom, and to whom all things belong!"

The *Song-Work* is an enormous poetic achievement: about 90 % of the total of 401 hymns came into being in this period, during which 8 booklets in all are published (24/10 1836-31/8 1837). The sermons in this period are characterized by considerable exuberance; they include the hymns before they are printed and become a particularly vivid commentary on them.

On October 16th 1836 Grundtvig presented his new hymn project from the pulpit. The old hymns are his model, but they are "static" and "must learn to adapt to our changed taste". It is no longer enough, as it was in 1811 (p. 162) that the hymns depict the great historical events. It has become his conviction "...since I learned to distinguish the loud and winged word from the static and deaf-and-dumb word and the Lord's quickening word to each of us from the historical description of what He once told His prophets, apostles and others who have passed away... Therefore a revision of our best old hymns and the finding of new ones is one of the most important Church concerns for us at this moment, and so I beg every one of you who share the faith and contemplation of the Kingdom of God in Jesus' name to join your prayers with mine, that with the aid of the Holy Spirit I may succeed to the glory of God the Father and to the resuscitation, growth and illumination of the little earthly trinity, faith, hope and love, which alone can join, bind and finally unite us with all that is heavenly, in whose name and living expression we know baptism to have been immersed and likewise uplifted so that God shall be everything in everyone!"

Already a month before this three major hymns had seen the light of day, in connection amongst others with the sermon on the resurrection of the Widow of Nain's son (Luke: 7:11-17). Jesus' words to the widow, *Weep not*, are repeated to the congregation now: "yes this is my testimony, and therefore I have said often and repeat now that in the spirit the Lord has met this congregation, just as He met the widow with her only-begotten son in the gospel of the day, stopped the bier, said to the Church, our mother, weep not and by resurrecting from the dead His Word through the grace of baptism and Holy Communion has resurrected the Church's hope and consolation, which in truth is Himself, the living Word of God..." Thus the congregation may sing:

> Jesus has visited his flock,
> Night has now turned into morning,
> The Son of Man, God's Comforter,
> Has brought an end to all mourning.
>
> In the dark earth the Saviour lay,
> Now on His throne He is sitting,
> Spirit and life are His Word to us,
> Joyful the tone of our singing!
>
> (DHB 308, 1 & 9)

This hymn was written around September 18th 1836. The following Sunday another great hymn was written on the epistle (Eph. 4:1-6) with the characteristic beginning:

> Our Church it is an ancient house,
> Stands though its towers may crumble,
>
> (DHB 280, 1)

a proverbial expression that reminds us of the symbolism around the shattered Church of Our Lady (p. 175). The Church that survives is the living congregation: it lives through the Word that here and now addresses it in baptism and Holy Communion. The Church may be a brick house on the outside, but "It is the Word that sanctifies the house".

The last of the three great hymns asks in tones of wonder how Christianity could be spread by the poor and uneducated Galilean men. The answer is that it is due to the Holy Spirit itself, is in fact "evidence" of the Spirit's power, and it is also the Spirit itself that now, through a renewal of hymns makes the Danish language its obedient tool:

> The mother-tongue bends deeply down
> Light and lively it complies
> To the thinking of our Lord;
> Sweet itself, but soft thereafter,

Borrows spirit, fire and forces
From the hero-song of Zion.

(DHB 242, 8)

VIII

If we follow Grundtvig's own programme as set out above we must first consider his translations of David's psalms, of which numbers 19 (DHB 350), 84 (DHB 378), 92 (DHB 4) and 103 (DHB 3) immediately invite our attention: corresponding translations are found in the DHB both from Luther and the Geneva-tradition, but Grundtvig's new versions are far more powerful. In addition to David's psalms Grundtvig worked on OT material (p. 162).

Moving from the Hebrew to the Greek church we find the material that without doubt was most congenial to Grundtvig. In all probability he did not know much about Greek hymnology beforehand, until, that is, January 23rd 1837, when he borrowed from the library an obscure collection, *Leiturgikón,* which contains a selection of hymns and prayers for the great holy days. There is evidence that it is the framework of this book that Grundtvig relies on in his subsequent reworkings of the Greek material.

The Greek influence has an explosive impact on him. Already in the booklet published on February 11th we find the first hymn "After the *Ancient Greek* Easter Verse", and from Sunday February 5th (Quinquagesima) up to and including the 2nd Sunday after Easter (April 9th) he was completely dominated by what may be called Grundtvig's "Greek awakening". On the first Sunday Grundtvig preaches on the baptism of Jesus (Matt: 3: 13-17) and says: We don't know whether Jesus' baptism took place on a Sunday, but great things happen on Sundays; Jesus rose from the grave, the Holy Spirit came over the apostles on a Sunday, "and on this very day five years ago, Grundtvig began his preaching ministry in Frederik's Church!" (p. 124) It is perfectly clear that Grundtvig was fascinated by the Greek texts, and in particular the so-called resurrection poetry or *anastásima,* which in the Greek liturgy is sung every Sunday throughout the year to establish the special position of Sunday in memory of the resurrection: "That is why it was a marvellous custom in days gone by for the Christian not to be satisfied, as we are, with noting in passing why they kept Sunday holy, assiduously reminding one another and the children of it, but to begin their public service every Sunday with a song

178

of praise to the crucified, dead and buried, but victoriously resurrected *Jesus Christ*".

This strengthened a feeling about Sunday that Grundtvig already had, which from now on received full expression: the resurrection is relived and made contemporary every Sunday; Christ is present in His Word. This is expressed in the Greek liturgy in all the hymns that begin with the word *simeron* (today), which allows the biblical event to happen *now*. It is characteristic that this is demonstrated in the sung hymns. It reinforced Grundtvig's idea of the hymn as the bearer of the resurrection testimony.

The "Greek awakening" reaches its highest point naturally enough at Easter. On Easter Day the sermon is introduced with a verse of Hades' Lament (not in DHB), after which the sermon is a commentary on the verse:

> Today Hell is sighing and groaning
> That Adam and all of his race
> Now stubbornly march in great numbers,
> Redeemed by the hidden God's Son;
> With pleasure I gathered them meanly,
> But He stole them back one and all,
> The Word of the crucified man
> Now sends them from hell up to heaven!
> Glory be to God's Elected,
> Crucified and resurrected.

"That is how, Christian friends, the happy morning-song of the Church rings in our ears from days long past, and although it is certainly sad that these triumphant tones died on the lips that gave birth to them, that these days belief in the resurrection is nowhere deader than amongst the Greeks, where the tender hearts must now sigh deeply at the old Easter hymn, whose words they hardly understand any longer and whose joy they cannot share at all, even though it is certainly sad in a way, yet it gives such great happiness to see that the Church's ancient hymns and songs of praise and spiritual songs can find a living echo in our hearts and on our lips, so that we feel and prove that the gates of hell have not prevailed against the house on the rock, that time, which otherwise consumes everything, has been unable to destroy the living memorial that our Lord *Jesus Christ* left behind Him here on earth, sanctified by His blessing and inspired with the Father's quickening Spirit. So, Christian friends, on this glorious festival of the resurrection, we who truly feel the Lord's presence must with diligence and joy recall to His honour that the life of His Church and Congregation on earth, the constancy of the people who devote themselves to Jesus Christ the Crucified, is not merely what is called a testimony to His resurrection and ascension but a constant reiteration of His victorius battle against death and crystal-clear proof therefore that Jesus Christ has the power to lose His life and the power to take it back again."

Here we find the content of the "Greek awakening" formulated. The resurrection is in the present; it happens today. It is the restoration of the whole of Creation that is demonstrated in the cosmic drama of the Easter service. This is emphasized in the last part of the sermon which leads in to a quotation from John of Damascus' great Easter canon: *Defte poma píomen*, in English, *Come, let us Empty a Cup once again* (only the last three of in all 6 stanzas are in the DHB (212); John's opening words probably offended the Church's sense of propriety!): "No, never before had the world been so openly disappointed in its expectation and clever calculations as it was to be now: for though it is over three centuries since the decisive battle took place, that quite extraordinary war that *Martin Luther* could still celebrate so wonderfully, when life made away with death (a reference to a verse from *Christ lag in Todesbanden* [Christ lay in the chains of death]), but when the worst of the battle was over, the world nonetheless was somewhat relieved and found it was not nearly so dangerous as had appeared. For no resurrection actually took place; Christ's body, which is His Church, did not rise from the dead but received only the resurrection pledge in the Holy Spirit, as is written: "put to death in the flesh, but quickened by the Spirit: by which also he went and preached unto the spirits in prison" (1. Peter 3: 18-19), so Christ has lived only in hiding on earth, unappreciated and in the end defiantly rejected and contemptuously forgotten by the world, but now victoriously reclaims His body and reveals His glory, just as in former times after His resurrection and ascension He revealed it to His ancient congregation.

> Come, let us empty a cup once again,
> Not from the fount that flowed out of the staff
> But from the quickening spring from the grave
> The spring of salvation that bursts into life
> Jesus, our life-force, who strengthens our hearts!
>
> Everywhere light in abundance now dawns
> Heaven and earth and hell are revealed
> The whole world's foundation is quickly discovered

180

Easter to all His creation is given
Feels itself strong through the Word's resurrection.

"Amen, in the name of our Lord Jesus, Amen"

In this context it is quite unique to find a Danish Easter hymn in translation forming the introduction to the Greek Easter morning service, the
antiphon between priest and congregation, in which the priest sings
Psalm 68: 2-3 and Psalm 118:24 verse for verse, while the people repeat
the chorus: "Christ is risen from the dead, death He defeated by His
death, and life is given to those in the grave." Grundtvig turned the
ceremony into a hymn:

> The Lord has awakened from sleep and arisen!
> Hearken now, hell, to our morning-song
> Christ from the dead is arisen!
> God resurrected has scattered His foes
> Like wax over embers they suddenly melted,
> Christ from the dead is arisen!
>
> (DHB 194,1)

In 1968 the present writer, unexpectedly faced with having to make a
speech for the current Russian patriarch, Pimen, chose to quote from
memory this hymn of Grundtvig, and gained a vivid impression from
Pimen's reaction of the close connection between the Orthodox Church
and the Danish Church – thanks to Grundtvig!

An absorption in the universal, all-embracing Church belongs to the
"Greek awakening". In these months Grundtvig speaks and sings without
reservation of the ancient Church as a communion of faith to which he
feels himself to be spiritually related, not just as a passing phenomenon, a
"national church", a stage in the road to something better and truer, but as
a Church that speaks a language that has an immediate impact on him.
He takes up the subject quite naturally on the 2nd Sunday after Easter
with the text on the good shepherd, and especially with the words that
there shall be one flock and one shepherd (John 10.16). The sermon
became the draft for Grundtvig's only "ecumenical" hymn:

> Christ and His Church are universal,
> A house of prayer for all mankind,
> His Spirit there alone is active,

God's love and truth interpreting;
Its faith and baptism it changes
With time as little as its Maker,
Its promises like its spirit last.

(DHB 285,1)

But the Church is definitely ecumenical on Grundtvig's premises; it is the common faith (=Apostolicum) and baptism that constitute "the Universal Church".

The "Greek awakening" is without doubt the most powerful stimulus for Grundtvig in 1837. It solved his final problem: the question of the Lord's real presence; the here-and-now character of the Greek hymns set him on the right road. The Lord's real presence was to be found in the direct and personal address of the baptism and Communion rituals. This explains why the real clash with the Lutheran view of Communion and the concentration of the Communion elements into the bread and the wine happens alongside and in conjunction with the "Greek awakening", In the very same Easter days he could characterize the Catholic, the Calvinistic and the Lutheran views of Communion as being "slippery dangerous and somewhat confused" respectively, and he adds "...that all Christians who believe in the Lord's real presence could and should agree that what we know or can know about the manner of the presence is that it rests on *the Word of God* alone, so that the presence must therefore of necessity be said to be spiritual, but is not therefore in any way incorporeal, since the Word is corporeal as well as spiritual and binds itself to the bread and the wine, which the Spirit therefore also with the Apostle Paul calls the communion or fellowship of the body and the blood, Amen in the name of Jesus, Amen!" (Maundy Thursday 1837).

IX

Parallel with the Greek influence we must consider Grundtvig's work on the Latin hymns, among which he had a strong preference for those with a dramatic content revolving around Christmas, Easter, the Ascension and Whitsun. This includes amongst others *Dies est laetitiae* (DHB 88), *Resonet in laudibus* (DHB 94), *Salve mundi salutare* (DHB 167) *Vita sanctorum* (DHB 201), *Mundi renovatio* (DHB 205), *Coelos ascendit hodie* (DHB 215), the Whitsun sequence *Veni sancte Spiritus* (DHB 263), *Qui procedis ab utroque* (DHB 249) and *Urbs beata Jerusalem* (DHB 289).

Grundtvig's adaptations were far from being "translations" in the usual sense; he produced a very free version, omitted what he disliked and added his own theological points, often in the form of extra stanzas. For example, whereas Arnolf of Louvain in *Salve mundi salutare* remains in meditation over Jesus' suffering and cross, Grundtvig is forced theologically to add the resurrection to the last stanza:

> I believe the Easter mystery,
> Saviour, through thy loving mercy.
> When I'm tempted, stand beside me!
> When my eyes close, come to guide me!
> Say: We go to paradise!
>
> (DHB 167,9)

Grundtvig created a new work of art from the old. He did, however, follow Arnolf's metre (with the exception of the last line of the new poem with its masculine ending). Above all, the work of 1836-37 shows how Grundtvig let himself be inspired to employ new and unknown metres in his hymns, which again created an enormous interest amongst contemporary composers who wrote the tunes to Grundtvig's hymns.

Among the hymns from the "English national Church" Grundtvig was particularly in sympathy with Anglo-Saxon hymns from the early Middle Ages, that is, the material which he himself had worked on from 1815-20 (p. 11). These include the great Easter Sunday hymn about Christ's descent into hell (by Caedmon) and not least Cynewulf's Ascension hymn (from the Exeter Book) (DHB 213). This tradition is, as we know, close to the Greek Church, and it fascinated Grundtvig because of the same cultic dramatic content.

Another distinctive group consists of translations of amongst others James Allen (DHB 401), James Montgomery (DHB 156 and 248), G. T. Noel (DHB 417), Isaac Watts (DHB 183 and 221) and Charles Wesley (DHB 660). Most of them were not first-rate poets, but Grundtvig's adaptations have an intensity and a drive that all but overshadow the originals.

A good example of this is his adaptation of Montgomery's "O Spirit of the living God", an English missionary hymn of the period consisting of 6 short 4-lined stanzas; in Danish it becomes one of Grundtvig's most powerful and most popular hymns, in a new metre with 6 6-line stanzas. The English iambics are replaced by the majestic Danish dactyls with alliteration and ordinary internal rhymes in lines 1 and 3 in each verse.

First comes the English original, followed by an English translation of the Danish adaptation:

> O spirit of the living God!
> In all thy plentitude of grace,
> Where'er the foot of man hath trod,
> Descend on our apostate race.
>
> You who go out from the Living God,
> Spirit of spirits on high!
> Flesh of mankind against God's only son,
> See how they battle before thee;
> But in thy mercy stay, O stay!
> Night is so gloomy and soon is here.
>
> Give tongues of fire and hearts of love
> To preach the reconciling word;
> Give power and unction from above,
> When'er the joyful sound is heard.
>
> Give tongues of fire yet a ministry mild
> To your assigned and anointed!
> With the apostles to earth's widest bounds
> Wanders the word of your blessing,
> So no man ever can set foot
> Where its loud voice has not been heard.

(DHB 248, 1-2)

Perhaps what first attracted Grundtvig to Montgomery's hymn was the heading: "The Spirit accompanying the Word of God", which was already a central thought in Grundtvig's theology. But there is a marked difference between Montgomery's theology of the Holy Spirit and Grundtvig's own. In the first verse in the English version the prayer is that the Holy Spirit should come – in the Danish version, that it should *remain*. For the Holy Spirit always *was* in the Church; it was the congregation who did not appreciate it, a theme that is taken up later in one of Grundtvig's great hymns about the Holy Spirit, from 1846 (DHB 250).

Even though as mentioned Grundtvig translated very freely, the material from the first four "national Churches" was nonetheless congenial to him to a remarkable degree. More complex was his relationship to the "German national Church", that is, to Martin Luther and the orthodox

184

Lutheran hymnwriters. It is true that it was the very tradition that had started him off as a hymnwriter (p. 162), but with the passing of time his relationship to Luther became more and more ambiguous. Outwardly Grundtvig wished to appear as the "Luther" of his day and age; inwardly he distanced himself from considerable areas of Luther's theology. The most obvious examples are his "translations" of Luther's hymns.

Luther's *Nun bitten wir den Heiligen Geist* (The Holy Spirit now we Pray) is a cry for help from the tempted in the midst of life's hazards, where sin, death and the Devil have besieged man. Luther's model was the medieval "leise" and in keeping with the message each stanza ends with the ancient cry for help – kyrie eleison.

In his version of the hymn Grundtvig goes a step further: the Holy Spirit is already in the Church, and the prayer to the Holy Spirit is based on that fact. Compare Luther's and Grundtvig's versions:

Nun bitten wir den Heiligen Geist
um den rechten Glauben allermeist,
dass er uns behüte
an unserm Ende,
wenn wir heimfahren
aus diesem Elende,
Kyrieleis.

The Holy Spirit now we pray
To bind us closely with the bands of faith
And until the world ends
To protect the Church
By thy grace avert
All distress and danger
Saviour, hear our prayer.

Du süsse Lieb, schenk uns deine Gunst,
lass uns empfangen der Liebe Brunst
dass wir uns von Herzen
einander lieben
und im Frieden
auf einem Sinn bleiben.
Kyrieleis.

O loving Spirit, now instil
The joy of love in our communion,

So we wander gladly
Jesus, with thy people,
Loving one another
As God loves His children
Saviour, hear our prayer.

(DHB 246, 1 & 3)

There can be no doubt about the quality of Grundtvig's hymn to the Holy Spirit, and it also occupies a powerful position in the present hymn tradition; but the tone of temptation has been shed and its lack is felt. The hymn is more Grundtvig's than Luther's.

The same situation can be observed in connection with *Gelobet seist du, Jesu Christ* (Praise be to thee, O Jesus Christ), where Luther compares Jesus' poverty with mankind's suffering and thus brings the incarnation into the present. With Grundtvig it returns to being an accomplished fact, which the Church is grateful for:

Er ist auf Erden kommen arm,
dass er unser sich erbarm
und in dem Himmel mache reich
und seinen lieben Engeln gleich,
Kyrieleis.

Poor were you when you came to earth,
Poverty you dignified,
Poor you willingly made yourself,
Rich we became for evermore,
O God be praised!

(DHB 89,5)

It might seem as though Grundtvig sang only of the ecclesia triumphans, but that is not quite the case; he could not assume the sufferings of *others;* elsewhere he could sing of his own in almost the same tone as Luther (p. 190ff).

Turning finally to the "Danish national Church" we find Grundtvig reprinting in the *Song-Work* his translations of the Danish version of *Puer natus in Bethlehem* (p. 163) and of *Dagvisen* (p. 172), and in general it is his adaptations of material from the 1569 Hymnbook that are the most successful, e.g. the reworking of the two Mary-songs (DHB 64 and 172) and in particular of the old hymn about the second coming of Jesus:

Lift up your head, all Christendom!
Lift up your eyes, and be not dismayed!
In heaven is your home;
There is your treasure, there is your heart,
From there in honour He comes with haste,
He whom you never can forget.

(DHB 229,1)

Otherwise one must admit that in this group Grundtvig reveals his limitations. From 1810-11 Thomas Kingo was his ideal (p. 162) and in the 1820's
his sermons were carried along by long quotations from Kingo's verses.
But when he began to adapt Kingo's hymns in the 1830's, as a rule he
changed the basic premise of their theology. Where, for example, Kingo
presents Christ's passion as an actual charge against his own sin and guilt
and continually talks of the imitation of Christ as mankind's battle against
all evil powers until the release of death, Grundtvig does not find "the trail
again until after Golgatha, where it has become glorified – not first and
foremost for the Saviour, but for mankind" (Magnus Stevns, see bibl.).
The Kingo adaptations are by and large failures, and only a few were
incorporated into the DHB; in one place an original Kingo hymn is
placed next to its adaptation (452 and 453).

Grundtvig had even less feeling for H. A. Brorson's poetic genius; in
this area we find real coarseness. Grundtvig also worked on his earlier
hymns, and in justice it must be added that he did not spare himself
either; here too there is a turn for the worse, which has unfortunately
been accepted into the work of the official hymnbook in the belief that
the poet himself must have the last word.

X

The *Song-Work* is thus stamped with Grundtvig's own wilfulness and
theological self-awareness. The high points are his renderings of Old
Testament poetry and the hymns of the Orthodox Church, together with
his own hymns. Actually it is difficult to distinguish between the adaptations and the original poems; he himself had a genre which he called
"echo-stanzas", i.e. original hymns that were clearly inspired by the
adaptations. This shows his working methods with poetry; the work on
the material common to the whole Church set up a chain reaction in him.

In 1839-41 came the *Song-Work for the Danish Church-School*, containing in particular songs based on Bible history and Church history for educational use; a few examples are to be found in DHB (127, 130, 230 and 283). Grundtvig's friends published a further three volumes of the *Song-Work* between 1871 and 1881 containing the hymns Grundtvig wrote from 1839 until his death.

Grundtvig's life as a hymnwriter is closely bound up with the course of his own life; his awareness of his own significance as a prophet and reformer turns his hymnwriting into a world which can only be entered on *his* conditions. Or to put it another way, his hymnwriting underwent a development from "Christmas" (1810-11 and 1824) through "Easter" (the beginning of 1830's) to "Whitsun" (from 1837), that is, precisely in step with his interpretation of the development of Christian life. It began with the cold and storms of winter, continued with the budding of spring at Easter and ended with midsummer. This whole world of imagery that he had developed and which was always present in his work, was gathered into his Whitsun hymn in 1843:

> In all its splendour now the sun shines,
> Above the mercy-seat the lifelight,
> Now is our Whitsun lily come,
> Now is there summer pure and soft,
> Now more than angel songs foretell
> A golden harvest in His name.
>
> In summer even's short sweet coolness
> The nightingale sings in the forest,
> And all the Lord chose once to make,
> May slumber sweet and softly wake,
> May sweetly dream of paradise
> And waken to our Saviour's praise.

(DHB 247, 1-2)

In the Christmas hymn from 1824, O, Welcome again... (p. 169) Grundtvig says of the angels:

> Spite ringing frost good year in sight
> for birds and seeds in winter.

(DHB 81,1)

And with Kingo as his inspiration he saw the sunrise and the resurrection, but with the Whitsun hymn came midsummer, and the harvest was

188

heralded with more powerful voices than the angels' (see above), and the slumbering were awakened from their sleep to the day that will never end in God's Kingdom. The Danish summer in all its splendour became an image of the renewing power of the Holy Spirit and a testimony to the poet's own feeling of his life's fulfilment. Grundtvig's imagery remained the same throughout his life; in the Whitsun hymn from 1843 he consummated the use of imagery that was first employed in the sermon for Whit Monday (p. 130f).

Grundtvig's greatness as a hymnwriter can hardly be evaluated on ordinary lines of comparative literary criticism. From a formal point of view he often made striking mistakes. Also as a hymnwriter Grundtvig was first and foremost an evangelist, and form and content in his hymns cannot be separated. His life was woven into the Christian tradition and history, in fact he was himself, in his own person, the tradition and the history, and as a result of his awareness of his own prophetic call he developed his own language.

This is quite literally true. He had his own universe of images, words and concepts. Words such as *heart, peace, faith, hope, love* etc. have their own particular value in Grundtvig's hands. They appear in his hymns in set patterns that may at times remind us of the formula for a structure of a tune. Or they are used as colour shades in a painting; each nuance – each word is a signal from his numerous visions. None of them are forgotten, and in the mature Grundtvig (from around 1837) all the shades are present. A strict economy of words and images is in control, which excludes coincidence. Nothing is superfluous – a testimony to the consistency of the content of his Christian poetry.

There is thus a micro-structure in Grundtvig's hymns, but his personal fusing of tradition with history also reveals a macro-structure. This appears too as a result of his absorption in the course of the service and of the individual ritual, especially baptism.

XI

Not long ago a hymnologist from another Scandinavian country said that Grundtvig's hymns were "dogmatics in verse". This critical comment can, however, be regarded as a compliment: in his greatest hymns Grundtvig time and again acted out the powerful drama of the salvation story with baptism as the fixed starting-point, but with a talent for variation that hardly ever fails; the theological and poetic motives multiply, even though he always remains within his own universe of words and images.

He thereby renewed the Danish language to such a degree that many of his hymns are partially incomprehensible for many modern Danes and almost untranslatable, because important nuances and points are inevitably lost. Finally therefore, using micro- and macro-structure in Grundtvig's hymns we shall go through one of his most central hymns, which also supplements the great hymns about the objective salvation that this article has already emphasized so strongly.

In the first half of 1844 Grundtvig fell victim to his second major depression. Its increasing strength can be observed in the contemporary sermon manuscripts; the handwriting is distorted out of all recognition, and in the last sermon before the final breakdown it is hardly legible. In this sermon (3rd Sunday after Easter) Grundtvig is conscious of his own approaching death and says, "'A little while and ye shall not see me: and again, a little while, and ye shall see me' (Jesus' words in John 16:16 – here used by Grundtvig about himself) ... that is where I am going; but only like the little children that are borne forward to be laid in the arms of the Lord, who blesses them and testifies that of such is the Kingdom of God. And so I go, borne by Him who bore our sins on His body on the tree, inspired by His spirit and wrapped in His righteousness, embraced by His love." This juxtaposition of the child's relationship and the fear of death determined the hymn under consideration.

It was written shortly afterwards and was called by Grundtvig himself "The child of God's cradle-song" (The complicated origins of the text are here omitted and the version referred to is DHB 488). The dactyls result in a three-four rhythm, just right for a cradle-song:

> Sleep sweet, little baby!
> Lie peaceful and gentle!
> So sweetly asleep
> Like birds in the wood
> Like flowers that bloom in the meadows!
> Our Father has said:
> Stand, angels, on guard
> Where my little ones lie a-sleeping!
>
> (DHB 488,1)

A superficial glance sees a sentimental picture from the nursery. But the image has other and deeper roots for Grundtvig. A particular vision from the baptismal ritual held him in its grip right through the composition of this hymn. In the ritual the minister read Mark 10: 13-16 about Jesus blessing the children; the pericope ends with the words: "And He took them up in His arms, put His hands upon them and blessed them." And the minister added: So let us also help this little child to the same blessing with our devout prayer to God", at which point the minister laid *his* hands on the child's head and said the *Lord's Prayer.*

The context was decisive for Grundtvig. To say the Lord's Prayer and be in God's embrace fused into one for him. The Lord's Prayer became an expression of the fundamental security in God, and the *embrace,* the warmest place the child knows, became a fixed metaphor for the relationship to God. Thus the hymn speaks of the adult who must return to the security of childhood. The bird in the forest and the flower in the field are not mentioned by coincidence; these are not just poetic pictures; we have only just heard about the flower and the bird in the Whitsun hymn (p. 188). They are also to be found in the Christmas hymn from 1824 (p. 188), and the bird was the fixed motif in *All Creatures that were Given Wings* (p. 164f). They are images that first and foremost come in on a biblical licence (Matt 6:26, see p. 164); they become an expression of the child's trust which all mankind is born with, and which baptism will restore again. The angels that are to stand guard by the child's cradle refer to a biblical text – Matt. 18:10. "Take heed that ye despise not one of these little ones; for I say unto you, That in heaven their angels do always behold the face of my Father which is in heaven".

A word-analysis of the first stanza shows that the images refer to very specific points in Grundtvig's view of Christianity. This also reveals itself in the following stanza:

> God's fingers so fine
> Make a cross on your forehead,
> The voice of His Son
> A cross on your breast,
> From henceforth no devil can harm you;
> And now you may bathe
> Your heart and your soul,
> Baptized with the hope of salvation.

> (DHB 488,2)

Grundtvig refers to the initial sign of the cross in the ritual: "Receive the sign of the Holy Cross both on your forehead and on your breast as a witness that you shall believe in the crucified Lord Jesus Christ." The two signs of the cross are made by the minister on God's behalf; therefore it is really "God's fingers so fine" that make them. This is one of the few exorcist elements which has remained in the present baptismal ritual –

not without a background in the stanza just quoted, which is often used during the baptismal act in the church. But it is not just God's fingers that make the cross and put the Devil to flight; God's own voice also makes the cross.

The last three lines are difficult to understand. They can of course be interpreted thus: now as a result of your baptism you can hope for salvation and thereby find comfort in heart and soul. But a closer analysis gives another result. The first five lines tell what happened at baptism in those days a long time ago. The last three lines tell what the baptized can do *now*. It is crucial how one interprets the expression the "hope of salvation". A total-analysis of this expression in Grundtvig's hymns reveals that it is equivalent to the phrase the "hope of glory", with reference to Colossians 1:27b: "Christ in you, the hope of glory". This hope, which is Christ Himself in mankind, gradually becomes for Grundtvig synonymous with the Lord's Prayer. For the hope is not an expression of human effort or achievement. The Christian hope is verbalized in the prayer. It has specific words to hold on to, namely the words of the Lord's Prayer which Jesus Himself says together with the worshipper.

The meaning of the last three lines is thus: at this very moment the baptized can through the Lord's Prayer repeat the sign of the cross on the face and the breast, i.e. the soul, and the body. Just as God's own voice made the sign of the cross for the child at its baptism, so can the baptized now repeat the sign of the cross with Jesus' own words.

It is this interpretation which is amplified in the 3rd stanza:

> Your hands put together,
> And thus add your amen
> To Our Saviour's prayer,
> Which rises unseen
> And sounds where the angels are praising;
> In heaven's great choir
> This little God's-word
> With joy is embraced by God's angels.
>
> (DHB 488,3)

When the worshipper puts his hands together, the *amen* is immediately given to Jesus' prayer. There is an important point here. This amen comes *to* the prayer. In one place Grundtvig compares the word "amen" with the King's granting of a petition: amen means "granted". In other words it is God Himself who adds amen to the prayer. The inspiration for this interpretation comes in the final count from Luther's little catechism

192

(at the end of the Lord's Prayer), where he says of "amen": "that is: that I must be sure that the Father in heaven receives our prayers and hears them, for He Himself has commanded us to pray thus, and has promised that He will hear us. Amen, amen means: yes, yes, it will happen thus".

On the strength of the divine amen the prayer rises up in secret to heaven and is embraced by the angels as the word of God Himself, which it is. True it is spoken by the worshipper, but the words are Jesus' words and ring with His authority. Whoever begins to say the Lord's Prayer is already in heaven with his prayer. It is this remarkable fact that stanza 4 explains:

> They shout and they sing;
> On the tongue of an earth-clod
> A word from God's son
> A prayer has become,
> On breath of the spirit here winging;
> In secret God hears,
> Says yes to the prayer!
> From lowland with joy it is ringing!
>
> (DHB 488, 4)

Since the Lord's Prayer, regardless of who speaks it, is a prayer from God's own Son, the angels can praise God because the clod of earth can pronounce one of God's own words. The reference is, of course, to man's creation from earth. Originally Grundtvig wrote:

> They shout, and they sing;
> On the tongues of worms ...

which he unfortunately rejected, when one of his pedantic friends pointed out to him that since "the whole race of worms is speechless, the image is, if I read it rightly, a failure". For Grundtvig's first phrase was by far the best: in the face of God man is no more than a worm! Anyway the same God who has added his "granted" or amen to the earthly prayer will also receive it in His heaven; it is a word of God's Son", because the Lord's Prayer is prayed "in Jesus' name", i.e. on Jesus' behalf, a phrase or truth that meant a great deal to Grundtvig.

The prayer rises up into the sphere of the heavenly songs of praise. When the granting takes place at almost the same time as the prayer is said, a song of praise is called forth:

And all the redeemed,
In our Saviour baptized,
Who have fought the good fight,
And suffered and died,
Passed on to the rest everlasting,
In unison shout
Their praises so loud
The angels stand silent and smiling!

(DHB 488, 5)

The beginning of the stanza takes its inspiration from Revelation 5: 9b, where "the Lamb" or Jesus is spoken of as follows: "for thou wast slain, and hast redeemed us to God by thy blood out of every kindred, and tongue, and people, and nation". All the dead who have been taken home into heaven unite their song of praise with the song of praise of the living on earth, in fact they drown the angels! (cf. *All Creatures that were Given Wings;* (p. 166).

The hymn was written in May – around the 12th, the 5th Sunday after Easter. Grundtvig did not preach that day, but the text of the day (John 16: 23b-28) always made a deep impression on him, and Grundtvig's relationship to the Lord's Prayer can be studied on the basis of his sermons on this Sunday over the years. Not until the end of 1830's did he reach clarification over the prefatory words in the sermon text: "Verily, verily, I say unto you, Whatsoever ye shall ask the Father in my name, He will give it you." The clarification consisted of a realisation that the granting occurs together with the prayer: "Indeed, my friends, this prayer also really belongs to the Word of Faith, about which the Spirit says that it must be heard and that at that point Christ is as near as the Word in our mouth and in our heart, so in this prayer we can feel Christ praying with us and for us, and by joining in it with Him out of a believing heart we become more convinced for every day vividly and clearly that whatever we pray to the Father for in Jesus' name He will give to us" (1837). It is this idea of the present granting of supplications which lies behind stanza 6:

And manna like dewdrops
Falls soft from the table
Of angels who smiled
On your sleeping child,
With joy you will find it tomorrow;
And clear-eyed you pray,

Goodnight you now say
To doubt and to fear and to sorrow.

(DHB 488,6)

The prayer gives immediate cheerfulness because it creates fellowship with the risen Lord. Whoever says the Lord's prayer is drawn back to baptism, makes it a present experience, and renews the fellowship with Christ in life and death. The Lord's Prayer came from heaven with Jesus, and together with Him it rises up to heaven again. But the granting and its certainty come again from heaven like dew in the morning (the image is from Psalm 72: 6) or like the manna for the people of Israel in days of old (Exodus 16). This comes from the angels' *table,* for in the centre of heaven stands the table where the faithful shall sit and eat with Abraham, Isaac and Jacob. The indissoluble fellowship with Christ in the Lord's Prayer and first and last in baptism offers the only attainable comfort and drives out all doubt, fear and sorrow.

The granting of the prayer which comes down from heaven like dew and manna, or comfort and deliverance, calls forth the song of praise:

Sleep sweet, little baby!
Lie peaceful and gentle,
And hum Jesus' name
With grace in your arms,
The whole earth is granted salvation!
Hum: Jesus is mine,
So fair and so fine,
The light and the life are my Jesus!

(DHB 488,7)

The ring is closed: the final stanza begins like the first. Whoever prays the Lord's Prayer renews his baptism and becomes like a child returned to the Father's embrace. And helped and comforted the "child" hums itself to sleep with its confession of Jesus, for the secret of the prayer was the fellowship with Jesus.

NOTE

The hymn translations are done by the translator of this book and do not necessarily correspond to other translations carried out to suit a particular melody.

BIBLIOGRAPHY

The Danish Hymnbook. *Den danske Salmebog 1953.*

Nikolaj Frederik Severin Grundtvig: Song-Work for the Danish Church. *Sang-Værk til Den Danske Kirke,* vol. I-IV (1944-64). Volumes I-V reprinted in 1983 by G. E. C. Gad's Publishing Company.

Uffe Hansen: Grundtvig's Hymnwriting I-III. *Grundtvig's Salmedigtning* I-III (1937-66).

Magnus Stevns: From Grundtvig's Hymn-Workshop. *Fra Grundtvigs Salmeværksted* (1950).

Jørgen Elbek: Grundtvig and the Greek Hymns. *Grundtvig og de græske salmer* (1960).

Christian Thodberg: A forgotten dimension in Grundtvig's hymns: the emphasis on the baptismal ritual. *En glemt dimension i Grundtvigs salmer. Bundetheden til dåbsritualet* (1969).

Christian Thodberg (ed.): For the Sake of Continuity. Words and Motifs in Grundtvig's Hymns and Sermons. *For sammenhængens skyld. Ord og motiver i Grundtvig's salmer og prædikener* (1977).

Grundtvig in the Mirror of the Early Church

by Niels Thomsen

In a Roman catacomb there is a picture of the dead wooden cross from whose root a strong vine is shooting. When I saw it for the first time I was put in mind of a line from one of Grundtvig's well-known Whitsun hymns *Oh Thou that dost Flow from the One Living God* (Du, som går ud fra den levende Gud), in which "The tree of life shoots from the foot of the cross". It became easier to understand the meaning of the picture in the catacomb.

One gains a similar insight from looking at the Byzantine mosaic in St. Clement's Church in Rome, where an acanthus vine is shooting from the foot of the cross on the hill of Golgotha which has become one with the mount of Paradise. The acanthus vine is spreading out to fill the whole apse and to give shelter to the birds, the animals and the people, and the same line of Grundtvig returns, or one similiar – "The tree of life took root in the grave" from the Advent hymn, *Welcome Now, the Year of the Lord* (Vær velkommen, Herrens år).

On to the church in Torcello in the lagoon of Venice where there is an enormous mosaic over the entrance depicting Christ walking into the kingdom of death after he had broken down the portals of Hell, so that the doornails and iron fastenings lie scattered on the ground and the Devil is writhing under the gate-leaves while Adam og Eve come forward towards Christ at the head of the innumerable prisoners of Hell. The picture is immediately recognizable if one knows Grundtvig's Easter hymn, *Last Night a Knock Came at the Portals of Hell* (I kvæld blev der banket på Helvedes port), where Grundtvig describes the same descent into the kingdom of death, Christ's victory over the Devil and his release of Adam and Eve and all the other souls in the kingdom of Hell. Grundtvig's poem and the mosaic interpret each other and together add weight and meaning to the part of the Creed that says "He descended into Hell".

197

Grundtvig never saw the mosaic – nor did he know the picture of the tree of the cross with its fresh shoots, or the acanthus on Golgotha; the model for his poem is taken from an Old English poem. But then so much the more striking is it that Grundtvig's poems spontaneously mediate an understanding of pictures and thoughts from the early Church and the Greek Church.

It is easily seen when it is a question of mosaics and pictures. But it is actually just as striking when it is a question of theological ideas. All the time, images are flashing into Grundtvig's hymns that build bridges to the early Church and the Eastern Church.

We find in the early Church, for example, reflected amongst others in Ignatius of Antioch, mythological ideas of the sky-kingdom's forces of destiny who become impotent when Christ triumphant from His victory over death ascends to Heaven at the head of the prisoners released from Hell and in the midst of the ascension subjects beneath him the sky-kingdom's forces and authorities. Grundtvig happened on similar thoughts in another Old English poem which he adapts into the hymn *Come, ye Souls, so Dearly Bought* (Kommer, sjæle, dyrekøbte). But he does more than merely adapt the mythological representations; he also interprets their meaning in such a stanza as:

> All the races of the earth,
> throughout their days are free again
> to choose again 'twixt life and death,
> light of day or dark of night,
> Paradise or wilderness,
> fires of hell or heavenly joy.

Again and with perfect naturalness the mythological ideas of the early Church have become a meaningful contemporary sermon, whilst the Creed's "He ascended into heaven" is at the same time shown to be loaded with meaning.

What is astonishing is the naturalness with which Grundtvig constantly speaks out of a harmony with early Church faith and thought. Most powerful of all is perhaps where he sings and speaks out of a faith in the Trinity. It must be emphasized that it is where he speaks *out of* his faith in the Trinity, not where he speaks *of* the Trinity; which is what he does in a whole chapter in *Christian Childhood Teachings*, with a rather flat and complicated result. But in the introductory prayers to the sermons he can vary his praise of the Trinity endlessly and in the hymns he can sing so naturally out of his faith in the Trinity that one can even forget that that is actually what he is doing. In his adaptation of the Latin Whitsun sequence *Qui procedis ab utroque* he writes:

> Spirit of all love and truth
> earth and heaven's living bond
> thou alone unitest.

The main idea of these lines is immediately accessible to everyone: the Holy Spirit brings love and truth and it ties earth and heaven together. But when one has sung a lot of Grundtvig's hymns and sung them often enough, one becomes aware that much more is reverberating. "Love" for Grundtvig is very often linked to God the Father, "truth" to God the Son. The "Spirit of love and truth" thus becomes a trinitarian wording that speaks of the Holy Spirit as He who issues from the Father and the Son and reaches out to mankind, uniting the living bond between God's loving father-heart and the human heart; and this heart is destined to be "a heavenly mirror on earth". Grundtvig is not attempting to explain the Trinity as if it was a difficult dogmatic problem; he is speaking of it as a natural pre-condition for the song of praise and the sermon, as he must also have understood it when he writes without further comment in *Christian Childhood Teachings*: "it goes without saying that the threefold human life in God's image must find its explanation in the threefold divine life, or as we usually put it: the divine Trinity".[1]

Thus Grundtvig has found the way for us to form a belief in the Trinity in a sense that is otherwise rare in our Church and which links him to the early Church, which shared a similar faith. On the other hand, we get nowhere by attempting to prove that Grundtvig had a particular theology of the Trinity – that, for example, he leant more towards the Eastern Church than the Western, or that he was more Athanasian than Arian or vice versa.

The whole series of examples of early Church motifs and realisations in Grundtvig's hymns shows how the Danish Church with Grundtvig as its mediator has access to the early Church heritage in a far more direct way than is otherwise known in the Lutheran churches. It has given the Danish Church a special character in the Lutheran world – one that is often unnoticed by Danes themselves – an ecumenical character.

But how has Grundtvig himself gained this access to the insights of the early Church? Let it be said immediately that the most important elements will not be understood through making a learned study of the early Church. It is true that Grundtvig had read a number of the Church fathers but the most essential background is his commitment to his own age. The starting point is his "unparalleled discovery" in 1825 that the Church is living and contemporary, that the Church came into being before the scriptures and that apostolic Christianity was alive and present in his own church in 1825 in the Creed as it was used at baptism. It is not my intention here to describe how Grundtvig made this discovery. But once he had done so, its significance for him was decisive. It is worth dwelling on the word "discovery". It indicates that in his own opinion Grundtvig in no way invented something new, but simply realised something that had been there all the time and which was as clear as day, so that it could be seen and understood by the simplest soul. Grundtvig wanted least of all to establish new theological dogma. For years he had fought to defend simple old-fashioned Christianity against the rationalists. He had tried to defend it on a scriptural basis but had run into the difficulty that the rationalists also used the scriptures and that the uneducated could not decide who was using them properly. It therefore came as a release for him when he discovered that apostolic Christianity did not have to be dug up from the writings of the past but was alive and present in the Church in the apostolic Creed. In this lay the Church's simple, manifestly clear expression.

Grundtvig's insistence that living Christianity was to be found in the apostolic Creed at baptism rather than in the scripture was understood by his critics and also by former defenders of old-fashioned Lutheran Christianity as a new and un-Lutheran teaching. That is perhaps not so surprising, for it is unusual in the Lutheran tradition to see the Church raised above scripture. But Grundtvig could neither admit that he had invented something new, nor that he had abandoned the Lutheran tradition. With regard to the former he himself would have answered that it was tantamount to saying he was wrong; he expresses this in the preface to a translation of the Church father Irenaeus published in 1827: "As for Christianity, everything that is new is indirectly false simply by being new, since in order to be genuine it must be as old as the Christian Church itself".[2] With regard to the latter he endeavours repeatedly to explain his relationship to Luther. This he does amongst others in some articles from 1840-42 that bear the characteristic title, *Church Enlightenment, especially for Lutheran Christians*.[3] Here for the first time he asserts his love of Luther, who was the only one of the reformers to reform in the spirit of Christ. However, for him Luther is no longer the teacher from whom he has learned what Christianity is: he is a witness to apostolic Christianity. Grundtvig stresses his childlike qualities and thus makes him a witness to the simplicity of childhood faith. As a witness to the sure fact that throughout 18 centuries there has been an apostolic

Christianity, Grundtvig places Luther in the line of Polycarp, Irenaeus, Augustine, Benedict, Ansgar and Bernhard.[4] He underlines as the virtue of Luther's conception of the Church that it possessed the sacraments after Christ's institution, but as its fault that Luther insists on having his own scriptural understanding incorporated into his conception of the Church.[5] This is not because Grundtvig disagrees with Luther in his understanding of the contents of the scriptures. It is even less because he looks down on them. On the contrary, he regards them as an unrivalled book of illumination; the point is that it is not in the scriptures that living Christianity is to be found but in the living word in Church. This Church belongs to Luther. Grundtvig never tires of emphasizing that Luther was in no way trying to create a brand-new Church, but that both before and after his break with the pope he was a clergyman in the same Church of Jesus Christ. Therefore it does not detract from Grundtvig's love for Luther that he has to reject Luther's theology of the scriptures, and he also believes that Our Lord will forgive him too, but it is necessary for protestantism to clarify the Church concept that Luther himself was unable to, precisely because he wished to have his own written wisdom included in it. He thus goes back beyond Luther but is convinced that he is doing so *with* Luther and not *against* him.

The discovery of the apostolic Church as being present in his own time is the essential basis of Grundtvig's harmony with the early Church. His interest in the apostolic Church begins from a factual point of view when he discovers it as a present reality. And because he knows it and is himself at home in it, when he speaks of it in its first centuries he feels free to pick and choose. He can polemize against "the Egyptian vinegar-brewer" Origen, and against the whole Alexandrian school of sagacity, and he can declare his love for Polycarp and Irenaeus. In *Church Mirror,* the series of lectures on Church history that he gave in 1861, he presents his picture of the Christian Church in the time before Constantine the Great. Then the Church was a kind of spiritual free state similar to the kingdom of Israel when Joshua led the people into it. In those days the Israelites were only subordinate to the judges they themselves had chosen, just as in the Church people were only subordinate to the bishops they themselves had chosen. However, the Church was superior to Israel inasmuch as within the Church there was no written law and no priest-hood, since all were equal through their baptism. Bishops, teachers and martyrs were in the Church to serve, not to rule over, the free community of the Church. Of course, says Grundtvig ironically, in those days too bishops and scribes were worried about what such freedom for the people could lead to, and they made every effort to limit it. But they did not possess the means to enforce it, and freedom was therefore preserved until bishops and scribes after Constantine the Great's victory in 312 could ally themselves with the secular powers.[6]

This is not the place to discuss whether the picture Grundtvig paints of the early Church is correct. It is a supreme way of writing Church history and it leaves him free to pour out the riches of the early Church. He does not believe he has discovered a special kind of early Church Christianity which he wishes to introduce. What he has discovered is the holy, Universal Church.

To all this it must be added that one of the things that helped Grundtvig to understand the Church was his discovery of Irenaeus, the Bishop of Lyon, who lived around 180. It was largely by coincidence that Grundtvig began reading him in 1823, but he then did so with great pleasure and speaks of him later with a love that is otherwise reserved only for Martin Luther. He translated the 5th book of Irenaeus' major work *Against Heretics* in 1827, praising Irenaeus in the preface as one of the few writers who has kept the child in mind; he also stresses how Irenaeus shows that the apostolic sources interpreted the scriptures according to the orally-preached and clear "Word of Faith". Nor is it a coincidence that he dates *The Church's Retort,* the work in which he first formulates his Church views, on "Irenaeus' day".

But in spite of his enthusiasm for Irenaeus there is no question of Grundtvig taking over his theology. It is doubtful whether Grundtvig would have cared at all to hear that he *had* a theology, for the word "theology" smacks far too much of a system and speculation. It is for precisely this reason that he emphasizes that Irenaeus keeps children in mind, and that he advises the overly wise Greek Church to "look again at Irenaeus, if you can look that low".[7] On the other hand Grundtvig does borrow a number of motifs and themes from Irenaeus and allows them to grow together with his own world of ideas. They are to be found in his sermons from the period when he is reading Irenaeus, and they remain there for the rest of his life.

One of the themes he adopts is the idea of growth. Like human life, Christian life must begin in the child-like and then grow to manhood. Irenaeus uses the image of growth against the gnostics, who thought themselves invariably perfect. Grundtvig finds that his own front against the rationalists is the same as Irenaeus' front against the gnostics. With Irenaeus as his starting-point he later allows his idea of growth to blossom so that it also comes to include a growth from faith to hope to love, and becomes a growth within the life of the Church. In this context it is not so

202

much a question of Irenaeus' ideas, but rather Grundtvig's own development of the motif he has discovered in Irenaeus.

A second idea that Grundtvig takes up from Irenaeus is the belief that man is made in God's image. He finds confirmation in Irenaeus that this image of God is never lost. This realisation is later converted into a polemic against the orthodox Lutheran image of man. The view of man which Grundtvig finds in Irenaeus is linked to what he has learned from romanticism, and thus it becomes again not merely a reproduction of a motif from Irenaeus, but the man himself becomes a tremendous inspiration for Grundtvig in his attempt to understand what it means to be a human being.

In general Irenaeus' emphasis on the world and man in it as God's creation – in contrast to the gnostic conception of the world as a waste product – or the work of the evil creator-god – plays a major role for Grundtvig because it enables him to legitimize this love of history, nature and the life of man as God's creation. He finds confirmation that it is possible to speak of the world in a different way from the orthodox Lutheran view, to see it in another light than that of the Fall alone.

Thus Grundtvig absorbed Irenaeus and made him one with himself, and there can be no doubting Irenaeus' great importance for Grundtvig. At the same time it is characteristic that in actual fact none of the motifs mentioned here, nor any others in Irenaeus that might be adduced, are completely new to Grundtvig. They are to be found in writings and sermons years before he began to read Irenaeus, so it is difficult to specify how much Grundtvig took from Irenaeus. With almost visionary force he seizes on the motifs that he needs and adapts them to his own context, so that they become part of his own understanding and linked to corresponding motifs which he takes from John's Gospel, from Paul and from the Bible in general.

Once more in his life he is demonstrably inspired by the Greek Church. In 1836 he is working on adaptations of hymns from the whole of Christendom for the Danish Church and he comes to the Greek hymns. There has been talk in this context of Grundtvig's "Greek awakening" and it is possible both to follow his enthusiasm for what he found and to see which motifs he seizes on in his sermons. Also here it is a question not of Grundtvig learning something completely new but of finding a confirmation of and developing something for which the stage was already set. What comes through to us is a theological, poetic insight into the drama of the Church service. In the Greek hymns he hears how the whole story of the salvation is condensed into the service. The resurrection happens, salvation is here and now, and the Christian hope is a present reality. This is actually something that Grundtvig knows very well. The hymns correspond to the insights which he already possesses, but they amplify and give body to them. The discovery of the apostolic Creed as a living word in the Church at baptism already contains within itself the possibility of understanding the whole service as the actual presence of salvation in the Church. This again makes it difficult to delineate what Grundtvig learns from his meeting with the Greek hymns, but none can doubt that he has grasped the meaning of the Greek service.

The strength of this feeling becomes apparent in the hymn he wrote during this period which has no Greek model but which has exactly the same character as that of the Greek hymns he met:

> Sunday morning from the dead,.
> Jesus rose victorious;
> now the dawn of every Sunday
> brings the penance for His death,
> wonderfully we relive
> all the Saviour's days on earth.
>
> Then His words are born again
> on thousand tongues throughout the land
> Wake ye now from sleep and torpor,
> hear Him, every ear that can!
> Rise up from the dead, ye souls, and
> greet the glorious Easter morn!
>
> Every Sunday death is quaking,
> darkness trembles under earth,
> for in glory Christ is shining,
> loudly sound the words of life;
> blessed in victory they attack
> the Prince of Death and darkness' realm.

This is Greek Christianity translated to the Danish Church. The Sunday service as a resurrection and Easter festival, the re-enactment in the service of all the days in the life of our Lord, the invitation to every soul to greet Easter morning in the Sunday service, the victory over death and darkness – all these breathe an understanding of the Greek service, and are simultaneously bound up with Grundtvig's own powerful emphasis on the words, the Lord speaking, which is reborn. It is not possible to

204

discover where the Greek influence ends and Grundtvig himself begins, for Grundtvig has absorbed the Greek into himself.

Once again it is his view of the Church that allows Grundtvig to make use of the Greek Church heritage. This is also the case with Grundtvig's understanding of the Eucharist. The Lutheran tradition before Grundtvig, and in fact the whole of the western medieval tradition had concentrated its understanding of the Eucharist around the forgiveness of sins, a mediation of grace in the Eucharist and the question of the real presence in the bread and wine. Grundtvig had never felt particularly comfortable with the Lutheran doctrine of the Eucharist, but over the years a wealth of Eucharist images blossomed in his hymns and one must go behind the Lutheran and the Roman church to find them. The idea of love, the idea of expectation, the idea of a union with the risen Christ and the anticipation of the heavenly meal are prominent motifs in Grundtvig, and in various forms he exploits the powerful imagery of bread and wine in a way that is new to the Danish tradition. He felt free to reach this breadth in his understanding of the Eucharist because he goes back to beyond the eucharistic problems of the Reformation and beyond the Roman Catholic doctrine of the Eucharist. It is difficult and not at all fruitful either to explain what Grundtvig's own teaching on the Eucharist was. He himself attempts to formulate one a number of times, but he fares no better than Luther or the Roman Catholic church. But in his hymns he is free to pour out the eucharistic imagery that corresponds to that of the early Church and thus it becomes the gospel message.

In two other areas where Grundtvig seems "primitive" it is even more difficult to determine how much or how little he has taken from the early Church.

The first is the relationship between faith and deeds. For western theology it has been a major task since Augustine's clash with Pelagius to clarify how faith, deeds and salvation relate to each other. Can salvation be earned by good deeds, and what role do the good deeds play in the light of God and in the sight of man?

Grundtvig remains strangely untouched by this basic problem in the western Church. He says in general very little about everything that can be called an ethical problem, but when he does so, it is with a wonderful innocence in relation to the whole tradition from Augustine to Luther and to modern protestantism.

By way of example we can take the following stanza from *The Pleiades of Christendom* (Christenhedens Syvstjerne):

A child's faith, the same for all men,

is Our Father's pride and joy,
and with faith a pure blend
of Christian teaching for the child;
for, with love for your neighbour,
is the Christ-child otherwise
like a bird free in the air![8]

Here is a beautiful picture of how childhood faith makes the Christian free as a bird and in a Lutheran context there is no surprise about that. What is strange is the insertion of "With love for your neighbour". What does he mean? Is this love a condition for this freedom – in addition to the childhood faith? Grundtvig does not seem even to sense the question. It is a matter of course that childhood faith and love for one's neighbour belong together, but *how* he does not make clear. One is reminded of the way the eastern bishops welcomed Pelagius when he sought support in the battle against Augustine, not because they accepted righteousness through deeds but because it was completely alien for them to speak of faith and deeds in the way Augustine and Pelagius were agreed on.

The difference is felt even more sharply in the hymn *Grace, she Comes from Royal Stock* (Nåden hun er af kongeblod), in which it says:

Each time we prayed the Lord's Prayer
deep in our hearts we were feeling,
grace only reaps the seed she sows,
nothing less is she content with.

And then:

The soul of kindness is our Lord,
who in His heart has compassion,
who when we fall before His feet,
will lift us up and embrace us,
this we must do in our own small way,
this we can all understand,
we who have human hearts.

It goes without saying for Grundtvig that we "in our own small way" must show the same love to our neighbour that God has shown us. It cannot be otherwise.

The background for Grundtvig's thinking in these terms is perhaps the idea that is expressed in the last two lines. Behind it lies the understan-

206

ding of man created in God's image that we have already mentioned. The human heart is intended to reflect God's heart, salvation consists of making God's image clear again. It is not therefore a question of man's love for his neighbour being a condition of salvation, but even less can one preclude the thought that love must revive the human heart. Therein lies salvation.

Ideas of this kind can be found in, amongst others, Irenaeus. They are not couched in the same terms and it is hardly possible to prove that that is where Grundtvig found them. But it is an expression of the fundamental agreement that existed between Grundtvig and the early Church.

The final theme with the ring of the early Church about it is the one that in a much-quoted conversation Grundtvig calls *his* contradiction: the contradiction between life and death. This comes in a conversation with the German theologian, Marheineke, who once visited Grundtvig. Marheineke wanted to know how Denmark was coping with the great contradiction between rationalism and supranaturalism. Grundtvig intimated that the contradiction did not worry him so much: "My contradiction is life and death," he answered. The conversation took place in 1836, when Grundtvig was already over 50. It is characteristic that the older he became the more clarity he sought, and it is obvious that the basic contradiction between life and death in these later years leaves its mark on everything he writes. Whether it is popular writings or sermons or hymns it is always a battle between life and death.

This theme is far too general and dominant for us to attempt to limit it to an early Church inspiration. The way forward to it also begins in quite different places. The preconditions are already to be found in the clash with Schelling in 1812-15, in which he accuses Schelling of attempting to resolve all contradictions between good and evil and light and dark – and of denying the reality of evil. Reason cannot and will not recognize these contradictions, but in the world of reality they exist. When Grundtvig comes to read Irenaeus ten years later, he finds him maintaining these contradictions against the gnostics, – and so in this regard too he becomes Irenaeus' ally, recognizing in Irenaeus' battle with the gnostics his own with Schelling.

But in Irenaeus he can also see how these contradictions are linked to the contradiction life-death, which we can see growing gradually and meaning more and more for Grundtvig from the end of the 1820's. There is nothing new here, for this contradiction is an expression of the same fundamental contradiction which exists between good and evil and between truth and lying and light and darkness, the fundamental contradiction which cannot be mediated or resolved out of existence. In the Greek hymns, which he was actually writing in 1836, he again finds life and death the most important Christian contradiction, which in the Eastern Church takes up a far greater position than the major contradiction between sin and grace that has become the basic theme of the Western Church. The contradiction life-death is by its very nature so dominant that Grundtvig would not narrow it down to one particular idea that belongs to one particular area of the Church. But he feels that it dominates the Greek Church with a particular force. He expresses all this throughout the section on the Greek Church the major poem *The Pleiades of Christendom*. As early as the first stanza he makes the Lord speak of Himself of the Greek Church as "once dead, now alive", and tells the Greek Church that "between death and you lies the struggle" and warns, "Hand not the bread of life to death". The theme is presented most directly at the end:[9]

> Life's constant risk of death,
> wherein dust and spirit merge,
> is responding to your call,
> with your mouth and with your hand.

This shows how clearly Grundtvig has recognized his own fundamental contradiction in the Greek Church, and even seen it as the particular calling of the Greek Church to "respond to" the contradiction. He does not give this task to any of the other Churches.

Which brings us to the last point in this article, namely, that in a peculiar way Grundtvig considers himself and thus the Church in Scandinavia to have a special connection with the Greek Church. Grundtvig's judgement on the Greek Church may often be felt to be more severe than on any other Church. The main reason is that the Greek Church has given up the apostolic Creed at baptism and is therefore only a churchyard without a church,[10] but the fact that it could do so is due to the self-conceit that already in the 3rd century was beginning to mark Greek scholarship. Almost as serious was that the Greek Church relinquished its freedom in the union with the empire. These reproaches of the Greek Church are to be found in *Church Mirror* and *The Pleiades* and in many other places, but in the midst of them one can also sense that Grundtvig feels a special attachment to his Greek Church, and that he fervently hopes for its reawakening in connection with the popular rising of the Greek people, whom he followed with a living interest.

It is more than a feeling. We can see it in his view of Church history as a course between the seven national Churches which correspond to the seven Churches in the first chapters of Revelation, a view that received its full treatment in *The Pleiades* but which appears already in the 1820's. In 1820 he expresses the hope that the Greek Church, just like the Jewish, will be reawakened, "so the seven-tongued Church can celebrate a golden year and a jubilee with joy".[11] Already here it is clear that Grundtvig's view of the seven Churches in a historical context is not just a matter of one succeeding the other. The aim is that they shall sing the song of praise together, as he attempts to make possible in the Danish Church through his adaptations of hymns from all the national Churches in the *Song-Work for the Danish Church*.

In *Church Mirror* he explains how the life of the Church and the Christian enlightenment is waning in the Hebrew, the Greek and the Latin Church, standing still in the English and again growing in the German, the Scandinavian and the still unknown seventh Church. This view is developed in the introduction to *The Pleiades* where the triangle of faith hope and love, which are of increasing importance to Grundtvig, have been woven into the history of the Church so that the Hebrew Church has become the Church of love, the Greek Church the Church of hope and the Latin Church the Church of faith. The English Church is the pivot. Then the rise begins in which everything that is lost will be regained. The German Church is the Church of faith, corresponding to the Latin Church; the Scandinavian Church becomes the Church of hope, corresponding to the Greek Church and destined to regain what was lost in the Greek Church. Then Grundtvig searches around for the Church of love which is to correspond to the Hebrew Church.[12]

From this it can be seen how Grundtvig feels linked to the Greek Church. The fellowship consists of the common hope that the Scandinavian and the Greek Churches share as their special lot. And thus from a historical and poetic point of view it seems natural for Grundtvig to build a bridge between the Scandinavian and the Greek Church.

NOTES

1. *Selected Writings*. Udvalgte Skrifter IX p. 469.
2. *On the Resurrection of the Flesh and Eternal Life*. Om Kiødets Opstandelse og det evige Liv. Copenhagen 1855, p. 2.
3. *Selected Writings* VIII p. 370-457.
4. ibid. VIII, p. 374-76.
5. ibid. VIII, p. 454.
6. ibid. X, p. 154-56.
7. *The Pleiades of Christendom*. Christenhedens Syvstjerne. ed. by Th. Balslev. Copenhagen 1955, p. 84.

8. ibid. p. 70.
9. ibid. p. 87.
10. *Selected Writings,* X, p. 150.
11. *The Pleiades of Christendom* p. 260.
12. ibid. p. 40-43.

While working on this article I have made special use of the following dissertations:

Jørgen Elbek: *Grundtvig and the Greek Hymns.* Grundtvig og de græske salmer. Gad. 1960.

Henning Høirup: *From Death to Life.* Fra døden til Livet. Gyldendal 1954.

Kaj Thaning: *Grundtvig's Meeting with Irenaeus.* Grundtvigs møde med Irenæus. Grundtvig Studies 1953.

ed. Christian Thodberg: *For the Sake of Continuity.* For sammenhængens skyld. Aarhus 1977. (Especially the articles by Lise Fibiger, Erik Krebs Jensen, Leif Kallesen and Morten Mortensen).

Grundtvig's Educational Ideas

by K. E. BUGGE

In accounts of the history of education and in educational handbooks there is usually a paragraph on N. F. S. Grundtvig, the "father of the folk high school". It must be pointed out from the start, however, that Grundtvig was not an educationalist in the way that all the other educationalists he is compared with were.

Grundtvig was not a *theoretical* educationalist in the sense that he was interested in developing an educational system or programme. On the contrary, his educational thinking was not very systematic at all. The ideas are not put together in any particular order or developed logically. He refuses explicitly to present a new educational programme and he does so with the characteristic explanation that life cannot be described before it has been lived. Actually, there *was* a continuity in his educational universe, a point to which we shall return. But there was no system or programme as the words are commonly understood.

Nor was Grundtvig a practising educationalist. The extent to which he himself was a good teacher is even debatable. There is evidence that his personality made a strong impression on the pupils he was dealing with, and of course we must not underrate him. But it is worth recalling a remark by his daughter-in-law, who had some knowledge of how Grundtvig taught his own children. She writes, "that it was not his way to enter into the thoughts of others". And to be able to do precisely that must be the prerequisite for being called a good teacher. It must also be noted that Grundtvig's personal knowledge of the practical realities of school life was limited. The only experience he had as a pupil in an ordinary school was his two years at Aarhus Cathedral School, from 1789 to 1800, otherwise he was taught at home by a private teacher. And the only experience he had as a teacher in an ordinary school was the three years or so he taught at a grammar school (for 14-17-year-olds) in Copenhagen. The rest of Grundtvig's knowledge of practical teaching comes from his post as supervisor to the school board in first Udby-Ørslev parish in 1811-

13, then to a couple of schools in Christianshavn, Copenhagen in the 1820's and finally to the Queen's Charity School from 1814 onwards. As far as can be judged from the remaining documents, the last-named was a long way from being a heavy work-load. He had some knowledge of home education, but this experience was also rather special and rather limited. As a tutor at Egeløkke Manor on Langeland he had taught a single pupil for some three years. Later he had taught his own two sons, but he soon handed this task over to a succession of tutors.

To sum up, it may be said that Grundtvig's ideas about school stem neither from the principle of a theory of education nor from comprehensive practical experience. They came into being in a quite different way: in the clash between his view of life and of mankind on the one hand, and a more or less random set of circumstances on the other. It is this state of affairs which explains the strange mixture of continuity and chance that is characteristic of his educational thought.

Let us first look at the relationship between Grundtvig's view of life and his educational theory. Then we must call attention to certain contemporary events that partly gave him occasion to express his opinion on upbringing and education, and partly contributed to a further development of his educational thought. A glance at some of his most important educational ideas, including both that of popular education and the teaching of Christianity, will be followed by some final remarks on what it all led to.

Views on Life and Education

The final clarification of Grundtvig's educational ideas takes place in the course of the 1830's. The decade 1830-40 is in general a particularly fruitful period in Grundtvig's life. A number of his works were produced which posterity has come to regard as major works. In 1832 came *Norse Mythology,* reckoned by some to be the most important of them all. From 1833 onwards came the comprehensive *Handbook on World History I-III;* in 1837 came the first volume of Grundtvig's *Song-Work for the Danish Church* containing some 400 hymns. In 1837 he was released from censorship and could now accept the request which had been made to him several years earlier by a group of young academics to give a series of public lectures on history. This resulted in the famous *Within Living Memory* – lectures given at Borch's College in the summer and autumn of 1838. The manuscripts of these lectures were not published until after Grundtvig's death, however. Last but not least it was in the 1830's – or more precisely from 1836 onwards – that his most important educational writings began to appear. The clarification of Grundtvig's ideas on the subject is therefore not an isolated phenomenon in his thinking. It is an integrated element in the general clarification that takes place in virtually every area of his thought during these years.

The process was initiated by a personal clarification. In the transition from 1831 to 1832 his impressions from the England trips in the three previous years began to fall into place. In England Grundtvig had learned to respect what he calls real life, as it is lived in trade, industry and politics. He also realised the crucial importance of freedom for the prosperity of a society. Most important of all, however, was that during his work on the book *Norse Mythology* he had been forced yet again to explain his view of the relationship between Christianity and the Christian faith.

In his introduction to *Norse Mythology*, Grundtvig distinguishes between faith and life-philosophy. Faith is thoughts or expectations that in a Christian view are closely bound up with Christ's person and calling. Life-philosophy, on the other hand, is a view of life and mankind that Christians may have in common with people whom Grundtvig calls "Naturalists". By this expression he means people who are not bound by a narrow biological, mechanistic view of man but who constructively believe that "spirit" is an important and a determining factor in being a person. On this point Grundtvig believes that the Christian is fundamentally in agreement with every person who has a "glimmer of spirit and a spark of truthfulness".

Grundtvig then explains this point of view. He expresses his conviction that the Christian and the Naturalist must agree that mankind is created in God's image and that at an early stage "a great accident" befell us. As a result of this "accident" mankind mistook its true purpose and the nature of man fell into "disorder". Thus far they are in agreement. The divergence between Christians and Naturalists, however, lies elsewhere, namely over how the damage can be repaired. The Christians believe that the purpose can only be re-established by a union between the person reborn through baptism and the Saviour Jesus Christ. The Naturalists on the other hand claim that salvation is to be found in man receiving Christ into his life as a divine pattern for moral behaviour. On this point, concerning the salvation of mankind, the discrepancy between the two views of life is insuperable. Here all mediation is impossible. It is a question of either-or.

The question now is to what purpose Grundtvig uses this distinction between faith and philosophy. It is notable that Grundtvig believed, as a consequence of this distinction, that Christians and Naturalists must be able to work together in the area of education. The disagreement about the path to mankind's final goal must be left aside until later. Only time can decide who is right. When it is a question of solving an urgent educational problem one must be able to cooperate on the basis of a fundamental agreement on a view of mankind.

However we evaluate the significance of these ideas, the fact remains that Grundtvig's distinctive view of the relationship between what is human and what is Christian gave him and those of his opinion an inspiring freedom to work in the area of education with colleagues who thought differently. It offered him a significant freedom to disregard specifically Christian conceptions of faith in determining the aim of education.

Contemporary Challenges

As mentioned above, Grundtvig's educational ideas came into being in the clash between his view of mankind and life on the one hand – and an external cause on the other. Of these external impulses we must take note of two political events and two running debates that each in its own way has proved a stimulus for Grundtvig's educational ideas.

In 1831-32 it was amongst others the political events on the European continent, and especially the July revolution in 1830 that made a tremendous impact on Grundtvig. He regarded them as symptoms of a profound crisis in which the institutions handed down to his age: the Church, the state, and scholarship, were in danger of being destroyed. It is not least to avert this crisis, "the great shipwreck" that in *Norse Mythology* he advocates a "reform of the school grave into a seed-school for life".

The other political event that was to be of crucial importance for the development of Grundtvig's thought was the establishment of the advisory Assembly in the provinces, which was announced in May 1831. The establishment of this advisory institution was, as the Danes saw it, an attempt to comply with the liberal "revolutionary" currents of the time as far as was humanly possible within the framework of an autocratic state. Suffice it to say that Grundtvig admits that if this new institution really is to be of benefit to the country then the members of the Assembly must be suitably trained. And this training could not take place within the existing school order. Something new was required. When the Assembly held its first session in Roskilde in 1835-36, Grundtvig therefore followed the proceedings with keen interest as they appeared in the newspaper "Assembly News". In the spring of 1836 he is struck by the thought that

214

the Assembly's existence and its negotiating structure have two consequences: firstly that Denmark in his opinion has thereby regained its lost, but natural constitution – i.e. the constitution it had had in bygone days, when the political set-up was characterized by "the King's autocracy" and "the people's freedom"; and secondly he notes that these negotiations are verbal. He can therefore speak of "the happy meeting at Roskilde", and he can characterize the negotiations of the Assembly with the expression "the mouth's accession to the throne" or as a resurrection of the word. In a letter to his friend and colleague, Gunni Busck (April 2nd 1836) Grundtvig writes "that the original Danishness and the voice of the people that quickens everything, a voice which I sought for in the old books and in myself, they too are truly resurrected in the new institution of the King in Council with the people".

Among the educational questions that were being publicly debated at the time there seem to be two in particular that have given Grundtvig food for thought: the so-called "monitorial system" (*indbyrdes undervisning*), a system imported from England in which educational advances were sought by dividing children into groups and letting the brighter pupils teach the rest. The role of the teacher was reduced to a sort of supervisor, seeing to it that the whole machinery was working properly. At first Grundtvig was strongly critical of the impersonal nature of the method, but after visiting the large central London school using the monitorial system he gained a more favourable attitude towards it. It appeared that in England the method had been further developed and they had worked out how to combine the monitorial system with a more active and personal commitment from the teacher's side. Furthermore, in Denmark a highly-respected educationalist, Professor Carl Mariboe, who was close to Grundtvig, had introduced into his school a new and more stimulating form of monitorial teaching. On the basis of these impulses Grundtvig began to consider whether there was not some good in the reciprocal principle in the monitorial system. The task that begins to loom before him is how therefore to draft a new form of monitorial teaching that could replace the form used hitherto, which had been rightly criticized.

Sooner or later Grundtvig had to cope with the question of the outer framework of the new school he was now beginning to visualize. At this point another discussion of the times comes to the fore: the debate about Sorø Academy. After a lengthy break, teaching at the Academy had once again been resumed in 1826. In the following decades there was regular discussion of a reorganisation of the education on offer at the school, which led amongst other things to the establishment of a practical (*réal*) department in 1837 alongside the grammar school and the higher, academic course that was also housed under the same roof. The reforms continued until 1847, when a royal resolution announced the opening of a practical high school in Sorø. In 1849 however the Academy was closed, and the practical high school plans put in abeyance.

Throughout the 1830's and 1840's Grundtvig followed the development of the institution with more than usual interest. In his educational writings he stated time after time his conviction that Sorø Academy was the place where his educational ideas could be realised. It is precisely because he had Sorø Academy in mind that Grundtvig speaks of *a high school* for the people. He uses this expression in accordance with contemporary usage to mean a higher educational institution, that is, either synonymous with university, or with an institution that teaches at university level. The first high schools in the present meaning of the word, for example Rødding, which was founded in 1844, were called in those days "higher peasant schools". Sorø Academy on the other hand was a high school in the contemporary meaning of the word. As mentioned previously, the institution comprised in addition to a grammar school an academic department that led to a university examination. What Grundtvig is imagining then is a sort of university, where the education is not based on "Latin" but on the specific Danish tradition, and which appeals not only to prospective government officials but also to broader circles in the population.

The continuing debate on Sorø Academy and the repeated reforms made Grundtvig's hopes less realistic. The possibilities were present at Sorø right up until 1849. Furthermore Grundtvig regarded a big, central, state-supported ("royal") institution as being on principle the ideal solution. The reason can be found in a group of manuscripts from 1834 with the title "State Education" (*Statsmæssig Oplysning*).[1] Here the opinion is presented that the state must take the business of education into its own hands, from top to bottom. Grundtvig considers it a too dangerous and demoralising sort of education for society. In Grundtvig's plans for Sorø practical and principle considerations go hand in hand.

Main Educational Ideas

The general content of Grundtvig's educational ideas used to be grouped under the following headings 1) Emphasis on *youth* – as opposed to

1. Grundtvig uses the same word *oplysning* to mean 'enlightenment' *and* 'education'.

216

childhood – as the real period of schooling; 2) Emphasis on *oral teaching,* in particular the inspiration derived from the stimulating, "spirited" lecture; 3) Emphasis on *the Danish-Norse cultural tradition* – as opposed to the classical-Latin – as the best foundation for education, and finally 4) that these ideas are somehow linked to *a Christian view of life.* There is no denying that this characterization points to something of considerable importance. But in the light of recent Grundtvig research we must make certain reservations.

With reference to the above sketch of the relationship between a life-philosophy and education the link to a Christian view of life must be depicted as an open and indirect relationship. Grundtvig specifically rejects the inclusion of Christian concepts in determining the purpose of education. But that does not imply that the view that the Christian faith takes of life is completely disposed of. That may well be the case for the time being – under temporal conditions. But as we shall see later, the possibility of understanding the faith asserts itself in an eschatological perspective as the final stage in the historical process that Grundtvig calls "the transfiguration of human life".[2] For the present, however, the conviction of faith can only exist in an educational context as "an unspoken dimension" (Niels Højlund). This open relationship between the work of the school and a Christian view of life is described by Grundtvig in various ways. The best-known formulation is to be found appropriately enough in the poem *Open Letter to My Children* in 1839. Here he expresses the hope that the children's life here on earth may be "Well aware of the deep desires, Only fulfilled by Eternity's glory".

One might then ask the question of the above four points: What is it that gathers these thoughts into a unity, into a distinctive world of ideas, which in relation to other worlds has its own specific character? What is the fundamental view that ultimately lies behind these ideas? An examination of the numerous drafts of Grundtvig's educational writings has revealed that the concept of "interaction" (*vekselvirkning*) plays a central role in his ideas about teaching and education. It seems appropriate therefore to direct our attention to this concept.

Of the adjectives that Grundtvig applies to "interaction" there are three that stand out: *free, living and natural.* Other adjectives could be mentioned, but let us dwell a while with these, the most common. It would appear that Grundtvig applies these adjectives to two different subject-areas within the category of interaction: partly the *function* of interac-

---

2. Grundtvig uses the Danish word *forklaring* to mean both "transfiguration" *and* "explanation".

tion, and partly the *conditions* under which it functions. The adjectives "free, living and natural" describe partly the actual function, what actually happens, the actual life lived at the new school he envisages; and partly the conditions under which this can take place. The supreme importance is attached to the actual function, the actual life as it unfolds, not what all this might eventually lead to. He rarely expresses himself on this last point, and when he does so it is only in the vaguest of phrases. For example, he can point out that it should serve "the common good".

With regard to the *freedom of interaction,* the lectures from 1838 – *Within Living Memory* are of particular interest. Here Grundtvig points out, for example, that it is a serious drawback of the lecture form that "no living interaction is reached between your thoughts and mine". He argues against a teaching method in which the teacher alone holds the floor: "I consider it to be cheating the service we do our audience so long as we speak alone and do not understand how to move on through living dialogue to a general participation and interaction..." And when he begins his lectures with the phrase, "My masters" he means it quite literally. He actually wants to regard the audience as his masters.[3] The teacher must in so many words give up all his gentlemanly traits and put on the guise of a servant. These ideas are later elaborated on in his description of the great joint-Scandinavian high school, "where everything that strongly attracts or awakes the spirit was in the form of a constant brisk interaction in the well-regulated conversation".

So much for the function of interaction when it is characterized by freedom. With regard to freedom as a condition it must be noted first and foremost that the freedom of interaction is conditioned by the freedom from an obligation to "the other life", i.e. life in the everlasting salvation. It was precisely this "whim", according to Grundtvig, that over the centuries had led clergymen and teachers to try to make people pious against their will. And the inevitable consequence was that they endeavoured to turn people into something out of their own heads. Grundtvig on the other hand maintains that the world must be taken for what it is, and all worries must be set aside about the possible consequences of education for mankind's eternal salvation. Education must be worked out exclusively for this life. It must contribute to the "transfiguration of human life", i.e. the explanation or clarification of the meaning and aim of human life. The "transfiguration" takes place within temporal life in a historical process that is progressing towards the end of time. Not until

3. Grundtvig's actual words are "Mine herrer" (My masters *and* my gentlemen).

218

time is no longer, will the final, everlasting "transfiguration" of the meaning of human life occur.

Another condition for interaction is freedom from "the Roman yoke". In Grundtvig's opinion the Latin-based education of his day rested on a mistaken assumption that mankind could be transformed. Thus the Latin education contains a strong dose of the "power-sickness" that is exactly what he wanted banned from the proper sort of school. He also believed that the freedom for interaction – the free interactive relationship between teacher and pupil is conditional on the freedom from the obligation to sit examinations. This well-known idea of Grundtvig's thus takes up a natural place in the category of interaction.

True interaction – or genuine reciprocal teaching – is also characterized in Grundtvig's educational writings by the word *life*. Both pupils and teachers must be animated, he maintains. It is first and foremost the use of living, oral communication that characterizes a living interaction. In the school for life education begins with the oral teaching by the experienced teacher and ends in a conversation between teacher and pupil, or amongst the pupils themselves. Here, as Grundtvig puts it, the purpose of education is manifested in a living interaction. What he is aiming for is a school "where the living word strives to recover its all-but-lost yet inalienable rights, and where everything is worked out in a living interaction, a genuine reciprocal education...".

The life of this interaction finds expression in other ways, however: Grundtvig places great emphasis on the appeal to the pupils' interest and on the conversation being diverted from the abstract to the here and now and the useful. In a word, "Cheerfulness is the life of the school." On similar lines Grundtvig emphasizes that "happy songs" are a sign of life at the school.

Among the conditions under which life can come to characterize the interaction it is above all the removal of the *book*, the written word, the traditional basis of education, that will define the new education. Books will of course be used, but they must be put in their proper place; they should be consulted "like good friends in reserve". We must fight the superstition that life springs out of books and that books can transform people. The living interaction presupposes that "when they talk on the people scholars can and will forget their books on life".

Another important assumption for interaction is the close link to folk-culture in the past and the present. Education must be *historical and poetical*. With the aid of the poetry, mythology and history of the nation it must guide the young so that they can hear the voice of the past talking to them about the true conditions of life. In the myths the poets have employed poetic imagery to achieve the expression of this deep recognition. And history is not a chance accumulation of events but at its deepest level an account of the gradual clarification of this recognition. History is "life-experience in its widest perspective". Education, however, also links up with folk-culture in the present. Education must desire "the welfare of the kingdom and the general good". And so the following subjects should also be studied at the folk high school: "folk-character, the Constitution, the fatherland in all respects... in brief, the living, the common and the general". A well-known expression of Grundtvig's efforts to put down the roots of education in the present life of the people is to be found in his idea that "the houses of clever and enterprising citizens" could become schools that were far preferable to Latin schools. But he does not regard this home education as a goal in itself. It too has a further aim – towards the general good. Its main perspective is "Mankind in general and society in particular".

Lastly, interaction is characterized by *naturalness*. In Grundtvig's ideas for a "natural" education two lines of thought converge: partly the demand that education should "help" and develop the existing "character" or "nature" in people and in individuals; partly the demand that education should respect a definite "order in nature".

Grundtvig's insistence that youth is the real period of schooling is closely bound up with his belief as to what is characteristic for the various stages in human development. The "nature" of youth, according to Grundtvig, is that the emotions are aroused. Within the framework of a natural interaction this awakening enters into a free relationship with the older, more experienced generation, whose "nature" is experience and reflection. Thus there arises an interaction between on the one hand "Light" in this context: experience and reflection, and on the other hand "Life", which here designates the heart's emotions or the "bright heads and fiery, burning nature" of youth. Corresponding ideas are advanced when Grundtvig takes stock not only of youth but of the Danish people in general. Their "nature", he thinks, is "warm, of the heart",[4] as he calls it. The Danish people are "the family of Love". In this context, too, there is a need for an interaction between light and life, between "education and knowledge" on the one hand, and on the other the warmth and the love, that are the people's nature. The warmth is not in itself able to create true education.

Anyone who has sung Grundtvig's line about "everything expected in the order of nature" will know that the concept contains an important

---

4. Grundtvig's word is "hjertelige" (the heartfelt).

element in Grundtvig's educational thought. But what is the content of the concept? When educationalists of the 17th and 18th century spoke of the order of nature they were pointing to an upbringing that was either in accordance with the child's nature, or following the laws that apply to the nature that surrounds the child. Grundtvig gives the phrase a quite different significance. By the "order of nature" he means the "law of life" which natural education must respect: that every human life passes through a particular historical process: from childhood through youth and maturity to old age. This natural order is the basic condition for all human life, and violation of this "natural law of the human life" cannot go unpunished, any more than violation of the other laws of nature. Thus the mark of maturity must not be stamped on the child. It would be the same as stamping the child with death.

The two lines of thought that meet in Grundtvig's idea of natural education thus express both a respect for human life as it is lived and an awareness that human development is promoted in the confrontation with an external influence. What enables these two lines of thought to be fruitfully contained in one and the same concept is the fact that they are included in the category of interaction.

Teaching Christianity

So far we have concerned ourselves exclusively with Grundtvig's ideas about the education that takes place on a level common to all humanity and based on a life-philosophy. However, when the opportunity arose, Grundtvig also talked about the teaching of Christianity that takes place on the basis of faith. The former, "popular" education is an offer to the people as such, whatever their faith or lack of it; the latter is an offer to the members of the Christian Church.

Some years before the division between philosophy and faith had been clearly formulated, Grundtvig had emphasized the necessity of the distinction between Church and School. Of considerable importance for this view was his discovery in 1825 that the Creed was the Church's rock. From then on he maintains that the Christian Church exists wherever the apostolic Creed is confessed at baptism. The Creed expresses the unchangeable nature of the true Church. "School" on the other hand is characterized by a progressive clarity, by a "free development to the recognition of truth". On the basis of this Grundtvig uses the word "Church-school" both about university theology and the catechism in the late 1820's. Later he seems largely to reserve the description for the teaching

221

of children by the Church. Thus his most comprehensive collection of Bible songs and hymns, published in 1870, a few years before his death, bears the title *Song-Work for the Danish Church-School.*

The distinction between Church and School receives further support from the awareness of the relationship between faith and philosophy that Grundtvig reached in 1831-32 during his work on *Norse Mythology.* In the mid-1830's these ideas lead him to write a polemical article, in 1836, which presents the following thesis: that it is a grave mistake to teach Christianity in state schools. Grundtvig refers to the fact, amongst others, that history has shown that it is lack of faith, rather than faith itself that has been strengthened in those centuries when Christianity has been taught at school. Furthermore, faith is a "matter for the heart", which cannot be learned and memorized as homework or be "hammered in through the catechism". Faith, in brief, is not a "school-matter". Faith is only asked for in church.

However, the question of the content and method of teaching Christianity was of great relevance for the parents and the congregations that took it upon themselves to bring up children with the elementary Christian teachings. The question became relevant for Grundtvig himself as his two sons, Johan and Svend (born in 1822 and 1824 respectively) grew up. In order to teach his sons Grundtvig produced two small books: *Chronicle in Rhyme for Childhood Teaching* and *Historical Teachings for Children*, both published in 1829. At the same time he drafted a plan to publish a collection of Bible stories in verse. It was abandoned at the time but resurrected ten years later in 1839 when he began publication of the second volume of the *Song-Work*, which contained a number of songs from Bible stories.

As far as the content of teaching Christianity is concerned the Bible stories and, for the older children the catechism, are obvious components. However, as is the case with his "secular" education ideas, so with the teaching of Christianity life comes before the knowledge that throws light on it. In a Church context life is the congregation's confession of "the living Word of faith". Thus the Creed becomes the key to biblical knowledge. The Christian life is there already; in the "Scriptures' treasure-chest" we can learn about this life.

With regard to method, Grundtvig refers also in the teaching of Christianity to the spoken word as the most important means of communication: "Only in the warmth of the oral word is the light living, and where it fails to accompany the divine Scriptures, these become nothing but a rack for the little ones", he says in a draft from 1828. We must further note that in Grundtvig's opinion, also the teaching of Christianity must be "historical and poetical". Whereas in secular education it is a question of illuminating the life of the people past and present through the aid of history and poetry, it is the task of the teacher of Christianity to throw historic and poetic light on the Christian life. In a letter from 1826 Grundtvig has therefore drawn a parallel between the aims of the two tasks of education: "poetically and historically ..., to illuminate the Christian as well as the the Danish folk-life". It must be noted, furthermore, that in both areas it is a question of developing or "transmitting" a life that exists – and doing so without confusing the two sorts of life and thereby bungling the task one was given. In a draft from 1836 Grundtvig thus emphasizes that although these two lives are admittedly different, they can nevertheless be reconciled. He himself lives both lives, "perhaps only poorly and on a small scale, but still really enough for them to strive to transmit themselves, no longer as they were in the past, mixed up and confused, but separately, each under its own name...".

Finally, it should be mentioned that Grundtvig's most original contribution to the content and method of teaching Christianity is his biblical songs and hymns. In this area a number of research assignments remain; for example, with regard to the genre-definition of the individual poems as songs or hymns, their use of popular proverbs and phrases, problems of tune-settings etc. Already we can say, however, that Bible-story *songs* move on a general, human level, the philosophical level, whereas the Bible-story *hymns* contain a specifically Christian message and therefore belong in the context of faith. Seen in a broader perspective the educational aim of the songs is to make children aware of the universal and historical context – and perhaps to offer an ethical upbringing as well. In a narrower perspective they aim to create an understanding that the Christian message can later build on. The Bible-story hymns also contain this latter perspective, but have in addition a direct Christian message, such as the possibility of resurrection on the strength of Christ's achievement. Whether in song or hymn Grundtvig strives for a Christian education that is characterized by life and happiness and which is thus completely free from the compulsion that promotes only hypocrisy and unbelief. In this specific area, the teaching of Christianity, Grundtvig also searches for freedom, life and naturalness.

Immediate Effects

Following this presentation of the main ideas in Grundtvig's educational universe it seems appropriate to conclude with a glance at the effects of all this, limiting our review to the immediate effects in Grundtvig's own lifetime.

In general Grundtvig's educational writings received little attention when they appeared in the 1830's and 1840's. It was as late as 1870, after the Grundtvig movement had made its mark, that interest in his writings became so great that the publication of the most important of them seemed opportune. The collection, edited by Grundtvig himself, appeared in 1872 under the title *Brief Writings on the Historical High School*.

But what then of the free schools and the folk high schools? They had already begun to spring up in the 1840's. The strange fact of the matter is that Grundtvig himself had certain reservations about both types of school. Christen Kold regarded a Christian revival as being the aim of the elementary schools. He declared that he would speak of "God's love and Denmark's happiness". And in his famous article *On the School for Children* in 1850 he wrote: "In the elementary school it is a matter of helping to develop what is already there: the Christian life, the shoot of which was received at baptism, and the folk-life, which was inherited from our forefathers..." On this point we can see an obvious disagreement with the main thrust of Grundtvig's high school writings.

Grundtvig had a strangely ambivalent attitude to the growth of the high school movement. On the one hand he could declare that it was excellent that the south Jutlanders had established a high school in Rødding, on the other hand he never visited this first of all high schools – despite repeated invitations. Roar Skovmand, who has made a close study of this strange course of Grundtvig's, is undoubtedly right to conclude that the reason for Grundtvig's cool attitude to Rødding was that he was still hoping to realise his old dream of a big, state-supported high school at Sorø. The small, scattered private schools were not the real thing, in his opinion. Not until rather late in the day, in the development that had taken place in the 1850's, did Grundtvig accept. The decisive events in this respect were the death of his benefactor, Christian VIII, in 1848, and the stranding of the Sorø project in 1849 (see p. 216). In 1856 Grundtvig was himself instrumental in founding a high school, Marielyst High School, outside Copenhagen, where he became a regular speaker.

Also with regard to the form of teaching at the high schools the results were different from what Grundtvig had actually imagined. Symptomatic of this was the development within the "Danish Society", a folk society founded in 1839. Here Grundtvig attempted to realise his ideas for a free, living and natural interaction. However, he was gradually forced to admit that the interaction was difficult, if not impossible, to put into practice.

224

Conversation simply never materialised in the Danish Society. The reasons were many. Perhaps the audience felt themselves uneasy in the presence of Grundtvig's powerful personality and colossal knowledge, as a result of which – as he himself put it – he always knew better than most. Furthermore, the average member of his audience at that time – around 1840 – simply did not possess the necessary qualifications for launching into a discussion on the subjects that were brought up. He lacked both the necessary courage to express himself as well as sufficient knowledge. Not until a hundred years later did the study-group as a form gain success in the folk high school, with its lecture or presentation followed by a discussion. Then and only then were some of Grundtvig's aims with the free, living and natural interaction put into practice. Until then it was the general belief that Grundtvig's means of communicating his message was the "spirited" lecture, even though Grundtvig himself had clearly made the point that the purpose of the lecture was to lead up to a dialogue – neither more nor less.

However, if the immediate reaction to Grundtvig's educational ideas was limited, then the long-term effects were so much the greater.

BIBLIOGRAPHY

Grundtvig's School World in texts and drafts, Edited by K. E. Bugge. Copenhagen 1968. Grundtvigs Skoleverden i tekster og udkast I-II.

The School for Life. Studies in the Educational Ideas of N. F. S. Grundtvig. By K. E. Bugge. Copenhagen 1965. Skolen for livet. Studier over N. F. S. Grundtvigs pædagogiske tanker.

Grundtvig's Ideas on the Church and the People 1825-47

by ANDERS PONTOPPIDAN THYSSEN

A. *The Period 1825-34*

The Church's Retort (1825-26)

In the first years of his ministry Grundtvig outwardly maintained the peaceful attitude that had characterized the period 1815-20. He had become less quarrelsome, he wrote in October 1823 as he was about to begin an essay defending Christianity. He preferred now to persuade rather than to overwhelm, to raise the shield of defence, not the sword of attack. In a later draft from the spring of 1824, which took the form of an exchange of letters, he dissociated himself completely from his previous attempts, especially in the *World Chronicle* (1812), to exercise spiritual force against opponents of the faith. A newspaper article from the same time (May 4th) emphasizes, like *World Chronicle* (1817) (see p. 108) that faith must not be forced on anyone but must be a matter of conscience which each must decide for himself.

On the other hand he was actively involved in the future of both the Church and the nation. It was a constant unrest, a swinging between *doubt and hope* which we have seen time and again in the period up to 1824, and these swings continued for many years. His long autobiographical poem, *New Year's Morn,* from the summer of 1824 had acted like a release on him as an interpretation of his life-path; but he wrote later of it that it depicted first and foremost "such a battle between black despair and May-green hope, in which hope is victorious", that his readers had never seen the like. Since the autumn of 1823 he had found peace in the thought that the future of the Church was a matter for God and did not depend on the clergy or the number of Christians. But even so he had to be on the look-out for signs of progress or decline in the Danish Church; and since

226

it seemed to be governed by rationalist preaching he must at least make clear what *true Christianity* stood for. This was the main idea in the above-mentioned imaginary *Exchange of Letters* from the spring of 1824 which underlined that this question had to be answered "absolutely historically" on the basis of the Bible and to be distinguished from the personal questions as to the credibility of Christianity.

The optimism of *New Year's Morn* was maintained for some months. Grundtvig had been greatly encouraged when in July 1824 a younger poet, B. S. Ingemann, published a lengthy poem on Valdemar the Great, which in the spirit of Grundtvig and on the basis of his Saxo translation praised Denmark's days of glory, Christian and national, in the 12th century. Although Ingemann was his only friend among poets the book became for Grundtvig an important sign of spring. Similarly, the appointment of another young friend to a parish in Copenhagen gave him high hopes that the churches of the capital would gradually become "Christian" (letter of September 30th 1824). Among his sermons we can find a particularly exalted one from the same period on the Spirit's quickening of the Bible's letter: God's Word must not be sought in the grave ("the written word"), it is risen: God will "bring alive again both His Word and all the friends of truth, all the children of light" (12th Sunday after Trinity).

But later that autumn and into the winter of 1824-25 the *tone changes*. *New Year's Morn* was overlooked and Ingemann's book was slaughtered by the Copenhagen critics. The bitterest blow came when Henrich Steffens, Grundtvig's ideal since his youth, during a visit in October 1824 declared Grundtvig's whole literary activity to be a major delusion. Grundtvig still stood alone "against the whole crowd of self-made viceroys in the Kingdom of the Spirit" and he lacked friends in Copenhagen, he wrote to Ingemann, "in the great struggle that these days is now being fought between life and death everywhere". (November 27th). Since the summer of 1824 he had been toying with the idea of leaving Denmark, and late in the year he dreamt in the poem, *The Dane-Shield,* of the glorious Norway as a place of refuge, for he was "sick and tired of the noise of arms" and was reluctant to "draw his sword again".

But just at that moment a number of young clergymen and theologians began to do battle with rationalism, and when the two most important of them, A. G. Rudelbach and Jacob Christian Lindberg, both leading scholars, asked Grundtvig in February 1825 to assist in the publication of a new periodical, *Theological Monthly,* he could not refuse. "Everything betokens," he declared in a letter on the subject, "that the long-awaited battle as to what is Christian and the truth to be trusted will now come alive." Grundtvig also wrote the main article in the two first editions, *The*

18th Century Englightenment in the Service of Salvation (published in April/May 1825). It was still characterized by moderation; enlightenment theology could not be stamped out; it was rather a question of proving its unchristian nature. Its supporters ought to be treated with gentleness in the hope that it must gradually give way to "as Christian a unity as can be expected in this world".

However, Grundtvig's attitude was altered by a debate on the so-called "devout meetings", which in the 1820's spread through Funen as an offshoot of the peasant revival from the beginning of the century (see p. 371). Grundtvig had not really had much sympathy for this movement. Partly he was bound to the importance the Lutheran State Church attached to the leading role of the clergy and to the fear of "pernicious sects", and partly the movement could not be reconciled with his own views: his rejection of the culturally inimical pietism (see p. 103), his belief in the link between Church and State, and his steadily increasing emphasis on the *Church* as a historical unity. On the other hand he disapproved of the logical demand of the State Church for religious uniformity, supervised by the clergy, since it involved numerous interventions against the revivalist circles through bans, arrests, court cases and fines. Several of the revivalists had written letters appealing to him as "spokesman" for the "old" Christianity and already in 1821 he had written to the rector of Kerteminde, which was a centre of the revival, warning him not to force people against their conscience and not to use secular power.

But it was not until January 1825 that he made a public pronouncement, incensed by a court case, the "Ellinge Case", against a revivalist group on Funen. They had been reported to the police by the rector and during the case they were treated as a fanatical sect and even mistreated by people in the area. In his speech Grundtvig depicted the meetings as poor substitutes for Church life, but nevertheless defended them as an expression of the "old-fashioned Lutheran Christianity" of the people, who had been let down by the clergy. The revivalists were not only harmless for society but in better agreement with the orthodox Lutheran basic tenets of the State than the clergy.

Grundtvig's tone was still controlled, but a newspaper article in April 1825 made a deep impression on him. It had characterized the meetings as a national plague, and intervention in the official rights of the clergy; the revivalists, who permitted themselves to read and explain the Bible of their own accord, were bunglers and quacks who "occupied themselves with what they simply ought to leave to the qualified doctors of the soul". Against this Grundtvig wrote a series of indignant retorts that wavered between "war and peace" (the heading under consideration); either an agreement "on *Church* freedom, *social* peace and *spiritual* conflict only as to what is genuine Christianity" – or war against the heresies of *the clergy*. Do they really regard us as so cowardly that we would not risk anything at all to acquire for the old-fashioned Christians amongst the peasantry the peace and the right that the law entitles them to...!" "When they attempt with *social* threats to frighten the peasantry from the Bible... then I must if possible be the first actually to accuse a clergyman whose printed writings conflict with the Augsburg Confession and Luther's catechism" (the Danish Church's Lutheran symbols according to the Danish law of 1663).

None of these contributions was printed. Grundtvig really did not want war but peace. As a young man he had fought tremendously hard on religious questions, but he was reluctant to do so now. And yet he was on the way to the bitterest battle of his whole life. When he visited Ingemann in 1825, he was in no doubt; now he had to draw his sword. A religious "edict of tolerance", he explained to Ingemann, could only be worked out by "threatening the persecutors who abuse the law with the law"; i.e. threaten "the heterodox, socially intolerant clergy" with the State's "Christian laws" which, applied strictly, would deprive them of their livelihood. Grundtvig declared that he had to "love the unjustly oppressed much more than the oppressors", stand alongside "the humbler folk who believe in the Lord", and "in the legal defence of his fellow-Christians employ a severity" that he would otherwise prefer to avoid.

Thus Grundtvig had crossed the Rubicon. The devout meeting participants had become *fellow-Christians,* whose cause he too was fighting for. This was the starting-point for his "Church battle" in the following years and it also had a great influence on his view of the Church. When in his sermons and notes he defended "true Christianity" against rationalism, he felt he was personally on safe biblical ground; on the other hand he was far from being unaware of the problems of interpretation, for the rationalists also appealed to the biblical evidence. But the question did not become pressing until the ordinary "old-fashioned Christians" came under pressure from the clergy, who claimed to represent the true biblical interpretation. Someone had to be the "rock in the sea of interpretation."

Two sermons from *July 1825* illuminate the problem. On July 24th Grundtvig raised the matter explicitly in a sermon on "the false prophets". They had become so many and so powerful that the remaining Christians had every reason to shout a warning to one another – be on guard against false prophets! But, he continued, you may ask: *how* shall we be on guard? He could only really answer this by referring to diligent Bible reading. But he himself was not satisfied with this answer. This is clear from his intense reflections in the following week in one draft after another (recently unearthed by Kaj Thaning).

The following Sunday he had a better answer: the Christian faith does not depend at all on scholarly biblical studies. Whenever this basis had been used to claim that Jesus could only be "believed in and followed as an intelligent teacher and virtuous man," those who lacked knowledge and insight sank back in doubtfulness. But they had no need: "If you still do not realise, then listen closely"! On this point he had himself been mistaken, he said; he had been deluded into thinking that having given up his childhood faith he had come after a long journey back to his home. For he *was already in the Church* when he awoke; this was the blessing of baptism and Holy Communion that then took effect. "So I reply to those who say that it is both idolatrous and unchristian to call Jesus Christ God and one with the Father and to worship Him: You are making a strange mistake, (for) as long as Christians exist there will also be people who are baptized in the name of the Father and of the Son and of the Holy Ghost." – "This is the creed that Christians have confessed in every age in every church; this and no other is the Christian Creed" in spite of every book and every claim as to what the Bible says.

This was what Grundtvig later called his "unparalleled discovery". But its significance first dawned on him when he received late in August a large scholarly book to which he had subscribed – *The Church Constitution, Teaching and Ritual of Catholicism and Protestantism* by H. N. Clausen, the newly-appointed professor in the Theology faculty (since 1822). Clausen was the young hope of the faculty who had now produced a fresh reason for the uniting of scholarship and reasonable Christianity advocated by the leading circles. Catholicism represented the Church orthodoxy that Clausen rejected, built up as it was as a historical and hierarchical institution; in contrast protestantism rested on the Scriptures, in order through the freedom of research to discover Jesus' spirit and teaching. Friedrich Schleiermacher in particular had helped Clausen to an understanding of Jesus' "frame of mind" as the bearing element in evangelical Christianity.

Grundtvig had long had his eye on "the young Clausen". Even though he was "up to his neck in water", according to Grundtvig, he was already the leading light in the faculty and influential with students, so early on Grundtvig was regarding him as a major opponent. "We find in the *youngest* theological generation, in the young Professor Clausen's disciples, the enemy at the door", he wrote to a friend in March 1825. In Clausen's book he saw the quintessence of the theology he must fight against, and he therefore immediately crossed swords with him by writing a bitter attack, a philippic from first to last which he called *The Church's Retort*. It was only a booklet written in a hurry but it became a watershed as an expression of Grundtvig's new understanding of the Church.

As early as the preface he makes good his plan to "threaten with the law". Clausen must either recant or abandon the title of Christian and thus his post as teacher of the future clergy. Otherwise Grundtvig would be forced "on behalf of the only true, historical and Christian Church" to declare him a false teacher, who was abusing his position in order to "undermine the Church which he pretends to be serving and strengthening!" On the other hand he was imploring the authorities for an edict of tolerance, so that Clausen's exclusion from the Church did not have social consequences, and this ought to be the case for all citizens apart from the clergy. Not until the end of the piece does he refer explicitly to "the law", however: that is, the Danish oath of clergy, the Augsburg Confession and Luther's catechism, which the government had bound the theologians and the clergy to. But he revealed already in the preface that his action rested on a new acknowledgement of "the unshakeable and unchanging foundation of the Christian Church", its "original creed". Only upon this basis and not on its scriptural interpretation – however certain that may be – did he dare to pronounce a "Church divorce".

This formal polemic was generally overshadowed in the booklet, however, by Grundtvig's new view of the Church, which is advocated as a contrast to Clausen's ridiculous "airy Church". Clausen wished to rely on the Scriptures alone, Grundtvig reports, but he regards them as obscure and indefinable; they can only be interpreted by scholars with a certain amount of probability, and can be used for anything whatever. His Christ is just as obscure, in fact merely the infinite in finite form – like Professor Clausen himself! And Christ's teaching is – according to "the Professor's unravelling" – only "the religious idea released from the picture forms of nature worship", left behind to the Church, which must keep itself in the background as no more than a medium for this idea, be as little active as possible and build on a dead man's spirit and a teaching that people have to guess at. This is "a quaint castle in the air" Clausen has conceived! His Christ is only a name by reason of his intellect, and his Bible but a shadow of his own thoughts, and his Church is in fact a temple of idols. What he overlooks is the Christian Church as a historical fact through eighteen centuries: "It is undeniable that a *Christianity has been born on earth,* since not only does it lie behind us in history but stands alive before us in which we hear faith in Jesus Christ confessed and the gifts of the Spirit bestowed in His name". This is the only true Church, "in which none is incorporated *through baptism and the Eucharist* without himself taking over the so-called apostolic Creed.

This was the main idea. But *The Church's Retort* is a strange work, in which new thoughts see the light of day that can hardly be reconciled. His "discovery" was not canon law but an inspired message; it would not lead to the Lutheran state orthodoxy by which Clausen was to be convicted but to a positive view of the Catholic Church that was unheard of at the time. The Christian Church was indeed the same historical-Christian Church through eighteen centuries: Justin, Irenaeus and the other Church fathers, Ansgar and Luther, are mentioned side by side. On the other hand Grundtvig rejects explicitly "the new exegetical papacy", the papacy of the Scriptures that the *reformation theologians* had laid the foundations of. This was the basis of Clausen's contempt for the historical Church and his "blind faith in the Scriptures", which completely denied the oral tradition, even a demonstrably "living Word" from Christ's own mouth! There were important new ideas on the way here, as yet only hinted at.

At any rate Grundtvig pushed this line of thought until it became a clear ecumenical appeal that was unique in its day: Let those of us who still wish to be Christians, unite on this rock which has defied the waves of time, "confine ourselves as a religious community, as a Church, to the crib in Bethlehem... withdraw to the Choir, offer each other and all who have fallen asleep in the Lord our hand over the font and our mouth around the altar, eating the one bread and drinking from the one cup". Let us "tolerate in one another all theological variety that can be united with that", with no other rule for interpretation than that the Scriptures must be understood after the Creed. "The school", theology, must therefore enjoy complete academic freedom. No Church can confess everything in the Scriptures, none of us can die on our own interpretation of the Scriptures, only on the original Creed of the Church. "To this the Church must adhere."

The Church's Retort created a greater stir than any other of Grundtvig's works. It was published on September 5th 1825, only a few weeks after Clausen's book, and immediately sold out; two more printings were made. According to a contemporary letter the book set the whole city alight. The students talked of nothing else and the majority of his readers "reprimanded" Grundtvig. Eighty-eight of them publicly expressed their feelings in a tribute to Clausen. Even at the Stock Exchange business almost came to a standstill when "the Retort" was published; and here there were many who sided with Grundtvig!

But the leading Church and literary circles could not but for the most part disapprove of Grundtvig's attack. The fact was that there had long been a more positive "Church" attitude in the offing; Clausen's book was itself an expression of this in its rejection of dry rationalism. J. P. Mynster, now a rector in Copenhagen and the leading light in the State Church, was far more conservative than Clausen but more or less took his side. He wished for a gradual, harmonious development with no break, and he published a sermon in October, *On Christian Wisdom*, which appealed for cool heads and condemned heavy attacks; such people caused only disturbances and were thus often "the enemies of the cross of Christ". In reality he regarded Grundtvig with inward loathing; "Who knows", he wrote shortly after to a friend, "where the impetuous and totally dishonest man may still end."

Grundtvig answered in a sermon, *On the Christian Struggle;* but the general antipathy he met was a heavy burden for him; in the last three months of 1825 he was "as one who lies in the grave". To Ingemann, who had sent a friendly letter, he wrote on November 4th that those were the first kind words he had so far heard from old friends and acquaintances; either they had raged against him or they had discussed the subject with a coldness that was even more intolerable. But he had no regrets, not even the hard words in the preface, which Ingemann had also complained of; "in a way I myself have written the book but the Lord has written the preface" – so it would hold its own!

H. N. Clausen's only response was a lawsuit for libel. His great book was his academic apprentice work, marked by learned and often arrogant self-conceit; so he was deeply offended. The case resulted for Grundtvig in a long drawn-out "judicial hell", which was the last thing he had wanted. Twice he tried to get the case thrown out, but in vain. In June 1826 he offered Clausen a compromise agreement with a declaration that he had wished neither to insult the professor's social honour nor condemn his purpose; but that too was rejected. On October 30th 1826 judgement was given – against Grundtvig. He had unjustly accused Clausen of false teaching, he was to pay the costs of the case and a fine of 100 *rigsdaler* – and in future his works were to be subject to censorship.

Before all this Grundtvig had given up the ministry. In his application to do so, dated May 8th 1826, he explains that he cannot condemn false teaching, which was his official duty, without involving himself in libel cases. There were other contributory causes; privately he referred, amongst others, to the burdensome nature of the duties of his office. Probably more important, however, was the opposition he had met. It had left a deep impression on him that on May 6th he had received a final ban on the use of a hymn-booklet he had published for the Danish

Church's millenary at the end of May 1826; the ban was instituted by H. N. Clausen's father, Archdeacon H. G. Clausen. In a pastoral letter in connection with the millenary, the combined bishops had also condemned him as a fanatical trouble-maker. The crucial factor was his audience with Frederik VI, to whom he appealed to quash the libel case. The King was unable to agree to this and Grundtvig wrote his resignation the same day. Frederik VI was on the whole sympathetic towards Grundtvig, but was himself marked by the views of the enlightenment. "Grundtvig is a fire-breathing volcano" he is supposed to have said.

The past year had been "a tough year of seriousness", Grundtvig wrote to a friend on July 8th 1826. But he would not change it for the most cheerful moment in his life: it has "created an epoch in my inner life that I have to call great". The conflict between the chaotic and the organising principle in him had ceased, to be replaced by an inner harmony with the Creed at its centre, around which everything that is Christian would soon fall into place. "You have probably heard that I have become catholic in the head, and that is very true" – but no less Lutheran, as truly as the Augsburg Confession was a confession of the holy Universal Church's faith and a protest against the pope and every abuse. "All the same it is perhaps most proper that I develop my Lutheran Catholicism in a free place... as a released Lutheran clergyman."

Grundtvig maintained this awareness of a new epoch until the end. The year of "the unparalleled discovery" was a new beginning, which had a decisive influence on the rest of his life. It opened new paths in several directions, and we shall follow the lines of development of the three most important in the years 1826-34: the continuing "Church battle", the working out of the new outlook on the Church and the further development of Grundtvig's cultural viewpoint.

The Church Battle (1826-34)

In the wake of Grundtvig's defeat in the case in October 1826 a straightforward religious war broke out between the little Grundtvigian-party and the much greater Clausen-party. With relentless attacks and counter-attacks, continually changing fronts, and many dramatic episodes it stretched on into 1834. Grundtvig's young supporters were the aggressors, in particular Jacob Christian Lindberg, a master of arts and highly qualified as a Hebrew philologist and numismatist, but now quite absorbed in the great clash. Even though Grundtvig was the object of the conflict his own behaviour was surprisingly reasonable.

His attitude was for a long time both clear and unclear. On the one hand he stood firmly by his main ideas from the autumn of 1825: "true Christianity" should make its presence better felt, and "the old-fashioned Christians" should be freed from the State Church's coercion; but he would prefer this to happen by peace and agreement within the State Church rather than by war. On the other hand he had himself started the battle with *The Church's Retort,* which in spite of his historical, ecumenical view of the Church must be regarded as a confessional accusation of heresy. At the same time he had raised questions of religious tolerance but maintained the old-fashioned Christians' exclusive right to the State Church. He felt a strong attachment personally to the State Church, in the sense that it was the Church of his forefathers which was of the Lutheran confession through history and by law. In *Important Questions for Denmark's Jurists,* published on September 2nd 1826, he was still stressing the importance of the tie between Church and State. The State needed these Christians and his great hope had been for "the quiet rebirth of the Christian-Danish life of the people". The State Church ought therefore to be freed of its "hostile elements", who in return should have the right to form free churches. But he now recognized that perhaps the enemies of the faith were the stronger; in which case the supporters of the Augsburg Confession must withdraw from the State Church.

A couple of contemporary letters to Norwegian friends illuminate his frame of mind at this time. They are concerned with, amongst other things, *haugianism,* a widespread Norwegian movement holding its own meetings, started by Hans Nielsen Hauge around 1800. Grundtvig had a lot of sympathy for the haugians, who had supported him financially in 1815-17. But now he wrote that he found himself in a hopeless dilemma between a generally unbelieving State Church and "something they regard as a church although it is not really one." They lacked an awareness of the importance of the ministry and should make sure that they got Christian clergymen who either led them back to a purified State Church or formed them "into a purely Christian Church with its own theological high school, which might perform miracles in the North". As a Norwegian clergyman he would have acted the same way – and in these years he actually often considered moving to Norway. Theoretically he was prepared to form a free church consisting of evangelical "meeting" people but in practice he retreated from this. The question was closely connected with his ideas on the Church and the people and therefore demanded lengthy consideration.

Lindberg on the other hand went immediately to work on a purging of the State Church. In September 1826 he created a stir with the essay,

What is Christianity in Denmark, a thorough demonstration of the official orthodoxy of the Danish Church according to its confessionary writings, with a rejection of the Clausen-party's "spiritual" interpretation and with a demand for the dismissal of all heretical clergy. An even greater sensation was created by a new essay from Lindberg in November which directly attacked the recent conviction of Grundtvig: this surpassed Clausen's notorious heresies, and if the bishops shared Clausen's opinion, as was claimed, then Lindberg had to declare the collected bishops to be false teachers! This was a provocation that alarmed the highest circles, but the Government wavered: a new court case might be difficult because of Lindberg's formal rights, and it might create discord among the people. The result was therefore a powerful threat in the form of an expression of the King's "extreme displeasure". However, Lindberg continued undeterred, and published two essays attacking Clausen in 1828 and 1829; the Government demanded that the latter be confiscated, but lost the legal battle in the high court in 1830! After that the essay went into five printings. Besides this there was a series of similar polemics in the same period from other young Grundtvig supporters.

At the same time Grundtvig's thoughts were moving in a different direction. Following his conviction and the royal disapproval of Lindberg he was inclined to regard the battle for the State Church as lost, and his first reaction was to write three long essays, largely on matters of principle, called *On Freedom of Religion,* the first two of which were printed in February/March 1827. They denote a turning-point. Here he acknowledged that the enlightenment had given rise to a widespread religious opposition which neither could nor should be suppressed. But since the old Church coercion laws were still in force, the result had been "Church chaos" with constant conflict between the two parties within the State Church on appointments, textbooks and rituals, and on top of all this hypocrisy and the forcing of people to violation of conscience with the compulsory participation in Church ceremonies by obvious "mockers". The solution must be religious freedom and "Church divorce". How the divorce was to be achieved was not made clear; but Grundtvig had many suggestions: the division of the State Church into two Churches, the abolition of the Coercion Act, the breaking of the parish-tie to the parish-priest (see p. 241), the withdrawal from the State Church either of "the deniers of the faith" or of the old-fashioned Christians. With this demand for religious freedom Grundtvig was making a clear break with his previous line of thought on the State Church, and he went a long way in his separation of Church and State, for example in his demand for civic confirmation, a civic taking of the oath, and civic marriage. Here he went even further than the political liberalism which gained influence in Denmark from the 1830's onwards.

The third essay was for the most part a bitter commentary on the libel process with a look back at his own achievement so far as a "patriotic writer" and a plea to His Majesty that he be released from censorship – "the criminal stamp on my writing". But the censor refused to allow publication of this part. It was a hard blow for Grundtvig that the censor really did wish to limit his use of "the writer's only weapon", and this undoubtedly contributed to his reticence about the Church battle.

But when he allowed *Theological Monthly* to fold in the summer of 1828, he justified it in another way that hints at a profound clarification. He concluded his last essay with a general rejection of the theoretical expositions concerning the Church and the School. We must not describe, but produce, what we lack! The 18th century was right to think that "the *practical* is and always will be the main thing in life, in spiritual matters as well as bodily", and therefore it is also true "that the Kingdom of God consists not of talk but of action". In an epilogue he thanked his associates but underlined for his own part "the unparalleled discovery" as the most important benefit. Through this it had became superfluous "to be afflicted by the Devil" on an interpretation of the Scriptures; on the contrary a clear distinction could now be made between the Church of Christ and the State Church organization since Constantine the Great. With no right to do so the State Churches regarded themselves as the Church of Christ and forbade withdrawal; and it was only the religious coercion of the State Church which had necessitated "the tiresome conflict" about what was true Christianity. But in Denmark the position of the Christians had become so awkward that they could not go on without religious freedom. They could achieve this either quietly by abandoning the State Church or by freedom within it through changes in the law. The latter required the enlightenment of the authorities over the sad situation as it existed; and since Grundtvig had now done what he could to illuminate them he would withdraw from the Church debate until further notice.

In the late 1820's Grundtvig was feeling thoroughly depressed by the course of the Church battle. Time and again "the enemy" had been supported from above, and the orthodox-theological tactics of his friends seemed to him increasingly problematic; in the years around 1830 he often sought to restrain them. He himself left the stage for a time in the years 1829-31, when he travelled to England to study the Anglo-Saxon manuscripts as a result of a special grant from the King. Apart from this, since 1826 he had only received a small fixed amount from the King (p. 114) and had found it difficult to manage financially with a wife and three children. The futures of Rudelbach and Lindberg as scholars had been ruined; Rudelbach, who was half-German in origin, became superintendent in Glauchau in Saxony in 1828, and Lindberg was suspended from his grammar-school post in 1829 and did not obtain another permanent post until 1844. But the Clausen-party marched on in triumph. From 1828 onwards, Clausen gathered a number of prominent academics, especially professors, to write for a reputable periodical as a counterbalance to "the activities of the Grundtvigian-party". His politically liberal tendency, which expressed itself in, amongst others, the demand for a representative Church constitution made him popular with the students; in 1832 they feted him with a torchlight procession. And the clergy in the capital stood alongside his father, Archdeacon H. G. Clausen.

But the indefatigable Lindberg continued the battle with a new periodical from 1830 onwards, *The Monthly Journal on Christianity and History;* and when it found only a few subscribers and had to fold in January 1832, he began all over again in 1833 with the weekly journal, *Nordic Church Times,* which enjoyed a wider reading public and continued right up until 1841. Amongst other things Lindberg used these periodicals to introduce a new tactic which proved to be of great significance for Grundtvig. It was based on direct contact with "the old-fashioned Christians" and specific attacks on deviations from the ritual and on injustices against the revivalists. When the "devout meetings" began in 1830 in Copenhagen, he made personal contact with them, and from September 1831 he himself held meetings in his own home. Through travel and correspondence he also achieved closer and wider contact with meeting-hall Christians throughout he country.

Despite the trips to England Grundtvig kept up with this development. He stayed in England for the summer only and his interest in the country was due to the fact, amongst others, that for a number of years now he had regarded the English religious freedom as a model: over there it really was allowed to form free churches outside the established Church. The sense for practical action that he saw in England corresponded with his own inclination over the past few years; but it had still not borne fruit, and, as he wrote later, it made a deep impression on him that he was regularly asked: What do you do? Even though he had reservations about Lindberg's popular agitation and the heavy and direct attacks on the rationalists he had to accept these reactions more or less as being necessitated by the Church battle. Originally he had dissociated himself from Lindberg's meetings but his regard for the oppressed "Christian peasantry" was the recurrent chorus in all his essays and letters on the subject, and the direct accusations were necessary as long as religious freedom was not permitted. In the winter of 1830-31 he decided to intervene himself, in the conviction that the time for new and decisive action had arrived.

First he wrote a new exposition of his view of the State Church, which was published in Lindberg's monthly journal around the turn of the year 1830-31, *Should the Lutheran Reformation Really Continue?* It reflected the main ideas in the essay *On Freedom of Religion,* only in a clearer form: the days of the confessional, uniform State Church are over; the Christians and the rationalists must part company, and H. N. Clausen's representative Church constitution is not a solution but a means of power for the vast majority of rationalist clergy. The necessary "divorce" could be carried out in various ways, but if a freer arrangement for both sides in the State Church could not be established, then the old-fashioned Christians should at least be allowed to meet together with "house-clergy" for a number of families, that is devout meetings led by a clergyman. As a reason for greater freedom *within* the State Church Grundtvig now stresses more strongly the importance of the Christians for society; here he referred to the description in the *World Chronicles* of the "beneficial consequences" of the Reformation for scholarship, education and social life.

After this Grundtvig was ready for action. In the spring of 1831 with Grundtvig's approval, Lindberg collected signatures from 83 families applying for permission to form a *free congregation* with Grundtvig as their minister. Already at this point Grundtvig was prepared for a battle against the State Church, if permission was refused. The knot "is close to being untied – or cut", he wrote to Ingemann on April 9th. Ingemann was horrified and strongly advised caution; Grundtvig's withdrawal from the State Church would arouse great confusion and indignation; it would be regarded as apostasy from Christianity! But Grundtvig replied that he had now been working to reform the State Church for 20 years, yet it had only got worse, particularly since 1825. When Christian peasants had to accept that the sacraments were falsified and their children seduced from their baptismal covenant – with the prospect of martyrdom in prison if they protested – then the *imprisonment* of conscience shouted to heaven that it must now come to an end. For six years he had fought with himself over the decisive step, which he had preferred to avoid taking; but now his decision was irrevocable.

The application was delayed for several reasons, including Grundtvig's third trip to England, but Lindberg put together a new one with nearly twice as many signatures which was handed over in November 1831. The applicants wished primarily to meet in the empty Frederik's Church, which stood near the Church of Our Saviour, where Grundtvig had been minister. But the basic congregation was Lindberg's devout meetings; only a third of the signatures were from Grundtvig's former congregation. Grundtvig's tremendous enthusiasm is clear from his accompanying essay, which did not attempt to hide the fact that the free church would break the ice for other free churches, and made it clear that in the event of a refusal the Government would be forced to use tough methods against precisely those in the State Church who had the law and history on their side. Grundtvig also included a contemporary pamphlet, *On the Clausen Libel Case,* a polemical masterpiece in which he underlined his principle of freedom: since the State Church could not be reformed he gladly handed it over to the Clausen-party; but then he and other old-fashioned Christians must be allowed to leave and form a little historical Christian Church.

After lengthy discussions the Government decided on a rejection, which the applicants were informed of on February 2nd 1832. Grundtvig attempted to appeal personally to the President of the Chancellory but when this too was rejected he himself began to speak at Lindberg's meetings, which were held every Sunday. This created a sensation and immediately resulted in such a tremendous rush to hear him that on February 25th Grundtvig hired the upper floor of a warehouse. The police, who were still following the activities of the meeting-people, now banned all meetings, but Grundtvig, who was personally informed of the ban by Copenhagen's deputy commissioner of police, insisted that he would speak at the warehouse meeting on Sunday March 4th. This made things very awkward for the authorities; they were on the verge of an open conflict with Grundtvig and his supporters, who would probably involve the whole of the steadily growing meeting movement.

The consequence was a sudden *change of course.* The deputy commissioner referred Grundtvig to the bishop, P. E. Müller, who personally enjoyed a friendly relationship with Grundtvig. He promised to request permission for Grundtvig's meetings, which were however to be called "prayer-hours". Two days later, on February 29th, the Government retracted, even agreeing to the application for the use of Frederik's Church. It was immediately handed over to Grundtvig, and the deputy commissioner personally ensured that this was publicly announced before the planned warehouse meeting on March 4th.

By going to the limits Grundtvig had thus managed to break the State Church coercion system. It was so great a victory that he immediately returned to his original main line: a calm and gradual development towards greater freedom within the State Church. He regarded the meet-

The march to the Royal Palace, 1848, to demand a new constitution. Grundtvig looks on from a window (top right).

The Constitutional Session in the Danish Parliament, 1848-49. Grundtvig is seated between the principal figures on the right. (Painting by Constantin Hansen, Frederiksborg Museum).

Silhouette of Grundtvig in the satirical magazine, *The Corsair*, 1853, with the following text by the editor: "This standard-bearer and idol of the orthodox is, and will continue to be, despite his colossal errors, his manifest egoism and his inextinguishable hatred of Rome, a respectable person. There is trumpet-power in his poetry, sounding-brass in his prose, a northern spirit and a northern tang to his bardic efforts. Orthodox Christian in his faith he is a heathen in his endeavour. What has he not managed to quarrel about? How many literary and other controversies has he not engaged upon? In brief, it is impossible to present a biographical silhouette of this wonder and phenomenon of nature.

I have been so furious with him that I think it incredible that a well-organized state police force has not long ago placed him in safe custody in Bistrup (a prison), and when I saw him on one festive occasion sneak up to Oehlenschläger, place the laurel-wreath on him, kiss him and say those apothegms of his, then it seemed to me that we were all more or less clever pygmies alongside this half-demented demigod."

ings in Frederik's Church as a transitional arrangement; the permission covered only a kind of afternoon service without baptism and Communion. Already in the summer of 1832 he applied to the bishop for the right also to hold baptism and Communion, and at the same time he limited his own reform demands to the breaking of the parish-tie so that lay people were allowed to choose their minister. The freedom of "the Christian peasantry" was still a major aim. On the other hand it did not affect him when the radical meeting-people withdrew their support and formed new meetings. But he followed Lindberg's battle against false teaching and infringement of the ritual sympathetically. It was waged in collaboration with the meeting-people and really did force more clergy to follow the ordained ritual. Even Archdeacon Clausen had to submit, following dramatic scenes in his church when meeting-people at an actual baptism protested at his self-designed ritual. The archdeacon replied with an application to the King from all the clergy in the capital for a general modernisation of the ritual (in November 1832). But Grundtvig's reaction was the opposite: the rationalists ought to have a free choice of ritual, but the "Christians" should have the same freedom, so that they could keep the old ritual.

In general Grundtvig himself now took charge of the Church battle. From 1831 to 1834 he wrote 13 major or minor contributions to the debate, and they carried more weight than Lindberg's vehement attacks. In the most important of them, *An Impartial View of the Danish State Church,* 1834, he summarized the result of his reflections. The State Church is not a Church at all, he maintained, merely "a social institution". On the other hand, Christianity is really a foreign guest, who in no way wishes to rule; but as "the faith of the Danish fathers" it had become identified with the State Church. The connection had in reality been broken in "the age of intellect", when the faith of the fathers, particularly of the clergy, had been ousted by "the heterodox sect", who freed themselves from the orthodox Lutheran teaching and liturgy. But the consequence of this was now to be taken in the legal *"freedom of clergy",* i.e. the freedom to teach, the free choice of liturgy and hymns and a simplified oath of clergy, supplemented by the law on the breaking of the parish-tie so that laymen could choose freely to form a congregation around the clergyman who appealed to them. No one was to be forced, not even the faith of the forefathers must be allowed sovereign sway – as in the time of orthodoxy and in the English Established Church, which was petrified in its contrary relationship to the sects outside. Only in a free State Church would the faith of the forefathers be able to benefit society, and what is more, be kept awake through conflict and competition with opponents.

Those of the clergy who were lazy and power-hungry would despair, but "for a clever, industrious minister of the people such a *free State Church* would be a little heaven on earth"!

Once again in this work as throughout the period 1825-34 Grundtvig stood alongside "the old-fashioned believers" against rationalism. The devout meetings are not attacked; the chief opponent as before is the power-mad Clausen-party who now together with the Church constitution and a new uniform ritual would revive the church state of the Middle Ages! The demand for breaking of the parish-tie was also supported by a letter containing the signatures of 581 meeting-people.

On the other hand, with this work Grundtvig concluded the Church battle in the Lindberg form that had so far prevailed – as a battle against false teaching and changes in ritual with the threat of withdrawal from the State Church. From now on the sole order of the day was "Church freedom".

The Clash with Protestantism (1826-34)

The Church battle was a bitter and important clash; but undoubtedly of even more importance for Grundtvig himself was his "unparalleled discovery" in 1825. This was the background for his greatest continuous theological work, *On True Christianity and on the Truth of Christianity*, twelve long essays in *Theological Monthly* 1826-27, 432 pages in all when they were published under one cover in 1865; and they actually are a unit with no clear distinction between the two viewpoints that are hinted at in the titles. The work was resumed and was not really finished until *Should the Lutheran Reformation Really Continue?* which as mentioned appeared in Lindberg's monthly journal 1830-31 (see p. 239). In addition to this and the shorter essays – there was the gradual incorporation of the same basic ideas into Grundtvig's preaching, *Christian Sermons or The Sunday Book* in three volumes, 1827-31, and his sermons in Frederik's Church in the first years, around 1832-34, which can be regarded as the conclusion of this line of development.

At first one notes some uncertainty in Grundtvig's theological understanding of himself. What was it actually that he had discovered? *The Church's Retort* was a leap forward, but in several respects so sharp a break with his previous thought that for the next six years he had to repeat and rethink his mental development in July-August 1825. The result was surprising; a clash not only with the modern theology of his age, but also with the orthodox Lutheran, of which he had so far been the spokesman.

The crucial development took place in *the twelve essays* 1826-27. Here we can follow directly the genesis of what was later called Grundtvig's "view of the Church", and we can see how it immediately cast new light on other important questions.

The clash with his age begins in classic Lutheran fashion – on the basis of the New Testament – in the first three essays on true Christianity (January-March 1826). They explicitly defend "the Christianity of our Lutheran fathers" in Luther's little catechism and the Augsburg Confession. That *this* is the real Christianity must be self-evident even for lay people who read the New Testament in translation. Grundtvig refers to the story and significance of Jesus according to the evangelists, not least John the Evangelist's words on the unity with Christ, on Christ as the true vine and so on, and to the apostles' teachings as the only true interpretations of Jesus' words. When the rationalists claim that the apostles did not understand Jesus, they are only proving that they are not looking – as the orthodox Lutherans were – for the real, original Christianity according to "the precepts of the New Testament", but consider their intellect to be the viceroy for Christ, just like the pope in Rome. In this way theologians make themselves masters of the faith of the Church and "what else is the papacy but a *selfmade* Christianity that they seek to impose on the Church of Christ"!

This line of argument is presumably linked to the libel suit going on at the same time. If Grundtvig was to make "the law" take effect, he had to build on the official basis of the Danish Church. When he set to work again, with a new series of six essays (June-December 1826), he had resigned his ministry and could therefore develop his "Lutheran Catholicism from a free platform" (see p. 234). Already in the June booklet he had reservations about his previous written theological defences of Lutheran Christianity. Many theologians, including younger ones, would answer that there is no way of deciding what Christianity actually is. Who says that the words of Jesus and the apostles have been preserved uncorrupted? And even if they had, they maintain, Christianity would disappear like dew in the sunshine after a historico-critical study of the original texts. In the face of this the untrained congregation is at the very least helpless and left to blind faith in the nearest clergyman. Nor does it help to follow the practical path out of the heart's desire and experience since that is an unsafe foundation carrying the risk of self-deception.

In this situation Grundtvig turns *against* orthodox Lutheranism. The desperate state of the Church is due to the fact that the Reformation did not destroy the papacy, but only dispersed it to the individual religious communities with their ratified symbolic books or confessionary writings and the corresponding dogmatic systems. This was the real revelation, i.e. a merely human testimony – and who cannot see here the roots of the dominant exegetical anarchy?

It is necessary to take *another path* – realize that true Christianity really is to be passed on by human testimony, but that it must be looked for in the history of the Church. That is where it is to be found.

This is where the New Testament belongs as a human testimony of the earliest history of the Church; it is not a revelation as the Lutheran theologians claimed. That way would not lead into a church but into a "school" which would grow old and pass away like all other human work. This had been Grundtvig's own worry in his relationship to his audience and the whole of "the scattered flock", since he stood "between systematic unbelief and undisciplined piety". But in the midst of this worry he found the answer: are you asking for true Christianity, and do you mean by that the *Christians'* faith and hope? Then the answer is easy, for if the Christians did not have that faith and that hope, which from the first they had confessed to and been baptized in, then of course they had nothing at all – which cannot possibly be supposed about the untold millions who have acknowledged the faith, many of whom valued it higher than life. *That* is the living testimony which has gone from mouth to mouth in Christ's Church, independent of schools and parties in Christendom.

This is amplified in the following essays. The Lutheran method of written theology has not merely been rendered impossible by biblical criticism, but is *in itself misleading*. It confuses the Bible with Christianity, whose fundamental concept has been found in the Church by all those who have been baptised, namely in the baptismal confession itself. This fundamental concept is not found quite so clearly in the Scriptures, and even when it is, it remains only "in a written confirmation by men who have long since passed away, men whose truth can only be confirmed by a living testimony". The Lutheran theologians therefore made a strange detour when they took the fundamental concept of Christianity down into the kingdom of death, to which all writing belongs by its nature. We "would be standing on the Bible, instead of placing it to be read on the altar, and we would be deriving Christianity from a *book,* which ... without the light of the Spirit and the life of faith serves only to create a snoring congregation, a thorny fence of sophistries, an iceberg of dogmatics and a flood of sermon-collections!" The Bible is an indispensable "Church Book", beneficial in relation to the degree of faith and enlightenment, but it does not defend itself (see p. 90), let alone the Church, whose cause cannot be decided by the feuding pens of scribes. On the contrary, it is the Church that must defend the Scriptures, the Church whose living concept is the Word of Faith that we confess and preach.

"Such a strange way this leaf has been turned over", writes Grundtvig. Before he was fighting "against thousands" for Lutheran Christianity as the only true one; now that he is contradicting that claim he finds himself even more on his own, accused of Catholic tendencies. But do not both Catholics and Protestants declare everyone a Christian who has been baptised with the same Creed and renunciation of the Devil? So it ought now to be possible to make *peace in Christendom*. Peace after "the great revolutionary war" of three hundred years, which has not only divided Protestants and Catholics but has given rise to innumerable internal conflicting religious communities and parties. The unity of the Church rests on baptism alone. There are other things that are part of the worship of the same God: the ten commandments, the communal service, the ministry, Holy Communion, the Lord's Prayer and the Holy Scriptures; but those who have "idiosyncratic" opinions about these can only be excluded by the brotherhood of communion, not by the Church.

Since it is the theologians who have created the division, Grundtvig places great emphasis on the difference between *faith and theology*, Church and "School". As a theologian he had to fight against the papacy and maintain the importance of ordination, including the unbroken episcopal ordination (with "apostolic succession"), which he misses in the Danish Church. But he will not accuse other interpretations of this as heresy. This point of view remains consistently radical; theology has dogmas, but the Church has none. As a community of believers it has only faith, hope and love, and is only answerable for what it "gives living expression to" in the Creed and the sacraments. The symbolic books of the Church must all be regarded as historical documents of the Church. The Church has nothing to do with the theological musings over "the incomprehensible Godhead", for example, on the doctrine of the Trinity, the doctrine of the Atonement and of the Eucharist. On the other hand the Church cannot do without "a theological high school" to throw light on the content of the faith; but everything over and above "basic Christianity" must only "go out to the Church as clarification, advice and exhortation, of which each must take what he likes."

In the spring of 1827 Grundtvig concluded with three essays (March-May). The first two do not contain much that is new; it is worth noticing, however, that now Grundtvig even declares himself in agreement with "the new theologians" at several points, for example, the fact that one cannot prove the truth of Christianity through the Old Testament prophecies and the miracles in the New Testament. In one of the previous essays he had rejected the orthodox theologians' explaining away of the discrepancies between the evangelists; he had become aware of the fact that they only increase the historical reliability of the evangelists.

But the final essay is an important one, because Grundtvig here for the first time in detail works out the difference between *words and writing* which was subsequently to take up such a central place in his world of ideas. This was a new realisation; earlier he had believed, he says, that every educated reader could see what Christianity was from the Scriptures. But he now saw that that was a mistake. The paper is dead and the letters are dead without faith and power. Faith comes from *hearing,* hearing "the Word of Faith that we preach". As he often did later Grundtvig is referring here to Romans 10: 6-17; but he maintains that the difference between words and writing is a common, *natural fact,* and "the natural always comes first", also among Christians.

The spoken word has a natural life and takes a natural priority over all letters – despite its abuse as parrot talk. Even the clearest book cannot be understood unless one knows the "word through hearing it". One reads as one is; a grammarian's and a "poet's" reading give widely different results. The poet takes life with him to the book, "listens in a way through his eye". It is impossible to see the spirit in letters without seeing with the eye of the spirit, that is, a poetic eye. In addition to this, every language has a particular spirit that controls the language of the people in all its glory. It is the oral word of this that the scribe can hide in books; but the spirit of the language hovers over all writing and and deftly puts the word into its reader's mouth that it took from the writer's. Thus the marvellous thing can happen that a book from ancient days puts a living word into our mouths which we are moved by and which we can move others with when we have a "language" in common with the writer. But it must be called a natural miracle since it apparently finds its explanation in "the wonderful nature of man".

From this viewpoint we must regard *the Bible.* Its supernatural origin is clear from the living effect it has had through its unique power, in all languages, even though it is written in a language long dead. It must be because all people are originally of one race with the same language, as the Bible says. When the apostles could speak every language it is due to the fact that the Spirit of Christ was the first spirit of the original primeval language, that is, the spirit of the human race. The "Word of Faith" in the Church is thus the renewed language of the human race; and with this language the Church is a special people, the "Christian people", who have the same relationship to the Bible as a natural people has to its own ancient books. Faith as well as the Bible can only come alive through supernatural means: baptism, Holy Communion, ordination, but in the Church of Christ there comes "a wonderful collaboration" of natural and supernatural powers. That is why the writers of the Bible can *speak* in the languages of the nations.

In the Middle Ages the biblical word became almost frozen at source, but then Christianity gave the languages of the nations a new "flexibility", corresponding to the biblical word: and for Luther, who had special poetic and prophetic abilities, the Bible became of a sudden "a gold mine, a sea of light, a source of life", in which spirit, word and writing fused together. Luther, however, gave priority to the individuality of the scribe, who should have been placed last; and the Lutherans adhered to his and the Bible's letter. But Luther cannot be systematised or imitated without creating a "kingdom of shadows". The error of Lutheranism was its lifelessness or its sickly life; but in spite of everything it far surpassed the "black death" of modern self-conceit. Through orthodox Lutheranism Grundtvig had himself acquired his childhood faith which led him to the Scriptures and on to seek *the chain*, "the living band" that joins the Church through all time with the apostolic Church, through the testimony of one generation to another. Now it is a question of "challenging death in all its forms", first and foremost through hymns and sermons in the spirit of the language as a living Church testimony that can set free, bear again and renew the shivering, sighing human race to a community with the God whose nature is love itself.

The essay ends with an optimistic look forward, and at many points it actually presages Grundtvig's efforts in the coming decades. But it also marks the distance from his starting point. Although heavy in its form there is a tremendous movement in his thought in these twelve essays. The clash with rationalism about written theology contains three different points of view. It is the Church's "border fortress", its invariable rule of faith, and for the individual an "oath of faith", which is to be taken on entering the Church. But it is also the essence of Christianity, uniting all Christian generations and communities. Finally, it is – particularly in the last essay – "the living Word of Faith" which must be proved by a corresponding oral declaration of faith. Grundtvig now maintained all three viewpoints in his "view of the Church", but with varying weight and various modifications.

The closest continuation was *Should the Lutheran Reformation Really Continue?*, which was published in parts during the winter of 1830-31. But in fact it is one long essay partly summarising and partly elaborating the result of the twelve essays assembled round their major subject: the attitude to the Reformation. The first part *defends* Luther against rationalism. He did not actually introduce anything new, but saw that "light and life in the ancient faith" were missing; he awakened the sleeping and the dead, and he cleared away what conflicted with the spirit of Christianity and hindered spiritual development in his day. This purification of the Church must "be continued with enthusiasm", this time as a purge of the philosophical, theological papacy, which was undermining the foundations of the Church: faith and baptism. Not one link in the Creed can be abandoned! In the second part, on the Church and State, this leads to the demand for a "divorce" between the Christians and their opponents (see p. 236).

The third and longest part, on Church and School (theology), resumes the attack on the *Lutheran scriptural theology,* illuminated in a historical perspective. The confusion of faith and theology began already in the early Church as a result of the clash with heretics and also internally between the bishops. This trend was strengthened in the Empire Church after Constantine the Great through a number of "spiritual assemblies", which became battlefields of Church politics. In the Eastern Church theologians from Alexandria also introduced an airy and arbitrary (allegorical) exegesis under the influence of pagan philosophy. The Western Church saw the rise of the hierarchy and the papacy, which attempted to recreate Rome's supremacy; this was a lesser evil since the bishops controlled the theology and adhered to the baptismal covenant on "the principle of life". But they introduced much that was new into the Articles of Faith, and in the face of this it was Luther's achievement to open the Bible to the congregation, to educate them in the unchanging Christian faith and to safeguard them from the "fairy-tales, silly dreams and lies" of the papal Church.

The error of the Reformation is then shown in more or less the same way as in the twelve essays. Even though Luther built in practice on the Creed, he used scripture as its basis; and in the interpretation the reformers took over the Alexandrian method, mediated by the Greek studies of the Renaissance. But the early Church did not have the New Testament: the apostles preached the word about the crucified man, just as in our Creed. Nor is it through reading the Bible that one joins the Church but by baptism; and even though the Bible is "the most outstanding book", being a book it can grant neither forgiveness of sins nor eternal life. With the Lutheran scriptural theology came the stigmatization of theological opponents and complete religious communities; but there is no essential difference between those who have the same baptismal covenant. The School, theology, should on the contrary enjoy full freedom within the limits that the baptismal faith sets. The Church must remain on its rock, but the school must go forward and keep pace with the times and its education of man, society and the world in general. Also in that sense the Reformation must be continued. With these words Grundtvig finished discussing his view of the Church for the time being. Its place in his *preaching* was another matter, however. His view can clearly be seen in the preface to *The Sunday Book* (September 1827), which begins, "To preach is not to write with pen and ink, but in the power of the spirit and with a *living* voice to preach *the Word of Faith:* the great gospel of the Saviour from the city of David..." Whereupon echoes sound of the twelve essays on the Creed as the basis for both "light and life", in contrast to the old orthodoxy. But apart from that, this line of thought has not left deep traces in the first two volumes (1827-28), which reproduce Grundtvig's sermons in the Church of Our Saviour in an expanded form, richer in thought and imagery. In these books Grundtvig has apparently not found it necessary to emphasize his view of the Church in his preaching. The sermons in the Church of Our Saviour were already a preaching of the Word of Faith in a broader sense, and already then they bore a certain "Church" stamp (see p. 119). Above all he discovered a long continuity in the central preaching (of the core) of the gospel, right back to the early Lutherans (in twelve essays); and at his anniversary as a clergyman in 1836 he assured the guests that he himself had been preaching the same faith for 25 years, ever since his ordination in 1811.

But when he began in 1828 on *the third volume of The Sunday Book –* which on account of his England trips was not finished until the spring of 1831 – he felt that there were still several things he had not "spoken out on". The result was that this volume continuously circles round "Faith and baptism in larger and smaller circles" (according to a letter to G. Busck). It is more or less independent of the sermon model; now it is the line of thought in the twelve essays and the essay on the continued reformation which break through in Grundtvig's preaching. The contexts are many and various, but there is only room here to hint at some of the main ideas.

The book has the same two fronts as the theological essays: not just against rationalism, but above all against Lutheran scriptural theology. *Rationalism,* says Grundtvig in one of the sermons, began around 1800 by declaring open war on Christianity, but it then tiptoed in gently with praise for Jesus' life and teaching, so as to fight the ancient Church faith with the help of the Bible; baptism and Holy Communion were out-of-date liturgy, and the old hymns were suppressed. "The living Church community with the Lord and each other" was to be replaced by the Scriptures. But the only true Christianity is the faith of the Church on the basis of the baptismal covenant, and that demands no more than childlike faith; it "calls all children and all those who labour and are heavy laden". The child's faith, which Grundtvig often stresses, is regarded without sentimentality; everything human is mysterious and Christianity is impenetrably mysterious, where the individual must begin like a child and grow to greater clarity just as natural human life grows and just as Jesus Himself grew up. Understanding must grow but the complete insight will not be achieved in the earthly life.

This line of thought is also used against the *Lutheran scriptural theology*. The Lutheran age resembled Christ's descent to the kingdom of the dead: "the body of the Church", which should embrace the whole Christian Church, was dead for us and our fellowship was all but broken down when the Church built on a book. All the content of Christianity was deduced by scriptural wisdom and focused on "the law's thunder" and Christ's death on the cross. It was poor fare for women and children and felt like a heavy and dead weight on the hearts of youth and the peasantry. But what our forefathers sowed with tears, we shall now reap. The angel of the children's faith has rolled the stone away from "the scriptural grave"; the body of the Church is resurrected and begins a new life, in which the Word of Faith "wanders alive on the wings of the spirit and of the breath we draw" and announces Christ's presence amongst us as the living Word, whose life is the light of man!" Already here on earth we can catch a glimpse of heaven and come to know in part what will there be revealed, when like children we believe in everything that has been shared with us in baptism and in Holy Communion through "the spoken Word of God". "The main cause is life, which through this discovery wells out of every believing heart."

This understanding of "the Word of Faith" as a present and recreating life is typical of the sermons; but it is no less a polemic against scriptural theology. This is taken up again and again, often with a sally against all forms of "book-learning". The academic world is nothing but a world of shadows, he says; you shrink up in the dead air of a study into a sort of mummy, thinking and talking like a book and treating everybody like a book. The more lonely a life you lead the more you centre on yourself. When all you do is turn pages and write letters, you even feel free of guilt. It is called self-denial to isolate yourself from other people and you find your own picture in heathen descriptions of paragons of virtue or biblical accounts of true Christians. Scriptural theologians in particular are tempted to self-conceit and self-righteousness but that righteousness belongs nowhere else but in the "monk's cell" and the study. "In fact, my friends, it is impossible to describe what a wretched, miserable, empty and lifeless, impotent shadow-picture their righteousness is!"

Later in the book he warns younger theologians in particular against trusting their own spirit, developed by Bible-reading and serious after-thought. The result may well be a worldly wisdom whose thinking about the divine things is dead and powerless, however "biblical" it may be. Nowhere does the Devil create havoc as in the study; every time a new light rises for us above the depths in God and man, we are tempted in many ways to kick over the traces. But stop; immerse yourselves in the faith which alone can bring salvation to both scholar and layman, put your hands together in Jesus' name and say the Lord's Prayer!"

This warning and criticism of study-scholarship was doubtless also directed at Grundtvig himself, just as similar thoughts in the twelve essays were. Grundtvig often called himself a "bookworm", and there is no denying that he was to a great degree; occasionally he also revealed – as in the period of his youth under Schelling's influence – a tendency to speculative theological thinking. His concentration on the "child's faith", the Creed and the sacraments can perhaps be partly understood as a personal counter-balance to this.

Through the third volume of *The Sunday Book* Grundtvig had in all essentials found the path that he was afterwards to follow in his preaching. The connection with his *sermons in Frederik's Church* is a close one, both in thought and in time; there are only six months between the publication of *The Sunday Book*'s third volume and Grundtvig's first sermons in Lindberg's meetings which from March 1832 continued in Frederik's Church. But the form of these sermons is different: they are on the whole shorter and in a simpler and calmer devotional style. In this respect they denote a new departure for Grundtvig, and are the basis for his uninterrupted activity as a preacher from now on. On the other hand there are obviously practical reasons for this change of form. The third volume of *The Sunday Book* contained meticulously composed "Sermon Studies", which, applying the arts of rhetoric and poetry and the style of polemical controversy presented Grundtvig's "view of the Church" for educated readers; but the sermons in Frederik's Church are only known from the notes that formed the basis of Grundtvig's oral preaching.

In addition to this he formed a new appreciation of *his audience*. According to its preface *The Sunday Book* was aimed at both Christians and "the multitude of baptized heathens", whom Grundtvig had also taken into consideration in the earlier sermons in the Church of Our Saviour. But the demand in the Church battle for full religious freedom and a "divorce" between Christians and non-Christians had changed his attitude. At the end of *The Sunday Book* he stresses the fact that Christians everywhere are a little flock, and it does not benefit "Sunday life" if others feel forced to go to Church, "that heathen and unbelievers imitate our customs". In an essay from about the same time on the continuation of the Reformation he directly disavows his former confusion of "talk with the world" and "talk to the believers".

The consequence was the wish to form a free church, a wish that, though illegal, was partly fulfilled in February 1832 when Grundtvig began to speak at the devout meetings. Here the divorce had been accomplished, so that Grundtvig could now "talk to the believers"; his first sermon or talk at Lindberg's meetings had as its theme, "It is good to be here". In the next he addressed the meeting as "friends, brothers and sisters in Christ"; he did not care much for the world's judgement, but for their sakes he would explain his ideas on Church freedom, which ought to be put into effect as peacefully as possible. And in his first sermon in Frederik's Church he gave powerful expression to his joy that now he was allowed to preach with no other link to his audience than their "common faith and mutual love and Christian friendship".

Considerations of space must limit a more precise discussion of the contents. The essential element everywhere is "the Word of the living God" in baptism and Holy Communion, which "develops out of itself the whole richness of the blessing Christ's gospel". This is strongly emphasized as being present reality as it is experienced; for example, as expressed in John's words: We have all gone over from death into life. But it is always a message that *fights* its way forward with death and damnation, doubt and the "mockery of the world" as its background.

The Word of Faith is the word of the cross, and at the cross is where we must always stand, he says; but the Word of Faith comes alive in our mouths and hearts, the crucified is resurrected in us and for us, and then the words of the Lord in the Bible are also revived one after the other, "they walk out of the grave and into the holy city". When the living word blazes up before our eyes, we see beside our own black misery the endless riches of God's grace; our soul is raised up from the abyss and thus we can regard nature and ourselves with controlled yet calm joy "which resembles most a summer's day in late harvest-time". Only with the Christian "hope of immortality" can we find this earth lovely and the temporal life glorious for those who have come to know the truth in Christ. The world mocks this hope, and we ourselves have moments when it seems to us unreasonable. Christians are not exempt from the toil and bitterness of the earth, but resurrected with Christ we must "not

252

regard what is on the earth but what is in heaven, where Christ sits at God's right hand".

Cultural Collaboration (1820-25, 1826-34)

The development in Grundtvig's cultural outlook in 1826-34 was not characterized so much by a new departure as by a gradual elaboration, furthered especially by his clash with the State Church and with protestantism from around 1826. But his point of departure was actually "the historical view" that he had reached in the period 1815-20 (see p. 107). The connecting line back to this period must therefore be briefly outlined.

The main idea in the periodical, *Danevirke* 1816-19, and his essays of the time was that Christianity and truth are not two things but one. Christianity may be a supernatural revelation but it involves human existence. "The historical view" implies, however, that this connection is not unchanging (as is the relationship natural-supernatural in orthodox and rationalist theology), nor is it a conceptual fusion (as in idealistic philosophy). The context is of a "historical" nature. The Creation itself involves history, in so radical a sense as appears in the *World Chronicle* of 1814: in spite of the fall God in Christ fulfils the destiny of man through history (cf. p. 109). This happens through struggle, the struggle of history, which is also the struggle of Christianity and of truth.

But the result of the historical outlook of *Danevirke* was a tremendous hope of victory, a hope for the future: who can doubt the victory of truth when he has felt the quickening of "the call to man from heaven to work and fight for truth, and out of that to bring that picture to life on earth"! And "whoever could regard with sparkling eyes the victorious path of truth through the passing ages" – and yet doubt "that true illumination will go on until the sun and all the stars melt into one eternal light; that mankind will reach its goal historically, as truth will reach her"! (1818).

This is the line of thought that forms the basis for Grundtvig's use of *spirit* as a human historical concept, as the power that drives mankind on in history's struggle, borne up by higher powers that lead on to the goal or destiny of mankind, of the nation and of history. Spirit is not an aesthetic or a psychological concept, nor is it a philosophical concept of the ideal; on the contrary it is closely linked to history. In opposition to this there appears to Grundtvig to be a *main opponent* behind all the separate battles, the crass materialism or "idiot-faith" which for many was the outcome of the 18th century enlightenment: "that man is in fact a beast, a two-legged creature... not created in God's image to eternal life but in the Devil's image to an earthly monkey who imitates what he never saw and covets what he cannot imagine" – a spiritual cipher, a spiritless rational fathead who signifies nothing (1818).

Grundtvig had fought this view of man historically by describing the achievements of the past, especially with the aid of the Chronicles of Saxo and Snorri, and in addition with a "philosophy" of the human condition based on experience. Both historically and philosophically he built on Christianity, but his view of history had far greater breadth than his Christianity, and it appealed to every intelligent reader of whatever faith.

Thus in the last volume of *Danevirke* he was able to advocate a *meeting on history's ground,* directed against the unhistorical revolutionary "somersaults" of youth which in Grundtvig's opinion were what characterized the contemporary German student movement and corresponding trends in Denmark and other countries. We are standing at a turning-point, he writes in 1818, can you not see that, history is the ground on which the battle must be fought, that it is on the course of history we must fight! ... make haste, vie with us to illuminate and fathom the depths of history." – "Unchristian you may be, but at least be *reasonable*": do not make yourselves ridiculous by pleading your infallible reason – a self-conceited, unhistorical "non-spirit", but "look to it that you find the historical way of reasoning". The appeal also builds on the national tendency in *Danevirke,* the praising of the ancient Danish humbleness, fairness, and "feeling for history" in contrast to grandiloquent ideas from abroad. All Danes should "unite to make peace with one another and support each other in the battle against everything that is un-Danish in literature and therefore unhistorical", unite in "a coherent and inspired effort", "a living battle for the true, the noble, the great".

This broad appeal to peace and struggle formed the background for reflections on the relationship between *Church, State and School.* For Grundtvig had to admit that he had failed to appreciate the distinction between eternal and temporal truth. Despite three long essays on the subject in the last volume of *Danevirke* Grundtvig did not reach a clear differentiation, bound as he was by his concept of universal Christianity. But he worked his way up to a stronger emphasis on the "temporal" and therefore relatively independent character of the State and School in relationship to the Church. In this connection an unpublished retrospect of the time (brought to light by Dr. Lundgreen-Nielsen) is of interest for its positive attitude to new Danish literature on the lines of Steffens and Oehlenschläger and for its resumption of Norse mythology. Grundtvig was now able to defend his youthful enthusiasm for "Aesir teaching", underlining it as a metaphorical anticipation of "mankind's historical path" and as an expression of the giant Norse spirit: the battle between the Aesir and the giants is "the historical, viz. temporal condition of life".

The idea of cooperation received clearer expression in a series of letters from Grundtvig to Steffens in 1818-24, for the most part unposted drafts, partly unprinted. Grundtvig had renewed his former enthusiasm for Steffens as a result of Steffens' new work: *The Present Time and How it came into Being* (1817). The most important drafts, from April 1820, are inspired by this book. Steffens had amongst other things stressed the advantages of "the living word" in his academic lectures, and Grundtvig, who never forgot Steffens' own "living words" in 1802-03, immediately applauded this idea. It did not really mean much to him until his clash with protestantism in 1826-27. But he was very much occupied by the wide-reaching agreement he had found between the two of them as regards a view of history: "not in any one or combined brain but only in history will we see one statute-book for the course and development of human life".

On the other hand, he did not attempt to conceal the fact that they were "in great disagreement on the Church" – for Steffens had been the standard-bearer for natural philosophy in Denmark. But even so they could "agree a great deal on the school", that is, on the cultural outlook. So Grundtvig proposed to Steffens "a literary union". In spite of their disagreement over the Church they must both be able to agree that "the course of historical scholarship follows the same path to reach its goal". – "Where the human spirit has its house and in what relationship it places the individual, self-aware, human being to the source, viz. to God, is a purely Church question; but that the human spirit, wherever it comes from, must find its way home again, and through history reach home, transfigured, that is not in question with us ... whatever is with the seal of truth written in history as the temporal statute-book of the spirit which we must abide by in order to move forward – that is a "School" matter to which all, with the same eyes, must answer alike".

Grundtvig had thus found his way back to the essence of the romanticism of his youth and also the basis for working together with all who shared the same point of departure as he and Steffens, all "Naturalists with spirit", as he called them (1832).

As a *minister in the State Church from 1821 to 1826* Grundtvig was bound by the many and various duties that were incumbent upon the clergy of the time, and in particular the major task he felt himself called to: to renew the ancient preaching of "God's Word" and to defend true Christianity against contemporary rationalism. But he did not abandon his historical and poetic interests. The last volume of the Saxo and Snorri translations was not published until June 1823, and a couple of months later he announced that the King had given him the job of writing a continuation of Saxo's History of Denmark. An unpublished subscription invitation shows a little later that he was now considering a complete history of Denmark-Norway in five parts. In the preface to *New Year's Morn* (August 1824) Grundtvig again announces his continuation of "the ancient Norse Chronicles" as well as writing hymns in an old style and historical poems. It appears that he now regarded this as his real "day's work" and his ministry as temporary; for his historical and poetic work he hoped to find "a friendly little place", probably Sorø Academy, an academic school with university traditions, where his friend Ingemann was working. From this point of view he was also able to regard his resignation in May 1826 as a release. He had now fulfilled his purpose in the State Church with his ministry in Copenhagen, and since the libel suit proved that opposition to false teaching was not tolerated, even though his oath as a clergyman demanded it, he could thus resume his historical and poetic work with a clean conscience.

There is much evidence to prove that also in his years in the ministry Grundtvig maintained and defended "the historical view" of mankind. This is clear from his sermons and especially in his many attempts in 1823-24 to defend Christianity from both historical and philosophical viewpoints; only a part of this work was printed (in *Theological Monthly 1825*, c. 200 pages). Here he again took up the fight begun in *Danevirke* against the spiritual death of the 18th century. This is the case in the essay *Rome and Jerusalem*, in which it is traced back to the Roman robber-state which was only interested in ruling and indulging and therefore tore apart the ancient "primitive peoples". From this sprang "the Roman spirit" which reached its culmination in the 18th century, characterized by the spiritless endeavours of reason to control and order everything, including all that is obscure and passionate in mankind. For the 18th century presupposed that the human race had reached a definitive point of clarity. Its opposite was the kindred feelings of primitive peoples and patriotism, and in particular the Judeo-Christian view of life, according to which human existence could not really be grasped or governed. Man is the "strange creature who cannot set his hand to anything or open his mouth to speak without revealing or reproducing something spiritual, something invisible, without showing what he is thinking and desiring".

At the same time he felt the need to clarify the coherence of his life, as he had done in the previously mentioned *Exchange of Letters* from the spring of 1824 (see p. 226). Here he defended in particular the time

Marie Toft, née Carlsen (1813-54),
Grundtvig's second wife.
(Royal Library, Copenhagen).

Rønnebæksholm, Marie Toft's manor-house, near Næstved. After her death Grundtvig wrote the poem *My Friend and Wife. In memory of my Marie on her birthday* (Poetical Writings VIII, p. 94) This includes the following verse: To me she was so loving/To me she was so wise/A lovely lioness she was/I never would have thought/Our land could be so rich/That it had such a woman/She was the threefold rose.

This refers to Marie's family coat-of-arms, which contains three roses on a silver field.

Grundtvig's home from 1859 to 1867, which he called "Happy Home". He was newly married, and although he was 75 he acquired a flock of small children in his household. In addition to Frederik (b. 1854), his son by Marie, he had a daughter by Asta Reedtz, his third wife, as well as the four small children she brought with her from her first marriage. The three children in the foreground are presumably hinting at this large family.
(From A Hundred Years. A Memorial Volume, ed. F. Rønning, 1883).

Grundtvig's study in his last home, *Store Tuborg*. It could only hold a fraction of his large library.

before 1811, his "mythological period": "the truth that everything noble, great and powerful in mankind is God's work and that the corporeal only finds its worth and its meaning when it is seen as an image of and a tool for the spiritual – this truth, which in fact all mythologies have in common with Christianity, was clearly the central point around which all my talk turned". To this period he added two more: "the theological" from 1811-15, in which Christianity became "the *only* means of salvation", and "the historical" from 1815, which was not yet in fact finished: "Everything I have written since is concerned with the claim that also in great matters one becomes wise only through experience", and that therefore only history, which embraces all things human, can connect and clarify it.

He wrote a similar retrospect the same summer in the preface to *New Year's Morn* and even in the long, often mysterious poem itself. When the preface speaks of Denmark as "the Palestine of History" the background is his efforts in the *Danevirke* period to revive the "wonderful heritage" of the people, and this line of thought plays a central part in the poem. Grundtvig imagines a continuous folk-tradition from the ancient songs of gods and heroes through legends, proverbs and ballads to Saxo's narratives on Christian achievements and the old hymns of the Lutheran period. Throughout the people have been searching for "the land of the living", which is the start and finish of history, and have listened to the words of the "father of the race".

> But little it pays
> To build on earth;
> Far better to follow
> The rolling wave
> That comes from the land of the living.

The rolling wave is the same as the "river of history", another favourite picture expressing the living tradition of the people, the oral nature of which is emphasized, and it is Grundtvig's hope that this "wave" will melt the "iceberg" of the age of enlightenment.

The poem also draws attention to the new literary movement in Denmark, which began with Steffens and Oehlenschläger and had been continued by Ingemann and Grundtvig himself. Not long after, in October 1824, a letter to Steffens praises his importance in high tones: spurred on by "the Norse spirit" you opened up to "us a glimpse of history's wonderful path, of Christ as the divine midpoint and our age as the whitewashed grave"; all Grundtvig's own efforts – which he briefly outlined – had sprung from this. The letter was his reaction to the unsuccessful meeting with Steffens (see p. 227), whose criticism had not moved him "a hair's breadth" from the path that Steffens himself had set him on.

He developed his view in greater detail in the unprinted essay *On War and Peace* from the autumn of 1825. The renaissance had been started by Steffens and Oehlenschläger in whom the spirit of the North arose again and showed how highly it valued Christianity; Oehlenschläger had since gone back on his principles, under the influence of the older Goethe, but the "ancient heroic spirit of the North" had also taken hold of Grundtvig and Ingemann, and there was no doubt that "its ancient words combined with new ones" had the power to "sweep out of the country all that spiritless lettering which ... is born on thoughts where the body is the main thing, that is, in the land of the monsters".

In Grundtvig's cultural outlook there were thus no serious obstacles to his establishing a friendly relationship with his literary age, insofar as it developed under the inspiration of Steffens. He had also expressed his *wish* for cooperation. His main obstacle lay with the Church, or rather, with the fusion of Christianity and ordinary life-philosophy whether it be of a rationalist or a romantic, idealist nature. Grundtvig could therefore do battle on behalf of "true Christianity", "ancient Christianity", without appearing intolerant and anti-cultural to contemporary eyes. But this obstacle disappeared to the same degree that Grundtvig reached clarification on "the historical Christian Church" as a given and historical reality that did not require a defence. It thereby became possible for him to distinguish more clearly between faith and philosophy for his own benefit.

The Church's Retort already hints at the new basis of cooperation through a return to the distinction between Church and School. It was a provocative challenge to battle, a sharp defence of the Church's faith; but precisely because of this background it demanded freedom "in the School", the right to differing theological views, and full religious freedom in the State for everyone "in a faith acceptable to society".

The gap between Church and School is also of crucial importance in the twelve essays in 1826-27, the detailed working out of "the Retort's" ideas. Early on, the introductory skirmish against rationalism is turned against the theologians' "spiritual power-madness"; "from that apparently all papacy and hierarchy have stemmed", the Roman, the Lutheran and the rationalist (March 1826). This point of view forms the basis for the major clash with the Lutheran scriptural theology, in which Grundtvig amongst other things allows the dogmas outwardly to disappear as points of controversy; they are for the "Church scholars only". The principle element becomes the oral transmission of the faith of the Church – with the "living words" of the sacraments as its focal points – which leads to a division between words and writing, both in the Church and in the popular tradition.

Several private letters from the same time (1826-c.1830) reveal Grundtvig's growing enthusiasm for the living oral word as being more important than all "written controversies", as the direct expression of what lives "in the heart that the mouth draws on".

The Church battle sharpened the controversies but also created the basis for an agreement through Grundtvig's demand for *religious freedom*. In his essays under this title from spring 1827 he took the decisive step of giving up the traditional link between State and Church and demanding a Church "divorce", but social equality for the conflicting Church parties. The fact that through this Grundtvig established a foundation for cultural cooperation can be seen from the important work *The Literary Testament of the Writer N. F. S. Grundtvig,* which he wrote in spring 1827 immediately after the essays on religious freedom.

In form it belongs to the series of retrospects begun in 1824, but here the new departure for the Church since 1825 has shed new light on his writing.

He began by saying that now he had clearly taken up his stand "under the banner of spiritual freedom and enlightenment" and he regretted that he had previously given the opposite impression. There was a long story behind this. The fundamental error of the medieval Church was to imagine that the spirit of Christian people could become the spirit of all people, even though many were only "forced confessors of the faith"; the result was a hostile ferment among the people against the Church. This was redeemed at the Reformation, but the Church's coercion continued also in the protestant countries with the suppression of "the spirits of the various peoples". The clash came in the 18th century and took the form of a general materialism with the Roman poets being taken as models. But where the ancient spirit of the peoples awoke, the people were recalled to a reverence for "the invisible forces that create living souls", and Grundtvig had followed the "reformation course" in his age, which began in Germany with Schiller, Fichte, Goethe and Schelling and in Denmark with Oehlenschläger.

All his writings were first and foremost a battle against materialism, "the anti-spirit's anti-historical course", whether he had been serving the spirit of the Bible, of history or of the North, all of which were an expression of the same view of mankind. His young readers in the North ought to understand this view: "Listen, younger brothers! ... if there is not by nature a mystery in man that contains within it what no hand has grasped and no pen described, and if there is no wonderful battle in secret between living and dead forces, between the spirits of day and night, a battle in which we ourselves must take a living part ... then I am not a man".

The mistake was that he had confused his work as clergyman and patriot and had dreamed of a complete rebirth of the old Christian popular "twin life in the North". Nowhere had "the Church and social unity" arisen so naturally and continued so undisturbed. But the confusion was nonetheless a mistake, which he had explained in *The Church's Retort* and especially in *Theological Monthly* (the twelve essays). The limits of the State and the Church no longer coincided; the Church community must now be dissolved and the spirit hostile to the Church must be forced into isolation. This had not become clear to him, however, before he had learned to distinguish between the Church and the Church School, that is, between Christianity and theology.

This distinction involves here in particular a dissociation from theological power-madness and uniformity just as in *The Church's Retort* and the twelve essays. But in reality the "testament" also takes up again *the broad concept of School* from the attempt at reconciliation with Steffens in 1820. He classifies most of his efforts so far under what he in those days called "School": the gradual "enlightenment of man", of "the human struggle", reflected in the battle between the Aesir and the giants which was played out in history and is quickened and governed by the spirit of the Bible. With regard to his Church polemics he is now willing to admit only to the one that began with *The Church's Retort,* which was to lead to a Church "divorce" and a gathering of the old believers. On the other hand he set great store by cooperation in civic society: on cohesion in the life of the people, on the connection between the people and the educated and on a spiritual society "with people of others beyond our own fellowship in faith and churchgoers".

Thus the new orientation and the idea of working together in the *Literary Testament* sprang directly out of the Church battle. In the midst of this Grundtvig also sought a *personal reconciliation* with a number of opponents in the knowledge that the clash was only of an ecclesiastical nature – these included Christian Molbech, P. E. Müller (Bishop of Zealand from 1830), Oehlenschläger and H. C. Ørsted. In the period 1811-15 Molbech and Ørsted had been his bitterest opponents when he attacked Schelling's natural philosophy (see p. 104); but now in a letter to Molbech he regretted that at the time he had tried to force the world to become Christian "like a Lutheran monk". His present clash with the Church was concerned with the opposite: that neither in the Church nor in the "School" ought one to "give unchristian material a Christian form"; and he hoped that the conflict would end soon so that he could pursue his heart's delight: "to illuminate both the Christian and the Danish life of the people in previous times", without intervention, linked only where they meet historically (March 1826). In a similar letter of reconciliation to Professor J. F. Schouw he wrote, "It is a time of spring and birth for scholarship, and all honest men who realize this should endeavour to be as good friends and have as living an interaction as possible" (May 1829).

Through his *England trips* (1829-31) Grundtvig came into contact with completely new circles and above all a broader horizon. In addition to his Anglo-Saxon studies they had a further purpose: it was clear to him, as he wrote in March 1830, that "the revival of history is the condition for a scholarship that is beneficial for and reconcilable with Christianity, and that England is the place from which the impetus in this respect must come. Perhaps he was thinking here of the Anglo-Saxon handwritten manuscripts which he was to publish in no fewer than 10 volumes, a task which he only relinquished because, on his own initiative, it was handed over to English research scholars. But his enthusiasm for England had a longer perspective. It was "the spirit of the North allied to Christianity which with the Northern settlers on the island created our people's world". The English "settlers" christianized Germany and the North and established a vernacular literature which has continued ever since with the English Bible and Shakespeare as its high points. Their "historical heroic spirit" expressed itself through the whole of England's history; in his own age Grundtvig had especially been impressed by the free conditions for the Church and society and "the powerful drive towards active effort in the cause of a great purpose" with a respect for their heritage and experience and with an immutable belief in Providence.

The influence of an alternative culture was the immediate background for Grundtvig's appeal on a grand scale for a cultural collaboration between the North and Christianity in his introduction to *Norse Mythology* (1832).

The actual idea of collaboration at this point presented no problem. Only a few weeks after he had raised the question through *Books and Ideas on Naturalism in the North, Past and Present* he could regard it as solved. He wrote about this to a friend, saying that he had now "referred our latest Naturalists to the temple that suited them better than the Christian Church" (October 29th 1831). According to the printed introduction this meant that although the Naturalists did not share Grundtvig's faith, they could – if they had any feeling for spirit – "go to school together" with him on the basis of the Christian philosophy, i.e.

261

the Christian view of man that was related to the Old Norse. Common to this view was that human nature had been damaged and must attempt to understand its disorder; but whereas the Naturalists believed that it could thereby heal itself and regarded Christ only as an ideal, we "old-fashioned Christians" believe that true health is impossible without uniting with "the Godhead's man, Jesus Christ" and experiencing an "ascension" into heaven, "whether we understand it or not".

By "Naturalists" Grundtvig was undoubtedly thinking of people like those mentioned above with whom he had sought reconciliation in the previous years, but presumably also the Clausen-party's "Naturalist clergy". For the collaboration presupposes, as is strongly underlined, that the two sides "each in their Church community" sharply maintain their differences of faith.

What greatly occupied Grundtvig on the other hand, was the aim of the collaboration: a general *cultural renaissance of the North and of the Christian view of man*. Actual work on the mythology began with a coincidence: his first *Norse Mythology* of 1808 had sold out. As he wrote in the letter quoted, he had thus found "a good opportunity to work out and develop many reflections I have long had." The introduction to the new work grew from draft to draft and ended up as a comprehensive attack on contemporary culture.

Since his youth he had perceived his own age as a watershed in history, a thorough-going cultural and social crisis in the wake of the 18th century's worship of reason (see p. 96 and 104). The French revolution would not be the last, and he saw this confirmed in the new French revolution, the July revolution of 1830. In *Political Considerations* (1831) he had warned against the Parisian "schoolboys" and "the wonderful views that will be revealed to us standing on the mountains of corpses, across streams of blood under wild screams of joy from escaped slaves". Where "unbelief, self-conceit and self-righteousness" assumed power they would constantly break out in acts of violence which in the end would disintegrate society. The introduction to *Norse Mythology* has the same point of departure but goes deeper into the problem. It could not be a question of faith, as it was in Grundtvig's youth, but a question of cultural derailment.

It began with "the Roman monster's" oppression of the people, which was continued by the Roman popes and the Latin schoolmasters. Since the Renaissance the consequence had been a literalist, classical learning, foreign to the life of the people and to the mother-tongue, and a view of mankind which insisted on seeing only the clear and the tangible, which dissolved everything spiritual into the four elements and which traced

262

man through the whole animal order to the worms. "Rome's anti-spirit" could therefore only develop animal selfishness and self-conceit. The contrast was first and foremost "the Mosaic-Christian view" according to which mankind is not an unchanging ape, but a "glorious incomparable creature in whom divine powers shall proclaim, develop and enlighten themselves through thousands of generations, as a divine experiment to show how spirit and dust can permeate each other and be transfigured into a common divine consciousness".

The corresponding *Nordic View of Life* was "as a constant battle which it is man's sole purpose to wage as nobly, as powerfully and as wisely as possible". The old Norse heroes were not flawless, but they were right to believe that the din of battle is much better than the peace of the grave. They did not share "the dear philosophers'" dream of eternal peace, but felt that life is the first condition for peace and the free development of energies the other – amongst a living people who feel themselves related to the gods and "are on fire with a higher life-warmth than the inarticulate". There cannot therefore be life in a people, a language or the individual's faith and philosophy unless they endeavour to manifest them. The Church society and the mother-tongue are not airy fragments of the imagination, but spiritual bodies that only survive through victorious battle. "If they are not inspired by a life-spirit which is always a heroic spirit" they can only sink into dissolution and decay as when soul and body are separated.

Therefore all men of the North, hopefully in England and the other Nordic countries too, should unite to lay the foundations of a new "all-embracing spiritual culture and scholarship". It should build on the Bible, the Norse and Greek mythology and on the history of the peoples, but incorporate every skilful endeavour, from mathematics to poetry, and aim at a "universal-historical" transfiguration of the whole of human life, "with all its energies, conditions and achievements". More practically Grundtvig wished first of all for an educated, scholastic training in which the study of Latin should be partly replaced by Icelandic, Greek and New Greek with particular regard for Homer, Herodotus and Plato. Secondly he proposed a "gentleman's academy, undoubtedly on the basis of Sorø Academy, as an education for the people's essential needs, an academy where prospective civil servants, teachers and others, who "would belong to the educated classes", could study the nature, history and language of the fatherland and in addition work for practical skills.

This line of thought was the starting-point for Grundtvig's educational writings after 1835. Of great importance too was an elaboration of his ideas on the difference between *word and writing* linked to his emphasis

263

on the importance of the myths. This difference, according to Grundtvig, is like that between life and death. Books in themselves are dead things, and life is transmitted not by the dead but by the living. Human life rests on spirit, "life-energy"; it expresses itself in words. "The inner living word is the spirit itself, and the corresponding oral word its life-expression". The myths are oral, inspired words in the original picture language of the peoples, sprung from their age of imagination, which according to Grundtvig's Christian view of history contained a higher truth; it was a "relatively innocent" age since it came after the Creation and the Fall (cf. p. 110). Just as he had done in his youth he distinguished between imagination, feeling and intellect, to which corresponded the ages of imagination, feeling and intellect in the development of the peoples and throughout history. The most recent age was on the whole an age of intellect, that is, the old age of the human race. That is why we have "torn down" with all our strength but only "built in ideas". The cultural renaissance presupposes that the inspiration from the myths can give "life-energy, warmth and richness" to the wide-ranging knowledge of the age of intellect, in other words, "the great school-marriage" between intellect and imagination which in the age of intellect must manifest itself in "dramatic poetry". Because intellect applied to human life comes only from experience, historical experience, and because since classical times the North has possessed the sense of unifying poetry and history, there is hope that 'the marriage' can succeed here through a "historical-poetic view of life".

In the North the necessary context of historical tradition is also to be found – in speech, at least in the images and phrases of the language – in writing, through books, by which "the spirit in a way actually mocks death". The introduction to *Norse Mythology* therefore ends – before dealing with the literature of myth – with the well-known popular line of tradition: folk-ballads and hymns, Saxo and the Icelandic literature, historical works and publications etc. – up to Steffens and Oehlenschläger as Grundtvig's own starting-point. "A new-Danish development" was to resume work on and "illuminate" the old-Danish and thus raise itself above the ruins of Roman spiritlessness! "That is what I have worked for all my life", Grundtvig could write in the same sense as in the *Literary Testament,* which in many respects forms the basis of *Norse Mythology.* But all the ideas and concepts found in the introduction build primarily on historical and philosophical considerations of Grundtvig's youth, especially in his "historical period" – 1815-20. Much had been explored since 1825 and much that was new had come into being, not least the demand for the "free development of forces", which is particularly stressed in the introductory *Rhymed Letter to the Norse Kinsmen:*

> Let *freedom* be our Northern watchword,
> Freedom for *Loki* as well as for *Thor*
> As freedom to our new world gave birth
> Let the *word* run free for evermore.
> Land of *thought* and *faith* and *knowledge...*

(With regard to *Norse Mythology* see also p. 212f and to the *Rhymed Letter* p. 272).

Immediately after *Norse Mythology* Grundtvig began on his major historical work: *Handbook on World History.* The first two volumes, on antiquity and the Middle Ages, appeared in 1833 and 1835-36, each of about 700 pages; the third volume began in 1842-43, but was not completed in the same size. In the preface and introduction to the first volume there are clear traces of the collaboration idea; together with a reservation about the *World Chronicles,* an emphasis on the difference between Church and School, temporally and eternally, and a criticism of the scriptural theologians' biblical orthodoxy. The *Handbook* was to be neither a history of the Church nor a history of ideas, but a "constitutional history", using the best sources and the surest facts. And it addressed itself to all Grundtvig's fellow-clergymen, in particular the student youth.

But the *Handbook* was first and foremost a continuation of the cultural battle as it has been waged in *Norse Mythology.* Just as in 1818 he was clearly aware that it is in history that the battle must be fought (see p. 253). He therefore threw himself into the task with a more than usual "fieriness", his own expression. The *Mythology* was published on December 22nd 1832 and contained some 700 pages; two days previously he had announced that the *World History* was going to be printed.

Both introductions, to antiquity and to the Middle Ages, are concerned with his *view of man,* and the same is true of the later introduction to *The New Year* (i.e. modern history). The question was whether man is "an ape of a kind", whether there was a solution to "the fatal disease of school": the tendency to dissolve and reform human life; or whether "Roman reason" should replace life with death and substitute violence and tyranny for justice and freedom. History will "lead the patients into real life", will show that human life really does exist; that man actually regards the whole earth as his kingdom and himself as master over the animals, on the strength of "the mysterious life innermost in us" we call spirit, which manifests itself in a multitude of ways and most powerfully in "the living word". But we receive the word from our parents, from the past, and therefore we must seek illumination on the here and now by turning to the past, if possible all the way back to our first parents. For man is not static like the animals, but changes from generation to generation, and so we must be able to trace a development throughout the history of man that corresponds to what we experience in ourselves.

The *Handbook,* then, is an attempt to "show the thread in the labyrinth of life". It has nothing to do with contemporary or past historical research; its "facts" are in reality the old historical stories in the Bible and in the chronicles of antiquity and the Middle Ages. By retelling these Grundtvig demonstrates "the life and the force" in the peoples and in the great events of history; and only in Christianity and the Christian belief in Providence does he find a reasonable explanation of the human "path": its creation in God's image, the Fall and expulsion from Paradise, which explains that many people "cast their eyes down to the earth and diligently buried themselves in it"; the special situation of the Jews amongst the nations and Christianity's victory over the Roman "kingdom of Hell"; the Church's development of the Germanic-Scandinavian people in the Middle Ages and finally "the New Year", which followed in the steps of the Reformation. History is thus seen in Grundtvig's world history too as a constant battle between belief and unbelief, good and bad, "Aesir" and "monsters". But even though "there will always be more bad than good". It is Grundtvig's hope that the "New Year" – with the aid of the heroic spirit of the North – will prove to be just as glorious in its achievements but calmer and clearer than in antiquity and the Middle Ages. (cf. a more detailed account p. 62).

From 1827 onwards, with the *Literary Testament* as his point of departure, Grundtvig consciously pursued two different courses in his work: a church course and a more "worldly" one. But the one presupposes the other, and they often approached each other. In his *sermons* he was also concerned with his view of man in the same way as in the *Mythology* and in the *World History.* Already in the first volume of *The Sunday Book* he therefore rejected the orthodox Lutheran understanding of the Fall as "a total transformation", as though mankind had thereby become an animal or a devil. He stresses that the true living knowledge of God does not exclude an awareness of the heathen and that it does not make us blind to "earthly beauty" or fearful of "friendly sociability with those who are outside it". A sermon in the third volume builds on the Old Norse myth of the tree of life, Yggdrasill, which is constantly attacked by beasts of prey and dragons and the teeth of time, but still keeps fresh through "drops from the secret well of life, in the hand of Providence". Other sermons inveigh like *Norse Mythology* against the spiritless endeavours of time "to explain away all spiritual greatness, depth and warmth from human life". Thoughts such as these were taken up again in Frederik's Church and throughout Grundtvig's later ministries.

On the other hand the efforts at cultural collaboration, as we have seen, had the *Church battle* as their precondition after 1825. The introduction to *Norse Mythology* was written at its climax, when Grundtvig had decided to start a free church even if it was "in a cave under ground". The Church battle also formed the background for the distinction in the *World History* between Church and School, which did not preclude the handbook's clear biblical-Christian outlook. And the difference between temporal and eternal must be properly understood: "the *temporal* life presupposes the *eternal* and must, wherever a power inspired by it fights *for* it also lead *to that goal*". But Grundtvig now distinguishes between history's long path to truth and the Christian Church's constant meeting with *full truth*, when it is *heard* in the "living word".

The work which for the present concluded the Church battle *An Impartial View of the Danish State Church* (1834), was at one and the same time a church work and a secular work. Like its predecessors it was a defence of the rights of old-fashioned believers, but it was addressed to the State and it stressed their importance in society. The reason given for this proves the coherence of Grundtvig's view of history right from the first *Chronicle:* every nation stands and falls with its religion. The ancient Greek and Roman societies decayed with their folk religion; but the Christian faith has achieved great things in Denmark, and the hope of a national renaissance must be bound up with it.

In particular the ending of the book seems to be related to the ideas of a collaboration in *Norse Mythology*. Whatever their faith the clergy in the State Church ought to form a middle link between academic training and popular education. The "heterodox" naturalist clergy could at least pass on the Bible's historical material in connection with "the main truths of natural religion". But at this point the book came into conflict with itself, for it underlines first and foremost the faith of the Christian forefathers as the basis for the correct "historical enlightenment". Furthermore, its bitter attack on the clergy, the power-mad Clausen-clergy, is sharper than ever.

Grundtvig soon gave up this solution too. Cultural renewal through "the School" could not be left in the hands of the ministers in the State Church. He had to seek another path. This was his main problem in the following years, the period of his educational writings.

B. The Period 1835-47

Patriotic Efforts

Until about 1835 Grundtvig occupied an *isolated position* in relation to the contemporary educated world. In 1834 he himself still regarded his position as that of a "hermit", sequestered in his study, where he buried himself in his work day and night. He had come into contact with several prominent men over the past few years, but Ingemann was still his only poet-friend; the literary world had not noticed his endeavours towards cultural collaboration. *Norse Mythology* and his history of antiquity and the Middle Ages had not even been reviewed, and in the preface to the last volume Grundvig threatened to give up writing, since his "Handbooks were only published with difficulty". Instead he would "make matches"! His own financial circumstances also remained a trial, dependent as he was on gifts and collections.

Together with Ingemann he lamented Oehlenschläger's abandonment of himself to "pleasant and comfortable Goetheanism". In literature, "cold, dead objectivity" held sway, reflecting just as soon the heavenly as the devilish, wrote Ingemann, and in like manner pantheism ruled philosophy: like Goethe and Hegel God actually "died last year", since the god-head's pursuit of consciousness – through plants, animals and men – had ended with them (letters to Grundtvig 1830 and 1833). However, Grundtvig answered this by defending pantheism as more tolerable than atheism and dualism; since pantheism finds God everywhere just as Christianity finds Him "in all that is good", we can "work together with the world" (November 1833).

"Naturalism" was therefore now no more than barely tolerable. There was not much left of the enthusiasm for the collaboration to be found in *Norse Mythology* and Grundtvig even felt that residue was hard to retain. In a poem from roughly the same time, *The Spirit of the Age* (1834), he places both the spirit of Christianity and the "spirit of the North" in sharp contrast to Goethe's spirit, the pantheism worshipped by the age. "We have long *attempted* to reach a compromise", but have merely discovered "that we can both only just manage to exist". He could go along with the spirit of the age in its fight for spiritual freedom against "the anti-spirit", but otherwise they found themselves "on opposite sides". Another contemporary poem, *Norse Gold* (1834), is deeply pessimistic. It looked as if the classical Norse age was about to be buried finally, with Grundtvig as "its last man": "Alas, must I, unappreciated / even by those with poetic insight / be but a name drawn on the black list / in the republic of scholars, / *There* condemned and tied and bound, / I, alone amongst these Romans / stand for the spirit of the North!"

But *from 1835 the picture changed completely.* Grundtvig came into contact with his contemporary age in a new way, through topical questions and through new circles of acquaintances; and although he remained a contentious figure he met a growing recognition from many quarters. This resulted in or coincided with his new view of the age. Having managed to maintain his "unreasonable hopes" in the years of adversity, sometimes in strong words, he now opened the flood-gates for a tremendous optimism which was not to be stopped by disappointments. It is above all this new attitude that separates the period 1835-47 from the previous one. The optimism was linked to his violent mental emotion. As early as 1918 a psychiatrist, Hjalmar Helweg, advanced the opinion that Grundtvig's mental condition was manic-depressive. But apart from the brief and clearly unstable periods in the winter of 1810-11, in 1844, 1853 and 1867 it is impossible to separate the "manic" or the "depressive" from Grundtvig's mental world in general. For him the hope of better times rested first and foremost on his Christian faith and view of man. "Believe me, my friend," he wrote to Ingemann in 1841, "Our Lord is making good plans for us, and however He may act, He will doubtless have His way from here on as before". Through his faith Grundtvig was inspired to a

> Longing deep as the wide sea,
> To hope, which swings itself higher
> Than eagles and angles on wings!

A point of departure for this period can be found in the preface to *An Impartial View of the Danish State Church,* that keywork from 1834. Here Grundtvig had to acknowledge that the present age had long been a foreign world for him. Only the Church battle as a defence of persecuted fellow-believers had sometimes dragged him out of his dream-world, the glorious world of the past, peopled with the shadows of the forefathers. It was not until he experienced England that he felt at home in the present, and learned to take note of "the undeniable advantage that both things and people actually exist, also outside the mind". Athough these words only apply to the book's evaluation of the State Church, they became indicative of the more extrovert, realistic attitude that characterized Grundtvig in the period 1835-47.

Even so, the present caught him by surprise, while he was still tied up with his work on the history on the world. As with the Church battle it

269

was not originally Grundtvig but some of his younger friends who took the lead in the outward action. In the autumn of 1834, Ludwig Christian Müller, a learned theologian who among other things was studying Old Norse literature began on a completely new course: public lectures on the history of Denmark in a free narrative form. These were held at Borch's College, where Müller was living, and they attracted a very large audience. He was closely acquainted with Grundtvig, who considered the lectures "an excellent sign"; but at this point he was only in the audience. The following year the country rector, Gunni Busck, also one of Grundtvig's young church friends, began a similar series in his parish, with *Norse Mythology*, Saxo and Snorri as his basic material. He had previously asked Grundtvig whether it was all right, for he was after all a clergyman. Grundtvig gave immediate approval to the project as being "harmless amusement", which would never be useless and might even be of some significance on the path of the kingdom of God. "Both those who can and those who cannot become Christians" ought to have better things to think about these days, "when filthy pleasure and ditto profit occupy more or less all their thoughts". These attempts to make contact with "the people" – "the Copenhagen ladies" and the country "youth and peasantry", as Grundtvig wrote – were the beginning of grundtvigianism as a popular movement. They were partly independent initiatives but they undoubtedly meant much to Grundtvig himself, not least for his high-school ideas.

Even more important, however, were the political developments. In order to forestall the emergent liberal movement the King had introduced in 1834 four advisory assemblies of the Estates of the Realm, one for each province. But they only served to add fuel to the fire. They gave rise to a hitherto unknown political interest in connection with the first election to the assemblies, at which farmers were also given the vote, and to a lively public debate particularly in the educated Copenhagen circles through old and new newspapers and magazines. For the liberals it was a question of arousing the sense of "the common good" through educating people in the nature, the institutions and the condition of the State. As the paper *The Fatherland* wrote in its first edition: "Without this assembly of knowledge, insight and awareness, and the living interest for the State derived from it, the people will always remain a mass of citizens instead of a union of citizens"; there will be "no energy, no common spirit and no patriotism ready for every sacrifice". Only thus will the citizens exercise "influence over the path of development that is man's lasting destiny on earth" (C. N. David, September 14th 1834).

Words such as these struck a kindred note with Grundtvig. Certain drafts on *Education for State Affairs*, probably from autumn 1834 should doubtless be regarded as a counter to the ideas of liberal education (cf. p. 214). Here Grundtvig acknowledged that a social education was required that could unite society. But it should have a historical and national perspective and be established by *the State* – on the model of Sorø Academy – in order to overcome the education that sprang from the individual's wilfulness.

Meanwhile he himself was in the process of overcoming his fear of democratic arrangements, at least with the assembly elections. In the same autumn Ingemann wrote a letter expressing his worry about the political turmoil in Copenhagen, like "an almost volcanic ferment". But Grundtvig answered that he nevertheless held out "good hope" so long as both sides agree to "approve" a reasonable compromise and allow the daydream to fade of an obedient and modest people and a wise and self-denying government (April 1835). A poem of the time, *The Golden Mean,* testifies to his new political course.

The year after he moved to a total support of the assemblies' constitution. The first assembly debates in the winter of 1835-36 had convinced him that it was the voice of the Danish people – which he had sought in ancient books – that really had been resurrected in this national council of the people. "My prejudice against the whole idea as a dangerous copy or imitation of a foreign concept was overcome", he wrote to Gunni Busck (April 1836). Royal power preserved and a purely advisory "council" – this was the original Danish constitution! The discovery filled him with inspiration; in the letter to Busck he even compared it with his "unparalleled discovery" of 1825.

In both the letters mentioned above he touched in the same breath on the necessity for a new form of popular education. When he wrote to Busck, he was in the middle of a draft of his first high school essay *The Danish Four-Leaf Clover* (1836), whose main theme is the same ideas as in the letter above on the assemblies' constitution. A new chapter was hereby opening in Denmark's history, he wrote; so from now on his own "social line of thought" will gradually become dominant! All the things he had dreamed of for twenty years had become everyday occurrences – since he now confined his "dreams" to society. True none had done the realm such sterling services as Christianity, which would continue to ennoble human nature in Denmark, "so long as the clergy through their determination to rule in the name of Christianity do not destroy the freedom of its activity". But "socially" the time of the Church is almost over. Society must build on the school; and the popularly elected King's Council requires a special "school for Danish life and society", "a high school for our young citizens".

In reality Grundtvig had himself come close to *the liberals' way of thinking*. The national conscience insisted on "freedom and peace", he wrote, using the same slogan that he had criticized in the poem on the spirit of the age (see p. 265). In contrast to his previous attitude he now found room for *political* slogans of freedom and equality: "national freedom" must develop calmly and "completely" through the free voice of the people in the assemblies, just like "national equality", which developed out of the absolute monarchy. The task of the high school is only determined in broad outline, but in accordance with liberal ideas of education; it was to produce an awareness of *"the national character, the constitution and the country* in all their aspects", and for the education to be genuine it must "spring from the individual's own life" (in contrast to "education in state affairs", see p. 271). But it must build on patriotism, so that the individual "places his honour at the disposal of the general good and gladly makes the sacrifices it demands" (cf. David p. 270). On the other hand Grundtvig also added here a historical-national perspective, partly through an account of the background for the assembly constitution in Danish history, partly through a proposal for an extension of Sorø Academy, the old "patriotic high school" from 1586, in fact according to Grundtvig from the time of Bishop Absalon (12th century). To the word *patriotic,* which appears regularly in the first high school writings, Grundtvig attached a connection with the past. Sorø Academy was particularly ideal because in the 17th century – as an educational institution for young noblemen – it had disseminated "a certain mildly patriotic education and warmth", and in 1826 it had been re-established as an academy by the Danish King. In addition, Grundtvig placed great emphasis on the use of Danish as the basis for the high school rather than Latin. It was right to stress the significance of the "general spirit", but Danish is "its body and the expression of its life", necessary as a bridge over "the gulf between the ordinary man and the scholars"; and for this Danish writers should be linked to the high school. The essay was nevertheless not particularly polemical, and Grundtvig admitted at the end that he had changed his opinion. The high school demanded a great change in the general way of thinking, but it could not possibly be greater than his own: the change that had now taken place "in the head of a clergyman from the old school".

However, in the most important of the subsequent educational writings *The School for Life* (1838) Grundtvig was once again on the warpath.

Here he resumed the argument from *Norse Mythology* against the spirit of Rome, "the foreign, stiff, forced and dead school creature from the Middle Ages on the basis of Latin and dead letters", and against "the German fancy" that life can be explained before it is lived and be transformed by learned heads. This attack was occasioned by a proposal from Sorø Academy to admit pupils without the necessary qualifications, but only to an introductory course in Latin. Grundtvig now demanded in contrast that civil servants should be educated at Sorø Academy – without Latin and without examinations. There was no need for more "schools for death", which destroy "the last remnants of our glorious nature", so that all educated people become slaves of animal nature and barbarism. The "school for life" on the other hand will develop the national character, "all the skilfulness that the life of man was predisposed towards ... all the industry upon which our earthly welfare, cheerfulness and common sense obviously rest according to the will of Providence and the nature of our being!".

Grundtvig further rejected a proposal to introduce practical (*réal*) schools with mathematics and natural sciences. This would be just as great a calamity for society as a Latin school for the civil servants. As "the terrible workshop for the death of society" it would create "bewitched citizens, who either cannot be bothered to work or can only be bothered to read, do sums on a slate, draw figures and make logical conclusions". For "the mathematicians preach a pure scientific spirit that is concerned in fact with neither life nor death nor any sort of human activity"; therefore they cannot possibly respect the needs of an individual nation. The proposal was a new reflection of the educated world's view of itself as "a pack of Romans who have all the rest of the world as slaves". This twin argument continued in all Grundtvig's educational writings right up to the last in 1847 (see also K. E. Bugge's essay p. 211).

In other areas, however, Grundtvig became reconciled with the age. Clear expression of this is to be found in the series of lectures which he gave for young academics at Borch's College between June and November 1838, published later as *Within Living Memory* (1877). They were historical lectures on the pattern of Müller and Busck, but they dealt with modern times, and here too Grundtvig had changed his mind. In the high school writings from 1836-37 the revolutionary "wilfulness" of modern times was still the great danger, leading to "the general shipwreck that threatens the people of Europe". But in the autumn of 1837 he realised that the excitement and rebellion of the times could also be seen as heralding "the resurrection of everything that is of the people and of mankind which has truly existed on earth". In this belief he could calmly "contemplate the earthquake". We must "be tolerant towards the mad and stupid war for freedom that as a counterweight to the rule of police chief and schoolmaster" is a necessary evil (according to a letter to Ingemann).

In his lectures, 51 in all, he expressly condemned the contempt he had shown in his youth for the "petty, philistine interests and puerile pursuit of freedom and self-conceit". He went over the history of the French revolution in detail, and even though it was "unpleasant", he found, "however, traces of what is essentially human even in the middle of Paris". Its political theories he rejected; only freedom was indisputable; freedom of conscience, freedom of speech and freedom of trade. As might have been expected, he called particular attention to his impressions of English enterprise, but with an eye on the dangers involved in industrialisation, which sacrificed "people in their hundreds of thousands to the machine". The same giant spirit that had created the machines ought to take responsibility for placing them at the service of man. Of Germany he was more critical, but he commended Steffens and singled out the romantic school of thought. As for the course of events in Denmark he had almost nothing but praise, and his hope of a new, happy era was linked in particular to Denmark and the North, which ought to "live and work in its *own* peculiar genius" and recapture a closer likeness to its youth ("the ancient North"). He had done this himself, he claimed; but in reality he was building very much on his "middle age" – not least on his historical outlook in *Danevirke* – and on a completely new and optimistic evaluation of the contemporary age.

The lectures were a great success. There was room for 250 in the lecture-hall, but numbers gradually increased until it was crammed with an audience of up to 600, and on the final evening Grundtvig was feted with speeches and songs. He himself counted these hours among the happiest of his life. At last he had gained access to an academic platform and the opportunity to work with "the living word" (outside the Church), which in *The School for Life* he had called "the great natural law for the working and spreading of the Spirit". He wrote to Ingemann that his lectures had been a success "beyond all expectation", even though his audience had been in "the black school"! "So what could not be achieved at Sorø. ... with young people, relatively uncorrupted and natural!" Since *Danevirke* Grundtvig had formed the habit of writing in a cheerful, broadly conversational style in his non-ecclesiastical essays, but the style of these lectures was more lively and natural than ever before.

"In my view the main battle has been won", he wrote afterwards to Gunni Busck, "so it is now really only a matter of putting the victory to good use". This he did by establishing a lecture society in Copenhagen in

May 1839 called the *Danish Society,* of which he himself became chairman. The society held public meetings with songs and lectures in a free form on historical and topical subjects. Of a meeting in 1842, for example, Grundtvig wrote: "This time I spoke mainly on youth and the constitution, yet most of all on the three 'folk festivals'", three national commemoration days, the most important of which for the Danish Society was the anniversary of the institution of the four assemblies. But there were other lecturers than Grundtvig, and the form of a society and meetings was copied in several places in the country; later they became of great importance for grundtvigianism as a popular movement.

1836 to 1839 were years of breakthrough in another sense. The liberals observed Grundtvig's enthusiasm for freedom, and in governmental circles his warm defence of the monarchy did not go unnoticed. Around the New Year 1838 he was lauded as a man of freedom in one of the leading liberal papers, and at the same time the Government removed the censorship on him. This was doubtless due to the influence of the heir to the throne, *Prince Christian Frederik,* who was the first to congratulate Grundtvig. The Prince would have been attracted by Grundtvig's liberal-conservative attitude, and the meeting led, according to Grundtvig, to "a long and extremely lively conversation with the Prince on Danish and Latin", which was influential on Grundtvig's writing of *The School for Life.* He was also presented to the Prince's consort, Caroline Amalie; and some time afterwards she urged him to give a series of lectures for herself and her ladies-in-waiting. It was "a strange audience", wrote Grundtvig, since it hardly understood Danish; it must have been Our Lord "who has put it into the Princess's head to hear the history of our country from me, a thought that the court will find very droll". The lectures were held at the palace in the spring of 1839 – three times a week – at the same time as Grundtvig was applying for the living at *Vartov Hospital Church:* and the influence of the heir to the throne undoubtedly contributed to Grundtvig's appointment, even though he was not recommended by the bishop. Vartov was only an institution for old people and the living was among the smallest in Copenhagen; but it meant from this point onwards – May 1839 – that Grundtvig was free of financial worries.

In Denmark the same year Christian Frederik became King under the name, *Christian VIII.* The liberals had great expectations of him since it was the new King who, as viceroy of Norway in 1814, had agreed to the Norwegians' desire for a free liberal-democratic constitution. But Grundtvig's hopes exceeded everybody's. There was no peace in him whatsoever, he wrote in private, "to do anything but what the day demands" since he was constantly occupied with what ought to happen in the new King's reign. The year after he praised "our age ... as a time of resurrection so poetic that it is only eclipsed by 'the beginning, middle and end of time', so whoever feels the urge and the ability to take part on the side of life in the great battle against death will find the lines fallen to him in pleasant places" (Psalm: 16:6). This was especially true of Denmark, "where the victory is certain".

Politically however, he found himself in clear opposition to *the liberals* around 1840. They collected thousands of signatures for a petition to the King demanding that the taxes should be granted by the assemblies. This would be a major step towards a free constitution; but Christian VIII had become more conservative, so he was no doubt pleased when Grundtvig immediately spoke out powerfully against the liberals' "constitution-making" and criticism of the Government. Grundtvig also exhorted those who shared his views to make a public effort, especially through meetings and societies, so that the people would not be forced "to regard the opposition as the only support for its freedoms and rights" (May 1840). Lindberg and other young friends followed the request and collected signatures on addresses *against* the liberals' demands, particularly from the members of the devout meetings.

Up to 1847 Grundtvig continued to warn against the liberals' constitutional ideas. But he only halfheartedly supported Lindberg's attempt to get up an address, even though his own name stood at the top of the list. Liberalism made swift inroads among the young students – the youth rebellion of the 1840's – and Grundtvig now preferred as far as possible to reach agreement "with the puppies for the sake of life ... just as we would still rather tolerate cacklers and burs than do without the spring sunshine", which also calls forth many weeds (to Ingemann 1841). On two points he could go along with the young people: the Scandinavian cause and the Schleswig question. *Scandinavianism* spread from 1838 via the Nordic universities as a movement to unite the Nordic nations, and the first Scandinavian magazine in Denmark (1839-42) was supported by both Grundtvig and the leader of the young people, Orla Lehmann. The *Schleswig question* came about in the 1830's as a result of the tension between a Danish national movement in North Schleswig – which was Danish-speaking but whose official language, being part of the duchy, was German – and a corresponding German-orientated counter-movement on behalf of Schleswig-Holstein (see p. 87).

In the 1830's Grundtvig had been disinterested in the Danish movement in North Schleswig, even though its leaders were inspired by him. But when the clash of interests came to a head in the 1840's, particularly concerning the right to use the Danish language, he burned with indignation; as did the liberals, who now became "national-liberals". On this cause Grundtvig could even agree with Professor Clausen, who took charge of a large collection on behalf of the Danish educational establishments in North Schleswig, in particular for a Danish-speaking grammar school; somewhat reluctantly he even agreed that this money should be used on the first attempt to realize Grundtvig's high school ideas by founding a peasant high school in Rødding. This opened in 1844, and in the same summer Orla Lehmann – on behalf of *The Scandinavian Society* – invited Grundtvig to join the young people's movement on a steamship trip to a big national meeting in North Schleswig. Grundtvig immediately concurred and both the trip and the meeting – at *Skamling Hill* – were a resounding success. The King disapproved of the meeting since these national demonstrations threatened to split the realm; but Grundtvig sought to overcome the ill-feeling by sending enthusiastic letters to the Queen on *"Denmark's resurrection* from the dead and the *rebirth of the language"*; never before had he spoken "so cheerfully and yet so thunderously" and to so many open ears as at Skamling Hill. Nor did he omit to point out that he was the only one among "the old royalists" who could talk to the young.

Altogether Grundtvig occupied a central place in the flourishing *public life* of the 1840's. He produced a generous profusion of poems and songs for every occasion: royal family events, meetings and parties, as well as for friends and acquaintances. His songs for the Danish Society came to fill four booklets and many of them were included in The Scandinavian Society's Songbook and in collections published by his friends. In the society and club life of the capital he was in demand as a guest of honour, even in distant circles such as the Copenhagen Printers' Anniversary Party, where he "proposed a toast that was interrupted by a great ovation following the singing of a song that he had composed himself". Time and again he was invited by The Scandinavian Society and from 1845 by the Student Union to a "Nordic Festival" every January. According to a newspaper report at one of these he rose "amidst prolonged applause" and proposed a toast "in a speech spiced with genuine humour and wit that was continually interrupted by storms of applause". At the first major Scandinavian student gathering in June 1845 H. N. Clausen spoke first, followed by Grundtvig, after the thousands of participants had sung one of his songs. A couple of days later those present at the meeting held a procession of honour to Oehlenschläger's house at Frederiksberg and thence to Grundtvig, who at that time was living at Brook House close by.

Among his many talks mention must be made of his lectures on Greek and Norse myths at Borch's College in 1843-44 *(Braga Talks,* published 1844) and his lectures on history for the Queen and her circle in 1842-44 (at intervals). Altogether he became closely acquainted with Caroline Amalie; she asked him to lead (from 1841) a "charity school" she supported; she attended the services he held, and she even visited him in his study. This influenced the cause that Grundtvig was most occupied with in the 1840's: the conversion of Sorø Academy into a "Danish" college. A lengthy series of pamphlets, recommendations, and private letters bear witness to this. In 1845 the King decided that a practical school should be opened at Sorø, and in March 1847 he issued further decrees that clearly bore the imprint of Grundtvig's ideas. In October that year he invited Grundtvig and Ingemann to dinner at court, an occasion which Grundtvig used not only to advance his high school ideas once again but to gain a promise from the King that he himself would assist in their implementation.

Shortly afterwards, in November 1847, a great party was held to celebrate Oehlenschläger's 70th birthday at which Grundtvig was given the principal role of presenting him with the laurel wreath. After many years' contempt from literary circles Grundtvig the poet was thus stepping forward as number two on the Danish Parnassus. But then two months later Christian VIII died, and a new era opened for both Grundtvig and the country.

Church Clashes

In September 1834 J. P. Mynster had been appointed Bishop of Zealand, and at about the same time most of the other Danish bishoprics were occupied by men who, like Mynster, represented a more conservative attitude. The rationalism of the Clausen-party was no longer in fashion; most of the young clergy were largely inspired by Mynster, who thus enjoyed great influence throughout his long episcopacy until 1854. This theological change of course made little impression on Grundtvig, but he realised that Mynster was introducing a line in Church politics that was the direct opposite of his own.

It was the old State Church that Mynster wished to strengthen through closer control and greater uniformity; and from his point of view the outlook was ominous. Almost at the same time as his appointment *An Impartial View of the Danish State Church* was published containing Grundtvig's two political aims for the Church: "release from the parish-tie" and "freedom of clergy" (see p. 241), presented as modest wishes but to Mynster's way of thinking revolutionary demands. And Grundtvig also appeared to be in alliance with the devout meetings, who at that point were spreading rapidly as a co-ordinated movement increasingly criticizing the clergy. Shortly after his induction Mynster had to face in his own palace the abuse of an arrogant Zealand schoolteacher, Rasmus Sørensen, who called him an enemy of the faith and left him with the pronouncement that he would be indicted before the King! But the same Rasmus Sørensen was the leading figure in a petition for release from the parish-tie got up by the meeting-people, in all 581 of them (see p. 242); and Lindberg's paper *Nordic Church Times* was the most important link amongst the revivalists. Furthermore, Lindberg travelled around in 1834 and 1835 visiting meeting-groups and holding large meetings in many places.

The first tightening up of the State Church line was thus directed in particular against Lindberg. His trips were watched by the police, and on the recommendation of the college of bishops the old ban on devout meetings was more strictly enforced in December 1835, in particular the regulations dealing with travelling meeting-leaders. It was these regulations that Mynster considered the most important.

On the other hand Grundtvig took up the battle on behalf of *"Church freedom"* together with a growing number of like-minded people. In December 1835 he wrote to a young parson in south-west Zealand, *J. F. Fenger,* that he "would (introduce) this evening rather than tomorrow the most unrestricted freedom in the Danish State Church". At this time he was also working especially for petitions from the clergy for release from the parish-tie to be presented to the assembly in Roskilde; and he managed to elicit just such an address from Fenger's area, where he had many supporters amongst the clergy. Both Fenger and Lindberg travelled to Roskilde in the hope of influencing the deputies, and Grundtvig wrote a number of letters with the same aim to leading members. But the member who had promised to present the question dragged his feet, and it was not presented for debate. In fact he had changed his mind on the matter, doubtless under the influence of Mynster, who regarded release from the parish-tie as a great misfortune; the individual's free choice of his minister would lead, in his opinion, to the disintegration of the State Church in its present form.

But that was precisely what Grundtvig wished to achieve through "free congregations" around the minister of their choice with freedom of teaching for the clergy and freer forms in the service. He therefore continued his attempt to arouse *"the spirit of opposition"* amongst the younger clergy, whom he thought were too compliant; and the following year he succeeded. At the next assembly meetings in 1838 and 1840 new petitions from the clergy were presented demanding release from the parish-tie, accompanied in 1840 by a demand for a supplement to the hymnbook from the time of the enlightenment. And Mynster ran into violent opposition when he produced a proposal in 1838 for a new, moderately modernized ritual that was to be followed throughout the country and thus put an end to the conflict concerning rationalist changes in ritual. The clergy of Grundtvig's persuasion rejected the proposal outright, particularly because it changed the baptismal ritual; and from the meeting-people there came a petition of protest in 1839-40 containing over 2,000 names. In 1839 Grundtvig himself published no fewer than three books on Church politics, two on his view of the State Church and one against the ritual proposal, which he slated from beginning to end; he also wrote a large number of articles on both matters.

These onslaughts had a disquieting effect on Mynster. In 1840 he prayed in the cathedral for God's protection against the "rebellious people, influenced with false zeal", who were rushing in to break the ties with which God had bound "the community of Christians" in the country. He spoke in Latin at the annual meeting of provosts, but the prayer was later published. For a while Mynster held off the storm through diplomatic ingenuity and his personal influence. At the assembly debates he managed to get the question of the parish-tie split up into insignificant matters of detail; his proposal on ritual was handed over almost unaltered to the Government in 1841, and the hymnbook was in reality left to Mynster himself to decide; he gained acceptance for a little supplement containing only one hymn by Grundtvig. In 1842 he also managed to institute a general obligation to infant baptism for the small baptist communities which had arisen around 1840. The baptists were harshly persecuted by the police who actually went around picking up their unchristened children for "compulsory baptism".

But from then on the course of events left him powerless, not least as a result of Grundtvig's influence. In 1842 the King granted the release of the parish-tie to confirmation candidates, and in the same year he set aside the proposal on ritual. The question of hymns was solved through the unofficial collections of Grundtvig's hymns, such as *Hagen's Hymnbook,* which went through six printings between 1832 and 1856. They were used particularly in schools, but from 1845 onwards there was tacit acceptance that non-recognized hymns were also used in church services. Grundtvig's battle for freedom of religion also bore fruit, with the support of the liberal papers. Attacks on the devout meetings gradually decreased and stopped completely after a large petition on the subject in 1843-44, signed by 1,300 lay people and 30 clergy. Grundtvig defended the baptists in the essay *On Religious Persecution* (1842); and his clergy friends refused to carry out compulsory baptisms. From 1845 the persecution of the baptists also began to wane and in January 1847 the King removed the "baptist label" that Mynster had inspired in 1842.

Thus the battle for "Church freedom" was also a defence of *the devout meetings;* but in the same period Grundtvig also repudiated them, for other reasons. The conflict was originally started by the meeting-leaders, who thereby broke the trust that the Church battle and in particular Lindberg's efforts had built up.

In Copenhagen the radical meeting-people withdrew after 1832 into separate groups, but in the rest of the country Lindberg had gathered the revivalists to him through his tour of 1834 and his praise for the movement in *Nordic Church Times* on his return. Soon afterwards, however, the meeting leaders began to criticize him. The attacks from Funen and Jutland were purely evangelical: Lindberg had been unable to share the revivalists' disgust for dancing and gambling and he contested the validity of their emphasis on conversion teaching by defending Grundtvig's interpretation of "Christ's descent into Hell" as a gospel for those who have died heathen (according to the Creed and 1. Peter 3:19). Around New Year 1836 the Funen and Jutland meeting-leaders broke with Lindberg when he refused to print a defence of an old evangelical catechism that the revivalists wished to use for confirmation lessons.

The west Zealand meeting-movement carried on under the leadership of the above-mentioned Rasmus Sørensen. He not only supported the evangelical attacks but also repudiated the "believers" among the local clergy who had links with Grundtvig; from the spring of 1835 onwards he was clearly heading towards a free Church of lay people. He therefore gave up the demand for release from the parish-tie (that is, in order to start free congregations with ministers who were "believers"), so much the more because Lindberg had refused to publish Sørensen's petition on the parish-tie. He publicly broke with the Grundtvig-Lindberg line in two articles from November 1835 and January 1836 (in *Nordic Church Times*), directed against a Copenhagen private school based on Grundtvig's principles and led by the theological graduate, J. P. G. Jensen. In an account of the school Jensen had written amongst other things that it was not really the place where faith should be imparted to the children; in contrast Sørensen strongly underlined his own excellent Lutheran evangelical teaching which led to the "religious awakening" of most children. He added a general attack on the clergy as "worn-out invalids", who ought to be replaced by "the rising popular class", that part of the peasantry who were developing the revivalist movement.

The articles were extremely provocative, in particular towards Grundtvig. Sørensen called himself an old disciple of Grundtvig and employed a great number of Grundtvig's phrases, but presented the man himself as a remote, bookish man who knew nothing of real life. At the same time he sent Grundtvig a private letter in which he praised and criticized his medieval history as though he was Grundtvig's equal. This situation formed the background for Grundtvig's clash with the meeting-movement. He who could hardly bear the criticism of close friends was being reprimanded by a schoolteacher! From Lindberg, who was still his close friend, he had learned of the lay rebellion in west Zealand, on Funen and in Jutland; and it made a particular impression on him that the movement was now failing him over his major demand for release from the parish-tie.

First he wrote a brief categorical rejection of Sørensen's articles on the school. Faith was *"in no way an educational matter";* the whole religious education in the schools was a complete misunderstanding and ought to cease forthwith. Most of the teachers were non-believers, and the orthodox were equally intolerable when they treated faith as a lesson to be learnt and "belaboured it" in dialogues on the catechism (as Sørensen had demonstrated). Confirmation, which ended a pupil's schooldays, should also be abolished, to be replaced by a "national ceremony", apart from special agreements between "the old-fashioned Christians and their ministers". The article was no less provocative than Sørensen's, both against him personally and the meeting-movement in general. It outraged many and Sørensen retorted with violent attacks on Grundtvig and Lindberg – to Mynster's delight: now "Satan's Kingdom" was being torn with strife!

Grundtvig's article was nonetheless not an unreserved expression of his opinion on religious education. That is to be found rather in Jensen's school prospectus and the prospectus for the charity school that Grundtvig was responsible for. The School's most important task was telling the Bible story, and then the history of Denmark and the world, with rotelearning only of verses. In this manner it would "doubtless serve the faith well" and teach everyone "to acknowledge the Christian outlook on life ... as a fief granted by God", to be used on the pattern of Christ. Nor would Grundtvig forbid teachers "to speak the word of life to children" in the public school. This he wrote by way of explanation of the article against Sørensen to a Jutland schoolteacher who was an old and far more modest

disciple of Grundtvig. The aim of the article, he wrote, was not to rein-
troduce paganism but on the contrary "to fight paganism and spread
Christianity" in a better way than the *"compulsory* Christian knowledge".

Publicly meanwhile, he continued his conflict with the meeting-movement. In the summer of 1836 he wrote against another west Zealand
teacher who had complained that the demands for release from the parish-tie and freedom of clergy overlooked the problems for teachers who
were believers. The answer was an abrupt rejection; the complaint was
due to an exaggeration of a teacher's importance, which could not equal a
clergyman's. The year after Grundtvig took stock of the situation in
Lindberg's paper: he still wanted freedom for the devout meetings,
amongst other things because they were thus easier to fight! Compulsory
schooling should also cease, since the teachers were apparently "on the
verge of putting themselves at the head of the devout meetings" and
would use "compulsory schooling" to this end. And anyway he regarded
these meetings as "a dangerous disease" which he had attempted to limit
for 25 years! He stated a similar point of view in his first article on Church
politics from 1839, *Speech to the People's Council,* where with apparent
satisfaction he emphasized that the devout meetings counted him among
their enemies. And in *Church Enlightenment,* which was published in the
form of periodical essays 1840-42, the last third of the work contained a
theological attack on the meetings. The community of the early Church
may very well be the aim of the Church, but "devout meetings and
brotherhoods" would not promote but hinder their development. They
were only man's work, destructive of the life of the Church, which should
grow peacefully on "the Word of Life everlasting" in baptism and Holy
Communion.

In the meantime Lindberg had resumed his connection with the meeting-movement in 1837, particularly as an adviser and a defender against
the authorities. Still more clergy of Grundtvig's persuasion followed the
movement through contact with the local meetings, and they often drew
large crowds to their churches. Nor did it help when Grundtvig sharply
criticized them for being influenced by the Lutheran pietistic thought that
governed the meetings. The clergy knew the local population better than
Grundtvig, and they took a sympathetic line towards the revivalists,
though not without some reservations. They saw that Grundtvig was
mistaken in regarding Rasmus Sørensen as a typical representative. In
spite of everything many meeting-people had greater sympathy for
Grundtvig than for Sørensen, and the great majority repudiated Sørensen when in 1839 he moved closer to the baptists and from 1841 to

political liberalism. But the attitude of the Grundtvig clergy was decisive. Through them large numbers of the meeting-movement gradually joined forces with Grundtvig.

In reply to Grundtvig's criticism one vicar protested that "the sincere Christians" whom he dealt with were of the same kind as those who in his student days had gathered around Grundtvig (1842). He thus touched on another side: the fact that Grundtvig himself worked as a revivalist preacher in his own way and was still looking for a renewal of Church life. In his sermons from this period Grundtvig stressed without reservation the "revival" that was now under way – in increasingly strong tones and doubtless on the basis of what he had heard from the clergy. Presumably he was imagining a Church revival that would be different from that of the devout meetings. Concerning the life both of the Church and of the people he wrote to Ingemann (1842): "it appears clear from every angle that if life is to return to our people it will come with gladness and with song"; so even if others find "the hanging of heads" heavenly, it is "still hell for us"!

There was yet another Church battle in this period, namely on the status of the episcopacy and the clergy, which Grundtvig himself had placed great emphasis on in the years following 1825 (see p. 245). This "High Church" tendency was taken over by Lindberg and his friends amongst the clergy and added to the tension between them and the meeting-movement around 1835-36; their assessment of the ordination of priests undoubtedly reflects Grundtvig's view at that time. On the other hand Grundtvig had been constantly at war with the clergy. From 1825 he had fought the craving for power both by the clergy and by the "scriptural theologians", and the antagonism was further sharpened from the mid-1830's onwards when Bishop Mynster took over. But it was an impulse from England that forced Grundtvig to reopen the question, namely, *the High Church movement at Oxford*, which he took a deep interest in from 1838 onwards.

The Oxford Movement could not but attract Grundtvig since it regarded the Church as a historical continuity with an emphasis on the sacraments and the early Church tradition, and because it criticized political and theological liberalism. But it was precisely Grundtvig's own thoughts on "the holy Universal Church" that gave him pause. In his great *Song-Work*, the first volume of which was published in 1837, he had adapted hymns "from all ages and climes" and had especially delighted in "the fusing of tones from all the major faiths in the Universal Church which during the work reached my ears and stirred my heart" (cf. p. 176). Grundtvig's line of thought was clearly ecumenical: open to both differences and unity. But the Oxford Movement wished to exclude from the Universal Church all communities of faith without "true" consecration of bishops (such as the English!), including the Lutherans, and they regarded their consecration of bishops as the foundation of the Church, the basis for the validity of the sacraments.

This was the crucial point for Grundtvig. Already in the spring of 1838 he stresses in a sermon that there is no other bishop on earth but Christ, who leads all believers, both Protestants and Catholics, with or without bishops, into the holy Universal Church. In a sermon from 1839 he describes all popes, bishops and clergy who want to be "Christ's viceroys" on earth as blind guides. We – the clergy – must on the contrary turn the congregation away from us towards "the Spirit of Jesus Christ as the only companion on life's path". In the attack on Mynster's proposal on the ritual he referred to the Oxford Movement's "episcopal ideas" and declared: "I hate every hierarchical remnant and must protest against every new hierarchical seed". *Church Enlightenment* and other essays also reject the Oxford Movement, in 1842 among other reasons because they did not understand the Creed as "being alive at baptism", but as having been found in the writings of the early Church fathers just like other "historical Church antiquities".

When the Queen granted him another trip to England in 1843 he immediately went to Oxford, where he had several conversations with Newman, Pusey and other representatives of the movement. But they did not change his opinion. He retained a certain amount of sympathy for the Oxford Movement as a justifiable protest against the "protestant enlightenment", and he did not fail to appreciate the importance of the Church's civil servants, as far as it went. He saw them first and foremost as teachers of the congregations in a *serving relationship* to them: "Church enlightenment is a free matter, as is the working of the Holy Spirit that must be diligently promoted by all the officials of the Lord but which *cannot be ruled* by the servants". The greatest amongst them will be known not as the pope "by *calling* himself but by *being* the humble servant of his fellow servants" (1845). Grundtvig hereby renounced his High Church tendencies; instead he now moves in a Low Church direction.

First a Man – Then a Christian

Grundtvig's "patriotic" and ecclesiastical efforts could be presented as two widely different spheres of activity, but he himself thought long and hard about their internal relationship. His efforts at cultural collaboration had already around 1820 led to a division between Church and School, after which Christians and Naturalists (such as Steffens) should be able to meet "at School" i.e. on the cultural level, in literature and scholarship. In his "Church battle" on the other hand he had strongly emphasized the difference between true Christianity and all kinds of naturalism, regardless of whether it called itself Christianity. He therefore demanded that the old-fashioned Christians be allowed to gather in special congregations, either outside the State Church or within it through the implementation of "Church freedom".

But then again his clear awareness of the special character of Christianity enabled him to resume his efforts towards cultural collaboration with even greater energy, though with a sharp emphasis on the antagonism *within the Church*. And on this last point his attitude began to change from around 1835. This is particularly to be seen in his sermons in the form of a milder view of those outside the Church and a greater stress on the link between "the Christian" and "the human".

Even in the summer of 1835 a sermon underlined that "being not far from the truth in spiritual matters" is "... still being outside it"; even if it was only a hair's breadth one is still "on the threshold of hell". A few Sundays later the whole of Christianity, so-called, is compared to Sodom and Gomorrah, a recognition that must rouse us "to work in earnest for our own and our brother's divorce from the world". Grundtvig never abandoned this gloomy view of "the world"; it always remained a basic element in his Christianity.

But in the same sermon it also becomes a reason for a powerful exhortation to enlighten the world, "employ every happy moment to enlighten it as to its failure to appreciate Christ", not in order to convert it but because it is wisest to keep peace with Him. "He is extremely cheap and good-natured, so if one just tips one's hat to him, He blesses the hand, and if one takes one's hat off, He blesses the head and heals the eyes so that one sees everything in the world much more clearly and much more beautifully". A similar attitude is expressed in his Christmas sermon that year, which reproaches the old-fashioned Christians for "the petulance and envy they show those who without taking possession of their faith wish to a certain extent to share their Christmas joy". We must generously tell them as much as they are willing to receive, without prescribing for them how much or how they should take part. This reproach he directs above all at himself: "I know it well because nobody within miles has contributed more than I have to embittering and frightening away many who wish in their little way to take part in our

Christmas joy; but I repent, because it was neither kind nor Christian of me".

In addition we find a greater emphasis on freedom in the personal faith. In a sermon from the summer of 1836 he rejects his own previous efforts to "repel opponents", "with blinding proof to force faith on the enemy". This can only lead to a dead faith, and it was "a false concern for the salvation of my neighbour that only insults truth and forfeits love". The gospel must not be preached "for the sake of its mockers and opponents, but only for those who have the heart to believe it". "Those who do not hear Moses and the prophets do not believe anyone rose from the dead either" (Luke 16: 19-31), which here in Grundtvig's interpretation means that faith must be a free matter because it is a matter of the heart. Since this was his personal experience he now felt "expecially called" to recommend this truth.

In the same autumn he went a step further in a sermon emphasizing that just as one can be Christian without being Danish, "so one can also be a good Danish citizen, and secularly speaking, a good person, without being a Christian". This distinction is presented as a new perception which he has still not "thoroughly" put into practice. But it remained a fact that we must "separate our Christian position from our natural position and from our position in society, by no means in order to withdraw from these but precisely in order to be able to give them their full due, so that they are left intact by Christianity and Christianity by them". Continuing in this vein he emphasizes firstly, as above, that faith is a free matter, not a civil right. All forcing of conscience in the name of Jesus is not the fault of the faith itself but of the various forms of "papistry". Secondly there is a stress on the positive relationship between "living faith" and "enlightenment and human well-being": the relationship is like that between the root and the branches, the source and the rivers, which can only "bless the earth", if the faith is alive. This was also true in the past, especially "amongst our Lutheran forefathers". But it is not demonstrated powerfully and clearly until we who belong to Christ "exceed all others in an active endeavour for all human enlightenment and all that can serve to make our fellow-man and fellow-citizen content and happy". Such a living faith will "thereby win all those who are of the truth, however blinded they may have been by the spirit of this world".

Thoughts such as these lie behind the poem *First a Man – then a Christian* from 1837. It rejects superficial christianizing through mission and book-knowledge (catechism teaching) and draws attention to Adam and a number of "faithful men of God" from the Old Testament who were not Christian. Heathens must not be condemned out of hand, and the gospel must not be preached for "animals and devils" (mockers and opponents). On the other hand the poem underlines the link between the truly human and Christianity, between first a man and then a Christian as the "order of life", especially in the concluding verse:

> Let each one strive upon this earth
> To be a human being,
> To open his ears to the word of truth
> And give to God His honour!
> If Christianity is the truth,
> Then if he is not a Christian today,
> He will be a Christian tomorrow.

If the sense for the human word of truth is developed it will lead to Christianity. This does not mean that Grundtvig will censure Christian talk to the ignorant who wish to hear (according to a private letter 1838). But first a man, then a Christian corresponded to his own life-course, and he later called it his motto in the sense that a Christian is neither more nor less than a Christian *man* (1867). The final verse should best be regarded as an expression of the same strong optimism that so often made itself heard in the period 1835-47. The verse must not be given a strictly literal interpretation since it would then cancel out the relative independence that Grundtvig in these very years was awarding natural human life.

This is true of the high school writings, which argue almost exclusively on the cultural level. It is equally true of the lectures *Within Living Memory*, which expressly counsel – in social life – a disregard for Christianity as being "something completely free and unpredictable". It is also true on the whole of all Grundtvig's public activity from around 1838 as a lecturer, festival poet and toastmaster. Here he spoke consciously to his audience as a fellow-countryman, not as a poet.

Altogether characteristic of the period 1835-47 is a marked preference for "the natural". This is not a new concept in Grundtvig; it has its roots in the worship of nature by the enlightenment, in the romantics' natural philosophy and in the philosophy of the organism, and particularly in the biblical depiction of man's creation in God's image. In his historical work one senses it early on in his understanding of the history of the world as "the course of the life of man"; it turns up again, for example in the twelve

288

essays (see p. 246), in the *Literary Testament*'s talk of "the laws of human nature" (1827), and in *Norse Mythology*, which perceives human life as "natural history", a combination of nature and history corresponding to the female and the male nature (1832). But the introduction to medieval history (autumn 1835) explicitly reduces history as the life of man to a mere image expressing *"the gradual development of human nature* towards enlightenment of itself"; and thereafter "the natural" comes out in his educational writings, especially from 1837, as a central educational, practical and cultural-political argument.

Grundtvig wrote to Ingemann in 1838: "I have learned to hate the unnatural far more than all natural defects, without thereby becoming less aware of these". A year later he went even further in *To My Two Sons*, a poem warmly praising human nature, which "must be honoured in all things". Admittedly it appears to have fallen amongst thieves and "is in bad need of a *water-cure*" (through baptism!); but by nature it is God's work, which cannot be bettered, but can only "grow, work, enlighten". The idea of a natural growth therefore becomes an important element in Grundtvig's view of man and in his educational thinking. "The course of life" is made actual in the individual's life and can in fact be likened to the course of the year as in the contemporary poem, *Open Letter to My Children* from 1839:

If fresh and green the shoot of early spring,
That flowers in summer's warmth to glorious prime,
Then to maturity the plant doth grow
And gladden with its fruit the harvest-time.

Another side of Grundtvig's joy in nature was his high estimation of *woman and womanliness* which he linked to both nature and feeling, the heart. In his introduction to medieval history he defended this period as the age of feeling: what should stop the intellect from underestimating the Middle Ages is the same as must prevent every mother's son from underestimating "the *depth* in *woman,* which, when it is filled by the power on high is the most heavenly on earth, that is, the *"mother-relationship"*, in which *feeling* harmonizes with *intellect"*. In the educational writings the "mother-tongue" stands at the centre; "the language" or Danish is more or less consistently replaced by this word, by "the housewives' language", which ought to put paid to the language of the scholars and "rule like a queen in the fatherland". A climax is reached in *Braga Talks* (1844), in which Grundtvig continues to compliment "the ladies" and to praise woman as the only creature that answers to the praises of poets of "the beautiful, eternally young, motherly and fertile nature".

That Grundtvig appreciated woman not just as mother was proved in the summer of 1844 when, after a fit of depression, he was attracted to a young lady, *Luise Hennings*. He only met her during a five-day stay at a vicarage, on the occasion of a family party. But those few days left their mark on a series of love poems from the same summer in which he also included the love of his youth for his wife, Lise, and the lady on Langeland, Constance Leth. One of the poems, *The Little Ladies,* also praises an English lady whom he only met once, at a party in London in 1830. A long conversation with her had made the evening unforgettable, but Grundtvig does not praise her anywhere else in such a way. In *The Little Ladies* Constance is given five stanzas, the English lady five and Luise Hennings seven, so the inspiration is just as clear as the discrepancy between them, since from a biographical point of view Constance was without doubt the most important. In addition everything points to the fact that these "relationships" by present-day standards were extremely decent. Grundtvig did not need a regular change of bed-fellows in order to extol "the eternally female". The poems are not particularly erotic, rather are they poems on the meaning of love, especially for the poet. Of the English lady (as a symbol of England) he writes: "With your smile and in your sight/ my poet's vision awoke!" And similarly on Luise Hennings: every time Grundtvig sings again "with the warmth of youth... the fire of your eye blazes up/ clear as a lightning-flash and mild as the sun!"

Grundtvig's high estimation of "the natural" was however closely linked to his Christianity. "The core of all my preaching is the Word of eternal light", he wrote in 1840, but Christianity will in no way corrupt human nature; it will rather heal it. The better we are as Christians, the more human and loving we shall be in all our relationships; and an appreciation of the temporal life that God gave us is a prerequisite for eternal life. A sermon from 1841 calls the new Christian life a new human nature, through which the Creator will complete his masterpiece despite sin and death: "to change dust to a likeness with the spirit of life that he blew into it". The sacraments are remedies for both the soul and the body and, as he writes elsewhere (1842), the new life has like the natural life "its obscure, unconscious conception and birth, and its slow development towards consciousness".

Also for pagans (non-Christians) it is "natural" that they "feel they are neither animals nor gods but human beings, created in God's image, with a call to be his children and a view to a heavenly heritage". This will set limits to the unnaturalness that has long emptied man of his powers and made life hopeless and unhappy. Then they would not treat one another like dumb animals that are bought and sold or trained to carry, pull, guard and do tricks, but as *people*. There is now much to prove that this will happen, he believes. The world will not be converted but through this it will nonetheless come "a step closer to the Kingdom of God so that none of its children that can be saved will be lost" (1844).

From the end of the 1830's *the nature of the people* becomes the most important link. It is all to the good that "Christianity" is split up and nations break away so they get the chance to prove what they are in their natural state. The peoples' "new year" will contain major errors but even so it will be "pleasant, fruitful, blessed and unforgettable for the heart". The Christians will be far fewer in numbers, but far better. And in the age of enlightenment and spiritual freedom Christianity will more than ever be in its element, so it "cannot but outshine and overshadow all else on the earth". It will be "admired wherever a human heart still beats". The Christians will work "on the pattern of Him who was in every way a natural person, only without sin and imbued with the divine nature that is well pleased to reflect itself in the human element". They must work hard and prove that "the new man" is in no way unnatural but absorbs the whole of the old man in his original "innocence and loveliness", all that is good in every nation on earth, just as "the whole human multiplicity" is contained in Christ. It will be "one of the most flourishing and enviable eras of the human race" (1838).

In other sermons Grundtvig's tone is more matter-of-fact; but optimism often breaks through with great power, justified too by the new "Christian enlightenment" (on baptismal faith). It is beginning "right now"; in the middle of the plain (Denmark) we shall see the mountain of transfiguration rise up! (1837).

In the relationship between Christianity and the people Grundtvig regularly returns to the figure of *John the Baptist*. Just as the Baptist revitalised the memories of the Jewish people and thus prepared for Jesus' coming, so will the newly-revived Danish national spirit reawaken the memories and myths of the people in Denmark. The world of the spirit will open to us when we see the continuity between the generations, and regard the here and now as no more than a crossing-over from the past to the coming, "so we stand in the midst of an eternity so all-embracing and therefore of necessity incomprehensible to us". This is the line of thought from *Danevirke* which is thus resumed, and Grundtvig can strongly emphasize the connection between the Christian and the national development and Christianity's meaning for the rebirth of the country. But since he now distinguishes between Christianity and Danishness, he places great weight on the task of John the Baptist. The spirit of the people will only "accompany us to the door"; the earthly fatherland is only a forecourt to the heavenly fatherland. The sound of "a word of the people in the mother-tongue" will be heard first. These thoughts took form particularly in the time of Christian VIII (until January 1848), but they assumed their greatest importance in Grundtvig's programme for the following years.

III
THE LATER YEARS
AND GRUNDTVIGIANISM

Grundtvig's Place
in Danish Intellectual Thought
– *with Particular Regard to Søren Kierkegaard*

by WILLIAM MICHELSEN

Grundtvig is not very easy to place in the history of Danish and European intellectual thought. It is true that as a poet he belonged to the school of Oehlenschläger; but his view of life was quite different from Oehlenschläger's. The romantic Ingemann was one of his closest friends; they shared a similar love of Danish medieval history – the "romantic" age – but they differed totally in their view of mankind and the relationship between the soul and the body. Grundtvig was neither a materialist nor an idealist. Finally there is so great a difference between the Grundtvig one meets in Danish literature as the poet of *The Hill by the Sea at Egeløkke* and the Grundtvig who conceived the Danish folk high schools and the free congregational churches (or "union" churches) that one is forced to ask whether it is in fact the same man. There are Grundtvig scholars who actually disregard Grundtvig's ideas in the first period of his authorship and consider the later period as being at odds with the first.

In fact, the whole of Grundtvig's corpus is at odds with his age, and the individual stages in his development are naturally enough at odds with the previous stage. A development that resembles the growth of a plant:

> If fresh and green the shoot of early spring,
> That flowers in summer's warmth to glorious prime,
> Then to maturity the plant doth grow
> And gladdens with its fruit the harvest-time.

as he writes in his rhymed letter to his children in 1839. From childhood and early youth he was a severe critic of his age and himself. This explains the changes of attitude we find in his writing and the changing faces he reveals.

A comparison with Søren Kierkegaard's works and Grundtvig's relationship to his age can throw considerable light on Grundtvig's place in Danish intellectual throught. Both opposed the dominant idealistic theology and philosophy, and both did so from a Christian angle; but Kierkegaard's attack was nevertheless directed at Grundtvig too, as well as against the whole of "official Christianity" in Denmark with no distinction between the grundtvigians and Grundtvig himself. Many have tended to evaluate Grundtvig from Kierkegaard's point of view; the main question is, however, whether Kierkegaard, his age and posterity have understood Grundtvig's thought and his place in Danish and European intellectual life and given him fair treatment.

The period 1800-1870, the so-called "golden age of Danish literature", was characterized by an agreement reached between Christianity and science, based on the philosophy of Kant and his followers. The assumption was made that Christianity could be reconciled with an idealist philosophy, first in Henrich Steffen's *Introduction to Philosophy Lectures* (1802-03) and then in H. C. Ørsted's dialogues and popular writings, published in 1849, under the title *Spirit in Nature*. Other characteristic expressions of this view are to be found in Oehlenschläger's *Gospel of the Year*, J. L. Heiberg's *Protestantism in Nature* and M. Goldschmidt's articles in the journal, *North and South*. J. P. Mynster protested against his friend Ørsted from a Lutheran point of view but Ørsted replied in turn in the second part of *Spirit in Nature*, published in 1851, the year he died. The gravity of the problem can be seen in H. C. Andersen's fairy-tale, *The Snow Queen* (1844), in his travel-book, *In Sweden* (1849) and in his novel, *To Be or Not To Be* (1857).

Distinct from this dominant ideology was B. S. Ingemann's consciously romantic philosophy and Steen Steensen Blicher's old-fashioned Christianity, which on occasion took exception to an idealist-philosophy, but took cover behind the short story, *Diary of a Parish Clerk* (1824). However, the most shocking breaks with the agreement between Christianity and idealistic philosophy were Søren Kierkegaard's *Philosophical Fragments* (1844), *Final Unscientific Postscript* (1846) and *The Moment* (1855). Rasmus Nielsen, a professor of philosophy, joined forces with Kierkegaard but maintained that faith and knowledge – precisely because they were two "dissimilar principles" – could be united in the same consciousness, a view that Georg Brandes challenged as early as 1866. In a university lecture in 1872 he said directly, "There is no doubt that Darwin's teachings will flatten the orthodox dogma; just as Copernicus' System robbed the orthodox heaven of its physical existence, so will Darwin's theory rob the orthodox paradise of its physical existence". The agreement between Christianity and science was thereby broken. Even though Brandes did not gain the professorship in literature he applied for, it was nevertheless his view of faith and knowledge that triumphed. Grundtvig died in the same year.

There has been and remains a general opinion, which Karl Marx believed, for example, that all religion including Christianity presupposes an idealistic philosophy and view of life, but that this cannot be reconciled with materialist philosophy, which natural science and social science (economics, sociology, politics) normally presuppose. One assumes either that religion is superstition or that it postulates an outdated theory of science and philosophy. This view was not unknown in Grundtvig's day of course; but it was kept in check by the philosophy of Kant and his followers, not least Hegel.

Against this Kierkegaard maintained that Christianity has nothing whatsoever to do with the views of the world developed by modern sciences and political systems, but only and exclusively with each individual person's existence in the individual moment, in which he or she can come into contact with eternity by acting independently of the causes that otherwise decide everything that happens – a line of thought which has been partially reinstated by modern existentialism. Grundtvig on the other hand insisted on the biblical view of mankind and of the world created by an impenetrable power, which we call God. According to Grundtvig, this power has created mankind in a likeness to himself and with the intention of realising his perfect kingdom in this world – a thought that even in the last century struck most thinking people as outdated – and still does. But both Kierkegaard and Grundtvig concentrated their efforts on fighting idealistic philosophy, because it showed a total misunderstanding of human existence. They also understood, each in his own way, what a misunderstanding of Christianity it was to make it dependent on idealistic philosophy and theology.

Grundtvig was 30 years older than Kierkegaard, so it is not surprising that his thought bears an older stamp. But both have sharpened their thought by forming it in opposition to an idealistic system, Kierkegaard against Hegel's, Grundtvig against Schelling's. The difference in the outcome is due to the fact amongst others that Kierkegaard took over the philosophical language that Hegel employed in order to beat him at his own game, whereas Grundtvig rejected not only Schelling's but also Kant's philosophical language, from the conviction that everything that is true must be able to be expressed in the mother-tongue and in concepts that can be understood by ordinary common sense. His view of life and man must be regarded as an alternative to the philosophical and theological systems and theories of knowledge which were erected on the basis of Kant's *Critique of Pure Sense*. Kierkegaard on the other hand presupposes these systems in his language and concepts and he can therefore only be understood with their help. So it is only in this way that Kierkegaard and Marx can be said to presuppose Hegel. Kierkegaard's existentialism assumes – just like Marx's materialism – Hegel's idealism. *Grundtvig rejects an idealistic as well as a materialist philosophy:* of course mankind consists of both the bodily and the spiritual; but not all of the spiritual in man is divine. He has a self-awareness, a soul, through which, at least to some degree, he has the ability to act freely, i. e. control both the bodily and the spiritual part of his being. He can be made responsible for his actions. The evil in men cannot be reduced to the bodily: for the body, like everything in this world, is created by God and is therefore in its origin good. But man has in his soul an ability to act freely against God's purpose as well as in accordance with it. This double possibility is the reason for the deviation from God's purpose which in Christian usage is called the Fall or the fall of man.

Perhaps it is now easier to understand why Grundtvig was for so long suspicious of every system that places a decisive weight on man's *freedom* to act, and which finds grounds for this freedom in human *reason*. According to the Bible it was through this freedom to act against God's will that the Fall occurred; man fell through abusing his reason, by setting it in place of God, if only for a moment. Yet it is also through this freedom that man is given *an ability to believe,* which is more than the instinct or drive of an animal, more even than the slave's obedience to his master. *Faith is the mature person's natural development of the child's trust.*

When Grundtvig realised that he had not become a clergyman merely out of obedience to his parents, and that his defence of true Christianity was not merely a legal duty, but that he could be a clergyman because as a free man in the Kingdom of Denmark he followed a call from God that he felt within himself and that a congregation wished him to pursue – with no ambitions to be a reformer or prophet and without being prevented at the same time from being a historian, linguistic and literary scholar and poet – then he chose freely to follow his call. Then he realised why the Fall is *not* the first expression of freedom. The first expression of freedom is the child's trust in its parents and faith in the God who has created both them and the whole world that we have been given to live in. He had actually forgotten this – like most people in our day. But when he again ventured to depict the religion and mythology of his pre-Christian ancestors, then he finally realised *what the situation of modern man is like:* he has the freedom to choose between Christianity and non-Christianity – "as an adult child".

It may be that Grundtvig did not read or understand all that Kierkegaard wrote, and that Kierkegaard did not know everything that Grundtvig had said and written; but they have both known the *situation* in which it was written, though each from his own side. Today the position of the Church vis-a-vis the people is quite different, inasmuch as it was more common to go to church then than it is today. Søren Kierkegaard was disgusted by the "official Christianity " of his age and he ended his writing career with violent attacks formulated in a number of newspaper articles and in the journal *The Moment* (1855), whose bitterness can still be felt by a present-day reader. It was re-published in 1961 and as a contrast to it the editor of the volume, P. G. Lindhardt, published Grundtvig's sermons for the same Church Year under the title *Confrontation* (1974). Grundtvig did not allow the name of Kierkegaard to be mentioned in his house throughout the whole of this period; he had felt himself under attack. So Lindhardt is undoubtedly right to see in the sermons Grundtvig's response to Kierkegaard, first and foremost in connection with the calling of J. P. Mynster to be "one of the real witnesses for truth" (the Danish translation of the word "martyr"): Grundtvig declares in his sermon for May 20th 1855 that his congregations neither are nor pretend to be "as capable and mature witnesses for truth as Our Lord Jesus Christ Himself or His apostles" and he names the Holy Spirit and Jesus' disciples as "the only reliable witnesses" about Him. The fault of the Church, says Grundtvig, is "that we who preached the gospel, neglected to take them along with us" – a statement which shows Grundtvig's solidarity with the clergy of the State Church. The day Kierkegaard died, Grundtvig preached on Matt. 22:15-22 ("Is it lawful to give tribute unto Caesar, or not?"). He said that each man must decide with his own conscience whether he can be a clergyman or go to church in the country he belongs to, or must worship God outside the State Church; but as the Danish law now "at last" stands, one can also make that decision without thereby giving up an iota of the right that God has reserved for Himself" – which is, to speak His Word to those who believe. Jesus confounded the Pharisees and "tore to shreds his enemies' false agreement" with His answer: "Render therefore unto Caesar the things which are Caesar's; and unto God the things that are God's;" for the battle "between the Kingdom of God and the kingdoms of this world" will continue "as long as the world lasts" and everyone must take part in it with his conscience, faith and conviction.

The difference between Grundtvig and Kierkegaard can be seen in their *attitude to time*. For Kierkegaard as for Kant time was a concept in human reason that is necessary for us to understand what happens (that it can neither be repeated nor altered): in human conception this pattern is "endless". Eternity is something quite different, something "timeless", which man can only momentarily link up with, that is, in a choice or a decision that expresses man's freedom. For Hegel and his Danish disciple, J. L. Heiberg, it was a question of teaching contemporary man to "leap" into this metaphysical concept of existence. For Kierkegaard it was rather a matter of forcing his age to leap out of every metaphysical system because it is an illusion. Man can only face eternity in the moment by choosing and acting freely.

Grundtvig on the other hand regarded time as limited – not merely for the individual through life and death but also for the whole world through its creation and final destruction. His major question, in the manuscript *On the Conditions of Man* (1813), was: is time dependent on man or is man dependent on time? – his attitude to an idealistic philosophy depended on the answer. And the answer was: man is dependent on time through life and death. Man is not an independent being, either in a practical or theoretical sense. With this line of thought Grundtvig broke out of the magic circle of idealistic philosophy in 1813. Only an independent being, God, is imaginable as living outside time, in a world of *unlimited* time and space, in eternity. And we cannot penetrate or understand such a being: we can only imagine him as creator of our world, limited as it is by time and space.

For Grundtvig it was not a complicated matter to imagine that God had revealed Himself at a particular moment in the history of mankind, in a person who was born, lived for a number of years, died, but returned to the eternal existence in which he belonged. And it was not a complicated matter to believe that this person spoke the truth about his fellow-beings and their existence in life and death. For Kierkegaard it became a philosophical problem: "Does a historical starting-point exist for an eternal consciousness?" (*Philosophical Fragments*). Only the individual living person can for a moment make contact with the eternal; people and events in the past could neither possess nor acquire any significance for the individual living person's gaining a life in eternity. This fundamental religious problem of Kierkegaard's is based simply on a concept of time. For Grundtvig it did not exist. Kierkegaard called on all his mental powers to solve it, and refused of course to recognize Grundtvig's uncomplicated explanation.

It is possible to think along other lines than those set down by Kant,

300

Hegel and Marx. One does not have to tie oneself down to an idealistic or materialist philosophy. One does not even have to make one's religion depend on an existentialism that confronts man with impossible demands. One can admit there are limits to man's knowledge and action that cannot be overstepped. One can see the limits to our material resources and the emptiness behind the annihilation of what they have given us so far, in the body and the soul.

It is possible to reconcile the idea of man's development in the past, present and future with the thought that neither man nor the universe have created themselves. In other words it is not unreasonable to imagine that the world has been created by a power that does *not* allow itself to be known by human reason. Nor is it unreasonable to imagine that this unknowable power has nonetheless enabled us through our senses, our imagination and our ability to think, which is developed by the feelings we have in common with the animals, to come to know this development, its former path and future possibilities. It is these ideas Grundtvig has seen expressed in the "Mosaic-Christian view of life", i.e. of "natural man", as he also writes. In the same place he calls man "a divine experiment" – using for once a scientific image.

For Grundtvig there was no clash between seeing man as a highly-developed animal and seeing him as created by God. But throughout his works he protested at seeing the experimenting and speculative reason as the embryo from which everything develops. Human reason is not God. Precisely because human intelligence is man's highest and most recently-developed faculty it cannot be the root from which the human soul, not to mention mankind and the world, have developed. Human reason and intelligence are, according to Grundtvig, just like human imagination in being developed by the *senses,* through which man, like the animals, familiarizes himself with his surroundings; in particular the ability to feel, from which the inner feelings have developed. "A thought is at heart nothing other than a feeling that has become aware of itself", says Grundtvig, adding that it becomes so in action. In these words lies the clue to his view of the human soul and human life – in a way that shows how he differs from the view that has been common in psychology since Voltaire and Rousseau emphasised reason and feeling respectively as man's most important faculties. In Grundtvig's psychology and anthropology this division does not exist. Instead he regards man as a *unity* in which "Spirit and dust can penetrate each other and be enlightened in a common divine consciousness" – i.e. where the spiritual and the bodily fuse together and enlighten each other in the human consciousness which can thereby gradually become what it was meant to be, because it is created to resemble its maker – and not just "an ape, destined to ape the other animals and then itself until the end of the world".

It is possible to see man in accordance with the "Mosaic-Christian view", as an alternative to the view that reduces man to an imitation of the next most developed animal. And the strange thing about Grundtvig's consideration of the biblical view of man is that it imagines a future development that counteracts every division in man and thus approaches a greater and greater likeness to the unknowable power that has created him.

Grundtvig gives only a few hints as to his view of man in the introduction to *Norse Mythology* (1832). Amplification must be sought in his philosophical considerations in the first three volumes of *Danevirke* (1816-19) and the drafts for them from 1813-15. The *impossibility* that Georg Brandes found of reconciling Darwin's theory of evolution with the Christian view of man as created and diverted from his divine destiny, was for Grundtvig a *possibility*. And the assumption of this possibility was for Grundtvig a precondition for working together with people of a different opinion. Those who could not accept the possibility had to be opposed – in a *free*, spiritual battle.

However, for Grundtvig the Christian faith was more than this view. Faith is based on the recognition that man cannot himself heal the wound that was inflicted by his divergence from his divine destiny; for this a new, super-human power was required: God's forgiveness, which Jesus has given all who believe in His Word. And for Grundtvig, there was nothing to prevent him cooperating scientifically, educationally and politically with people who had a different faith from his own.

Grundtvig and Grundtvigianism as a Political Factor

by BIRGITTE THYSSEN

Both Grundtvig himself and his supporters or friends, the so-called grundtvigians, left their mark on Danish politics in various ways in the last century. In the following article we shall take a closer look at their achievements, ending our study with Grundtvig's death in 1872, by which time the formation of the United Left Party in 1870, splitting the grundt-vigian movement into two wings, marked the beginning of a new era in Danish politics.

Grundtvig's Political Activity

In the years 1829-31 Grundtvig undertook three trips to England, where he gained a vivid impression of the enterprising life of English society and the emphasis on the rights of freedom enjoyed by the middle class, a factor which was to be of crucial importance to his interest in Danish social life. He caught a glimpse of the present and became a 'realist'. He studiously observed the bustling social life with its restless human activity and its extrovert initiative. He realised that all the many and varied activities in trade and industry belonged to "what the nobility call the pleasure of life". His experiences in England contrasted oddly with what he knew from home: Copenhagen was a peaceful, sleepy provincial town compared to London. He wondered at the difference and gradually moved towards an explanation that was of great significance for his understanding of human life; namely that it was freedom, personal and national freedom, that lay behind English initiative. From now on it became a principal element in Grundtvig's overall view of human life that the spirit can only live and flourish in freedom. Thus his experiences in England became a basic premise for his later efforts to improve the life of the people; his stay in England made him a champion of freedom.

During his work on *Norse Mythology* (1832), in which he developed his view of the people based on his English experiences, he finally clarified the relationship between the Christian and the human. He later formulated his view of the intrinsic value of human life in the motto "First a man – then a Christian". True humanity is a precondition for being able to hear God's word. From the 1830's onwards Grundtvig widens his commitment to cover other areas, including political matters.

But Grundtvig's use of language is different from modern political usage. He speaks, for example, not of *samfundet* ("society" in our usage) but *borgerlige selskab* (lit. the society of the burghers – or middle classes), which is more or less the same thing. Grundtvig offered many opinions on economic, social, political and national matters, but he did not use these expressions; instead he spoke of *det folkelige* (= the popular/what is of the people), which included the national, the social, the political, the historical, the poetic etc. Another very common expression was "Danishness"; everything was to be as Danish as possible. Danishness embraced the whole question of Denmark's future as an independent nation, which Grundtvig was passionately interested in.

"The popular" is thus a central concept for Grundtvig, and at the same time an extremely far-reaching and complex concept. The concepts "spirit of the people" and "Danishness" are inseparably linked to it. Behind "popular culture" and the "spirit of the people" lies the hidden conviction that a nation is more than just a randomly composed group of people who live in the same place and are bound together by political, economic and social ties. Within the nation lies a mysterious and invisible power, the spirit of the people, which penetrates and activates the nation from within and makes it flourish. And this spirit of the people has created the nation's history and the whole of its development. The spirit of the people is the deep motivating force that makes the nation a unity in spite of every difference. The spirit of the people expresses itself through the native language, the living language and the living word. Every nation has its own specific national character which is peculiar to that nation and which manifests itself in that nation's language and history; and the aim is, through the activity of the spirit of the people, to develop and deepen that national character. It is therefore not a coincidence that the Danes speak Danish. Only through the Danish language can the power and activity of the spirit of the people rouse the Danish people spiritually and politically. Grundtvig believed in a national revival and that is why he entered politics.

Even though he expressed himself differently from politicians nowadays when he was engaged in political matters Grundtvig was nevertheless still talking politics. For in his day and age he had a view on every subject under the sun, including politics. He had in fact once written to one of his sons that he "always had a firmer grip on things than most people". He was not one to hide his light under a bushel.

Grundtvig's general view of the government and the constitution of the state underwent major changes in the course of his life. His work as a writer and speaker stretched from his death in 1872 right back to the start of the century. Originally he had been a supporter of absolute monarchy, which until 1848 he had believed would guarantee the Danish people the best and freest development, and therefore he disapproved of any form of popular representation. The people were not yet mature enough to take power themselves; what was first needed was a popular national revival and maturation, or what we would call in modern usage – political consciousness. He feared that government by parliamentary majority would lead to the lowest living well at the expense of the ablest. On the other hand he had complete confidence in the monarchy.

However, this did not prevent him from approving whole-heartedly of the moderate popular representation that found expression in the provincial assemblies in 1835-36, because they returned to the people their ancient right to vote. But the provincial assemblies were to be advisory only, and as an opponent of majority rule, known in those days as the "free constitution", he had no desire to see them develop into a legislative assembly. The legislative power must remain with the King, as this would ensure stable development. He expressed this desire for a free and independent monarchy, supplemented by the "free voice of the people" in a song from 1839 – "A royal hand and the nation's voice, both strong, both free". This was the order of things that he wished to continue. He therefore opposed the liberals' constitutional demand, raised after the crowning of Christian VIII in 1839, for a free constitution in Denmark. Similarly he was much displeased over the great public demonstration in March 1848 that ended with a mass procession to the King. He was sceptical of the wishes of the March movement as regards both constitutional matters and the Schleswig demands, where he feared the consequences of incorporating Schleswig into Denmark without first asking the people of Schleswig what they wanted. So on that March 21st he regarded the mass procession to Christiansborg with mixed feelings.

However, his finger was sufficiently on the pulse for him to realise which way things were moving – that absolutism was irrevocably lost and that the day of popular government had arrived; "Whatever we do, the rule of the common man and the whole population has come", he writes in 1848. And so once again he entered actively into politics. He understood that the time had arrived for the national revival that he had dreamt of since his youth – and therefore he did not join the nation's liberals. They imagined that the victory of freedom and democracy would mean that the common people who had lived under absolutism and the guardianship of government officers should now move on to being governed by clever, educated and highly-cultivated freedom fighters. They had a fundamental distrust of the people, whom they did not know much about, and they wanted control over the country reserved for themselves. Grundtvig on the other hand, throughout his childhood and his youth, had been very close to the peasant population, which needed only to be awakened to independence and responsibility. For him the education and awakening of the people on the one hand and their political freedom on the other were two sides of the same coin.

In England he had learned how much freedom means for the people's skills and their development, so that when he became a member of the Constituent Assembly in 1848 he was the parliament's most radical member; he wanted the maximum freedom possible. His election programme was expressed in the words: "Denmark and Danishness above everything, genuine blood brotherhood with our Northern neighbours, war and no truce against all Germanity on Danish soil, and bold demands for the freedom and validity of the popular voice, and thus in every way a popular and true Danish government". He was a member of the constituent Assembly until its dissolution, after which he had a parliamentary seat with brief interruptions from 1850 to 1858, and again in 1866 as an opponent of the revised constitution.

In parliament he was a warm advocate of freedom in every area of life – not only in the Church and at school, but also in business and trade and in government and legislation. However, he was far too one-sided and far too little a pragmatist to exert a direct influence on the legislative process and political life in general. At the same time there is no doubt that despite his age – he was already 65 when he entered parliament – Grundtvig performed his duties well. He was known as the bard and educator of the people, and his efforts in Church and national life had already left such a deep mark that his presence and forceful personality were difficult to avoid. He stood there as the others' guilty conscience and when he spoke, everybody listened. On the other hand he also annoyed his associates with his rambling, one-sided and pugnacious style: "The peculiar method of negotiation which the honourable member permits himself," the National Liberal, Krieger, once said of Grundtvig, "will not cause me to forget the respect I owe the assembly or the respect I owe Denmark's bard, N. F. S. Grundtvig". The other prominent politician, Monrad, called Grundtvig and another politician, Tscherning, "The only two members whom we would deem geniuses. It is as if I was watching a beautiful, natural phenomenon, as if I was seeing active volcanoes."

We shall now take note of Grundtvig's views on various matters that were being dealt with in parliament and which show how his belief in freedom left its mark:

1) On the General Military Conscription. Before the 1849 Constitution conscription was for the most part the responsibility of the peasantry. It might be imagined that Grundtvig with his fondness for the peasantry would support a general conscription, thus removing the gap between the social classes by making conscription a duty for everyone. But instead he demanded the abolition of conscription and the establishment of all national defence on a voluntary basis. What he had in mind was a general voluntary arming of the nation.

2) On Economic Freedom. He was also a supporter of the greatest economic freedom possible and regarded private property and freedom of trade as cornerstones of economic life. He thus made himself a spokesman in parliament for the abolition of all compulsory guild membership. Trade was to be completely free.

3) On Church and School. Church and school matters in particular enjoyed Grundtvig's interest and favour. Here too he asked for a wide-ranging freedom. Already in the 1830's he had supported the expansion of Church freedom in the belief that the individual's attitude to matters of faith and to the Church should not be influenced by society. Also at that time he had put forward a proposal that would make it possible to obtain release from the parish-tie (the "obligation to avail oneself exclusively of the services of the incumbent of the parish", – Danish-English Dictionary – Vinterberg and Bodelsen, Gyldendal 1966), and to go to another church than the parish church; in 1855 with Grundtvig's support this was made law. On the educational side he opposed all compulsory schooling and supported the law of May 1855 which increased the freedom of schools.

In his old age he was again given the opportunity to prove that he took the battle for freedom seriously. In 1858 he had concluded his parliamentary activity, but he returned after the defeat by Prussia in 1864, when reactionary forces with the wind in their sails prepared a revision of the constitution on the basis that the best and safest exercise of power lay with the "educated, the wealthy and the gifted". Grundtvig, who was by now nearly 83 years old, allowed himself to be elected to the *landsting* (the upper chamber of the national parliament) in order to protest against the *landsting* itself with all its privileges. He became the spokes-man for the Left party's opposition against the new restriction of the general franchise. With great energy and conviction he spoke against "the privilege, the purse and arithmetic" and prophesied that the new propo-sal would offer a miserable future to King and country. When the law was nevertheless passed, introducing a limited franchise to the *landsting,* Grundtvig and Tscherning went to the King to urge him to use his right of veto. But they were not even allowed to see him.

With this battle against the revised constitution Grundtvig's political career came to an end. What gave him his independent profile in Danish politics was his stubborn insistence on the cause of freedom, which at the same time made him parliament's most radical member. Through his participation in politics he had opened the way for his supporters, the grundtvigians; and his political beliefs and popular ideology were the starting-point for the political movement that bears his name.

The Church Society

In the 1860's the Grundtvig movement made a political and popular breakthrough. Around 1860 grundtvigianism still played no genuinely independent part in Danish politics. But as a result of the growing popu-lar support that grundtvigianism was gradually gaining there arose amongst a number of grundtvigians a desire to make their presence felt in Danish political life, a presence that bore the particular stamp of Grundt-vig, based on the grundtvigian view of life and the popular enlightenment that it entailed. The grundtvigians thus began on a politicisation and organisation of the movement.

Their first real society, formed in the 1860's, was the Society for Free-dom in the Folk Church, called "The Church Society". Since Grundtvig's formulation of his programme of Church politics in the 1830's, demand for freedom within the Church had been on the grundtvigians' agenda. A milestone was reached in 1855 with the law on release from the parish-tie, but there was still a long way to the free formation of congregations which Grundtvig had in mind and which was also to include "the freedom of the clergy".

At the first of the Grundtvig "friends' meetings", organized in 1863 in connection with Grundtvig's 80th birthday, the demand for full freedom of the clergy (including full dogmatic and lithurgical freedom) was again made by Grundtvig, who in front of the 700 or so grundtvigians who had gathered from throughout the country expressed his view that the free-dom of the clergy could be achieved "so long as all the clergy wish for it and express that wish". But it had been his "greatest sadness" to have found amongst his "clergy friends" the "keenest opponents" of this demand, which, according to Grundtvig was a condition for the continued existence of grundtvigianism in the Folk Church. Several leading grundtvigians were well-disposed towards the thought, but others rejected the demand for dogmatic and liturgical freedom, which in their opinion would only lead to confusion and dissension in the local churches. They could however agree on an extension of the other area of the freedom of the clergy, namely the minister's personal freedom and right, for example, to refuse on the Church's behalf to serve people in church whom he considered to be non-believers.

At the end of the meeting the landowner, H. R. Carlsen, rose to say that the discussions had made it clear that the disagreement was particularly over the range of freedom the clergy should be allowed. He would therefore propose that the assembly called upon the conveners to set up a committee that could consider what legal freedom it was desirable to acquire for the clergy in the Folk Church. The majority of the assembly gave their consent to Carlsen's proposal.

The 22 conveners of the friends' meeting followed Carlsen's proposal to form a committee and handed the task over to those conveners who lived in or around Copenhagen. Sofus Høgsbro, the former principal of Rødding Folk High School, now a member of parliament and more than any other the driving-force behind the political efforts of the grundtvigians, proposed a meeting on September 23rd to which in particular the grundtvigian members of the *landsting* were invited. The meeting discussed amongst other things a legal proposal drawn up by Høgsbro on "the right to free activity by the clergy within the Folk Church", and it was agreed at the request of Høgsbro to form a proper society for Freedom in the Folk Church instead of just setting up a committee. The provisional committee of the society constituted itself with Carlsen and Høgsbro as the political leaders and the clergymen, Gunni Busck, Peter Rørdam and Kristen Køster as the Church leaders. As the society's secretary, Høgsbro was given the task of writing the invitation to join the society which was to be sent to amongst others the participants in the friends' meeting.

Høgsbro worked on the invitation in October 1863, discussing it with both Grundtvig and Carlsen. It was debated at the two committee meetings on October 30th and November 5th, where it underwent a number of changes; Grundtvig and Høgsbro, for example, wanted a more radical approach to the question of the local church's participation in the choice of their incumbent, but they ran into opposition from Peter Rørdam who refused to go so far. It was decided to print 600 copies of the invitation and Køster was requested to send it to participants in the friends' meeting and to other "friends of the cause".

The invitation bore the stamp of the contradictory ideas that the five conveners appear to have had. On the one hand one can sense the antipathy towards organising, a feeling many grundtvigians shared and which finds expression in the introduction to the invitation, where it looks almost as if regret is being felt at the need to establish a society. On the other hand the relatively solid structure which is hinted at for the society's activity seems to suggest a firmer hand behind the proceedings, probably Høgsbro's.

The aim of the society, according to the invitation, is to work towards the state of affairs which Section 80 of the national constitution allows ("the constitution of the Folk Church is governed by law"), whereby the Church secures as much freedom from State control as possible, that is, "especially in the preaching of the gospel and the rejection of all papacy in matters of faith". The law of 1855 on the release from the parish-tie would form a reasonable starting-point for the Church constitution, which should also include the following points:

1) Full release from the parish-tie also for the clergy, i.e. the clergy should have the right to refuse the sacraments.

2) The right to release from the parish-tie in order to join a non-established Church, so that a clergyman without an official appointment could gather a congregation anywhere in the country.

3) A majority of Folk Church members in a parish should have some influence on the choice of, and dismissal of, their incumbent.

4) Total freedom for the clergy to teach, on a biblical basis, in accordance with their "honest convictions", i.e. dogmatic and liturgical freedom.

5) The State must be responsible for the theological training, appointment and remuneration of the clergy, so that they did not have any financial relationship to, and thus dependency on, their congregations. Relations between the incumbent and the congregation were to be "mutually free". Finally the State was to make a grant towards the stipend of the non-established clergy.

The pivot of the programme was the desire for the freedom of the clergy and for making the relationship between minister and congregation completely free. The layman's influence was to be increased through the demand for a free choice of incumbent and free activity of clergy in the parish, and in general the demand for "freedom for the congregation". Above all lay the desire to help towards undermining the minister's social position as a government officer in the parish; this is not so far from the

310

plan put forward by Høgsbro, who believed that only in this way could the clergy become "the natural spokesmen of the local churches".

With regard to the society's method of activity it was the aim of the conveners to get "the necessary and modern" bill put before parliament. In addition the society would expound the idea of Church freedom at public meetings, which the society would attempt to get started in the different areas of the country; at the same time pamphlets on the subject would be produced and a monthly journal published for the society.

The committee had not worked out a proposal for the society's laws, but at the constituent meeting on September 3rd, it had been decided that the society's executive committee should be centred on Copenhagen and elected by the Copenhagen group and by the members of the national parliament who had joined the society and who lived in or around Copenhagen. But the conveners hoped that members in other parts of the country would form branches of the society with independent committees. The members of the society had no other obligation to the society than to give it their "spiritual support". There was no fixed subscription, only voluntary contributions.

At the committee meeting on December 16th Køster could announce that 316 people had joined The Church Society, and by the meeting on January 29th 1864 membership had risen to 441. A list of these members must have been drawn up, but it has proved impossible to trace. Køster also stated that 250 members had agreed to subscribe to the projected society journal and that 205 *rigsdaler* had been sent in as members' voluntary contributions.

The Grundtvigian Organisational Structure

The society did not send out a public invitation to join The Church Society, but only to participants in the friends' meeting and other "friends of the cause", who were urged to spread the word to other "friends". In other words, it was personal contact and influence within the grundtvigian circles that were to build up the society's membership. A similar method of approach had been used in connection with the invitation to the first grundtvigian friends' meeting, where the appeal had been made to relatively few, but these "representatives" must have supported the idea of a friends' meeting and in their local areas encouraged others to take part, with the result that the number of participants far exceeded the conveners' expectations.

There is much to suggest that the life of the grundtvigian political organisation as it found expression in the 1860's followed a similar pattern to the one above, with a number of forward troops in and around Copenhagen who started the work and reliable grundtvigian representatives out in the local areas who through their personal contacts and their status in the parishes, at private meetings and the like could bring "the word" out to the Grundtvig-minded laymen on the spot, whom they knew better than the Copenhagen leadership. These spokesmen were also responsible at a local level for carrying out the proposals that the Copenhagen leadership agreed on.

This view is confirmed by a new initiative that took place in June 1865. Carlsen, Høgsbro and Grundtvig planned to cooperate in the publication of a political weekly which was to be the press organ of the grundtvigian left, and in this connection Høgsbro sent out requests to roughly a hundred leading grundtvigians to take up subscriptions in the projected magazine. He enclosed subscription lists which these grundtvigians were to present in their parishes in order to promote local support.

It appears that this organisational structure worked according to plan. The magazine, which was given the name *Danish Folk News,* was launched in October 1865 with Høgsbro as editor, and it made a decisive contribution towards the strengthening of grundtvigianism's political influence. A large majority of the representatives reacted to the appeal either by becoming subscribers themselves or by returning the invitation with the names of more subscribers.

The fact that in 1865 these men are expressly chosen as useful contacts in the establishment of a political weekly based on grundtvigian views must indicate that also in previous years these people had shown an interest in a grundtvigian political commitment. There is much evidence that they were typical of the spokesmen that the Copenhagen leadership based its organisational efforts on.

Resumption of The Church Society

The society's work in its first phase lasted for a very limited period. Its inability really to establish itself is apparent from the lack of local support for the committee's proposal in the invitation to hold public meetings and spread news of the society and its aims. There also appears to have been an internal conflict within the committee which as far as can be judged was split into a popular (political) wing around Høgsbro and a more Church-orientated wing. The dissension surfaced in connection with amongst others the publication of the projected monthly magazine. At the committee meeting on October 16th 1863, by which time 165 subscribers had already come forward, it was decided to publish as quickly as possible.

The magazine, which at Høgsbro's suggestion was provisionally called *The Folk Church, a Monthly Magazine for Church Freedom,* was to contain articles by Kristen Køster, Grundtvig and Høgsbro. In addition the first number was to include a general appeal for membership of the society, a draft of which Høgsbro had drawn up beforehand. It was in particular on this draft, which supposedly represented the whole of the committee, that disagreement arose.

The result of the committee members' discussions in the new year was a decision to stop all activities of the society until further notice. Officially this was justified on the grounds of "the war situation", but the closure was in fact largely the doing of the Church wing on the committee; this can be seen from the fact that the more popular wing around Høgsbro refused to stop the society's activities and even in May were considering publication of an appeal for support at the parliamentary election in June, although they gave up the idea again in the face of opposition.

The background to the resumption of committee work was the politically motivated dismissal of Vilhelm Birkedal from his post as vicar of Ryslinge on September 22nd 1865. The broad movement of support that followed in grundtvigian circles created a realistic possibility for the resumption of the society's activities. Vilhelm Birkedal was invited to a new committee meeting on February 20th 1866; he had been an opponent of the society in 1863, but now wished it to restart.

It is characteristic that on its resumption in 1866 the society placed less emphasis on appearing as an exclusively grundtvigian society, preferring if possible to involve other forces. This was due to the fact amongst others that in the second half of the 1860's the grundtvigian political initiatives increasingly bore the stamp of the "popular" grundtvigians, especially the peasants, the free school men and the high school men, who through the constitutional battle had become more politically conscious. They wished for a more outward-looking policy to reach new circles.

They were not alone in their belief that Birkedal had been unjustly dismissed, for leading members of the left who did not hold grundtvigian views nevertheless expressed their sympathy for the cause. Further evidence that the committee were determined to involve more people than before in the society is to be found in the decision to write the new invitation in more general terms of greater independence and freedom for the local churches.

The main point of view in the public invitation that Høgsbro composed was that the Folk Church, 17 years after the introduction of the national constitution, still preserved the major features of the old State Church constitution in spite of Section 80 of the Constitution, and that the only significant progress that had been made was the law on the release from the parish-tie. Thus it should be the aim of the society to reform the State Church constitution by law (on the basis of the principle already enshrined in the law on release from the parish-tie) and achieve a true people's Church with free congregations around free clergymen. The society gave Birkedal's "arbitrary dismissal" as the direct occasion for its resumption, as well as the danger that "the constitution of the projected *landsting* presents a threat to the development of our Church freedom". Neither the invitation nor the rules of the society contain much information about its structure beyond the fact that there was a committee of 5 members in Copenhagen who were to be elected at annual general meetings.

Despite the society's loose structure the grundtvigians nevertheless knew where they were going, as is proved by the swift rise in membership. Numbers increased from 711 on April 21st to 940 on May 1st and 1095 on May 15th.

The committee's function was outwardly very limited, with the result that the popular meeting in March at Nykøbing Mors, called after Birkedal's dismissal, made a direct appeal to the committee to organize public meetings.

Not until mid-May did the committee respond to the request; then they pointed out that since the society's resumption they had deliberately stayed in the background because of the battle in the offing against the revised constitution; all efforts must be put into the parliamentary elections in June. At the same time the committee emphasized that it was through public meetings that the society could best be served, though this must be left to the members to decide. This was the last public statement from the committee; committee members took part in some of the popular meetings which were arranged locally on the subject of Church freedom, but the committee apparently preferred to hand over the initiative to the local representatives, and to work behind the scenes from now on. The society's accounts book shows that it continued until 1868. At the same time it is worth underlining that many of the grundtvigians who arranged the popular meetings worked as representatives in connection with the founding of the *Danish Folk News*.

The Question of the Free Congregations

In spite of his dismissal Vilhelm Birkedal was determined to continue his ministry in Ryslinge. This decision called forth many expressions of sympathy from grundtvigians and paved the way for a grundtvigian initiative to change the law in favour of a free clergy. A large meeting in Odense in January 1865, called by grundtvigian peasants, teachers and clergymen, resulted in a declaration recommending that the Government revive and support the proposal for free clergy activity within the Folk Church and thus meet a real need amongst local congregations.

At the March meeting in Nykøbing Mors a headmaster, Hr. Poulsen, stated that the reason for the meeting was the government's "ruthless and arbitrary behaviour" towards Birkedal, and that in order to oppose Birkedal's dismissal from the Folk Church, "his co-religionists" around the country should work for an extension of the law on the release from the parish-tie. The meeting ended with a declaration sent to the Society for Freedom in the Folk Church, who were urged to ensure that views were expressed on the subject at public meetings throughout the country.

On November 26th 1866 during the first parliamentary session after the change in the constitution Høgsbro proposed a bill on the free churches question. He had drawn it up himself at the end of October after which he had discussed it with the Church Society's committee and with Birkedal and Grundtvig, all of whom agreed that it was very moderate in its demands compared with what the grundtvigians could have wished for. But if it was to have a chance of passing through both chambers and especially the *landsting,* where opposition was greatest, it was necessary to limit it to meeting the immediate requirement of being able to form free congregations within the Folk Church, a point particularly pertinent to the Birkedal case. The bill would enable a minimum of 20 households, provided they had acquired a church building or prayer-hall and lived within 3 miles of it, to be released from their parish-tie and join an authorized clergyman to form a congregation around him; and this congregation was still to be regarded as a part of the Folk Church.

In support of the bill Birkedal sent a petition to the *Rigsdag* signed by 189 members of his free church in which they asked to be recognized as part of the Folk Church. The proposal was also supported by 72 vicars – mainly of grundtvigian persuasion – with Grundtvig at their head. In 1867 he addressed the *Rigsdag* in support of the petition from the Ryslinge congregation.

But the bill also had its opponents, led by Bishop H. L. Martensen, the

High Church leader. Between the high churchmen and the grundtvigians there was a fundamental disagreement on the interpretation of Section 80 of the 1849 Constitution which stated that the Folk Church constitution was governed by law. Martensen and many others interpreted this as meaning that the Folk Church should have a constitution passed in a single bill and not bit by bit; all the minor Church bills should be stopped until representation for the Folk Church was created by a constitution. The grundtvigians understood the expression "by law" to mean "by laws" or "by legislation" as could already be seen from their initiative for a law on release from the parish-tie; they thus supported a bit-by-bit settlement within the Folk Church. What annoyed Martensen most was that in their Church politics he believed the grundtvigians were simply feathering their own nest. On top of this many official Church people feared that the grundtvigian initiative would lead to the dissolution of the Folk Church. Martensen therefore worked to persuade the *landsting* to oppose the proposal and suggested that the "Church's own voice" be heard through a Church commission. In accordance with Martensen's line of thought the convention of Copenhagen clergy issued an address on February 20th proposing a postponement of the adoption of the suggestion until "expert advice" had been called; at the same time they recommended the establishment of a Church Commission. The address, which was sent to every parish, received the support of 758 clergy and about 70,000 laymen. This protest had a specific effect on the further debate in the *landsting*, where the bill was refused a third reading.

In the course of the summer of 1867 the proposal for free congregations and the whole question of an extension of Church freedom, including the bill on the participation of congregations in their choice of an incumbent, was made the subject of diocesan conferences around the country on the basis of a circular letter on April 15th from the Minister for the Church, Rosenørn-Teilmann to the country's 7 bishops. Apart from Bishop P. C. Kierkegaard, who was a moderate grundtvigian, the combined bishops expressed their opposition to the free church law and its "disintegrating tendencies" and to the bill on the choosing of a minister; a majority within the clergy were of the same opinion.

Incensed by the diocesan conferences and the attitude expressed above, the grundtvigian representatives organized a number of popular laymen's meetings at different places in the country in the course of the summer and autumn of 1867. Here there was strong support for the proposals on free churches and the participation of the congregations in the choice of minister and a point-bank refusal to settle for a special law to cover Birkedal's case alone. A common feature of the meetings was that they could see a close connection between the two bills; many stressed that it was a condition of their support for allowing lay influence in the choice of a minister that the free churches bill was carried, so that a minority in the congregation who were voted down were not forced to accept the majority's choice of a minister but could themselves choose another and start a new church. The meetings also resembled one another considerably as regards subject-matter, but they are interesting as a guide as to which grundtvigians expressed an opinion publicly, or in other words, who the local representatives were; and they are an example of how the grundtvigian organisational structure (outlined above) worked out in practice. Thus the existence of The Church Society committee is barely noticeable; the meetings were arranged solely on local initiative, though presumably on the inspiration of the committee, and at a number of meetings committee members were invited to take part. This is precisely how the grundtvigians appear to have worked: the initiative came from the local group but on the basis of a request and with support from the central group.

A summary of these meetings reveals that a lot of the grundtvigians who acted as conveners and who spoke at them were the same people who functioned as representatives in the summer of 1865 on the occasion of the foundation of the political weekly *Danish Folk News,* which must indicate amongst other things that they pursued the grundtvigian initiatives or in other words were among the grundtvigian representatives in the organisational structure outlined above.

The powerful stir around "the free church question" caused the Frijs government itself to take up the matter and amongst others to appoint as Minister for the Church the moderate grundtvigian Bishop P. C. Kierkegaard, who was the only bishop not to oppose the bill on free churches within the Folk Church.

In December 1867 he presented to parliament a bill on the free churches that grundtvigian circles were far from satisfied with, since it took too little notice of the *folketing's* (the lower chamber) previous decisions and too much notice of the *landsting's* reservations. They were particularly opposed to the requirement that the choice of minister should be ratified by the King; there was however approval that the government had actually presented a bill. It passed quickly through the *folketing* but met stiff opposition in the *landsting,* partly as a result of the protest movement that grew up. Meetings were organized to fight it and clergy and bishops sent addresses and letters to the *Rigsdag* protesting against the "dangerous and disintegrating" proposal. All this turmoil was too much for Bishop Kierkegaard, who resigned, to be followed as Minister for the Church by Aleth Hansen, a rural dean. When a majority in the *landsting* was prepared to defeat the bill, the Government took the matter into the cabinet, with the result that since no one dared to bring the Government down, the bill was passed with a couple of amendments at a meeting on April 28th and made law on May 15th.

In grundtvigian circles in many parts of the country there was great dissatisfaction with the final wording of the law. Carlsen in particular was bitter and spoke of a "deformed" law worth nothing. Birkedal and the Ryslinge Church, however, regarded it as a kind of victory.

At about the same time as the free church law passed through parliament the Society for Freedom in the Folk Church ceased to exist. Its account-book was kept up until October 1868. The demand for free clergy (dogmatic and liturgical freedom), which had been in the Society's original programme in 1863 but which as a result of opposition from various grundtvigians was omitted at the resumption of the society in 1866 was never met in practice; but the original aim of "free clergy for free churches" was achieved in limited form through the Free Church Law.

The importance of the society lies in its being the first real, organized gathering of grundtvigians in the 1860's; indirectly it also paved the way in the battle for the free church law, which attracted a large number of the Left party to the grundtvigians and proved that grundtvigianism had become a political force.

The National Left in the Rigsdag

Through the political efforts within the Church and the debate in the constitution, political grundtvigianism had become so powerful that after the change in the constitution in 1866 a grundtvig-orientated group could also be formed in the *Rigsdag* – this was the National Left. Together with the political weekly, *Danish Folk News* founded in 1865, which helped to form opinion and had a great influence on the movement's progress amongst the population, the *Rigsdag's* group was the most distinctive expression of political grundtvigianism of the time.

During its lifetime to 1870 the group consisted of roughly 20 members. In the contemporary press and colloquially it was often known as "the grundtvigians", a word which was only partially applicable since not everyone in the group held grundtvigian views. But throughout the period it generally included grundtvigians in its leadership, and as a majority of its members were actually grundtvigians the term is on the whole defensible. Either way there existed a powerful, distinctively grundtvigian group in the *Rigsdag*.

What particularly distinguished the National Left from other groups in the *Rigsdag* was the grundtvigian ideology, which in adapted form can be characterized as the core of the group's major ideas. For it was not everything in the grundtvigian view of things that in the eyes of the leading political grundtvigians could be used in the political context of the times.

One of the leading grundtvigian politicians, Sofus Høgsbro, who was at the time editor of the *Danish Folk News,* used its columns in 1867 to explain how the National Left saw themselves. Here he asserted that it was necessary to make a distinction between grundtvigianism's views of the Church on the one hand and of the people and politics on the other. The grundtvigians in the *Rigsdag* laid particular emphasis on the best possible development of the social life of the people. Similarly one had to distinguish political from Church-orientated grundtvigians. It was possible to agree with grundtvigianism on how best to serve the "special character of the people" and to demand Church and School freedom, without having to go along with Grundtvig's view of the Church. Whether one accepted the Church view was, in a political context, up to the private individual; what could be used in a political context were Grundtvig's ideas for the people. He stresses that it was the task of the *Rigsdag* to establish the outward forms and conditions for the development of society, and on these specifically outward forms grundtvigians could co-operate with non-grundtvigians (for example in the National Left) even though they had different views of life. For it was not the *Rigsdag's* task but the Church's and the School's task to create a "life-content" in society.

But even though Høgsbro was keen for the National Left to be regarded as one of the genuine people's left-wing groups in the *Rigsdag* the truth was rather that the group took up a centre position between the peasant-left groups and the national liberals. As Høgsbro himself maintained, on most domestic policies the National Left could work together with, for example, the Tscherning Left, since both Grundtvig and Tscherning wished to develop the life of the people as far as possible. The difference between them was that they wished to reach this goal along separate paths: "Tscherning by starting from the physical world, Grundtvig from the spiritual". Grundtvig, who in this context is to be regarded as synonymous with the National Left, could thus go along with much of Tscherning's programme, which Høgsbro characterized as thrift with the state finances, a fair distribution of the burden of taxation, social and political equality, freedom of trade etc., that is, Tscherning's Left Party programme. But Grundtvig did not believe that it was enough just to take care of people's material needs. If the goal of the best possible life for the people was to be reached, broad sections of the population would need to be awakened and liberated. The ordinary man must "thus be trained to use his spiritual powers; only then can we expect him to realise how to use his physical ones and to acquire for himself the outward necessities that support human life and the greatest possible development". A consequence of this spiritual and political liberation was that the State's grip on the Church and the School would need to be loosened.

Thus on a large number of questions the National Left was in reality closer to the National Liberals than the left groups. This was true not least in foreign affairs, especially in their views on nationality, on a common policy with the other Scandinavian countries and on national solidarity with Schleswig. What they had most of all in common was scorn for the "materialists" and respect for the "spirit". They agreed that the most important currents in their day were of a spiritual, ideological nature, a view that the despised "materialists" – i.e. the other peasant-left group – could not see the meaning of, according to the National Liberals and the grundtvigian politicians.

To summarize, an alliance between the National Left and the National Liberals should have had a good chance of working as a result of their common ideological attitude – in contrast to other left-wing groups, which found their basis in socio-economic conditions. But in connection with the formation of the United Left in 1870 the National Liberals joined with the farmers' party while the main part of the National Left joined the other left groups to form the United Left.

This was the signal for a period of struggle within the grundtvigian movement, which provoked an actual split between the more national-liberal wing and the leftish wing who were sympathetic towards the peasants. The tensions between the two wings had been latent throughout the period, without ever coming seriously into the open. But now the battle broke out in full force and protests were heard from the national-liberal grundtvigians against "the false alliance", which was deemed a connection between "spirit and flesh", between "Aesir and giants". This conflict continued for several years and the gulf between the two wings was never really bridged.

The conflict reached a sort of conclusion at least on the surface at the general election of 1876 when the national-liberal grundtvigians lost ground to the left-grundtvigians, a sign that the left's politics were now dominant amongst the grundtvigians.

Rødding Folk High School, the first of its kind in Scandinavia, was founded in 1844 and remained in its original form until 1864. (Lithograph by A. Nay from a prospect by F. Richardt, ca. 1850, Royal Library, Copenhagen).

Ludvig Schrøder (1836-1914), the founder and first principal of Askov High School, at the lectern surrounded by Askov teachers and pupils. (Painting by Erik Henningsen, 1902, Frederiksborg Museum).

A serious man was Christen Kold (1816-70) from Thy, at least if we are to judge from the only known portrait of him, reproduced here from a lithograph. And it was doubtless not intended as a joke when he said that the difference between his own high school and those established by academics like Ernst Trier and Frede Bojsen was that whereas *they* told their pupils about the Persian Wars, *he* gave a lecture on Mr. Larsen's wife in Ryslinge! (Royal Library, Copenhagen).

Grundtvig and the Folk High School Movement

by ROAR SKOVMAND

1. The Folk High School at Rødding

The first folk high school – not just in Denmark but in the whole world – was founded in the autumn of 1844 in the little North Schleswig village of Rødding.

What had it got to do with Grundtvig? It was not some sort of sudden realisation of his educational ideas for a "high school for the people"; nor was it the large folk university with a strongly Danish flavour in the venerable buildings of Sorø Academy that K. E. Bugge has previously described. Nevertheless Rødding was recognized by Grundtvig himself when in the summer of 1844 he made what was for him an extremely rare trip to south Jutland to speak at the biggest popular meeting that had so far taken place in the country.

The meeting was held on July 4th – American Independence Day – on the highest point in south Jutland, Skamling Hill near the Little Belt. In the recent past the poet-priest Steen Steensen Blicher had established the custom of holding annual national popular meetings at Heaven Hill (*Himmelbjerget*) near Silkeborg. The summer of 1843 saw the first meeting at Skamling Hill, when as the North Schleswig leader Peter Hiort Lorenzen put it, the people "in a single night moved Heaven Hill twelve miles to the south". (1 Danish mile = 7.532 km).

The background for these Skamling meetings was the sudden awakening of national consciousness among the two national groups that lived in the duchies of Schleswig and Holstein. From time immemorial Schleswig had been linked to the Kingdom of Denmark, and throughout half of the duchy, the language of the common man, the Church and the school was Danish. The legal language was German, as it was in South Schleswig and in the purely German Holstein, which nevertheless belonged to the Danish monarchy. In the 1830's a powerful movement had spread out from Kiel University to unite the two duchies and free them from the absolute power that the Danish King still maintained.

In the counterthrust to this Schleswig-Holstein movement the leading light was the Danish lecturer at Kiel University, Professor Christian Flor. He was strongly influenced by Grundtvig and had reviewed his major work *Norse Mythology* (1832), going so far as to claim that he was the only one to make sense of it. On the other hand Grundtvig himself had told Flor that in the review of over 50 pages Flor had understood his intentions exactly.

Flor undertook in the spirit of Grundtvig to rouse the North Schleswig peasants to safeguard their Danishness. He was reluctant to step forward publicly, least of all as a speech-maker, but behind the scenes he knew how to summon the forces that would best promote the Danish cause.

He found them in the common man. In 1836 he persuaded a North Schleswig peasant, Nis Lorenzen, the newly-elected member of the first Schleswig Assembly of landowners, burghers and peasants, to demand the use of the Danish language in the law and the public authorities in North Schleswig – a demand that was in fact agreed to by the new king, Christian VIII, in 1840. Flor's next step was to get Danish newspapers established in North Schleswig. The first of these – from 1838 – was given the "grundtvigian" name of *Danevirke* – taken from the border rampart that since Viking times had protected Denmark against German advance. Twenty years previously Grundtvig himself had published a journal of the same name. When Christian VIII appointed his brother-in-law Prince Frederik of Nör, a man with Schleswig-Holstein sympathies, to the position of viceroy over the two duchies there was much anger in Danish circles. In protest against these Schleswig-Holstein tendencies, Flor persuaded the Liberal, Peter Hiort Lorenzen, a grocer, to speak only Danish at the Schleswig Assembly. Others had done this before, though only men who had no command of German; Hiort Lorenzen had. But now, on November 11th 1842, he spoke Danish. The demonstration could not go unchallenged, and the German minutes of Hiort Lorenzen's Danish speech were struck out in the record book and replaced by the sentence, also in German: "The deputy from Sønderborg spoke Danish – he continued to speak Danish."

This incident had a powerful effect, not least on the Liberal circles in Copenhagen, who already called themselves National Liberals. Hiort Lorenzen was feted both in Copenhagen and at the first festival at Skamling Hill on May 18th 1843, where North Schleswig peasants who had bought the place celebrated the King's agreement to their demand for Danish as the official judicial language. Their spokesman was himself a south Jutland farmer, the young Laurids Skau from Sommersted. The speech he made was probably written by Christian Flor, but what impressed the audience of 6,000 was that here was an ordinary farmer standing up unabashed in public and proclaiming in ringing tones that whoever wants to talk to us in the name of the State is under obligation to address us in the national language. And when the State requires us to speak, wherever that may be, we must have the right to use our mother-tongue.

This was exactly what Hiort Lorenzen had demanded in the Schleswig Assembly Hall, and the climax of the Skamling Festival came when J. C. Drewsen from Copenhagen, a manufacturer, politician and friend of the peasants, handed over to Hiort Lorenzen a silver drinking-horn with the inscription: He continued to speak Danish.

In the very same month that the festival took place Drewsen and others of the same liberal opinion founded in Copenhagen a "Society for Schleswig Support", which set out to obtain funds for the establishment of Danish educational institutions in North Schleswig. Shortly after the Skamling Festival Flor set up the "Schleswig Society", with Laurids Skau as secretary. This society also had as its main aim the establishment of Danish educational institutions in Schleswig, in cooperation with the liberals in Denmark. But whereas the friends in Copenhagen imagined something like the practical school (*réalskolen* for children of burghers, emphasizing the 3 r's), Flor aimed in the first instance to start a school in the spirit of Grundtvig.

Already in 1841 Flor had written to the editor of *Danevirke,* Peter Christian Koch, who was himself influenced by Grundtvig: what Flor regarded as the spiritual and political salvation of the ordinary man was the same "high school idea" that Grundtvig had advocated in his latest high school publication, *Prayers and Ideas for a Danish High School in Sorø.* Flor managed to win over to his way of thinking the committees first of the Schleswig Society, later of the Copenhagen Society.

On August 14th 1843 he presented a draft to the Schleswig Society which ended as follows: "If this idea does not alarm you by its novelty, then we hope you have been given the vague but happy feeling that also for the peasant class and the burgher class there ought to be an educational institution where the pupil's everyday mood is not one of feeling oppressed: a responsibility will be laid upon you, but it will be an exhilarating one; the light will dawn on you! And without a shadow of doubt you will be able to see that in the future such a folk high school will be the strongest safeguard of all against all oppression in the community and all oppression of the spirit."

Here the words "folk high school" are used for the first time. Once the Schleswig Society had found and acquired a suitable building in Rødding close to the northern border of the duchy, Flor, as the national chairman of the school's first governing body, formulated the programme for the new school in 1844. It was based on the idea that "peasants and burghers can receive such knowledge and skills as can be of use and for pleasure, not so much with regard to the individual's particular occupation and business as to his position as a son of the nation and a citizen of the state … We call it (the institution) a high school, because it will not be any ordinary sort of boys' school, but an educational institution partly for young people past the age of confirmation, and partly for the fully-grown young farm hands and men, and we call it a folk high school because members of every trade and profession can gain entry into it, even if it is to be established mainly for the peasantry and expects to draw its pupils mainly from that class."

A few days after the publication of this programme another meeting took place at Skamling Hill, on July 4th 1844. Nearly twice as many turned up as the year before. There were speakers from North Schleswig – Laurids Skau and Hiort Lorenzen – and from Denmark – the National Liberal leaders, Orla Lehmann and Carl Ploug, and the Jewish author, Meir Aron Goldschmidt. But it was Grundtvig's speech that made the greatest impression. He praised the men of North Schleswig for "continuing to speak Danish", but he added that if the fight to reinstate the mother-tongue to its rightful place was to succeed, there must be yet another sort of school with the particular aim of preserving Danishness; its main emphasis should be on education through awareness of the people, the fatherland and the mother-tongue. He therefore congratulated the Schleswig farmers on taking the first step, the giant step, towards establishing such a school. You must, said Grundtvig, build a high school in your midst which "you can see is Danish from a hundred miles away and whose message can be heard throughout the world". It must not dishearten you that in the whole of the Kingdom of Denmark no model or likeness of it is to be found. Just as in days gone by, it must be the task of the people of Schleswig to build the model for us in the rest of the kingdom.

On November 7th that autumn Rødding Folk High School was opened, again with an exuberant speech, this time by the school's first principal, the young theologian Johan Wegener. He gripped his audience right from the beginning of his inaugural speech by quoting the first lines of a historical poem by Grundtvig's close friend, B. S. Ingemann, urging that the spirit of the past should

> shake the soul and wake the spirit,
> strengthen the heart and arm the hand
> to many a glorious Danish deed,
> to rescue Denmark in time of need.

It was a historical and poetic speech in the spirit of Grundtvig and it contained the future programme of the folk high school in a nutshell.

However, Rødding High School did not enjoy the easiest of fortunes. Hardly had it opened with a score or so male pupils in the first winter and even fewer in the following summer, before the 1848-50 war put a stop to all teaching. By then the school had already had three principals, including Flor himself for a year. When the war ended, he again put the school back on its feet, this time with a fourth principal.

Sofus Høgsbro was 28 years old. As a friend of Grundtvig's sons he had been a regular guest in the family home, and he identified himself completely with the core of Grundtvig's high school ideas. Høgsbro's inaugural speech in November 1850 was published in Grundtvig's own journal *The Dane*. The gist of it was that now that the army had secured Denmark against the enemy in the south, the task was to give the ordinary man an "insight into what serves the general interest best". It was a programme that laid greater stress on the democratic rather than on the national aim.

Høgsbro remained principal for 12 years, and in the mid-1850's the winter role rose from 35 to around 50. The pupils came not just from south Jutland but from the whole country, and they lived in a special pupils' house built in 1845. Høgsbro was closely connected with the Friends of the Peasants and the Left Party in parliament, and was elected in 1858. He was a keen advocate of Grundtvig's ideas on Church and school, and he soom became one of the Left party's leading politicians. This led to criticism of his school and a dwindling in numbers, with the result that Høgsbro resigned as principal in 1862.

His successor was yet another young principal, the 26-year-old Ludvig Schrøder. He too was close to Grundtvig, but placed greater emphasis on Christian evangelism than Høgsbro cared for. However, when Flor in his capacity of chairman of the governing-board – of which Grundtvig also was a member – heard Schrøder talk about the school to the Danish Society in Copenhagen, he realised that Schrøder was the right man to carry the school forward. Schrøder had said that the school must have three aims: through the mother-tongue and the history of the country to awaken the national consciousness – through a description of social conditions to educate skilled and able citizens – and finally to help the peasant to be cleverer at his work.

But hardly had Schrøder made a good start at Rødding before a new war broke out in 1864. This led to the loss of the duchies to the Germans and put an end to Schrøder's efforts in Rødding. Flor, however, secured the continuation of the school by acquiring a building in the little village of Askov, close to the north bank of King's Brook (*Kongeåen*), which had now become the country's border until 1920.

2. The Folk High School at Hindholm

Eight years after the establishment of the high school in Rødding a "folk-high school for adult sons of farmers and smallholders" was opened at Hindholm Farm near Fuglebjerg on Zealand. The background for Hindholm was quite different from Rødding. It was not a university professor but a smallholder, Peder Hansen, from Lundby in south Zealand, who was the driving-force behind its foundation. The idea came not from Grundtvig but from a school teacher, Rasmus Sørensen, who in 1843 had published a plan for establishing "a school for the bright lads of peasants who with the aid of further education could come to represent the peasantry".

In the 1840's Peder Hansen had travelled from village to village on Zealand, urging the smallholders to free themselves from the oppression of the landowners. In 1852 at a well-attended meeting of a south Zealand local council he proposed that they ought to get "a folk school for the adult sons of peasants and smallholders" started in the south Zealand counties. There was general support for the idea, and Peder Hansen emphasized in print the socio-political significance of the matter: "If our class are not to get the worst of it in the continued struggle against better-informed and educated opponents, it is high time that we ourselves did something so that the peasants ... have some men who ... partly as farmers, partly as smallholders can be leaders and protectors of our class in every area."

It was the head of a children's home, Anders Stephansen from Holsteinsminde, who with the support of Friends of the Peasants became leader of the new school at Hindholm, a neighbouring farm to the children's home. He himself was deeply influenced by the ideas of the enlightenment, but for his senior teacher he chose N. J. Jensen, a graduate and supporter of Grundtvig's ideas. The pupils at Hindholm came from a simpler level of society than those at Rødding, and for more than two decades Hindholm became the high school for the Zealand farmers and smallholders. It was the only folk high school in Denmark before 1864 to have more than 100 pupils in a winter season. From 1860 to 1875 it had more pupils than any of the other schools in Denmark, and teachers from Hindholm founded folk high schools or agricultural schools at eight other localities in Denmark. Both Anders Stephansen and Christian Nielsen, who replaced N. J. Jensen in 1864, were a far cry from Grundtvig, but their aim was the same as his: to awaken the pupils' social consciences and make them realize that a nation must not be split up into separate trades and professions but must develop together and blend into a unity.

3. Christen Kold's High School

In 1851 at the end of the Three Years War, Christen Kold, a trained teacher, created his own little "school for confirmed children" at Ryslinge on Funen. Here it was not a question of the local people demanding their own school, but of a teacher who wanted a school wherever the opportunity arose to start one. In addition to the money he himself had saved up he received support from evagelical circles, from clergymen of Grundtvig's persuasion and from Grundtvig himself. In a letter to a friend Kold writes: "As far as teaching theory goes, I have got it from Grundtvig ... and the practice will take care of itself. It is best learned through life."

However, the educational theory was Kold's own. He did not know Grundtvig's writings on the folk high school, and even if he had, he would hardly have used them as a guide. It is true that he dictated to his pupils long passages of excerpts he himself had made of Grundtvig's history of the world, but it was for him a sort of text for the day, an underlay for the declaration of his own ideas, which bore a strong Christian stamp.

However, Kold did follow Grundtvig's dictum to build on the living word and not on books. In 1862, long after the school had moved to Dalby near Kerteminde, Kold received a visit from the coming principal of Rødding, Ludvig Schrøder. In a letter to his brother Schrøder described him thus:

"It is a sort of Socrates who sits in his chair surrounded by a large number of farmers and farmgirls who come from far and wide to visit the school. And all the day long – apart from when he is lecturing in the school – he talks to all these people in such a way as always to stir something in them. He has a wealth of experience and of stories, and with these treasures he enriches his audience, with the clear purpose of encouraging their active efforts. They are establishing free schools for children round about in the parishes. He lets them have his former pupils as teachers, but the peasants take care of the teachers' board and lodging and consider it a privilege to be able to sacrifice something in a good cause. He lectures for an hour or an hour and a half every morning, at which time the schoolroom is full of pupils and visitors. He prefers to take a chapter out of world history, but the main point is its practical application, which he has a particularly good grip on. He aims to stir us ... to open our hearts to the spiritual world so that it can come to use us as willing instruments to proceed with the task of our people and the whole of humanity."

A comparison between Kold's school and Flor's and Høgsbro's reveals immediate differences. With Kold there was evangelism and encouragement to effort, but perhaps too little education. At Rødding there was education but perhaps too little encouragement to effort. With Kold the material revival was united with a Christian message of "God's love and Denmark's happiness". In the 1850's his roll in the winter term never exceeded 30, but in 1862 – after the school had moved to Dalum near Odense – it increased to 55 and grew to over 100 in the last year of his life, 1870.

At Rødding and later at Askov there was a group of teachers of equal ability. Kold also had a good staff who looked after the more elementary subjects of reading, writing and arithmetic, but the school rested entirely on his personality and when he died its days were numbered.

Kold's folk high school on Funen was not the first in Denmark, but it was the one that made the strongest mark on the future. This was due to his inspired knack of organising the school so that it corresponded to the conditions and environment of the farming class. Whilst the pupils at Rødding had servants to polish their shoes every morning, Kold and his pupils wore clogs, ate their porridge from the same bowl and slept in the same dormitory. To prevent the pupils from being separated from their own soil Kold limited school time to the five winter months, when the pupils could best be spared from domestic work. Kold was also the first to open a three-month summer school for girls. And finally it was he who gave the impetus to the establishment of Children's Free Schools in large numbers, schools where the everyday grind was banned and stories and story-telling given first priority.

328

We have just heard Schrøder on the subject of Kold, and those of his friends and colleagues who after 1864 chose to work in the folk high school sought out Kold and used him as their model. Kold himself, however, was critical of all other schools apart from his own. In the 1850's he once told a young man whom he wished to admit as a pupil to his school that there were three high schools to choose from: Rødding, Hindholm and his own. Rødding's aim, he said, was to develop heroes to safeguard Denmark against the advancing Germanity. Hindholm was founded by friends of the peasants to educate heroes in the struggle for equality and freedom against the landowners. "My school on the other hand was founded for life. It educates heroes for the never-ending battle between life and death." Later Kold added that in the true folk school – for that is what he now called his own school – the influence must be Christian, because the national character can only be kept alive by Christianity.

What would the principals, the teachers and the pupils of Rødding and Hindholm have said to such a characterization if they had heard it? Presumably that firstly they did not like being called heroes, and then that the daily life of the school was not determined exclusively by the conditions that had given rise to its foundation.

But Kold's personal charisma was so powerful that the grundtvigian folk high school that gained ground in the late 1860's was in fact an amalgam of Grundtvig and Kold.

4. From Peasant High School to Folk High School

There were other schools apart from Rødding, Hindholm and Kold's school that were called peasant high schools or higher peasant schools. In the winter of 1862-63 there were in all 14 "peasant high schools" receiving grants for upkeep from the Ministry of Church and Education – out of the funds of Sorø Academy. The total winter roll at these schools was 449. Of these Hindholm had 110 and Kold's, as stated, 55. The average number of pupils at the other schools was 24, and only three schools, including Rødding, exceeded this number.

Many of these schools were in reality continuation schools for boys. When Christen Kold began his school he did not want any pupil over 16. He discussed the age of the pupils with Grundtvig himself, who insisted that the pupils should be over 18, but Kold stubbornly maintained that that was the "watch-and-pipe period". At that age they start courting and the spiritless approach to life has already taken "firm seat". In Kold's first

329

intake only one was over 19, but in 1862 nearly all his pupils were at least 18. Kold had to admit Grundtvig was right. In the period 1852-62 the percentage of pupils over 18 at all the schools that received state grants rose from 43 to 70.

The 14 schools that were operating in 1862 differed considerably, but none of them would or could live up to Grundtvig's high school plans from the 1830's and 1840's. The large school he had dreamt of came to nothing, even though a few of the small schools that were built instead were raised above the simple level of the higher peasant schools, inspired by the thought of the bigger school. It was of great benefit that schools for mature youth were built wherever the need for them was felt in the country, and it was the fact that instead of one major high school several smaller schools were opened, experimenting in different directions and originating from enlightened circles in the country, that offered the possibility of a healthy selection of the best.

But if predictions had had to be made in 1862 about what sort of future the high schools would have, none would have dared to dream of the development that would take place after 1864. It was also impossible at the time to judge which direction within the high school movement would prove to be the strongest and bear the richest fruit.

Might it not easily have been the higher peasant schools, which were called the "bjørnbakker" schools, after their founder? When Lars Bjørnbak, a country teacher, established his "higher agricultural school" in Viby near Aarhus in 1857, he chose the motto "Knowledge is power, ignorance is slavery". Like Peder Hansen his aim was to educate the peasants to full equality with the "privileged professions". One of his methods in this direction was to teach pupils how to behave in respectable company, how to drop their Jutland dialect and speak the King's Danish. The course ended with an examination. In its first few years Bjørnbak's school had only a small roll, but through the talks he gave, the newspaper he published and the tough anti-militarist attitude he adopted, he gained considerable standing amongst the peasants and reached an influential position in the Left Party. He fought the grundtvigians just as hard as he fought the conservative burghers.

In 1866 Ludvig Schrøder's close friend, Captain Jens Nørregård, a graduate and a Grundtvig supporter, used his own funds to open his own high school at Testrup – a neighbour to Bjørnbak's school at Viby. Other grundtvigians in the area, whom he had tried to make contact with, demanded a formal pledge from him: "Whether or not you support the Friends of the Peasants do you agree that it is the peasantry that must make progress and be educated and grow up to become the backbone of the people and bearers of the new age?"

Nørregård could easily answer in the affirmative, but in the next few years meeting after meeting turned into a battle between the Aesir and the giants, names borrowed from Norse mythology. The Aesir were the grundtvigians, the giants were the bjørnbakkers. This battle led to an increase in the intake at both schools, at Bjørnbak's from 36 in 1866 to around 100 in 1878, when he died – at Nørregård's from 21 in 1866 to over 100 in 1877. The result of the duel between the two movements was an enlightened population in the Aarhus area. In the 1830's and 1850's it was this area more than any other in the country that sent most pupils off to high schools. But after Lars Bjørnbak's death, the pupil roll at his school fell to under 30.

In the long run it was the grundtvigians who set the tone in the high school movement. They were presumably livelier and more dynamic than the bjørnbakkers. Already in the 1850's they were making their mark on the school at Uldum near Gedved, and at the school at Marielyst near Copenhagen which Grundtvig's friends later presented to him on his 70th birthday in 1853 and to which they gave the name Grundtvig's High School. Marielyst never had many pupils, and Grundtvig himself did not play much of a role in its life. It was not the school he had dreamt of.

The high school movement did not really get going until after the national defeat by the Germans in 1864. In the years 1865-70 no fewer than 25 new high schools were established, and now they were no longer called "peasant high schools", but "folk high schools" – Flor's name had won the day. A former pupil of Grundtvig's high school was appointed to the government Finance Committee, where he immediately secured increased support for the *folk* high schools. A grant from the Finance Bill had been given to the peasant high schools since 1851, but from 1868 a further grant was made for the provision of "talented but poor pupils" at the folk high schools.

This led to a sharp increase in pupil numbers, but apart from at Bjørnbak's school and at Hindholm the increase took place only at the "grundtvigian" folk high schools, which blossomed after the war. Askov went from 42 pupils in the winter term of 1865 to 197 in 1876, Vallekilde on Zealand from 31 in 1865 to 172 in 1876, Ryslinge on Funen from 23 in 1866 to 111 in 1876, Testrup in east Jutland from 21 in 1866 to 102 in 1876, Vejstrup on Funen from 25 in 1867 to 67 in 1876 and Vinding near Vejle from 39 in 1867 to 70 in 1876.

In 1866-67 the number of pupils at high schools and agricultural schools was not quite 1,000. By 1869 it had risen to 2,000; in 1872 it was close to 3,000, and in 1876 it passed the 4,000 mark. Two-thirds of them were the children of farmers, over a fifth the children of smallholders. To some degree the schools were still "peasant high schools", but the fanfare to be heard in the name "folk high schools" corresponded to the aims of the grundtvigian and Kold schools, and three-quarters of the Danish population still lived in the country. In 1881 16 per cent of the young people from the country were attending a high school. In Aarhus county, where the "battle between the Aesir and the giants" had fired the imagination, one in four young men was at a folk high school. The large percentage of children of smallholders proved that the high school was not just a farmers' school.

5. The Revival Schools

When the government appointed Dr. Mathias Steenstrup as supervisor of high schools in 1876, he had the bright idea of informing the schools that he would like to "visit" them. He did not wish to inspect them. In his first report of his "visits" he divided the schools into two groups, the "revival schools" and the "proficiency schools". The grundtvigian-Kold schools were placed in the first category, the Bjørnbak schools in the second.

What was revivalist about the schools? First of all there was the *song* which began every lesson. The songs were taken from Grundtvig's song collection and from contemporary poets, several of them – including C. Hostrup, Christian Richardt and the Norwegian, Bjørnson – were closely identified with the folk high schools. The songs were so many and of such merit that there was nearly always one that fitted in with the theme of the lesson. The young Grundtvig followers who established the new schools after 1864 at Askov, Testrup and Vallekilde each published a songbook from their school between 1872 and 1874. The first one contained historical songs, the second Scandinavian patriotic songs, and the third, biblical songs and hymns. A teacher at Askov, H. Nutzhorn, arranged the tunes, and twenty years later the three song-books were gathered under one cover, edited by Nutzhorn. Including the new edition the Folk High School Songbook has now sold in two million copies.

The kind of folk-song contained in the Folk High School Songbook owes a special debt to Grundtvig. In the autumn of 1838 he gave a series of lectures on contemporary history which he called *Within Living Memory*. When he reached the war against England and the Battle of Zealand Spit *(Sjællands Odde)* in 1808 where the naval hero Willemoes had fallen, there was a sudden silence. It was not broken until one of the audience proposed that they should sing Grundtvig's own song about Willemoes to the composer Weyse's new tune. They immediately began to sing. This was the breakthrough of the "folk song" in Denmark. And five years later, when Grundtvig drafted his teaching programme for the "adaptation of Sorø Academy to a school for the people", he emphasized the natural position of song in a high school: "For although one must no more set out to train all our young people to be concert singers than to be scholars, it is still the folk song, used naturally, that from days of old has been the most fruitful means of teaching, and it must play a major part wherever young people are to and learn with pleasure."

But the song was only the prelude to the real purpose: the *lesson*. Skills such as writing and arithmetic were demanded, and in Danish lessons pupils could get to know the best examples of Danish literature. Only the irreligious side of literature was kept out, the sort of literature represented by Georg Brandes and J. P. Jacobsen – the grundtvigian high schools were worried that it would undermine their pupils' morality.

First place in the curriculum was given to the *lecture*. In 1931, the centenary of Grundtvig's first publication of his high school ideas, the editor of the High School magazine asked Holger Begtrup, a folk high school man and a Grundtvig scholar, to write about the event in the magazine. Begtrup wrote the article, but insisted loud and clear that the origin of the folk high school should not be sought in Grundtvig's century-old "paper plans", but in "the living word" which had been heard at his lecture series, *Within Living Memory*, at Borch's College in 1838.

It was as if the grundtvigian folk high schools and high school circles in general were close to identifying the lecture with the living word – an idea which, as K. E. Bugge has previously pointed out, was far from Grundtvig's intention. It is a quite different matter that the best men at the grundtvigian folk high schools had the talent to speak refreshingly and with substance – and thus often left a deep mark on the minds of the impressionable pupils. There was also room, though it happened far less often, for an interplay between teacher and pupil.

A peculiar example of this is to be found in the diary which a young carpenter, Niels Nielsen, kept during the winter term 1884-85. He was a pupil at Vallekilde during that politically troubled six-month period, at the end of which the right-wing government under the leadership of a landowner, J. B. S. Estrup, violated the spirit of the constitution and passed a provisional finance bill that allowed the Government to build defence works with the money which the left-wing majority in the lower chamber had refused to grant. But before the storm clouds gathered,

Ernst Trier, the principal of Vallekilde, had told his pupils one day about a picture from Norse mythology that had just been painted on the gable of the new gymnasium by the young Norwegian artist, Louis Moe. It depicted the wolf Fenrir, who would only allow himself to be tied up if the Aesir-god Tyr put his hand in his mouth. Trier urged them to recall that Tyr was the young god amongst the Aesir – it is youth who must sacrifice and put all their efforts into tying up the monster."

It was a speech that left its mark on young minds. Trier was probably thinking of Germany and Bismarck when he spoke of the monster, but the young people thought of Estrup. The provisional government measure was not the only one. Others followed, and by way of reaction rifle clubs were formed with programmes directed against the enemy without – and within. Was this not Tyr's battle against the Fenrir-wolf? The young carpenter at any rate joined the rifle movement. But the following year, when he returned to Vallekilde, he heard Trier issue warnings against the "revolutionary rifle clubs". He comments in his diary as follows: "So back he went to Tyr ... and said that that was how we young people ought to sacrifice ourselves, but I don't understand how it will come about, because Trier condemns us the moment we take action and venture to do something ...". The carpenter asked Trier for a further explanation, which he was given in private, "but it's no easy matter to maintain an independent opinion to his face". Trier insisted that the rifle movement was just as dangerous as the French revolutionaries, because the undergraduates, the followers of Brandes, "and the whole mob of freethinkers" would infect Danish youth and suffocate all the good shoots that were planted in them at the folk high schools. The carpenter argued in his diary: "So perhaps it's right to have misgivings ... but if you are aware of the danger, you can be on guard against it".

The carpenter's diary reflects both an attraction and a criticism, and doubtless both made their presence felt in the minds of mature pupils, but it was probably exceptional for a pupil to dare to contradict his principal, even though it would have been in accordance with Grundtvig's ideas for an interplay at the high school between teachers and pupils.

In another respect the grundtvigian folk high schools were completely in tune with Grundtvig's line of thought, namley *the communal life at the school*. On his visits to England around 1830 Grundtvig had received a powerful impression of how valuable the college life lived at Oxford and Cambridge is for academic youth, not least the communal meals between students and professors. Kold had introduced communal meals when he opened his school in the 1850's and since the founding of Askov in 1865 it had become the norm at grundtvigian high schools for teachers and students to eat at the same table. As leader of the housekeeping, the principal's wife was often "high school mother". The young Norwegian poet, Bjørnstjerne Bjørnson visited Vallekilde in the late 1860's, and when he had given his talk and was ready to dine, Trier informed him that here they all ate out of the same porridge-bowl. "This really is a community!" exclaimed Bjørnson. But when he had seen the person sitting next to him dip the spoon into the same butter-pat he gave up: "No, I really can't manage that, my friend!" But the teachers and pupils did.

Living together for months at a time gave teachers and pupils its own satisfaction. Friendships were stronger and purer and raised the level of home life throughout the country, not least as a result of the high school mother's efforts. When the pupils returned home to their daily business they took the high school experience with them, built village halls and free schools, held annual autumn conferences with high school teachers as speakers, took part in church and political life, and established co-operative dairies, shooting and gymnastics clubs and occasionally, as we have seen, rifle clubs.

6. The Scandinavian Folk High School

The name and the concept of folk high schools was not confined to Denmark. In the rest of Scandinavia folk high schools sprang up in the second half of the century on the Danish pattern – started in villages by local groups or by an individual with their support. Everywhere the schools were run by experienced principals with skilled wives by their side, and they were assisted by a more or less permanent staff who frequently moved on. Although most of these schools called themselves folk high schools from the start, the majority of their pupils came from the peasantry, and in particular from its middle class. However the name was synonymous with the school's aim of raising the peasantry to a position of responsibility and influence in the life of the nation – just as in Denmark.

Everywhere in Scandinavia the schools established themselves either immediately or soon after as boarding-schools with a domestic character, often with the principal's wife as "high school mother". The schools claimed independence and curriculum freedom from the State and local authorities, but soon began to seek government aid both for upkeep and

for pupils of limited means. It took some time before the State acknowledged them, and this happened only gradually alongside the increased
influence of the peasantry in the parliaments.

The folk high school moved first to Norway. It was picked up, so to
speak, by two young theologians, Olaus Arvesen and Herman Anker. At
a Scandinavian Church Conference in Lund in 1859 they had met the Danish students, Ludvig Schrøder, Ernst Trier, Jens Nørregård and Christopher Bågø, who in the previous year had got together in a group they
called *Little Theology Group* (*Lille Theologicum*). All four of them
became leading folk high school figures in Denmark a few years later. At
that time they had still not declared themselves grundtvigians. But the
two Norwegians on the other hand had, under the inspiration of their late
compatriot, Ole Vig, who had dreamt of building a folk high school in
Hamar, close to Lake Mjøsen.

After the Lund Conference the new friends journeyed together to
Copenhagen to pay tribute on Grundtvig's birthday to his Scandinavian
visions. They persuaded Grundtvig to give a weekly lecture in his home
the following winter, when Arvesen and Anker would be staying in
Copenhagen. The lectures dealt with the history of the Christian Church
and were later published under the title *Church Mirror*. Here Grundtvig
gave pride of place to the Apostles' Creed, and the Norwegian and
Danish friends were initiated into the high school calling. Under the
influence of these lectures and the Sunday services of Vartov it seemed
natural enough for the high school men to emphasize the link between
the popular and the Christian view of life. The inspiration from their
second teacher, Christen Kold, influenced them in the same direction.
On the basis of Grundtvig's motto "First a man, then a Christian", they
regarded the task of the high school to be the implementation of a John-
the-Baptist role amongst young people.

In 1864 Anker, who had come into a rich inheritance on his father's
death, established with Arvesen the first folk high school in Norway at
the place Ole Vig had singled out. They set out to create a "historical and
poetic" high school, and therefore named it Sagatun. The school's
interior, with its pictures of Norse mythology, suited the name – just as it
did 20 years later with Vallekilde high school's gymnasium. From the
start Sagatun was well-attended, and in 1871 when Grundtvig celebrated
his 60th year as a minister Anker invited all the Norwegian pupils from
Sagatun and other schools to accompany him to the party. His retinue
consisted of 128 high school lads.

At that time there were only 5 folk high schools established in Norway,

The gymnasium at Vallekilde in north-west Zealand, with the gable painting by Louis Moe
– *Tyr and Fenris*. (Drawing by the architect of the house, Martin Nyrop, 1884).

**Testrup Folk High School in Jutland, the venue for the first Scandinavian folk high school
meeting. (Based on a drawing from 1876).**

Left: The Norwegian poet, Bjørnstjerne Bjørnson (1832-1910), who joined the grundtvigian movement in the 1860's and 1870's. He was originally known for his peasant tales and historical poems, but later he became deeply involved in the movement, both as a poet and as a politician in cultural affairs in the contemporary debate. Nobel Prizewinner in 1903.
Right: The farmer, Peter Larsen (1802-73), the most important leader of the meeting movement. He broke with Lindberg and Grundtvig around 1835, but later became Grundtvig's "good friend". From the name of his farm on west Funen he was known as Skræppenborg. He combined warmth and wit with a somewhat dominating nature; his voice was apparently so powerful that it could be heard "over half the parish". (Royal Library, Copenhagen).

The Danish movement in North Schleswig led to the two big Skamling Hill meetings in 1843 and 1844: Grundtvig spoke at the latter. (Lithograph, Royal Library, Copenhagen).

all on the Danish pattern. The most distinctive was the one run by the theologian, Christopher Bruun. He had previously visited Schrøder's, Trier's, Nørregård's and Kold's schools, and once he had started his own school he wrote to Schrøder: "The Danish school is the father of mine ... so when I write to you, it is like a soldier reporting to headquarters." Bruun's school in Gausdalen was given the name Vonheim, the home of hope. Whereas the name Sagatun pointed to the past as its source of inspiration, Vonheim pointed to the future, and it was in addition a name with a Norwegian ring to it. While Anker and Arvesen supported Classical Norwegian *(bokmål)*, which was close to Danish, Christopher Bruun was a firm believer in New Norwegian *(landsmål)*. The dialects in the valleys where the pupils came from lay closer to New Norwegian than Classical Norwegian.

The most ardent and most influential spokesman for the folk high school in Norway was Bjørnstjerne Bjørnson. He himself had been excited by Grundtvig's ideas and by the meeting with his followers, "these young, grundtvigian graduates, their faith, their enthusiasm, their poverty – yet their happiness". In 1875 he settled down at Aulestad Farm, only a few minutes' walk from Vonheim, where he immediately became almost a daily guest. At Bjørnson's suggestion Bruun gave a series of lectures to the Student Society in Kristiania which were published in 1878 under the title *Ideas Fundamental to the People*. They formed a caustic attack on the alienating culture of the intelligentsia. This was in the spirit of Grundtvig. Not so much his message of "the inspired view of life" perhaps, but *Ideas Fundamental to the People* was later regarded as a gospel in the minds of the grundtvigian high school teachers in Denmark and Norway.

Then in the same year, 1878, Bjørnson and Bruun went their different ways. There was an element of fanaticism about Bruun, personified in 1866 in the figure of Ibsen's Brand, and Bruun's propensity for evangelism also repelled Bjørnson. Bjørnson himself went through a religious crisis, reflected in his play, *Above One's Ability,* in 1883 which involved a break with both Bruun and Christianity.

Bjørnson's desertion damaged the high school cause in Norway, and the authorities added their opposition, including the national parliament which in 1875 had granted state funds to government-controlled county schools *(amtsskoler)*. These received more applications than the folk high schools, whose pupil clientele was limited to the sons of well-off peasants. The crisis which the Norwegian high schools thus ran into was not overcome until after the turn of the century. The preferential treatment of the county schools then gradually ceased and the shire schools *(fylkeskoler),* as they were now called, moved closer to the folk high schools in their aims. Young high school teachers from the two different types of school continued to travel to Denmark, and particularly to Askov, to gain inspiration for their work.

Right from the start the Swedes' relationship to the Danish folk high school had nothing like the character of the close personal friendship of the Norwegians. As late as 1883 – when a Scandinavian folk high school conference was called for the first time – Ludvig Schrøder wrote to one of his colleagues that he would like to invite the participants to visit Askov, but he did not know any of the Swedes apart from one – who was not of the first rank.

By coincidence it was Christian Flor in his old age who persuaded the Swedes to take the idea of a folk high school seriously. On a trip abroad in 1867 he met August Sohlman, the editor of Sweden's most widely-read liberal newspaper, *Aftonbladet* (Evening Paper). Flor, who owned an ironworks in Sweden, complained at the lack of interest shown by the Swedish peasantry in the welfare of their society. He impressed upon Dr. Sohlman the necessity of awakening nobler powers and instincts – either through the sort of great and imminent danger that Denmark had been exposed to in 1864, or through an immediate effort towards popular education.

Dr. Sohlman at once took up this challenge. He organized two big meetings in Stockholm where he advocated the establishment of peasant high schools in Sweden, so that amongst the peasantry men would emerge who could worthily represent their class in all political matters – with enough insight not to be led astray by agitators who wanted to exploit them for their own selfish ends. Dr. Sohlman told the meeting that he had already sent an experienced collegue to Denmark to study the Danish schools and file a report in *Aftonbladet*.

Shortly afterwards, in December 1867, the paper carried a series of reports from Dr. O. W. Ålund. They covered his visits to Marielyst, Hindholm and Kold's high school. He had not managed to visit the new schools established by the friends of the *Little Theology Group*. Kold's enthusiasm had had the same powerful effect on Dr. Ålund as on Schrøder five years earlier, but he doubted whether a school that relied on its leader's personality to such a degree could survive his departure. The doubt was confirmed when Kold died two years later. At Marielyst Dr. Ålund found rather too strong an emphasis on history lectures. But Hindholm fulfilled all his expectations. Here importance was attached to

338

the history of Denmark, to the Danish language and to the pupils' needs in practical life.

So Hindholm became the Danish folk high school that the Swedes took as their model. Almost immediately following Dr. Ålund's stay, Hindholm's principal, Christian Nielsen, received a visit from two delegates from Kristanstad county in Skåne. Here they had considered establishing what they called a "higher folk school". But immediately on their return, one of the delegates, the erudite rural dean, C. A. Bergman, published an article *On the Danish Folk High Schools Compared with the Swedish Higher Folk Schools,* in which he sided strongly with the folk high schools, in particular Hindholm, where a middle path was being trodden between a one-sided development of the intellect and a one-sided development of the emotions. He persuaded Christian Nielsen to speak on the folk high school at a big open-air meeting in Skåne, and already on November 1st 1868 Onnestad folk high school, the first in Sweden, opened its doors to fifty new pupils.

The following day another Swedish folk high school opened. It was established in the former coaching-inn at Hvilan between Malmø and Lund. Here the originators of the project, from Bara Agricultural Club, managed to persuade the young scientist, Dr. Leonard Holmstrøm, to take over the leadership. The main aim of the school – as it was for nearly all subsequent Swedish folk high schools – was "social education". It was something sorely needed, since following on the local government reform of 1862 and the democratic reform of parliament in 1865 the State had put greater power into the hands of the people and in return demanded an increased awareness of the language, history and constitution of the country.

In the same year, 1868, a third folk high school was opened by the "scout", Dr. Ålund himself, in the Vadstena area. He too modelled his school on Hindholm, but his successor, P. A. Gödecke, in his article from 1872, *On the Aims, Curriculum and Methods of the Folk High School,* rejected "the rather one-sided grundtvigian schools in Denmark and their copies in Norway", and their effort "to impose on the pupils a view of life that on the one hand is a most peculiar poetic and religious one and on the other hand a political and Scandinavian one". Dr. Gödecke personally reproached Dr. Ålund for attempting to introduce "the living word" and other whims of Grundtvig. Nor was Hindholm otherwise considered to be a particularly grundtvigian school.

For 12 years the Swedes kept the grundtvigian folk high school at arm's length, and the two did not come any closer until a Scandinavian School

Conference in Stockholm in 1880 where Jens Nørregård from Denmark and Dr. Holmström from Sweden each spoke about their countries' folk high schools. They did so in a baking hot lecture-hall, but the atmosphere between the Swedes and the Danes was cool at first. Not until a Swedish principal intervened to advocate passionately the folk high school cause did both sides spontaneously walk over to one another, introduce themselves and warmly shake hands.

Moved by this mood of friendship, Jens Nørregård soon invited his Swedish and Norwegian colleagues to a Scandinavian folk high school meeting at Testrup. It was to take place early in September 1883 so that participants would have the opportunity on their return journey of celebrating the hundredth anniversary of Grundtvig's birth on September 8th.

Before the Testrup meeting was held, two of the Swedish folk high school's leading figures, Dr. Holmström from Hvilan and Teodor Holmberg and his wife, Cecilia Bååth-Holmberg, visited Denmark and the Danish folk high schools. On his return from his study-trip in 1882 Dr. Holmström published *Notes from a Trip to the Jutland Peninsula*. Here he maintained that Jutland was a generation ahead of Sweden in the area of agriculture – and that this was due to the folk high school. In the homes of the most able farmers he had noted that either the husband, or his wife or the children had attended a folk high school.

At the Testrup meeting itself Holmberg claimed that there was an advantage in the different attitudes from country to country. But the Swedes were not too pleased when Nørregård said he wished they would undergo a popular spiritual revival such as the Danes had experienced. He said, "It is the Christian revival and the life within the congregations here in Denmark that has kept the high schools going and given them their best pupils." Schrøder went even further in the direction of teaching the Swedes, "The life-source of mankind is only to be found in the covenant between Christianity and the spirit of the people." It was not that he wanted a real war to wake the Swedes up, but the Christian revival in Denmark could benefit Sweden. The Danish chairman, Christoffer Bågø, had to smooth things over. In accordance with Grundtvig's own high school ideas he said that a high school vocation could be undertaken and be blessed without it resting on a Christian foundation.

Despite this discord, the Testrup meeting and especially a subsequent excursion to the southern part of Jutland led to a warm and lifelong personal friendship between leading Danish and Swedish folk high school men and their wives. The year after the Testrup meeting Swedish and Norwegian folk high school teachers set up a memorial to Grundtvig on

Skamling Hill. But there continued to be a more distant relationship between the Swedish and Danish folk high school than between the Norwegian and the Danish. The Danish grundtvigians maintained, on the basis of their view of Christianity and the people, that the Swedes did not really know how to run a folk high school. And is it not likely that this attitude resulted in the Swedes not even attempting to concern themselves with Grundtvig's educational ideas? And this in spite of the fact that the aim of their own folk high schools was not so different from the one Grundtvig himself has sketched out in his high school writings.

Finland acquired her first folk high school in 1889. Towards the end of the 1860's, when the folk high school was gaining ground in neighbouring Sweden, Finland was so poor that the poet, Zachris Topelius, called it the poorhouse of Europe. By the 1880's things had improved. Sofia Hagman, the Finnish-speaking headmistress of a girls' school had attended the second Scandinavian folk high school meeting at Sagatun in 1885. In 1887 on her way to Askov and Vallekilde she visited Holmberg's folk high school at Tärna, but with unfortunate consequences. During a coffee break the question of the language conflict between Finnish and Swedish in Finland was raised and Sofia Hagman was so shocked by Holmberg's pro-Swedish attitude that she suddenly quit the company and the following morning caught the train for Askov.

After her visit Sofia Hagman returned to Finland and in January 1889 she established the first Finnish folk high school, for girls only, at Kangasala near Tammerfors. In the three-month term needlework was taught alongside history and literature and the school quickly gained many pupils. In the same year a Swedish-language folk high school was opened in Borgå by J. E. Strömborg, who had been a close friend of J. L. Runeberg. This later became one of the leading schools in Swedish Finland.

Otherwise it was the various provinces' student organisations in Helsinki who were behind the establishment of both Swedish-language and Finnish-language folk high schools. From 1890 onwards the student organisations awarded scholarships annually to philosophy graduates fresh from college, so that they could travel to Sweden and especially to Denmark to study the folk high schools. In return they had to promise to work at the newly-established folk high schools in their district when they came back. 12 of the 16 folk high schools that were established in Finland between 1891 and 1895 were founded by the student organisations in cooperation with the local population. And nearly all of them were run by principals who had been to Askov.

Then in 1890 the Russian emperor decreed that the Finnish postal service should be transferred to the Russian Foreign Ministry, thus pushing the Finnish-Swedish language conflict into the background. Now it was a case of both language groups in Finland making common preparations on behalf of the "mother country" and its constitution, which the Russians were busy violating. And in this situation the Finns could use Askov high school as an armoury. The school attracted them not only by its skilled staff and versatile pupils but also by its close links with the Danes in south Jutland. They were at the time under the forced yoke of the German emperor and the Prussian officials, but it was in these very years that the south Jutlanders under the energetic leadership of H. P. Hanssen-Nørremølle and began a well-organized cultural battle against the Germanization of North Schleswig. H. P. Hanssen had been a student at Askov and all his life he remained in close contact with the school.

The Finns were immediately attracted to the high school song. When four scholarship students, including Niilo Liakka, later Minister for Education, and Hjalmar Nikander, later a school supervisor, came to Askov in the autumn of 1891 they were welcomed by the pupils singing verse after verse of Runeberg's *Our Country* (Vårt Land) which they had learned by heart. The Finns were used to singing only the first and last verses, but they managed to join in the song contest by repeating the first verse – in Finnish! And they took the joy of singing back home with them.

The Finnish scholarship students wanted to copy the Danish folk high schools once they had returned home. One of them wrote to Schrøder that Grundtvig's plant was now acclimatized to his country and that his picture was hanging on one of the school walls alongside Kold. The revival aspect was if possible even more urgent than in Denmark. But the government in Finland did not accept schools like the Danish. Bitter easterly winds were blowing in over Finland with the result that history lessons had to be taught with great care and preferably be limited to biographies. The Russian governor-general was on his guard. When a newspaper revealed that at one of the schools there were lessons in "local government and political science" he had to remind the school authorities that teaching constitutional law at a folk high school was forbidden. Subjects such as needlework, housecraft and agriculture on the other hand presented no danger. By 1896 there were 19 folk high schools in the country, including 13 speaking Finnish. They also differed from the Danish by being mixed schools with roughly the same intake of male and female pupils. Term was limited to the winter months.

With Czar Nikolai II's manifesto in February 1899 Finland's old constitution from the days of Swedish sovereignty was annulled. The principal of a newly-established folk high school in the neighbourhood of Turku (Åbo) wrote to Dr. Holmström: "What will happen to the folk high school nobody can predict. But it is after all a matter of fact that it won't receive any government grant. From a certain quarter comes the question: What are you teaching in geography, general history and the history of Finland? You send a letter with your heart in your mouth and by roundabout ways and with translations added addressed to the highest or rather the ethically lowest authority – and you have to wait for more questions – or no answer."

The folk high school in Finland was placed in the forefront of the battle, but it survived and experienced a renaissance when Finland was freed from the Russian oppression in 1917.

By the turn of the century the folk high school in the four Scandinavian countries had been given a distinctive character, and within each country it had developed in its own direction. But however different the schools were, their leaders and teachers continued to gather at intervals at Scandinavian folk high school meetings to confirm their mutual connection and to acknowledge the inspiration from Denmark and its grundtvigians – or from Grundtvig himself.

Grundtvig's Ideas on the Church and the People 1848-72

by ANDERS PONTOPPIDAN THYSSEN

The Danish Cause

In 1848 Grundtvig reached the age of 65, but for him the year was the beginning of a new period in his life which included two more marriages and a new and major achievement. It is through this that the picture which lasted beyond Grundtvig's lifetime was formed. The same main lines were preserved as before but they were strengthened and deepened and new features were added. In his attitudes and manner he continued to be marked by the optimistic, extrovert outlook that had characterized him since the end of the 1830's. His volatile temper could still blaze up into anger and harsh comments and answers, but on the whole he now became milder and more conciliatory. In 1849 a debate with Meir Goldschmidt – who was the publisher of the outspoken paper, *The Corsair*, and whose satire Kierkegaard was so affected by – took such a peaceful course that Goldschmidt made particular mention of Grundtvig's "deep, good-natured heart". "I become less quarrelsome with each passing year", Grundtvig himself wrote in 1856. But in many respects his views acquired a more radical and categorical nature.

Politically a new epoch began in the wake of the *February Revolution in France* in 1848. The revolutionary movement spread like wildfire through Europe, not least in Germany, where demands for freedom and democracy were combined with efforts towards national unification; and this had a momentous consequence for the Danish-German "United Monarchy" of the time. In Holstein and Schleswig from the beginning of March people began demonstrations for a common Schleswig-Holstein constitution in association with the confederation of German states. Only Holstein belonged to the German confederation but now both duchies were to be separated from Denmark, joined only by a personal union.

Prompted by this the liberal ferment that had long been brewing broke out in Denmark, especially in Copenhagen. Also here great crowds gathered at political meetings led by the National Liberals, who demanded that Schleswig should be joined to Denmark with a free constitution. The culmination was a procession of thousands to the new king, Frederik VII, on March 21st. When the King complied with the Copenhageners but rejected the Schleswig-Holstein demand the result was a National Liberal ministry, which amongst other things was to prepare elections to a constituent assembly and for war against the Schleswig-Holsteiners, who were receiving support from Prussia and other German states.

At first Grundtvig was at a loss over these events, "the boundless confusion" that he saw everywhere, in both Europe and Denmark. He did not take part in the demonstrations, which resembled the revolutionary "shipwreck" that he had feared for so long, and he had no confidence in the National Liberal academics and their political and national theories. Political developments were running counter to his ideals from Christian VIII's time that he had so far cherished.

Crucial to his attitude was a powerful and painful feeling that the future of the Danish people was at stake. A unified nationalist Germany would be a big and dangerous neighbour who might swallow the whole of Denmark. The question was whether the Danish people *wanted* to survive at all. The duchies had had a large German bureaucracy in Copenhagen, and many had regarded everything German as a model. For 400 years the Germans have been our schoolmasters, Grundtvig wrote in March 1848, "so that all our so-called '*intelligence*' is *German*". But he was aware that the days of the Danish-German double-state were over. Everywhere the nations were awakening and the task now was to rouse the Danish people to an awareness of "*the Danish cause*": that Denmark and Danishness is "something in itself".

With this view in mind he started publication of a weekly magazine which he called *The Dane* on March 22nd. The first editions were marked by the stirring political events in Copenhagen, which Grundtvig now took a more positive view of, since they proved that everybody was prepared to make common cause against the Schleswig-Holsteiners. But the questions of Schleswig and the new constitution which occupied the age were not for him the main problems. Everything depended on whether "Danishness" itself was worth fighting for. "If the country of *Denmark*, without Schleswig, was nothing whatsoever, then the Danish cause was apparently already determined and already *lost*". A distinction must be drawn altogether between the state and "the country of Denmark". The state is only a made-up foreign word for everything that stands under the same whip, whereas the name of the fatherland "was so bright in the eyes of numerous generations as the beech trees in May ... that for two millenia it had given the clog-people wings when the risk of life was at stake". Grundtvig could no longer build on the monarchy: "it is no longer enough for me to have a *king,* but I would myself like to be a little king and see nothing but little kings all around me" who have learned the royal art of controlling oneself: "the little self-denial". And what else can unite the many individual men with a certain degree of self-denial than the national feeling, the common patriotism. Through this every people acquires the courage to be itself without imitating others, and the Danish people have a particular need to wake up to an awareness of their own special character and task as a *people.* The country needs all its strength now and "all its skilled, hard-working and active children, however insignificant their work may appear at first glance". If patriotism can burst into flame again, everyone will seek illumination regarding their native language and "all that touches on our common beloved fatherland, both in times past, present and future".

In a way *The Dane* was a continuation of *Danevirke,* Grundtvig's first periodical from 1816-19, (see p. 108). *The Dane* also points to the nation's great past, the ancient Denmark and the mythical world of images. But one difference comes immediately to mind: *Danevirke* was aimed at a higher level of education, at the educated and widely-read, whom Grundtvig called in those days "the nobility and spirit of the people"; in contrast he had explicitly distanced himself from "the mass", the broad public. This attitude still held good in the 1830's. In *Norse Mythology* (1832) the rebirth that Grundtvig hoped for would be spread by "the clergy, the statesmen and the professors", and even the high school writings were chiefly aimed at the leading men in the country. They were also able to emphasize that the general public was the basis for the high school, however, and from around 1840 onwards Grundtvig often showed an interest in the peasant class, though mostly in the spirit of the enlightenment, with a reference to Frederik VI's peasant reforms and the four assemblies that also included the peasant class. But Grundtvig had still only superficial contact with and knowledge of the peasants and the villagers; the "people" he spoke to in the 1840's consisted largely of students and educated circles in Copenhagen.

On this point *The Dane* introduced a change of direction. Here Grundtvig sought to write as simply and straightforwardly as possible. The people became the whole Danish nation, "the ancient community on field and heath and blue waves". Already in the second edition he impressed upon the Copenhageners that Copenhagen was not Denmark;

instead of turning up their noses at peasant coarseness and servant's hall jokes they ought to go to the defence of the ordinary man. For "the mass" formed the core of the whole nation; and being purely Danish-speaking *they* would be easier to win to the Danish cause than the Copenhageners. With this viewpoint Grundtvig became the leading spokesman for the *farming* class, which constituted 80 per cent of the population. Politically it ought to have the upper hand, he wrote in September 1848, and in *The Dane* he stresses its importance time and again. The whole nation badly needs the advancement of the peasantry, he declared in 1849. Even though the land belongs to the people as a whole it is best used by owner-farmers; he therefore warmly supported a continuation of the peasant reforms of the enlightenment. And only amongst the country youth could he find the life-energy that – when it was stirred – could turn the machinery of the state into "a free and natural party of friends" with the stamp of the people (1850). The words *folkelig* (= of the people) or *folkelighed* (= the people's character), which became characteristic for Grundtvig, were not just the essence of the people's specific character and particular talents and tasks, but were now linked especially to the ordinary folk and most of all the farmers and peasants.

With this enthusiasm for the people and "the Danish cause" – as an urgent matter of life or death – Grundtvig's optimism returned in full measure. "The *youthful* hope of Denmark's happy future" was to be the hallmark of his magazine, and this became very much the case. Everything in Denmark is wonderfully prepared for an unparalleled golden age, which will also come if we just have the courage to await it and enough love for our country to bring it the sacrifices that we can anticipate which will repay themselves a hundredfold to our children and grandchildren!" (1849). For his own part the foundation remained as before his Christian faith, his "trust in divine *Providence*, which seeks the best and is master of "happiness". Typical of this is the poem *To Denmark*, printed in *The Dane* in May 1848 which ends:

> Fatherland!
> On the edge of the abyss,
> In the midst of blue waves
> You will flourish and last, ...
> Your best is still before you
> That lay hidden with the *ancient* of days!

> (cf. Daniel 7:9).

347

"The Danish cause" also meant that Grundtvig intervened in public life, which thus provided the basis for a *political change of heart in him*. It did not take him long to give way to the new constitutional ideas, though not without reservations. In *The Dane* he dealt with current affairs and kept up a running commentary on political and national events, both in verse and prose. The result was four volumes (1848-51) of in all 3,136 pages; since he himself wrote nearly all the contents this represented a considerable effort. At the same time he entered the political scene with great energy, first as a member of the Constituent Assembly (1848-49), then as a member of parliament until 1858. He had never been so busy as now, he wrote to his son Svend in 1849. But his energy appeared inexhaustible. He lacked neither zest for life nor vitality, he said on his 67th birthday; and he remained busy for years.

Among the electors Grundtvig acted as an old friend of the farmers and made a good impression especially in country districts with his warm and cheerful talk on "the Danish cause". It created a stir at the elections to the Constituent Assembly when Professor Clausen lost to an unknown weaver; but Grundtvig was elected unopposed in the same constituency at a re-election shortly afterwards. Under the growing party divisions in parliament between the "friends of the peasants" and "friends of the civil servants" (the National Liberals) Grundtvig preferred the former. With the friends of the peasants he also joined the common cause as a supporter of a general franchise and freedom in all affairs. But he was actually an opponent of party formations and as early as 1848 had considered founding a "Danish Society", which should form a "living centre for all that is natural and rests in itself historically". In the spring of 1853 he realized this plan by establishing the "Danish Association", which with "Danish enlightenment as to the common good" was to build a bridge across the class divisions and the gap between town and country. The Association gained about 2,000 members divided into local districts, and it published the magazine *The Danish Flag* (*Dannebrog*) containing as its main contribution – naturally enough – a series of articles by Grundtvig on *"The Danish Cause"* (1855). But its programme was too imprecise; the magazine folded at the end of 1855 and the association followed suit in 1856. (On Grundtvig as a politician see also p. 303).

Measured by the yardstick of the age Grundtvig did not have great influence as a politician. He did not have the sense of what is politically possible: his proposals were as a rule defeated, and his many parliamentary contributions consisted mainly of wide-ranging speeches to the Danish people. But on certain important matters he was more clear-sighted and realistic than most in his time.

On *the Schleswig question* he strongly repudiated the Danish demand for the incorporation of Schleswig into Denmark in 1848. One cannot treat living people like runaway slaves, he wrote, and Denmark would never gain peace with Germany if she suppressed the Germans of South Schleswig and their language as *they* had suppressed the Danish. Everything depended on the wishes of the Schleswig people: "To a nation they belong/who consider themselves so/With an ear for their *language*/and fire for their *country*" (August 1848). In practice this meant some form of division of Schleswig. In the following years he was himself seized by the unconciliatory atmosphere of wartime and maintained Denmark's right to the whole of Schleswig when the war ended in the defeat of the Schleswig-Holsteiners in 1850. But the power that the Danes had won they should "use as humanely as possible", with freedom of expression for both German-minded and Danish-minded (1851). Later, therefore, he turned time after time against the compulsory arrangements the Government had introduced in order to strengthen the Danish language in central Schleswig. On the other hand, after 1864 when both duchies had been conquered by Prussia he was a powerful supporter of the national right of self-determination. His line of thought was now considerably influential on the politics of the Danish minority in Schleswig, and the goal was finally reached in 1920 when following a referendum North Schleswig was reunited with Denmark.

Grundtvig took up a similar position on *the Scandinavian question*. This acquired political significance in the 1850's and 1860's when student scandinavianism and the National Liberals cherished the hope of a unification of the Scandinavian countries into one state with the same king. As late as 1851 Grundtvig was the centre of a joint Scandinavian student meeting in Norway on the invitation of the Norwegian student society. The Norwegian students had been interested in him as far back as the period 1815-20, and he himself had regarded Norway as his second country, so the trip was a tremendous experience. In many places, both in the capital and in the country, he made eloquent speeches; the Norwegian parliament interrupted a session so that its members could hear him, and on his departure he was given a great ovation by the students; he had in a way been the youngest in the whole crowd!

But after his homecoming he emphasized in *The Dane* that the Scandinavian fellow-feeling was of a spiritual and cultural nature; politically the peoples ought to grant one another complete freedom and independence. He was thinking here especially of Norway, whose separation from Sweden he anticipated (achieved in 1905); in the same year, 1851, he worked in the Danish parliament for the independence of the Faroes from Denmark. In articles on "the Danish cause" from 1855 he defended the small and weak nations. To condemn their patriotism as injustice against other nations was about as humane and Christian as warning poor people not to love their neighbours so as not to do an injustice to the rich and great! The more strongly each nation safeguards its independence and its language the more vigorously human life will develop in every direction, and the more beneficial will be the interaction between the nations of the earth.

In Danish home affairs Grundtvig played a significant part through his demand for freedom within the Church and School, and by his position on two important controversies: on *defence* and on the *constitution*. Already during the negotiations on the new constitution he had rejected the idea of a standing army, which in peacetime could only serve to oppress the people. Instead of general conscription and the military training of young people in "barrack prisons" he wantèd a general arming of the people with weapon training in local surroundings. He also opposed the division of parliament into a *folketing* (lower chamber) and a more conservative *landsting* (upper chamber) but after the war of 1848-50 he defended the constitution against plans for a conservative United Monarchy constitution which would be superior to the Danish parliament. This was the direct reason for his establishment of "The Danish Association" in 1853; and after 1864 he fought with all his might against a revision of the constitution, which nonetheless was carried in 1866, giving the *landsting* a more privileged position (see p. 308). In both respects Grundtvig's main ideas became hallmarks of the large left-wing people's party, *Venstre* (the Left); and the controversy split the population into two enemy camps right up until around 1900. Grundtvig was therefore right when in negotiations on these questions he anticipated a threat to what he called "the Danish cause".

Church Ideas

Throughout the period 1848-72 Grundtvig developed his thinking on Church matters. In print they appeared partly in theological essays, which became especially well-known through the major book *Christian Childhood Teachings* (1868, from the years 1855-61); and partly in surveys of Church history, whose most detailed work was *The Pleiades of Christendom* (1854-55, collected 1860) and *Church Mirror* (lectures 1861-

63, published 1871). But it must be added immediately that his "Church view" actually received its best expression in his sermons and hymns, i.e. linked to the service and the biblical texts.

One example from 1857, a sermon on *the good Samaritan,* stresses that Christianity must be regarded first and last as "a new life-source". It is therefore no wonder that it is despised by "the unbelieving world", which "in fact prefers death to life", and finds life so unsure and in the end so boring that it throws itself into the arms of death as a refuge from life's troubles. But the gospel of Christ is welcomed by all those who hold life, human life, dear and yet feel deeply that it "is besieged by fear and anxiety and with every step is approaching death, just like the man who went from Jerusalem to Jericho and fell among thieves", was robbed and beaten and left half-dead. The good Samaritan is a picture of Jesus himself who sacrificed himself for us; and the parable was told for the scribes, who knew the law of love on their fingers but to no avail since no sinner can give himself the love of God and his neighbour that he lacks. But the essence of Christ's gospel is "that what was impossible for *the law of love* is performed by the *life of love* ... which revealed itself in Him with the good deeds of the Father and the self-sacrifice on the cross". "This life of love is furthermore actually present in the Word of the Lord to us at holy baptism and Holy Communion" and pours out eternal life upon all those who believe in it, in and through the love of Christ.

Grundtvig's ideas on Christian *childhood teachings* began with the view that the knowledge that is necessary for Christianity is very simple and can in the main be taught orally. His first attempt, in 1840, took the form of a conversation between a clergyman and "a Christian mother" who wished to know what she should teach her children. It rejected the "book-reading" of Luther's catechism, which for the most part was Luther's own ideas; childhood teachings and all Christianity should build on baptism with the renunciation and the Creed, the words of baptism and the blessing after baptism ("peace be with you"). Grundtvig published a similar conversation in 1849, this time between an old and a young man; and in 1847 he proposed a handbook for church-goers, clergymen and teachers to replace the catechism: "a simple guide" to the Church, the minister, Sunday, the Church festivals and services, to baptism, confirmation and Communion and other Church ceremonies, to family prayers and Bible-reading, supplemented by a little biblical history and Church history.

But only here and there does the book *Christian Childhood Teachings* deserve its title. The main view in this respect is that even though books may be of use in childhood teaching they must be subordinate to the "united, audible and living testimony of the *Lord* and His *Church* at baptism and Communion", and particularly to the apostolic Creed at baptism, which "expresses *everything* that we must believe in order to be true Christians". The content of the Creed is to be sure the same as John 3:16: For God so loved the world, that he gave his only begotten Son, that whosoever believeth in him should not perish, but have everlasting life. But this is only a written word, and we must presuppose that Christ still has a Church on earth, so it is that which we must ask, "what is the foundation that the apostles have laid on behalf of *Christ* and laid *not* in a book but in the *Church* itself as a gathering of Christian people".

On the whole *Christian Childhood Teachings* is a somewhat heterogeneous collection of articles which were in no way a "simple guide" but rather a summary and development of Grundtvig's ideas on the Church since 1825, a year which is stressed time and again as the great turning-point. Furthermore the essays are all more or less polemical. In the 1840's and particularly the 1850's and 1860's Grundtvig's views on the Church came under increasing fire from the more orthodox Lutheran theologians and clergy, who closely followed Mynster and his successor as Bishop of Zealand, H. Martensen (1854-84), known also in Germany as a conservative Hegelian. This conflict undoubtedly sharpened Grundtvig's views and his criticism of the "scriptural theologians".

The first seven articles deal mainly with the Creed and the sacraments, that is, his "Church view" in the strictest sense, which was later taken up in other contexts. Here mention can only be made of certain new features or those not previously dealt with. Grundtvig now maintained quite definitely that the Creed is a word "from the Lord's own mouth", both historically as given by Jesus to the apostles after the resurrection, and when it is heard here and now as the Lord's word "*to us*", the present Church. This was also true of the blessing after baptism, the Lord's Prayer and the words instituting baptism and Holy Communion. But he acknowledges that in 1825 he had misused "the testimony at baptism" as a weapon of attack, "a sword of the law in the hand of the State Church". It is in itself "the gospel of peace", which can only be used in defence (cf. p. 236).

On the other hand he persisted with his "ecumenical" view: the words of the sacrament are, as the Word of God, the common faith of the Church, and *they* alone are the Word of God; it was the error of Luther and his successors to regard their sermons and the scriptures as God's Word. The individual must build "his salvation on his *participation* in the *whole* of the faith, hope and love of the Christian Church", corresponding to baptism (faith), the Lord's Prayer (hope) and Holy Communion (love). He also maintained the division between faith and teaching, Church and School (theology) and thus had reservations about his own Church views that belonged under "teaching". But his repudiation of scriptural theology led to his attempt to base his own reflections almost exclusively upon the words of the sacraments, supplemented by views taken from his philosophy of history and of man; and they therefore often took on a categorical and speculative stamp.

The middle section of the book contains a series of articles which constitute a clear and emphatic defence of his well-known reflection on the link between *the old and the new life,* "the inborn and the reborn human life" (cf. e.g. p. 110). It is the created "human life in the image of God" that is restored; and the faith, hope and love of the Christian life are not much different from faith, hope and love in the human sense. The Christian life must be regarded as a real life, a new creation on a par with Jesus' human life, but with "the same seasons as the old human life", so that it develops only gradually "from the most obscure life of the child to the strong and clear life of manhood".

New for him was the idea of *"the Christian signs of life"* in the confession of faith, the preaching of the gospel and the hymn of praise (1857). Grundtvig does not thereby wish to reduce the Christian life to words as opposed to action; but precisely because no clear distinction can be made between faith, hope and love in the Christian sense and the "heathen" or "jewish" sense, we must point to the confession of faith, the preaching of the gospel and the hymn of praise as the "expressions of life", even for the "present, frail, weak and obscure, yet Christian life". The basis was in reality a new understanding of the significance of the *congregation,* which we shall deal with later. With the *"signs of life"* Grundtvig connected the Word of God with its fruits in the words of the congregation and he experienced them increasingly as "visible expressions of life" in the Vartov congregation. It is a happy truth, he says in 1861, that through the illumination of the Word of the Lord for us "a new young life has come into being in the confession of faith, the preaching of the gospel and the hymn of praise, which goes from strength to strength and from clarity to clarity".

The last section of the book deals in particular with Grundtvig's *ideas on Church politics,* also often touched on in the first sections. Most of the new viewpoints characterizing this period he had already developed previously in a long series of commentaries and essays since the Constituent Assembly. The new constitution introduced religious freedom, but the State Church continued as the "Folk Church" for the large majority, with a promise – vaguely expressed – of a representative Church constitution (1849). Grundtvig turned against the latter with all his might, and it now became clear that his demand for Church freedom had a wide-ranging principle aim. A Church constitution would mean a continued "clergy pressure", a continuation of the centuries-old "church-pressure" "with rigid uniformity". Many clergymen actually maintained that the old Church laws were still valid for members of the national Church; but Grundtvig found it outrageous that people should be forced "to confess some sort of faith and follow certain Church customs", "to lie and dissemble on the most solemn matters". Free will must be the fundamental law for every Church community (1851). His conclusion to this was a demand for an almost unlimited freedom of clergy (particularly on liturgy and dogma) and the right of every minister with his voluntary church-goers to form a free congregation, who could freely "order their own spiritual matters" (1854). The implementation in 1855 of Grundtvig's old demand for release from the parish-tie was therefore only the first step.

The motive now was first and foremost the desire "to awaken and sustain the religious life", especially "living Christianity". Only ministers who were both clever and had the common touch would be able to gather a congregation, once the demands for church freedom were implemented. In addition Grundtvig would preserve the Folk Church system partly in order to maintain the interaction between the Church and the people, partly in recognition of the dangers of a free Church, the temptation to an "appearance of Christian perfection" and the danger of a new deterioration in the next generation. He also understood the many "moderately enlightened" Christians who ought not to be forced to choose between "following us" (by leaving the State Church) or by remaining. On the other hand he did not give up his long-standing criticism of the State Church as a confused ,mixture of believers and unbelievers, where the clergy were also obliged to serve the "obviously ungodly", for example, at the Eucharist. But this did not lead to practical ideas of Church discipline, apart from the demand for personal "freedom of clergy", that is, freedom from the obligation to serve everybody. Doubtless Grundtvig reckoned that this problem would solve itself through "Church freedom".

In a number of the articles in *Christian Childhood Teachings* Grundtvig touches on Søren Kierkegaard's attack on the Church in *The Moment* and other essays from 1854-55. This greatly interested him since he was himself in conflict with the official Church, and he often spoke about it – according to his closest associate in these years, *C. J. Brandt*. He also made direct capital out of Kierkegaard's attack on the "play-acting" of the State Church in his battle for Church freedom. But Grundtvig and Kierkegaard did not understand one another. To Kierkegaard Grundtvig was "the bellowing blacksmith"; and Grundtvig called Kierkegaard "the little hairsplitter". Kierkegaard's New Testament Christianity could not affect Grundtvig since he had long ago given up building his faith on scriptural theology, which in his opinion was being pushed to the limits by Kierkegaard. It was for Grundtvig a peculiar and false interpretation to believe that Christians should regard all that brings "happiness in this world as the Devil's work", and should "torment themselves and each other and the whole world every night and day in order to please the Lord Jesus Christ". That Kierkegaard was only aiming at a comfortable and quiet "confessionary Christianity", as has later been claimed, was not easy to reconcile with the passion that characterized his attacks. Grundtvig's thoughts on Kierkegaard, or occasioned by Kierkegaard, can in all essentials be explained on the basis of his own beliefs.

Several of the final articles in *Childhood Teachings* also deal with *the history of the Church,* which for the older Grundtvig overshadowed the history of the world. Biblical and Church history now frame world history in a similar fashion to his first two *World Chronicles* (1812 and 1814). The biblical history of the Old Testament informs us (the Christians) of the preconditions for Christianity as "the *ancient* history of *man* in his best clothes and in his highest relationship"; and with Christ "the *new life of man* amongst Christian people" begins, i.e. in the history of the Church. The Christian people are neither a worldly people as they are for the Roman Church, nor an invisible Church as they are for a spiritual Christendom of air". But they are a real people who "in the Spirit have *life, language* and *country* in common"; and following Grundtvig's discovery of its hallmark (the signs of life) "in the *Word of God* fused with the *Word of the Church"* we can now continue the history of the Church after the time of the apostles. The Bible throws light on the history of the human race in its "childhood" (until the Tower of Babel), through its "youth" (the history of Israel), into "the beginning of the history of its manhood" with Christ. And with Him began also the Christian people, "who through manhood and old age shall complete the course of man".

Such ideas had a long *previous history,* however. In *Church Enlightenment* (1840-42) Grundtvig still did not regard the time as being ripe for "a history of the Christian Church". But by the summer of 1842 he was ready. He wrote to Busck that he longed to finish his history of the world and "get to grips with the history of the *Church"*, which he had always regarded as "the major book" he would write. But first he had to learn to "sort the wheat from the chaff" and examine the history of the world as the Church's stage and as "material to create something new from". Around 1850 he published several synopses of Church history and already in the first of these, from 1847, he sketches the main outlines that he later followed.

His point of departure here is the view that Jesus and the history of the early Church in the New Testament could be seen as a prophecy of the purpose and the course of the Church's history. The historical life-stages are determined on this basis. The Christian people began with a childhood, which like Jesus' childhood was full of spirit and wisdom. Then followed "an obscure interval" – corresponding to Jesus' youth – where things "went downhill" in the old Christendom but "uphill" in the new: the English, German and Nordic Middle Ages. With Luther "an incomparable light" shone over the Spirit, the Word and the Faith – just as when Jesus stepped forward in Nazareth. But when the application failed, no progress followed, but a time of regression. This was temporary, Grundtvig assumes, necessary as the run-up to a great leap forward so that we could reach the goal, which is "the fully-grown Christ". To this is added an interpretation of the seven churches in Revelation as images of the leading peoples in the history of the Church. After the fifth, the German Lutheran (Sardis), where everything is a matter of Scripture, comes the Nordic Baptist-church (Philadelphia) and finally the presumably Indian Eucharist-church, "after which the consummation follows", so the last Church reaches the same height as the first.

Grundtvig continued this line of thought in the long poem *The Pleiades of Christendom* which characterizes the six churches to which he attached greatest importance: Jewish-Christian, the Greek and Latin, the English, German and Nordic, corresponding to the first six churches in Revelation. In an introduction from 1860 he pointed out that he would not place too much emphasis on his textual interpretation, which might be doubtful; the essential thing was whether the poem gave an apposite and beneficial overview of "the course of the Christian people". It should be regarded as "a spiritual people", who have continually interacted with the main peoples and languages through which the Christian life has revealed itself in the confession of faith, the preaching of the gospel and the hymn of praise. Nor did he seek to hide the fact that the poem pointed to the Danish-Nordic church as the most important of the time. The North has its own people's spirit – "which is one of the highest"; and "since amongst us in both the people and the Church there has been a *living revival* we dare now to speak of it as a *settled matter* that *our hour has now arrived*".

Grundtvig's last attempt, the lectures on Church history from 1861-63 (*Church Mirror*), is only a broader presentation of the same pattern. Here he maintained that it is not really the Christian life he seeks to depict, but the history of the Church on the basis of baptism and Holy Communion, the confession of faith, the preaching of the gospel and the hymn of praise. The various Church communities are judged in accordance with their attitude to baptism and Holy Communion, which leads to severe judgements particularly on the Greek Church (which does not use the apostolic Creed at baptism) and on the reformed Church communities. The account bears the mark of Grundtvig's growing self-confidence. The Christian "regeneration" which the Reformation and evangelicalism had vainly attempted, had now begun in Denmark, where as a result of Grundtvig's efforts "a core for a Christian Danish free Church" had been formed. The Lutheran community in Denmark was to be "the womb for a popular Church life and for an enlightenment through Church history"; therefore "we can calmly look back on the desperate circumstances under which the new order of things had to be prepared".

This interpretation shared the same assumptions as Grundtvig's view of history in general: that the course of the world is nearing its conclusion. According to an early Church chronology which Grundtvig adopted it covered only 6,000 years, corresponding to the six days of creation, and in Grundtvig's time there were only about 400 years left to run. But one must ask whether Grundtvig has not forgotten his own "historical view" from 1815-20 in these late reflections on the history of the Church. He is close to surveying history as a whole and thus placing himself outside time. Either way there is a considerable distance between the old Grundtvig's self-importance and the modesty of his view of history according to which every man must acknowledge his own insignificance as being only a part of the history of mankind that will soon be invisible.

The Church and the People

In the winter of 1847-48 Grundtvig was accused by two clergymen of confusing Danishness with Christianity. One of the two was his old comrade-in-arms from 1825, A. G. Rudelbach, who unlike Grundtvig had remained an orthodox Lutheran. By way of answer Grundtvig wrote two articles claiming the exact opposite: "I am not *confusing* Danishness with Christianity, but separating them more sharply and clearly than any pen has ever done". In this he was right in a way, as a short retrospect will prove.

In the years after 1810 he had made the distinction between Christianity and culture sharper than anyone else and had fought for the *specially* Christian against the fusion of the rational truths of the enlightenment

357

and all forms of romantic pantheism. The specifically Christian was first and foremost the message that he found in the biblical stories and images and in the orthodox Lutheran hymns. But as long as he attempted to define and defend it conceptually as the true theology, it remained in an undefined and competitive relationship with other views. The distinction became much clearer in 1825, when he "discovered" that true Christianity is given historically in the baptismal Creed, in baptism and Holy Communion, mediated by "the historical Christian Church". This meant that the specifically Christian has been given in advance, before all understanding, as a mysterious "Word of God", which creates what it names. Faith does not tempt with silver and gold, but "merely says God's peace! arise/and join the King's guests!" (see Matt. 22:2-10). As "a wondrous power" it cannot be a general truth, a state religion that embraces everybody; the numbers of the faithful are hidden and of no importance (cf. the poem, *The Christian Faith* 1828).

Thus Grundtvig introduced his distinction between faith and progressive understanding; and as a result he began his long battle for "Church freedom", which formed the basis of his distinction between Christianity and Danishness in 1836 (see p. 287), and which also characterizes the above articles. They stress that Christianity originally came to the people as a "a heavenly guest", not in order to be served, but in order itself to serve. It came in the form of a defenceless monk (Ansgar), with no other influence than what "*the Word itself*" could obtain. It was not Christianity but the papists' Roman spirit that oppressed the people and made them pretend that they were pervaded by Christianity. However, the clergy pressure was perpetuated by the Protestants, who sought by force to maintain the appearance of Christianity. But since "spiritual slavery" is just as unchristian as it is inhuman, the Christians must now make a common front with "the Naturalists" against the clergy pressure so that Christianity and the people can once again "return to their original, free, only true and natural relationship".

But the two articles did not hide the fact that there was also a *connection* between Church and people, summarized as follows: "the spirit of the people is the necessary precondition for *living* Christianity". The reason was, as so often before, Jesus' relationship to Israel and John the Baptist. The prerequisite for the Coming of Christ was that God had formed His own people and thereby "the whole life of the people of Israel", reawakened by John the Baptist, who prepared the way for the Lord and made ready for Him a "well-prepared people". In a similar fashion pagans must be educated and mature to Christianity.

The word *precondition* is in itself too weak and vague to express

Grundtvig's meaning. Behind it lies his long-standing battle against on the one hand the rationalist, materialist philosophy of man, and on the other hand the "thoroughly superterrestrial and supernatural Christianity of the strict Lutherans". Not just Christianity but also mankind is a divine wonder. "Even the most wretched living person is a great work of art in a quite different sense than is the loveliest statue." Through language and speech we have "a mysterious connection with the whole of the *invisible* world"; the invisible Word "comes from above and goes right through us and reveals on its way what lives and moves invisibly inside such strange creatures as we are". It excludes "the sharp dividing-line between divine and human that our theologians usually draw".

It is not "the true and living 6ut the false and dead Christianity that will set the great gulf between heaven and earth, between God and man, and between time and eternity". The same God who created heaven also created the earth; and from the dust of the earth He created man in His image and "*blew* into the dust his heavenly life-spirit, so it is clear that He wished to link heaven to earth and unite Himself with mankind". "This great and wonderful work of God" is accomplished despite the power of the Devil and sin. Thus in the fulness of time He sent His son, who is the only one to unite God and man, so also the man of dust can be cleaned and transfigured and the earth filled with the glory of God. As a consequence of this it would be contradictory foolishness for a Christian to set aside the human in order to strive for the divine. "The more kindly and more inwardly we can link the divine and the human, the heavenly and the earthly, the temporal and the eternal, the spiritual and the corporal, the better it is and the more we are like our Lord Jesus Christ who was one with His heavenly father and yet a human being like us in every way, though without sin" (1841).

In its main features this line of thought can be traced back to Grundtvig's youth, for example, the *Chronicle* of 1814. But the practical application of the relationship between the human and the Christian is characteristic of the period after 1835; and the emphasis on "the people and the popular" in the 1840's can be regarded as a further realisation of this relationship: the human is linked to a particular people with a particular language and a particular history (cf. p. 285, esp. p. 291). The peoples of the world too are created by God, and are encompassed by His Providence; and according to the articles on Christianity and Danishness from 1847-48 Christianity must either find "the spirit of the people" or create it itself where it is lacking. Thus from 1848 Grundtvig could speak in his sermons of both the human and the popular as a basis for Christianity and of the significance of Christianity for the people and the national tasks before them. This was also the case in the articles from time to time in *The Dane* and *The Danish Flag,* but here he tried to distinguish between Christianity and Danishness. In "the Danish cause" he disregarded Christianity on principle – but not "Our Lord"!

A few examples will illustrate this. In his New Year sermon for 1848 Grundtvig assumes that even the "worldly wise" are hoping for "a great spiritual revival", so that the people come to appreciate their fatherland and their mother-tongue (country and language). But it is the Christians who now in the name of *Jesus* are to do the job of work which the spirit of this world has dabbled with in vain. The servants of Christ used only to say to the people: "Wake up, you who sleep, and arise from the dead, so that Christ can shine for you!" – "Awake in all the natural feeling of the sweetness of life, the inspiration of the mother-tongue, the loveliness of our country. And then decide for yourself whether you will thank Him who awakened you," or be satisfied with the life that is blown away like the flowers of the field. "All is ready for an awakening of the people, if only the power is there, His power."

Another sermon from that spring illuminates the question from another side: "If we do not believe in earthly things, we believe even less in heavenly." When our everyday speech is hot air, that is, our talk "of what by nature lies closest to us: our heart's feelings, our sorrow and joy, our fear and hope, our own mother-tongue and country", then the Sunday talk of the Word of God and the Kingdom of God is also hot air. Such a view is often presented: that Christianity presupposes words in the mother-tongue about what "lies closest to us".

Another frequent motif appears in a sermon the following autumn: in particular "the little, mild and peaceful Danish people" are the home of the "warm heart". It is threatened by powerful enemies, but far more by a growing wilfulness and selfishness; in parliament everything is usually decided by "the cool calculation, the heartless wisdom", and yet it is "in the warm heart of the Danes that our patriotism has its source and our happiness its foundation". God looks into the heart in spite of all its defilement, "the human heart, which from the beginning he quickened with his breath". "If only the Danish heart continues to beat, feels the danger to its life and sighs for the heavenly Father", then the country is saved. It resembles a ship in distress, but a ship that has held close to the Church ship by a mysterious drift; so that the same Lord "that saves his own great ship also saves the little Danish one which for a thousand years has sailed alongside enjoying the calm sea He has created!"

This trusting attitude gains the upper hand completely in Grundtvig's New Year sermon for 1849, after the year of "the great earthquake". In

360

spite of all wilfulness and self-conceit it had been one of the happiest years for many centuries. For it was the bonds of darkness that had burst; so from a Christian point of view "through the hand of Providence human life has been made and is making giant strides to *victory, freedom* and *enlightenment*". Furthermore it appeared that in Denmark there was "a loving bond between the King and the people and between us all as fellow-citizens from ancient time and children of a common mother".

He therefore also praised the soldiers who sacrificed their lives in war for their family and their nation. Christians must not raise themselves above the soldiers as children of the world in the false assumption that Christian love is of a different nature from the love these "noble warriors" showed. "For truly they were not far from the Kingdom of God, and ... whoever is not stirred by love of his country will never enter the Kingdom of God". There is an indissoluble connection between faith and an "untiring proof of love for our family" and a fundamental unity "of all true and genuine *human* love from the very lowest to the very highest degree".

In 1851 he looked more closely at this connection in *The Dane*. Christianity demands an "everyday relationship" between parents, children and brother and sister. But if there is the least life and strength in Christianity it must give the "home life" in the family a much richer content so that we look more at the heart than at the clothes and the livelihood, "more at what the life of man in heart and soul is nourished by, is capable of and can bring about, than the life of the world, which we share with the dumb animals". Christianity can also "create a heavenly community life on earth, where with love, spirit and wisdom Christians engage actively in the community life they are appointed to participate in". This admittedly has a far-reaching perspective, since it demands Christian enlightenment and a clarification of the confusion which the so-called "Christian State" has left behind; but Danish Christianity has already enlightened the people as to the necessity of religious freedom and thereby removed a great obstacle to a free and healthy community life.

In *The Danish Flag* Grundtvig describes his view of Christianity quite simply as "the *human* that fuses together with the divine". Christianity is created for the sake of mankind as "the only good that helps": the proof of "*God's* love of mankind". It leaves those who belittle it to themselves; but where love is missed and appreciated it gives "its great sign" and gradually dessicates "self-love, which is the source of all our sin and misery".

In the years from 1848 until the mid-1850's there was a considerable change in Grundtvig's relationship to the *devout meeting movement* and his clergy-friends who were attached to it. In 1847 he fiercely repudiated

Vilhelm Birkedal, who in a newspaper debate had defended "the revival-ists", as the supporters of the movement were called. Birkedal had main-tained that the invisible society through baptism and Holy Communion also requires a society turned outwards, in which the common spirit and faith comes to consciousness; and he found this best realised in the meet-ing-movement – with all its faults. But as before Grundtvig totally rejected the "self-made devout meetings" and declared that the commun-ion of saints was created solely by "the Lord's work in the Holy Com-munion".

By that time, however, he had already met his destiny in *Marie Toft* (b. 1813), a widow and a landed proprietor out of a noble family but known in particular as a prominent leader of the meeting-movement in south Zealand together with a number of clergymen who were close to Grundt-vig. In 1845 she approached Grundtvig to discuss the movement and had a friendly reception; but their conversation became strident and she was deeply wounded by his words. Nonetheless she invited him in 1846 in connection with a talk he was to give the local Danish Society; but when Grundtvig continued to denigrate the devout meetings she also refused to take part in his "meetings"! However, she did not break off the connec-tion, which continued via conversations and letters on religious ques-tions. Marie was "more spirited and undaunted than most", and already in 1848 she was the superior partner in their internal relationship. Grundt-vig's first wife died after a long illness in January 1851. In the summer of that year he became engaged and then married to Marie. In spite of their age difference it was a very happy marriage; they were like "a loving couple" who could not do without each other. It was, wrote Grundtvig, as if they had "stolen away into Paradise" (1854).

She proved of great importance to Grundtvig as a "spiritual friend". "Never have I met a man or a woman with whom it was such a pleasure and a comfort to exchange words and thoughts about all the matters of the spirit and the heart as this wonderful woman, who never tried to elude anything of that nature and who never said I was right until she saw that she was wrong" (1855). His enthusiasm for woman as such received a new impetus. He closed down *The Dane* in December 1851 with a cele-bration of woman, "who believes in spirit" and who "committed herself to words with spirit".

The final words are:

> So long live the woman!
> Who bore us into *Denmark's people*

A blessing on the female spiritual friend
And the tongue which is the heart's interpreter.

In the same year he was the only writer of note to defend Matilde Fibiger, the pioneer of the women's cause in Denmark with her controversial book, *Clara Raphael*. In the following years she also made the personal acquaintance of Grundtvig and Marie.

In his second marriage Grundtvig enjoyed a grander way of life, partly in Copenhagen, partly at her manor. And yet at the same time through Marie he came closer to the *country people*. Although according to Grundtvig she was a queen in her appearance – "the woman who could control a whole kingdom" – she had so simple a manner "that every Zealand peasant and smallholder, not to mention their wives, could not but regard her as one of them". Grundtvig listened in wonder to her talking for hours about agricultural affairs with peasants and smallholders explaining everything to them and laughing "so gently at all their clumsy objections that in the end they themselves had to join in the laughter and more often than not give way". She felt "even more sympathy than I did" for these Zealanders, talented and cheerful, but lazy and neglected as they were. After her death the peasants and smallholders from her estate raised a monument to her because she had abolished villeinage, given up her hunting rights and helped many of them to become freeholders on very favourable conditions.

"Truly the lady is revived!" wrote Grundtvig in one of his many poems to Marie (1851) and she never abandoned the "revivalists". But according to Grundtvig they came even closer to a complete understanding on this and to "fundamental agreement" on the essential: "I have never known a woman who could hold her own so well on the *human* connection to the *divine* and the *popular* to the *Christian*" (1855). Without having talked to Grundtvig about it she became just as eager as him in 1848 for "the Danish cause" and in the same year she worked for his election to parliament. She drove me, he wrote, to a living participation and a radical activity wherever a door was open to all that is noble in heaven and earth, and she was in every way a wonderful helpmate for me". He was on the way to becoming "unfair to everything in this world that was not like her, and sullen about everything that was not *for* her" (1854). According to Grundtvig it was Marie who drove him into founding the Danish Association, though here she was supported by her brother, H. Carlsen, and the clergyman, Peter Rørdam, who was married to her sister. "My wife believes, and it is certainly most desirable, that many of the revivalists will be won over to the cause, if they are spoken to properly, and it is clear that they more than any must feel what a disaster it would be" if the mother-tongue became dead and powerless in the sermon, song and Bible as was the case in Schleswig, where the clergy spoke German or were German-educated (February 1853).

Marie was right; local branches of the Danish Association were often established in the revivalist areas or around grundtvigian revivalist ministers. And she was right in a wider sense: in the years after 1850 large sections of the meeting-movement ranged themselves behind Grundtvig and grundtvigianism as a Christian people's movement. Mention can be made of a few features of this trend (see also p. 373ff).

When Grundtvig celebrated his 70th birthday he received a present of 7000 *rigsdaler* for the establishment of a high school, in a letter signed by 379 contributors from Denmark and 92 from Norway. His plan for a state high school had been shelved by the National Liberal government in 1849. The collection was continued in *The Danish Flag* at the request of a circle which included both spokesmen for the meeting-movement and the clergymen who had cooperated with it. One of the largest contributions came from the Jutland-Funen meeting-movement's overall leader, the farmer Peter Larsen, who in 1835-37 had supported Rasmus Sørensen's clash with Grundtvig and Lindberg (see p. 281). Peter Larsen had to ask in *The Danish Flag,* however, what the purpose of the high school actually was; and he explicitly challenged Grundtvig to compare his societies for Danishness with the devout meeting's importance for Christianity. But Grundtvig's reply to Peter Larsen, whom he called his good friend, was very friendly. The high school should "revive, nourish and educate *the life of man* which one must presuppose for Danish youth", while not losing sight of either devoutness or patriotism. And seeing as the devout meetings would only work for a living Christianity and did not wish to be a Church within a Church, they corresponded quite rightly to the Danish Association's work for a living Danishness. More important than "these self-made connections" were nonetheless living Christianity and Danishness in themselves, "which for me, and as far as I can judge for Denmark in general, have become inseparable, and for a valid reason, namely that on the one hand living Danishness has a good eye for Christianity's omnipotence, and on the other hand Christianity always borrows the spirit of the mother-tongue from the people it dwells with, inspires and enlightens". For Grundtvig "Danish" was a broad concept, just as, according to a reply to Peter Larsen, "purely human" was the same as "Christian"! (1854 cf. p. 353).

In 1856 Peter Larsen even invited Grundtvig to one of the large meetings he held at his farm. Grundtvig regretted that at the last moment he was prevented from coming but assured Larsen that he wished he could be there; and that he "really did want to speak personally to God's children over there about the things that belong to the Kingdom of God". A year later Peter Larsen attended the Scandinavian Church Assembly in Copenhagen and astonished the theologians who had gathered there with an hour-long speech in defence of Grundtvig's view of the Church!

Another example is Grundtvig's relationship to *Christen Kold*, who first became known as the leader of the devout meetings and always bore the stamp of this. He had been trained as a teacher, and during a period as tutor in west Schleswig around 1840 he had independently put into practice Grundtvig's ideas on oral, narrative teaching. At the same time he worked energetically for a "Danish Society" similar to Grundtvig's one in Copenhagen. In 1849-50 as a tutor with Vilhelm Birkedal he conceived the plan of establishing a "higher peasant-school", especially for children of the "revivalists". Birkedal had become the rector of Ryslinge in southeast Funen, and revivalist numbers grew rapidly in response to his ministry. But Grundtvig's "Danish cause" was of great importance for Kold at the time; what he later described as his aim: to revive faith in "God's love and Denmark's happiness" was, properly understood, the same as Grundtvig's aim with *The Dane*.

For his initial outlay Kold needed 600 *rigsdaler,* and his trip to Grundtvig to seek support was not in vain. Birkedal gave 10, Grundtvig gave 50, and Marie Toft 100 *rigsdaler* (in the spring of 1850). Kold's description of the school, which formed the basis for the collection, made it clear that the purpose was a "peasantry that was educated about both Christianity and the people"; and Kold also acquainted Grundtvig with his essay, *On the Elementary School* (cf. p. 224). In 1852 Grundtvig donated another 50 *rigsdaler* to Kold's school and in 1853 Kold was the first to be considered as the leader of the high school for which Grundtvig had received support on his 70th birthday. But in the same year Kold opened a high school near Kerteminde in north-east Funen which was the starting-point for the meeting-movement. Here he added a free school for children and he also became the central figure in a flourishing local Danish Association. It was from this same area that Grundtvig was urged in 1855 to seek election to parliament, when the member for the constituency, a leading representative of the revivalists, wished to resign. The election day was a triumph; there were election speeches, Grundtvig was elected by an overwhelming majority and afterwards there was a popular celebration with numerous speeches and songs and ending with folk dancing. Grundtvig was supported in particular by Birkedal, who had great talent as a platform speaker. As a contemporary exchange of letters shows, their former differences over the meeting-movement were forgotten and replaced by a close friendship.

In the summer of 1854 Grundtvig suffered the terrible blow of losing Marie, who died after giving birth. But he continued along the same path. In 1847 he had disclaimed the title of party-founder on the basis that his supporters represented two irreconcilable parties: one that extolled only his sermons and his hymns and defended the devout meetings, and one that praised his "mythologicalness, historicalness and his tremendous Danishness". But the latter "party" soon lost its influence. It consisted of students and the educated circles in Copenhagen who had applauded Grundtvig as a public speaker in the 1840's; for the most part they joined the National Liberals and in the 1850's and 1860's became opponents of Grundtvig as a "friend of the peasants". The core of grundtvigianism was formed by "the revivalists" among the country population and their clergy. But as has been seen, they abondoned the pietistic tendencies of the meeting-movement. A number of pietistic meeting-people turned away from Grundtvig, but the majority joined the grundtvigian ministers and the meetings were replaced by church and popular meetings. Grundtvig's supporters were still "revived" but in the broader sense of "in many areas" – and in this sense like Grundtvig himself, they followed in the steps of Marie.

There was one point on which Grundtvig had never quite been able to agree with Marie. According to him she had the eloquence to be able to "speak of our Lord" far better than the clergy, and with regard to "*wisdom by examinations* and the self-appointed *clerical dignity* she was not merely unbelieving, like all wise women, but quite merciless". Grundtvig, however, had thought that the congregation was best served by deferring to the proper Christian officials (1855). But over the next few years he too often dissociated himself from the clergy and theologians, as he did from provosts, bishops and popes, both in *Christian Childhood Teachings* and in his sermons. Instead he emphasized the importance of women for "the Christian enlightenment", "the general clergy" in the main and the congregation as such. The clergy had neither a monopoly on preaching the gospel nor ownership rights over the sacraments. The devout meetings should in no way be called in question on the clergy's behalf, but should be judged, just like the ministers, by their attitude to the Christian Creed, the preaching of the gospel and the hymn of praise in connection with baptism and Holy Communion (1857).

Until 1847 as we have seen, Grundtvig had great reservations about the Church as a human fellowship (see p. 362). The "*external community of believing and loving people*" was characteristic of the time of the apostles, but it would first revive close to the end of the world (*Church Enlight-enment,* 1842). But in 1854 he announced an imminent "interim", in which the servants of the Lord should "prepare for the crossing over from death to life of the whole Church through faith in God's son". A year later he went even further: the text on the pouring of the Spirit on the Church (John 16: 5-15) was now to be preached more powerfully than at any time since the days of the apostles. "For now is the great *crossing over* from *dark* to *light* and from *death* to *life* ... which has had no parallel since "the forty days" (between Christ's resurrection and ascension). In *Christian Childhood Teachings* he has reservations about even the word *church* as being an imprecise foreign word that had been exploited "when cunning *priests* and *popes* wanted to set themselves in place *of the Lord* and place the *external* above the *internal*". This should be replaced by "congrega-tion" or "people's assembly" and "the communion of saints" should be replaced by "the fellowship of saints" (1855-56). In *Childhood Teachings* he also introduced the expression "the Lord's free congregation" or "the Danish free congregation" as a designation for the living congregation in contrast to the State Church.

In the 1860's the congregational fellowship became a chief concern for Grundtvig and the grundtvigian congregations. We see, through the light of "the living Word of God to us ... the Christian congregational life arising in the midst of us and revealing itself in the common creed of the whole congregation," he preached in 1860. In contrast to individualistic Christianity, Christians should strive for "the inward, mutual love with its life-fellowship or community life" (1862). The delusion that Christ lay in the Scriptures as in the grave "and could not help Himself" drew a veil over "the whole organization in the spiritual house of God on earth, which Christ's living Church is" (1865). The following year he called the revival of the almost "dead and powerless congregational life in the common faith and mutual love" his "real task in the service of the Holy Spirit"; but it was first through "Christian marriage" that he had "learned to feel really what the life of the Church congregation is" and to nourish the hope of its flowering.

The "Christian marriage" refers in particular, as previous statements show, to his marriage to Marie, but also to his third marriage to *Asta Reedtz,* whom he married in 1858. She too was the widow of a landed proprietor from the nobility and like Marie a Christian "revivalist", in fact from the same circle, since she was acquainted with Marie's family. She brought four small children with her from her first marriage, and since Grundtvig had had a son by Marie and a daughter by Asta, in his old age he had six small children in his house. It was strange for his eldest sons, but Grundtvig happily accepted the whole flock rushing into his study. Through Asta Grundtvig acquired a capacious house, which he called "Happy-home" *(Gladhjem),* and she opened her home to his growing circle of "friends", especially members of parliament, students, peasants and smallholders in large numbers, not least former meeting-people.

Grundtvig was also glad to have his new friends around him, and the great party for his 50th anniversary in the priesthood in 1861 provided the impetus for a more or less annual "friends' meeting" in Copenhagen, as a rule around Grundtvig's birthday on September 8th. They lasted a few days and Grundtvig himself led the way as a speaker and participator in the discussions. In addition there were large communal meals and outdoor parties in the evening with numerous speeches and songs, the scene being illuminated by coloured lamps or torches, even fireworks. Most of the participants were visitors from some distance, especially common villagers from the whole country, and as a rule from Norway too; at the last friends' meeting in 1871 there were 3,000 present. For the people of Copenhagen – apart from the Vartov congregation – the grundtvigians were now a strange "sect", who were known as "the happy Christians".

The rallying-point was Grundtvig's view of the Church, but there were other hallmarks. Everything was inter-dependent for this circle. One important subject was the battle for "Church freedom", which gave rise to organisational efforts that culminated in the formation of a grundtvigian party in the *Rigsdag* (see p. 308). On the second day of a friends' meeting there were often discussions on "school matters", which Grundtvig placed great emphasis on, especially after the unfortunate war in 1864. Also from the pulpit he exhorted his audience "to strive with renewed effort to promote popular education in the mother-tongue in every human direction". "Wherever the voice of the Son of God that has awakened us is not heard, there the people are now as a rule so stone dead to the Spirit that they do not even believe any Spirit exists." So the Christians must lead the way; the clergy too should "work zealously for *popular* enlightenment ... without asking about the faith of the young people"; there was no point in using bigger words than people could manage. As a model he pointed in particular to Christen Kold, who was also his personal guest. A number of young people took up the challenge and opened peasant high-schools which resembled Kold's school, rather than the state school that was originally Grundtvig's aim.

For Grundtvig and his friends it was a "spring time" without equal. The large Vartov congregations around the country testified to this, as did the

368

N.F.S. Grundtvig in 1862. (Painting by Wilhelm Marstrand, Frederiksborg Museum).

N.F.S. Grundtvig, 1872. (Photo by Lønborg, Royal Library, Copenhagen). From the summer of 1872 the English writer, Edmund Gosse, has given us a description of Grundtvig as he appeared in Vartov Church (in *Two Visits to Denmark*). He writes as follows:

»For a man of ninety, he could not be called infirm; his gestures were rapid and his step steady. But the attention was riveted on his appearance of excessive age. He looked like a troll from some cave in Norway; he might have been centuries old.

From the vast orb of his bald head, very long strings of silky hair fell over his shoulders and mingled with a long and loose white beard. His eyes flamed under very beetling brows, and they were the only part of his face that seemed alive, for he spoke without moving his lips. His features were still shapely, but colourless and dry, and as the draught from an open door caught them, the silken hairs were blown across his face like a thin curtain. While he perambulated the church with these stiff gestures and ventriloquist murmurings, his disciples fell on their knees behind him, stroking the skirts of his robe, touching the heels of his shoes. Finally, he ascended the pulpit and began to preach; in his dead voice he warned us to beware of false spirits, and to try every spirit whether it be of God. He laboured extremely with his speech, becoming slower and huskier, with longer pauses between the words like a clock that is running down. He looked supernatural, but hardly Christian.«

new hymns and the new high schools and free schools that were established in several places. Grundtvig used powerful words to describe the
development.

In 1866 he could "say with the patriarch: with my staff I passed over this
Jordan; and now I am become a large company" (not "two companies" as
in Gen. 32:10). It was precisely in the Nordic countries that the apostolic
Church should be reborn; the Danish Church was "obviously the last stop
on the way to the new Jerusalem"! On the other hand he also had reservations about his "visions" and "illuminations" and he warned of an
increased enmity from "the world". The prophecies of happiness from his
old age were at heart of the same kind as the "unreasonable hope" of his
youth and his powerful vision since 1835: a personal faith linked to a
poetic inspiration that goes from the small to the large, from the concrete
to the deeper meaning, a comprehensive context. As in the following
poem in old age:

> Cool falls the evening dew
> A night frost is heralded,
> Day had carried its disease
> From the cradle to old age,
> Mournful sounds the evensong
> Even in the Happy-home!
>
> But where life and light *reside:*
> In our Father-God's embrace,
> Love can never there forget
> Life's dangers, light's distress.
> Daily presage *morning-light:*
> So there *is escape from death!*

From the end of the 1850's Grundtvig suffered from a number of infirmi-
ties; he found it hard to walk, his eyesight was weak, and he also had
bouts of illness. But apart from these he was mentally alert and active to
the last. Like the old Northern warriors he regarded the "straw death" (in
bed) as "death in its worst, most boring form". Strange as it may sound,
until 1867 he did not usually go to bed at night but lay down on the sofa
where he also sat when he was working. On Sunday September 1st 1872
he preached as usual and then had a dinner party with members of
parliament, with whom he enjoyed a lengthy conversation. The political
course was a controversial subject amongst his friends and invitations
were again issued to a big friends' meeting around September 8th, when

Grundtvig would be celebrating his 89th birthday. But the day after, on September 2nd, he died sitting in his study. The friends' meeting was thus combined with a grand funeral which ended on Køge Ridge, where Grundtvig was buried in a vault alongside Marie.

Grundtvigianism as a Movement
until around 1900

by ANDERS PONTOPPIDAN THYSSEN

Grundtvigianism as a Church Movement and a Popular Movement (1825-1860's)

Grundtvigianism regarded as a "party" can be traced back to the Church battle, 1825-34 (see p. 226 and 234). The lengthy debate gave both sides the character of a party; but it was especially Grundtvig's opponents who gained a hearing when they spoke against "the party", Grundtvig's little party of neo-orthodox fanatics. It was hardly a party as such and was certainly not a large grouping, consisting as it did of some young theologians, originally with *Theological Monthly* as their rallying point (1825-28), and a student-circle that gathered around *Lindberg*. Some of them later went off in different directions but most of them entered the Church as the first generation of "grundtvigians".

Through the Church battle Grundtvig also became an important name in the meeting-movement, and the congregation he led from 1832 began as a devout meeting. It consisted mainly of artisans and other common folk who did not make personal contact with Grundtvig; it was said that he was "ill-equipped to talk to the common man" (1832). But everyone knew Lindberg, whose modest home became a centre for the "revivalists" in Copenhagen. From 1833 he also came into contact – through the paper *Nordic Church Times* – with the meeting-movement in the rest of the country. On his long tour in 1834 he built up considerable sympathy for the revivalists, who gave him a warm welcome wherever he went. On the other hand he could share completely their critical view of the clergy. Most clergymen were "unbelieving, conceited, under-educated, and basically lecherous dogs". They neglected the meetings, he writes, preferring to play with the lord of the manor until late in the night, and they would rather look after their cats and dogs than the salvation of their congregation!

At this point the meeting-movement was regarded as part of the grundtvigian party. But the picture changed in 1835-36, when the leading meeting-people rejected Lindberg and Grundtvig; and Grundtvig's rough criticism of the movement over the following years seemed to exclude any contact between him and the revivalists (cf. p. 281ff).

At the same time a new form of grundtvigianism begins with the lectures by Ludvig Christian Müller and Gunni Busck around 1835, with Grundtvig's High School writings from 1836, his "Within Living Memory" lectures in 1838 and the founding of the Danish Society in 1839 (see p. 275). This was "popular grundtvigianism", which appealed to the people in general and which aimed to awaken a love for Denmark and a sense of the "common good". But from the beginning it had a Church background, for it was led by the clergy, who according to Grundtvig had "our Lord up their sleeve". Seen from this angle he could overcome his reservations about the "alien task" that regarded the fatherland on earth as its goal: "the earth is the Lord's and the fullness thereof, and He gave it to the children of man, so it is a question of gradually *renewing* the "form of the earth" in ourselves according to the image from above and through the Spirit he sends out!" (November 1835).

Out in the country the new popular style began to make its presence felt around 1840. For example a Zealand minister, J.F. Fenger, wrote to Grundtvig in the summer of 1841 on the subject of a large folk festival he had held in his parish on the Queen's birthday. It began in a yard near the school, which had been decorated with greenery and flowers, garlands and banners. Here Fenger made a speech for the queens of Denmark and many songs were sung, including new ones which had been rehearsed at the school. The large gathering had then moved off to a neighbouring wood, carrying the Danish flag before them followed by the flags of seven other nations on a long row of wagons. The party continued in the wood until sunset with no more than coffee and cakes to keep the villagers going; so no one can be accused of drunkenness, wrote Fenger. But perhaps people will say we are mad, "for we sang from the bottom of our hearts and regularly shouted hurrahs for all the people we like. I saw many happy faces and not one sullen expression." Fenger was inspired by the Danish Society, and the same was true of a folk festival held in the same style which Christen Kold and Ludvig Christian Müller arranged in west Schleswig in 1840. It was held at the same place several years running.

Grundtvig himself stresses the part played by the young Peter Rørdam as a minister "for the people". He had an "unequalled success in pleasing people", when he became a minister in south Zealand in 1841. Grundtvig writes in 1842 that Rørdam could "walk in and out of their hearts with his clogs on. When he feels like it, he says from the pulpit, 'I think it would be nice now to sing A Child is Born in Bethlehem (or whatever). I'll give you the first verse and you can join in!' –, and the whole church joins in. Even when they met to elect the parish council he spoke to the peasants in such a way that he got them to sing a verse or two for Frederik VI. That is the way it should be".

But as Grundtvig emphasizes, it was still only "in the corners" that the new movement could be glimpsed. Relations with the *meeting-movement* had to be sorted out first, for it was a truly popular movement in the sense that it had sprung from the common folk, who also provided its leaders; by 1840 or thereabouts it covered large areas of the country. As a rule it formed only a minority, but it evoked considerable attention. A south Funen farmer complained in 1838 of the 60 Langelanders who "were wandering through village after village" holding meetings; one or two were enough to "throw the whole house into confusion", so if the movement spread, there was "fear of a religious war"!

At the end of the 1830's Lindberg was still the most important link between Grundtvig and the meeting-movement. In spite of the antagonism in 1835-36 he had maintained contact with the movement through *Nordic Church Times*, which remained its mouthpiece to the authorities while simultaneously disseminating Grundtvig's ideas on the Church (cf. p. 283). Around 1840 the revivalists and the grundtvigian clergy joined forces in three causes: against Mynster's proposal for changes in the ritual, against the liberals, and against a separatist baptist movement that had arisen in a number of meeting-circles. At this point Lindberg became the central figure in two nationwide petitions, one against changes in the ritual, the other against the liberals' constitutional demands (see p. 276). Both collected around 2,000 signatures. The latter also received support from outside the meeting-circles, for in and around the country areas there was general distrust of the liberals; but for both petitions Lindberg worked in close cooperation with Peter Larsen, who was the leading light in the meeting-movement at that point. At the same time Lindberg began to introduce Grundtvig's ideas from the Danish Society, whose meetings were often mentioned in *Nordic Church Times* with reproductions of speeches and songs. In the spring of 1841 he even changed the name of the paper to *The Danish Flag* (Dannebrog); its aim now was to "promote Christian and popular enlightenment", while continuing to defend the meeting-movement. In this form the paper lasted only until 1842 when

373

Lindberg had to give up, disheartened by the bitter opposition and his own poverty over many years. But the line the paper took was a determining factor in subsequent developments.

On *Zealand,* outside Copenhagen, the meeting-movement was strongest in the south-west (from c. 1830); from there it spread north and east. In its early years it was led first and foremost by Rasmus Sørensen; but in the same area a number of young Grundtvig-inspired clergy were appointed who, despite Grundtvig's warnings, began to hold meetings. Already in the 1830's therefore differences arose between the "clergy-inspired Christians" and Rasmus Sørensen's supporters, and at the start of the 1840's most of the revivalists joined forces with the clergy.

The following years were a time of unrest during which ideas from the Danish Society became popular through the clergy. Thus J. F. Fenger held both popular meetings and devout meetings in the 1840's; Rørdam dissociated himself from the meetings, but worked in his parish for both a Church and a popular revival. In 1844 he actually spoke at a devout meeting at Marie Toft's (in south-west Zealand) and was extremely impressed by the large meetings in that area, which not for nothing was known as "the holy land". He told Grundtvig in a letter that he ought to experience such a gathering of 3-400 revivalists; their "inspired song" was without equal! As their leader Rørdam singles out his friend F. Boisen, "a fine vicar", who was "like a fish in water" at the meetings. But the same Boisen met much opposition from among the revivalists when he began in 1845-46 to hold "ungodly meetings",[1] that is, popular meetings and meetings in the newly-established Danish Society. He continued to be a highly-respected vicar, however, and was elected member of parliament for the area in 1848 and 1849. He became known in grundtvigian circles throughout the country as the publisher of a devotional paper, *The Messenger,* from 1852 onwards.

Funen was even more strongly marked by the meeting-movement, which was led mainly by lay people. When it spread to the island of Langeland at the end of the 1830's it was a veritable conquest, commanded by at least 20 visiting lay preachers, most of them from Funen. It was precisely for this reason that there was unrest on Funen when a number of the new revivalists on Langeland formed a baptist congregation, a move that met with sympathy in many places on Funen. The Funen lay preachers responded with a powerful counter-offensive in cooperation with Lindberg and ministers from south-west Zealand; with the result

---

[1] The Danish *gudelige forsamlinger* means literally "godly gatherings" or "gatherings of the godly" – hence Boisen's "ungodly meetings".

374

that many Funen meeting-leaders, in particular Peter Larsen, adopted the grundtvigian view of the Church as a counter-balance to the baptism movement. In and around Kerteminde, the focal point of the meeting-movement, matters were taken even further; here in the 1840's the meetings centred on Grundtvig's sermons, hymns and songs (from the Danish Society), and on his historical works and high school writings.

In 1841 Peter Larsen moved to *Jutland*. There he had long enjoyed great influence at the devout meetings, which he visited on long tours every year. But already in the autumn of 1841 he made contact with the grundtvigian clergy. This happened at a meeting of the Foreign Mission, led by Vilhelm Birkedal, who was then a vicar in west Jutland. Here Peter Larsen met 11 ministers who, as he writes, were all "young healthy men whom I thought the dear Lord could most certainly use in His service". At the meeting a missionary society was set up which spread quickly to east Jutland, and from 1842 Peter Larsen held meetings at his farm in south-east Jutland in connection with the annual mission meetings. At these a number of ministers also spoke to 3-400 revivalists. At the same time, from July 1846 the Birkedal circle of clergy began publication of a newspaper, *Christian Folk Paper,* which aimed to forge links among the meeting-people and actually did achieve a wide circulation among the Jutland meeting-people. The paper was used in particular to discuss the meeting-movement, with sharply divided contributions for and against; but the clergy's attitude remained by and large approving. The paper was to be both "truly for the Christian and for the people," though it is doubtless characteristic that it did not carry many subjects "for the people" until 1848, when articles appeared on national and political questions.

1848, with its great events, was altogether a turning-point. The change of political system, the war, and the general franchise at the elections to parliament (*Rigsdag*) also seem to have evoked a response from the meeting-people on behalf of "the Danish cause" and grundtvigianism.

The change in attitude has been registered in reports to the Moravian Brethren in Christiansfeld in North Schleswig. Their emissaries had been visiting the Jutland-Funen meeting-circles for many years, receiving a friendly welcome in spite of their declining influence in the 1840's. But when in 1852 the Brethren attempted to re-establish contact through a new emissary, J.P. Lund, he ran into major obstacles as a result of the widespread national and grundtvigian-inspired attitude that rejected the Brethren as being a German and a pietist movement. According to Lund's account, from 1852 to 1854 Funen and south-east Jutland were more or less overrun by the grundtvigians, and in the other areas of

Jutland there was a fierce battle. There was apparently a general breaking-up in these areas with a predominantly grundtvigian trend, even though the old pietistic meeting-movement held on in certain central and north-western areas. The emissaries did not come to Zealand, but a private letter from 1854 informs us "that the revivalists in west Zealand had declared at their last gathering that if any Christian minister was dismissed, they would leave the State Church". In its context this declaration referred first and foremost to Grundtvig. It was feared that he would be dismissed on the grounds of his antagonism to the then conservative government which did actually have several rebellious officials removed.

On the other hand interest in the devout meetings was on the wane in many areas in the 1850's; they no longer had the lustre of sensation or martyrdom, and more and more "Christian ministers" were being appointed around whom the revivalists could gather. Among these ministers Grundtvig's ideas on the Church and the people won increasing respect. There is plenty of evidence of a change in their preaching. Previously even those ministers who had been close to Grundtvig had preached powerful Lutheran revivalist sermons; but now they recognized, as one of them put it, that a sermon can be highly revivalist without one harsh word being uttered merely by emphasizing Christ's love and the glory of life in the baptismal covenant. The preaching was given a freer form, and the services a livelier character, undoubtedly more or less according to the pattern in Vartov: with large gatherings regardless of parish boundaries, a constant flow of new hymns and tunes, stronger communal singing in faster tempi, "not at all the slow song of the State Church"; with baptism and Holy Communion as the centres of gravity and with far more communicants than normal.

Then there were the Church and popular meetings that in grundtvigian circles replaced the devout meetings; these had a much broader programme and were open to everybody. In the 1860's Grundtvig's battle for a revival of the Danish-Norwegian cultural heritage seems at last to have called forth a response in large areas. Proof of this comes among others from the following description from this time: "The old folk songs were brought out and sung again in cottage and castle, we studied Saxo and Snorri, the old myths and legends, Grundtvig's history books, everything was new for us who knew only the Latin education, so to speak ... The presentiments of Christianity in Northern paganism as they appeared in the myths were powerfully underlined." This also affected the preaching of the day; on Funen it was even claimed that every Sunday the grundtvigian clergy were preaching on Odin, Thor and Freya.

Naturally the Church side of grundtvigianism was not neglected. The meetings also included "Church enlightenment" and contributions to the debates on Church matters, especially "Church freedom". The size of the friends' meetings in Copenhagen showed how wide-ranging the programme could be. They were at one and the same time Church and popular meetings.

The Major Advance (1865-76)

In the development we have been following, from a little "party" of theologians to a movement within the Church and the people, Lindberg is the first and greatest name alongside Grundtvig himself. From the 1860's onwards two others must be raised to the same level, namely Christen Kold and Sofus Høgsbro. They achieved a similar importance as the link between Grundtvig and the ordinary people. Kold became the mediator of his high school ideas, and Høgsbro shaped his main political ideas into a practical programme. It is especially through *their* efforts that Grundtvig gained a wide influence as a source of inspiration for the Danish peasantry.

Whether *Christen Kold* knew Grundtvig's high school writings is debatable. My own opinion is that it is at least probable. They were read by a circle who laid the foundation for his educational activity in Dalby near Kerteminde, with both a free school for children and a high school for the mature youth (from 1853); and it is unthinkable that these writings were not in the possession of some of the grundtvigian-inspired clergy whom Kold had been in close contact with in the previous years, partly as private tutor. But it is clear that Kold's model was not the large state high school at Sorø, which was Grundtvig's great hope until 1848. Kold was only interested in building up a "higher peasant school" that corresponded to the life-style and way of thinking of country youth.

The goal was "to awaken and illuminate the Christian and national life" (1852), "to open the eyes and ears of young people so that they are capable of gathering experience" (1854). The teaching content at his high school also included practical subjects, but the most important teaching activities were lecturing, narrating and story-telling, and reading aloud, especially the Nordic myths and sagas, Bible stories and other historical material, as well as contemporary literature. Of crucial importance, however, were the school's close links with the peasantry. It was an independent peasant culture Kold wished to create. The pupils were told they would not become grand by going to high school – they were merely farm hands under farmer Kold; and they lived together with him as though in a farmhouse. He remained on his guard against every external refinement, every imitation of town manners. In contrast he praised the peasant virtues of hard work, frugality and plainness; and what the "grand" considered too simple in the peasants' way of life he presented as their advantage. It was a question of being oneself and raising oneself and one's class. On religious questions Kold took an independent line, especially in the 1860's. He was even content with a cool relationship with the grundtvigian clergy. Respect for the clergy in general should be broken down so that the peasant could be free and independent in spiritual matters.

The intake at Kold's high school did not really begin to accelerate until the school moved to Dalum near Odense in 1862. Thereafter he also gained wide-ranging influence through the so-called free schools, whose number rose from around 20 in 1860 to at least 49 in 1870. The background for this was as a rule the revivalist circles, who were dissatisfied with the teaching of religious knowledge in the public schools, with the dry learning by rote and the tough discipline. But under Kold's influence it became a conscious movement, sharpening its criticism of the public schools and placing great weight on the free narrative style of teaching and the parents' right to decide their children's schooling for themselves. Kold's high school became the focal point of the movement. All his high school pupils should be missionaries, he declared; "we contemplate nothing less than the conquest of the whole of Denmark". The free schools became the most important medium; a large number of their teachers were Kold's former pupils and they often returned to the annual meetings at the school. These took place, with Kold as the central figure, from 1865 until his death in 1870.

Kold's influence ranged even wider through the large number of new high schools that were founded in the 1860's, especially after 1864. The majority modelled themselves on Kold's high school and thus became "revivalist" schools, serving the needs of the peasant youth. The leaders were well-qualified since most of them were theologians, and they were to a high degree inspired by Grundtvig's original school programme; but they worked like Kold for a new school reform with the same front against the Latin school and academic education (see R. Skovmand's article). In addition, both Grundtvig's and Kold's educational ideas gained increasing importance in the elementary schools, especially through a number of teachers' training colleges with a grundtvigian stamp.

Sofus Høgsbro began as the principal of Rødding Folk High School and differed from other high school men such as Kold in his more practical and down-to-earth attitude. But as a politician, from 1858, Høgsbro also worked to establish links between grundtvigianism and the peasantry. He had learned from Grundtvig that Christianity and freedom belonged together, in the Church, in the school and in politics; and if the efforts to awaken and raise the nation were to be more than words they must have political consequences.

Høgsbro therefore regarded it as his task to draw the Christian and popular revivalists into politics and to create a large grundtvigian people's party which secured the peasantry political power but with a feeling for the people at large and a responsibility for "the common good".

In grundtvigian circles Høgsbro ran into opposition from the clergy in particular, sharing the same fate as Kold. On the other hand, like Kold he received full support from Grundtvig himself, whom he visited regularly every Sunday. However, many of the older grundtvigian clergy had reservations about democracy, which had been introduced in the new constitution of 1849. They doubted that the peasantry were capable of running public affairs. The social gap between peasants and clergy was still wide and the clergy felt more attracted to the National Liberals, the party-grouping of civil servants and educated circles centred on Copenhagen. In contrast, Høgsbro wished to unite all true "friends of the peasants" into a common front. His programme was ready in 1865: "Above all, let all democratic parties join together in one party! The leadership will fall upon Grundtvig's disciples of its own accord ..."

This was optimistic in 1865. But it was precisely at this point that *grundtvigianism began to make major advances* with the country population as its basis; the movement continued over a broad front for more than ten years. Its background was a period of socio-economic progress for the owner-farmers, the leading class in the general agricultural population. Through the agricultural reforms they had achieved economic independence and had enjoyed a long period since 1830 of increased productivity and rising prices for agricultural products. Furthermore they had acquired political influence through the new constitution and a series of municipal laws. Alongside this came a growing desire for political and social self-assertion in relation to the higher social classes.

But grundtvigianism was not just a weapon in the farmers' "class war". For in the period after 1865 grundtvigianism was at one and the same time a political people's movement, a movement within the Church, and a cultural battle primarily inspired by Grundtvig's ideas on the Church and the people, not merely by class interests. The farmers were an important element, also among those who led the way as spokesmen and promoters of the cause, but equally important were the clergy, the high school teachers and the common folk in general, until the rapid growth of the towns towards the end of the century. For a number of reasons the farmers stood in the forefront of the battle for a genuine "democracy", but all research has shown that the local grundtvigian circles maintained a broad recruitment, with a numerical preponderance of the lower social classes.

It must also be borne in mind that a political left-wing party, the Left (*Venstre*) already existed, fighting exclusively for the political and economic interests of the peasantry, and that this party rejected the grundtvigian "daydreams". The Left had been agitating since the 1840's, and until 1865 it was their politicians in particular who made their presence felt as "the friends of the peasants" in parliament. In the same way there existed peasant high schools which set out solely to raise the social status of the peasantry by teaching them useful skills, partly through preparing them for the class war, for example by practising the language and manners of educated townspeople (see esp. p. 330). One would have thought that the farmers ought to have preferred these alternatives seen from the point of view of the "class struggle". The fact that they did not makes the forward march of grundtvigianism somewhat surprising; the social interests were here incorporated into a general outlook on life which proved to have a greater appeal than the programme of the older "friends of the peasants".

Høgsbro's first triumph was the battle against a conservative revision of the constitution in 1865-66. There was agitation throughout the country with broad participation from the grundtvigian circles; Grundtvig supported it personally by allowing himself to be re-elected to parliament. The revision was carried with the aid of leading peasant politicians who wished to pursue an "agrarian policy" together with the landowners; but the opposition was so great that Høgsbro could form a grundtvigian-orientated party-group of "noes", the so-called National Left, who became the largest of all the party-groups in parliament at the 1866 election.

The next major clash concerned "Church freedom", prompted by the dismissal of Vilhelm Birkedal as the vicar of Ryslinge in 1865. Again the affair led to a nationwide campaign demanding the right to form independent "free congregations" linked to the official Church. The grundtvigians' position was by now so strong that the government actually passed a "free congregation" law in 1868 despite massive protests from the clergy, among whom Grundtvig's "friends" were still only a small minority (cf. p. 316).

Two years later, in 1870, Høgsbro achieved his major aim: to unite all the left-wing groups in parliament around the National Left. In reply the landowners united with the National Liberals to form a new government and this alliance became a solid right-wing grouping from now on. In opposition to them was the new "people's party", calling itself *The United*

Left. Its programme embraced both grundtvigian and "peasant" demands, but the overriding demand was that every government should rest on a majority in parliament. The United Left had nearly half the votes in parliament and the aim was to acquire a majority and thus form a government.

The result was a bitter political battle which forced everyone to take sides. Not a few of the older grundtvigian spokesmen. especially the clergy, now repudiated Høgsbro's policies. The fiercest criticism came from Vilhelm Birkedal, the first free congregational minister, who had hitherto been the hero of the National Left. In his eyes the new party was a false alliance. We have nothing in common with the "earth-crawling" peasant politicians, he maintained. They are governed solely by class prejudice and envy. Cooperation with them would be like cooperating with the Aesir when they used a giant to help them and thus took the path of destruction. The chief aim of the grundtvigian "people of the spirit" was that "the nation should be filled with a great and good life-content".

Naturally Birkedal was applauded in the National Liberal papers in Copenhagen. But he was rejected by the entire grundtvigian press, which now comprised at least five papers. Høgsbro himself confirmed that "the political-grundtvigian line" stood firm in its convictions and for that very reason would win greater sympathy through political collaboration. "The spirit and the truth" will win on their own merits and gradually "carry the majority of the people with them"!

The corresponding *cultural-political conflict* reached a climax in 1871-72. In 1867 the National Left had resurrected Grundtvig's proposal for a state high school in Sorø, but without success. On the other hand the grundtvigian politicians had prevented an expansion of the elementary school and in 1870 they proposed the introduction of two new branches into the grammar-school: a nordic-historic and a mathematical-scientific branch. The National Liberal minister for cultural affairs reduced the nordic branch to a few lessons per week in the Old Nordic language, but the proposal provoked widespread debate. From the grundtvigian side came a unanimous criticism of the old classical education, and university education in general: it was foreign to the people, a one-sided training of the intellect and an examination-orientated learning, yet it dominated the whole of the public school. By way of contrast a new kind of education was on its way centring on the high schools, which "will develop the innermost nature of the people". Below these the free schools were also gaining ground, and along with the big Sorø high school the new educational system would be fully expanded.

The National Liberals, who were now the government's spokesmen on cultural affairs, rejected all this as pure nonsense. There was only one kind of education, an academic one. The most one could expect of the people was that they respected its fruits. The National Liberal papers scorned the politicians of the left for being worthless, anti-cultural barbarians, so the debate had a clear, political perspective: the Left, they maintained, were far from possessing the education that was demanded of a government.

But the academic front faltered. A professor of philosophy, *Rasmus Nielsen,* made common cause with the grundtvigian line on cultural affairs and reformulated it in the language of the educated classes, partly in talks and lectures, partly in a literary periodical, *For Ideas and Reality* (from 1869). And through the Norwegian poet, *Bjørnstjerne Bjørnson,* grundtvigianism and the Left found an enthusiastic and belligerent champion in both Norway and Denmark. At a Norwegian students' meeting in 1869 he even attacked the "student body" as being alien to the popular movements of the time. A year later he became chairman of the Norwegian student society, which was then guided into the "popular framework" through talks on the new popular education.

Politically he worked with great energy along the same lines as Høgsbro, as well as for the collaboration between the Nordic parties on the left. His paper, *Norwegian Folk Paper,* began a close collaboration with Høgsbro's paper *Danish Folk News* in 1871. In the National Liberal circles in Copenhagen he had been a popular, almost idolized, guest, but in the spring of 1872 he cut them to shreds in Rasmus Nielsen's periodical. They had failed on all accounts; instead he appealed to the young people to take up the "national concerns". It was the special call of the North to show the world a free society, built on faith and patriotism. Shortly afterwards he held a large meeting for the high school cause in Oslo with Ludvig Schrøder from Askov as the main speaker. Bjørnson followed him with such a thunderous attack on "scriptural theology" and Norwegian pietism that the rostrum shook and the ladies wept in terror!

Through the spring of 1872 the clash was sharpened by the approaching general election in September. The tone of the National Liberal papers became even harsher; Høgsbro became "the shortlegged coachman of egoism" and Bjørnson "the foaming beserk of hate", undermining intelligence to the detriment of society and culture. The United Left worked on throughout the summer, giving numerous election addresses particularly in the country, and finding support in the grundtvigian tradition of popular meetings. Grundtvig's own position was a much-debated question. Several of his old friends came to him complaining of the Left's "passion for the party", right up to the end of August. But Høgsbro had the last word when he and other Left politicians took part in Grundtvig's dinner-party the day before his death.

The political strife hung like a threatening cloud over the memorial ceremony. The leaders of the large meeting of friends did what they could to keep it free of politics; but Bjørnson, who was representing Norwegian grundtvigianism, would not be subdued. A free school teacher who had come from Funen with a special army of 300 men arranged an unofficial meeting with him, and in his main speech Bjørnson touched on the sorest points. He stressed in particular Grundtvig's "spiritual capaciousness", his ability to see friends amongst enemies and make full friends of half-friends by showing confidence in them. This was true in the high schools, which had only one major enemy, the education that says to the peasant: Come into the Latin school, then you will be a man, but not before! It was true in politics, where the Norwegian grundtvigians were joining the "freedom movements and their parties" as a matter of course, thus assuring rapid growth. And it was true of relations with Germany despite the injustice of the defeat in 1864. Reconciliation with the German people was also necessary so that the light from Grundtvig could "go round the world"!

The speech was accompanied by loud applause and strong protests from the meeting; one participant said it was like "a glowing stone in the water, so that all around it foamed and sizzled". The mention of reconciliation with Germany provoked an intense debate over several months. But the chief event was *the election* shortly after the friends' meeting, where the United Left gained a parliamentary majority. Already at this point they had won indisputable power since they could now stop all law proposals and prevent the passing of the annual finance bill.

In the spring of 1873 the Left thus demanded governmental power explicitly. But the King, Christian IX (1863-1906) only had full confidence in the landowners, and his aristocratic advisers considered it unthinkable that any Left politician should be worthy of a ministerial post. On the other hand, that autumn the Left also employed its most powerful weapon when it rejected the finance bill. This caused a great scandal even outside the Right's usual areas of support. The government called an election, and although the Left maintained their majority in parliament, they did not increase it. Their opponents among the grundtvigian spokesmen now moved onto the offensive with joint declarations and a number of inflammatory pamphlets (1873-75); they claimed that Grundtvig had never gone in for "majority rule" and would have disapproved of the Left's ruthless power struggle. Birkedal was on guard, however; if it could be proved that Grundtvig really had supported the United Left, then in this matter he was "more grundtvigian than Grundtvig himself".

But these grundtvigians had in actual fact become right-wing men and they were generals without an army. The Left's power, according to a National Liberal politician, stemmed from "the grundtvigians' lay army with the young clergymen" (1873). The main body of grundtvigianism merged together with a broad grundtvigian-inspired goal. The task was not just political, but as a young grundtvigian politician put it, "one of emancipation, which would contribute to the abolition of everything that ties down human life and prevents it from stirring". Høgsbro's *Danish Folk News* was at one and the same time the main popular organ of grundtvigianism and the leading political paper of the Left. In addition, there were a large number of new left-wing papers and numerous more or less political people's meetings. As a speaker and organizer Høgsbro was overtaken in the 1870's by *Chresten Berg,* a grundtvigian schoolteacher; he was a more colourful personality who knew how to rouse the still passive country-dwellers to fight for the people's cause. Bjørnson contributed from a distance through letters, articles and poems, such as *Song to Awaken Freedom's People in the North,* dedicated to Denmark's United Left (1874). The first lines run:

> Despised by the great, but loved by the small,
> Say, is that not the path that the new must tread?

The new begins as a sighing in the corn, but now goes "like a roar through the roof of the forests"; and "it will turn to a storm before anyone knows". For "a people which feels the call is the greatest power on earth". The long chorus is characteristic:

> For democracy
> stand up, stand up,
> for the Church and School
> for freedom!
>
> Set free what is waiting
> in winter mists,
> in the slumber of habit,
> it is waiting for you!

This combination of democracy, Church and school, with "freedom" as its common sign, stemmed from grundtvigianism and was a reality on the left of the grundtvigian circles. New free congregations were still being established; there were not a great number of them but they attracted the most enthusiastic Left people and functioned as a model for many parish congregations. The grundtvigian high schools were increasing rapidly in number (see p. 331), and the same was true of the free schools, numbers of which rose from 49 in 1870 to 270 in 1880 (with 7.197 children). There

Grundtvig during hymn-singing at Vartov Church, Copenhagen, where he was rector from 1839 to his death in 1872. (Painting by Christian Dalsgaard).

Grundtvig's Church, Copenhagen, built 1921-40 and designed by P.V. Jensen Klint. The picture gives a frontal view of the tower, which reveals plainly the architect's intention, namely to create a cathedral in the style of the traditional Danish village church with Late Gothic corbie gables and vertical lines. Homage was also paid to Grundtvig as a hymn-writer by making the front reminiscent of a gigantic organ. The cost of this huge church – the largest to have been built in this century in Denmark – was met through collections held all over the country. Donations were made by a wide cross-section of the Danish people.

were also a number of other institutions such as local lecture societies and meeting-houses, public "autumn-meetings" at high schools and a network of shooting associations that spread after 1864; these had a national background but contained a strong grundtvigian element.

In parliament the battle continued against the government, whom the United Left put "on starvation rations". This was particularly true of the Right's wish for military grants. The Left preferred a general arming of the people, but the government wanted a major defence works around Copenhagen. After a long and fierce debate the government proposal was definitively rejected in parliament, and the government therefore called an election in 1876. But the result was a great victory for the Left. The opposition then had 74 votes in parliament, whereas the government could only number 28 votes.

The Neo-grundtvigian Period

From the end of the 1870's a new period begins for the grundtvigian movement. In several respects there was a "change of climate", as it was called. This was true politically for the Left in general. Against expectations the right-wing government hung on with the same leader, *J.B.S. Estrup,* for the best part of twenty years. He did not allow himself to be affected by the Left's majority in parliament, but when necessary promulgated finance bills outside parliament. The support of the King and the *landsting* (upper house) was sufficient, and there was in addition an effective organization of right-wing societies in 1882-83. In the towns they created a sort of nationally-minded grouping around the Right and an expansion of defences, especially the fortification of Copenhagen, which Estrup turned into his major aim.

Culturally a new trend began to make its mark from the end of the 1870's, led by the literary historian, Georg Brandes, who had made himself spokesman for a "modern breakthrough" on the basis of natural science, positivism, and the critical literature on the Church and morality that was appearing in France and other countries. These ideas provoked a corresponding "realistic" literature of the novel in Denmark and a "literary Left" that gained increasing influence in intellectual circles, that is, in Copenhagen. It attacked in the first place the National Liberal attitude to culture but also created trouble in grundtvigian circles, particularly when Bjørnson joined Brandes in 1877-78.

In the country a new pietist revival gained widespread support in the 1880's and 1890's. In was an organized movement, led by ministers through a society for "Home Mission" (*Indre Mission*), established in 1861, which formed local communities with "mission houses" and paid lay preachers. It expressly rejected grundtvigianism and politically tended to join forces with the Right.

These competitive elements put a brake on grundtvigianism's forward march as a united movement. This first became apparent in the political struggle. Already in 1877 the Left was weakened by a split into two sharply divided party-groupings, a moderate Left which was led by Høgsbro amongst others, and a radical Left, led by Berg, who supported a more aggressive line. After a gradual reconciliation they were able to run a successful election campaign in 1884 without internal disputes, and under Berg's leadership the Left once again made a concerted assault on the government. The political stir on the left reached a new highpoint and led to the formation of numerous rifle associations as a safeguard against a coup from the Right. However, Estrup responded in the spring of 1885 by proroguing parliament, issuing a "provisional" finance bill, limiting freedom of speech and banning the rifle associations. Berg was even given a prison sentence, which contributed to the breakdown of his health. In October 1885 a young member of the left attempted to assassinate Estrup but failed; this led to the establishment of a gendarmerie corps and to further limitations on freedom of speech. The onslaught had failed: the Left retreated from a direct clash and split again in 1886-87, when moderate circles preferred negotiations to achieve at least minor concessions while Berg continued to pursue the politics of the battlefield. Estrup, however, remained a virtual dictator right up until 1894.

The divisions in the Left also split the grundtvigian movement. The concerted advance in 1885-86 received widespread support from grundtvigian circles but on the whole the political development was marked more by the internal strife in the Left's ranks and the fierce power struggle between the Left and the Right. Opinion was also divided among the grundtvigians with regard to both the cultural radicalism inspired by Brandes and the forward march of the Home Mission. Many older grundtvigian spokesmen rejected the literary Left, and a right wing of the grundtvigian Church movement sought cooperation with the Home Mission.

In a way however, this split was an advantage. There was no longer any danger that grundtvigianism would be identified with a particular political party. It still proved capable of providing inspiration in many areas in collaboration with various other groups. The closest model remained the optimism of Høgsbro and Bjørnson together with the political cooperation in the time of the United Left. Already at the time this attitude was called *neo-grundtvigianism*, a designation given by the right-wing grundt-vigians meaning for them false grundtvigianism. But the younger grundt-vigian spokesmen, who began to make their mark around 1880, were well aware that they were living in a "new age", whose tasks could only be achieved through a renewal or a "continuation" of grundtvigianism. They were therefore often called neo-grundtvigians. With no derogatory con-tent the word neo-grundtvigianism can in fact be used to summarize the efforts which first and foremost characterized the history of the move-ment in the period up to the end of the century. They found expression in different ways, but can be explained in brief as liberal Christianity and a resumption of the battle for "Church freedom", together with a cultural openness and a contribution to the solving of the social questions of the day.

In Church affairs it may seem surprising that Berg's radical Left at one and the same time depended on the enthusiastic supporters of the grundt-vigian view of the Church especially in the Jutland congregational chur-ches, and on an alliance with the liberal Left. But this was a sign of the same "spiritual capaciousness" which Bjørnson had advocated. The allian-ce with the literary Left became official at a party held for Bjørnson in 1878, but Berg had beforehand secured friends of Brandes for his main mouthpiece, *Morning Paper*, published in Copenhagen. On Berg's re-commendation Brandes brother, Edvard Brandes, was actually elected to parliament by grundtvigian peasants even though he declared himself an atheist (1880). The election was attacked by the moderate Left but stren-uously defended by a grundtvigian congregational minister: faith and politics must not be mixed. For Berg the literary Left was of value as a counterweight to the National Liberal refinement; but he did not fail grundtvigianism. When Edvard Brandes wrote a critical article on Grundtvig on the occasion of his centenary (1883) in *Morning Paper*, he broke off the connection.

The debate on "Church freedom" was raised in 1880 by young grundtvi-gian theologians, brought about by the descriptions in realist literature of the State Church's hypocrisy. They demanded in particular freedom of clergy (doctrinal freedom) in order to prevent hypocritical preaching; a minister should only be bound by his personal convictions. But they also criticized the theology course at university and linked up with a broad current amongst grundtvigian lay people who sought a greater lay influ-ence, especially in the choice of minister, access to the priesthood with-out examinations and the liberation of the free congregations from cer-tain State Church regulations.

A large meeting at Askov High School formulated these wishes in the form of a petition to parliament (1881), but in government circles it was regarded as the Left's politics in disguise. The Minister for Cultural Affairs sent a rebuke to the clergy who had signed the petition and brought a court case against them when they protested; in addition he sought support from the Church by gathering all the bishops into a conservative Church Council. The unrest in connection with "Church freedom" culminated in the same year when the large free congregation on the island of Mors refused to exclude children from Holy Communion as the rules demanded; it was therefore itself excluded from the official Church. The Left's spokesmen immediately signalled a political protest, but were persuaded to rest content with a general vote of confidence in the Mors church. This petition, which received extremely widespread support, meant that the grundtvigian circles approved the development on Mors, and in several places they now preferred the same independent position as "free churches". In all nearly 30 free congregations or free churches were established before 1900.

The neo-grundtvigian ministers also attracted attention with their criticism of university theology, which at the time defended the old dogmatic system and, as far as possible, the Bible's infallibility in the face of scientific criticism. This led to repeated newspaper controversies with the older grundtvigian spokesmen, who maintained their conservative view of the Bible. A young free church minister , V. Brücker, even sought to convince the "freethinkers" (i.e. atheists) of the difference between scriptural theology and Christianity. This happened at a much-discussed high school meeting in Norway in 1886, with the broad Left collaboration as its background. According to Brücker scriptual theology led to academic conceptual structures which clung to scientifically outdated ideas. But Christianity is a reality in the living Church as a life in the "Word of Faith"; and this does not preclude scientific investigation of the external, "objective" reality. For instance, belief in God's creation of the world is not incompatible with natural science theories of the origins of the world. Brücker did not manage to convince the freethinkers; but the opinion to which he gave expression was of importance to many young people, especially at the high schools. Other neo-grundtvigian spokesmen proposed more radical views; but in 1893 Brücker could still attract almost the whole grundtvigian left wing of the Church to a large meeting.

The general attitude to "current affairs" needed to be debated by the *high schools* in particular, and this partly changed their character. The neo-grundtvigian trend found an important mouthpiece in the weekly paper *The Current of Time* (1884-95), which was aimed primarily at the high school circles. It attacked the older grundtvigian high school for developing merely a poetic, introvert life; the teaching should now concentrate on the history and social problems of recent times. Grundtvigianism should be developed "with the conditions and demands of the present before our eyes". The paper discussed both the Church and education, politics and literature, and not least the relationship between faith and knowledge and thus the relationship to natural science and the historical biblical research.

A typical representative of the new high school direction was *Alfred Poulsen,* who already in the 1870's had left "the land of visions" and had become a grundtvigian "realist". In 1884 he took over the high school in Ryslinge, which under his leadership became one of the largest in the country. But during his first years at Ryslinge Poulsen's realism found expression in a powerful political engagement, which was characteristic of the majority of young high school men. Among other things he championed the rifle movement and was chairman of a big rifle association. This, however, led to a clash between the new and the old grundtvigianism in Ryslinge. For Birkedal, who was still a congregational minister, agitated equally strongly for the Right's defence policy and all the grundtvigians in the area were members of the free congregation in Ryslinge. After an Easter service in 1885 Birkedal actually read out a proclamation by the Right; but his audience walked out of the church in protest. A subsequent public meeting turned into a bitter clash on the rifle question. Birkedal thereupon declared that he would not be a minister for rebels and resigned as a congregational minister, followed by Alfred Poulsen's brother, who had supported the rifle movement.

Among the older high school principals *Ludvig Schrøder* at Askov was the one who best understood how to keep up with "the current of time". Already in 1878 he appointed a natural scientist to the school as a teacher on a new two-year course. Schrøder rejected the realist writers, yet in 1881-82 he appointed two young teachers who soon afterwards began to teach realist literature and other current affairs. From 1885-86 Schrøder himself made social studies a major subject in his lectures, and when he also allowed the Left to elect him to parliament, the school acquired a reputation for being particularly left-wing. This, however, gave rise to such problems with self-aware, radically-minded pupils that in 1890 the school had to introduce a kind of limited entry. Askov maintained a central place among the grundtvigian high schools; but from the 1890's Alfred Poulsen became the leading light in the high school movement.

Although the running political battle from 1885 played a decisive role it also undoubtedly contributed to the widespread interest in other social questions that came in its wake. Economic developments increased the

389

social differences; the farmers became relatively well-off, while the peasants and the growing working class in the towns lived in poor conditions. However, many grundtvigian spokesmen realized these social problems. *The Current of Time* warned against the possibility of grundtvigianism turning into a farmers' movement; the farmers ought to secure access to society's benefits for the workers too. The paper therefore carried many articles on social questions, wage standards, the poor law and child welfare. The high school movement's oldest and later the most influential organ, the *High School Magazine*, often concerned itself with the position of the farmworkers; here the wage-earning young people in the country found numerous advocates of shorter working-hours, better housing conditions and the abolition of special "servants' halls". It also published a lengthy, impartial and understanding account of the main ideas of socialism. Furthest of all went the new paper, *Every Man His Due* (1886-90), which had a wide readership in the young political societies out in the country. With its grundtvigian background it made itself spokesman for a simplified social Christianity and its chief editor supported the Social Democrats, who were on the way to becoming the major workers' party.

In the 1880's and 1890's no fewer than three young neo-grundtvigians attempted to found high schools in Copenhagen with particular emphasis on the working-class. Only the last attempt succeeded, in a new high school form begun in 1891 by Johan Borup more or less as an evening course; yet it was "something like the high schools, something free, something cheerful, thorough and comprehensive, yet unpedantic and non-academic and especially up-to-date, something that aims at current trends" (Borup 1893). Originally he attracted mainly office people, but later he established good contacts with working-class groups.

Other social questions were also debated with support from the grundtvigian side. Interest in *Henry George's* criticism of land speculation was aroused by the *High School Magazine* in 1888 and thereafter gained numerous supporters in grundtvigian circles. The *women's movement* originated in the educated circles in Copenhagen, but when a son of Høgsbro joined the committee in 1884 he immediately proposed a campaign on "the living word", especially in high school circles. An exhortation to the high schools to take the matter up was responded to by so many that it was difficult to secure speakers in the numbers required. The women's movement then became a grundtvigian cause too. At about the same time, from 1885, the *Danish Peace Association* also registered an advance, supported from the grundtvigians by no more than the paper *Every Man His Due*. But after 1890 the peace movement created wide interest in grundtvigian circles, especially through its promotion by Birkedal's son, Uffe Birkedal, and encouraged by the antipathy to the Right's militarism. The *temperance movement* had a similarly cautious reception when it began to spread in the 1880's; the demand for a ban and for total abstinence conflicted with the grundtvigian concept of freedom. But it was nonetheless supported by a number of high school teachers, and temperance societies were also formed in grundtvigian circles.

Among the other new "causes" the *co-operative movement* was of the greatest importance, especially the co-operative butchers. The background for this was the falling corn prices, which necessitated a reorganization into animal production, and the dislike of the right-wing grocers and wholesalers, from whom the peasants wished to free themselves through economic co-operation and independence – corresponding to the political struggle for democracy. This development was promoted to a high degree by grundtvigian circles, especially the high schools and the agricultural schools.

When the representatives for the Jutland co-operative societies met in 1887 in order to discuss an amalgamation, it turned out that the meeting consisted almost entirely of high school people; they therefore chose the *High School Magazine* as their joint organ. The driving-force at the meeting was the leader of a co-operative society in Brücker's free church. In 1896 he became chairman for an amalgamation of all the country's co-operative societies and thus for a number of years the leader of the movement. The establishment of the co-operative dairies was especially inspired by two grundtvigian principals of agricultural schools, and the dairies were often linked to grundtvigian circles. In 1888 Ryslinge free congregation was called "the dairy church", as it was said to include all the dairy-workers on Funen. The co-operative dairies' chairmen had for the most part been pupils at high schools or agricultural schools; this was true of 71 per cent of them in 1897. The first co-operative butchers was established in 1887 by a grundtvigian principal of a teacher training college, and the following co-ops owed much to his energetic activity for the cause. He was therefore the obvious choice as chairman when the co-operative butchers acquired common representation in 1890.

How strong the grundtvigian contribution was in all these "causes" is difficult to decide; and that is typical of this period. The "grundtvigian" was not a clearly delineated concept, and the movement embraced many different and even partly conflicting efforts. The fact that in spite of this grundtvigianism maintained its special character was due not least to its peculiar *form of local organization*. The starting-point everywhere was the local group initiative, often inspired by a single "activist", but the first activity was to gather co-workers and local support in "a grundtvigian circle". It is characteristic that grundtvigians of the time spoke rather of "the grundtvigian circles" than of grundtvigianism. The group that took the original initiative continued to produce new shoots and was able to ramify into many branches, but the local collaboration and the community spirit continued to play a decisive role. A few examples will illustrate this.

When a free school was established in the village of Egebjerg on south Funen in 1863 its background had been a grundtvigian circle which gathered in a private home. All the free schools drew to some degree on such a circle, which would organize and finance the foundation of the school. In Egebjerg the free school teacher at once undertook to run a reading society and an evening school for young and old alike. In 1871 the free school circle formed a shooting association, and in 1882 they built a village hall by the side of the free school: this became the centre for a lecture society and served as a meeting-place and practice area for the shooting group. In 1882 a communal dairy was also established, followed in 1883 by a co-operative stores and in 1889 by a temperance society and a co-operative dairy which replaced the communal dairy. These institutions were of course not reserved solely for the free school circles, but the initiative emanated exclusively or largely from them.

A similar development could take place with the public school as its basis. At the beginning of the 1880's the village school in Sundby on Falster acquired a grundtvigian senior teacher, P.K. Pedersen, who turned the parish into a centre of folk culture. There was no grundtvigian background on Falster, and Pedersen began by bringing together the peasants for lessons in agricultural economy. He then set up a co-operative stores which attracted the majority of the parish and he extended the co-operative stores house with a village hall. He moved on to establish a song society and later a choir for the whole of north Falster, as well as bringing together his former pupils for evening classes. This led to a lecture and young people's society, which became the focal point of folk life in the area.

The larger grundtvigian circles also built on local circles. Ryslinge free congregation included members from many parishes, but they gathered around 12-15 local free school circles. The free congregation on Mors, later a free church, was established in 1871 by a lay circle under the inspiration of grundtvigian clergy. It had a powerful central position on the island through possessing a big church close to a high school and a village hall that could hold an audience of over a thousand. But just as in Ryslinge the free congregations soon attracted members from miles around, who organized themselves locally in free school groups or in some other way. "The free", as they were called, took the lead in the island's popular institutions, not least politically as supporters of Berg's radical Left.

Another large west Jutland circle developed around a congregational church in Bøvling, established when a majority in the parish had applied in vain in 1874 for a grundtvigian minister. This free congregation became the starting-point for two other congregational circles in the area, which together with the Bøvling group totalled nearly 500 families around 1900. Nine free school circles had also been established. There was a close link between the free congregations and the development of political and economic organizations, as a single example will show. Just like the congregational church building plan the Left started their paper in the area in 1874, and the chairman of its committee also became a member of the free congregation and of its committee for a while. Furthermore he was a member of the local party leadership, and in the 1880's and 1890's he helped in the establishment of a savings-bank, a co-operative dairy and a fire insurance company; he also sat on the board of a building society and in a committee for a temperance society. Most of these institutions were brought into being by church and political circles as a counterweight to the influence of the Right and of the Home Mission in the local area.

The formal organisation model was as a rule extensively democratic, with a vote for each member or subscriber whatever the size of his contribution. For example, the Bøvling congregation had its members as the highest authority, gathered at the church meeting, which with voting rights for both men and women elected a financial committee and a church council. The difference between this and the hierarchical State Church was therefore conspicuous. The State Church congregation had no influence at all.

When Estrup resigned in 1894, the Right retained governmental power. The Left were deeply split, and Berg was dead. In 1895, however, a new left-wing party was formed which resumed the battle. It had Høgsbro as its chairman, but the real leader was a west Jutland schoolteacher, *J.C. Christensen,* who had Berg's party-grouping as his background but who for the most part pursued a moderate line. With a firm and level-headed leadership he managed to unite the Left under a steadily increasing share of the votes, and his policy of negotiation undermined the government's power. When it had been reduced to 8 parliamentary seats in the 1901 election, the King handed over the reins of government to the

Left. This represented a change of system; parliament and the Left had finally won.

J.C. Christensen did not present himself as a grundtvigian, even though he had originally come from a grundtvigian background. But it was characteristic that as a minister he immediately concentrated on Church reforms which on significant points satisfied the grundtvigian demands: the abolition of the Church Council of bishops, the establishment of local church councils (vestries) with the right to elect their own ministers and access for the free congregations and other "free circles" to use of the parish church. The long-standing clash of interests between grundtvigianism and government power was at an end. Thus the change of system was also a triumph for the large majority of grundtvigians who in so many ways had taken part in the battle for the victory of democracy.

A Brief Survey
of Grundtvig Literature

by Jørgen I. Jensen

I

The influence of Grundtvig's work has been different from that of every other figure in Denmark's history. His achievements have not only given rise to a vast amount of literature and research, but they have also penetrated, often through underground channels, into the very heart of the Danish mentality. It is generally agreed that a figure from the past really shows his calibre the moments his ideas live on without any longer needing to be linked to his name. What can be said about Grundtvig's importance on this more general semi-unconscious level is not very precise, particularly because as a Dane one has no chance of distancing oneself completely from one's own tradition. But perhaps Grundtvig's general importance for our day and age can most easily be traced in the kind of guilty conscience that can make its presence felt when developments within public and institutional life, particularly in the schools, appear to be moving in a quite different direction from the one indicated by Grundtvig. If things go too far, politicians who are dissatisfied with one thing or another can still be heard complaining that this or that really is too bad "in Grundtvig's fatherland" – from which we must conclude that an invocation of Grundtvig is still regarded as having a general appeal.

The difficulty of saying anything more precise about Grundtvig's significance under one heading is increased by the fact that the impulses from Grundtvig, which are linked to something specifically Danish, in particular the Danish language, are crossed by influences from other, more internationally-orientated schools of thought, such as liberalism, cultural radicalism, socialism and existentialism, not to mention the more imprecise but absolutely vital secularization that did not begin to gather momentum until after Grundtvig's death. The picture is complicated even more by the capacity of Grundtvig's ideas to be linked to both liberalism and cultural radicalism (ideas of liberty), to socialism and marxism (emphasizing the community), to existentialism, existential theology and secularization philosophy (the division between the human and the Christian).

Even when we attempt to deal with the area of Grundtvig's influence for which written sources exist, the situation remains confused. No single person has an overall knowledge of what is available in the way of essays and brief articles from Grundtvig's lifetime until today in Church and popular periodicals, church newsletters, newspapers, year-books from high schools etc. – not to mention the sermons and letters in private and public archives – even though within the area of the church debate extensive studies have been made in certain periods (by amongst others A. Pontoppidan Thyssen og P. G. Lindhardt). The mass of material that they present makes one realize how much remains to be brought to light from the other periods. The breadth of Grundtvig's writing is thus quite different from, for example, Kierkegaard's, who has had a far greater influence than Grundtvig but whose importance for Denmark cannot begin to compare with Grundtvig's. His exceptional position can be seen most clearly in the fact that his name appears more often than any other hymnwriter both in the Danish Hymn Book – over a third of the book consists of hymns written or adapted by Grundtvig – and in the High School Song Book, which is the most widely used song book in Denmark and continues to be published in new editions.

It might be wise at the start to dwell a little longer on the relationship between Kierkegaard and Grundtvig so as to gain an impression of Grundtvig's position in Danish intellectual life. For it has given rise to a particular sort of interference, as can be seen from Danish theological literature, that two such important yet incompatible figures as Kierkegaard and Grundtvig should belong to the Danish tradition. The Danish theologian, K. E. Løgstrup, whose so-called creation theology has had such a powerful influence since the Second World War on both theology and culture in general, said in an interview shortly before his death in 1981 that we in Denmark must respect the difference between the two giants from the 19th century, Kierkegaard and Grundtvig, and that he placed himself alongside Grundtvig against Kierkegaard's existentialist thought. Everywhere we can see that no matter which wing of the Church theologians belong to they feel duty bound to take up a stance on Kierkegaard and Grundtvig or incorporate them both into their thinking. This is as true of theological writers who continue the classical dogmatic tradition, such as Regin Prenter, as it is of P. G. Lindhardt, who in the 1950's and 1960's was regarded as the most radical theologian in Danish public life and who was the Danish theologian most discussed in this period. In Lindhardt's sermons we can see how the relationship between Grundtvig and Kierkegaard creates the tension that helps to give the sermons their particular dynamic. Characteristically Lindhardt has also undertaken a collected edition of Grundtvig's sermons from 1855 – the year in which Kierkegaard attacked the Danish Church with unprecedented vehemence in the periodical *The Moment,* and shown how these attacks received an immediate response in Grundtvig's sermons.

If we move away from the area of theology to the general cultural and literary debate we again find the Grundtvig-Kierkegaard constellation, for example, in the following introduction to a 1980 radio series on Danish poets by the modernist poet and critic Poul Borum, who may be called a representative of the typical Danish attitude to Grundtvig and who formulates the problems that are involved in giving Grundtvig's achievement as a poet the place it deserves; "It is strange to think that Denmark's greatest contributors to world literature, Grundtvig, Hans Christian Andersen and Kierkegaard, were all active in Copenhagen in the 1840's producing works that lie outside the three main genres – drama, the novel and poetry – that are dominant in the European literature of the time. Grundtvig wrote hymns, Andersen fairy-tales and Kierkegaard philosophical writings that often approach intellectual novels and poetry of ideas – in the big wide world Kierkegaard is known and respected as a philosopher, not as a poet, Andersen is "merely" a writer of children's stories, and Grundtvig, our greatest poet, is unknown.

Yet Grundtvig is not really known within Denmark either. We read Andersen as children and take him with us through life; some of us discover Kierkegaard and plunge into him from a giddy height; but Grundtvig is so enormous and formidable and mysterious and remote, and seems to be reserved, as it were, for two strange races called grundtvigians and Grundtvig-scholars. Even so there is of course a Grundtvig for the people; many of us have been connected with the folk high schools he inspired, and we are all influenced indirectly in our upbringing by his educational ideas. Then there are the hymns that we have all met in Church and at school and cannot help remembering bits of, bits that turn up at the most impossible moment."

II

It has been calculated that Grundtvig's writings would fill between 120 and 150 volumes in a collected edition; and the nature of his work has caused writers and researchers with widely differing approaches and from many and varied fields of study to concern themselves with him. He thus occupies a central position in both Danish literary history and Danish Church history. Every Danish literary history and Church history has a relatively large section on Grundtvig. This is true, for example, of the most comprehensive portrayals to date – Vilhelm Andersen and Billeskov Jansen's literary histories, together with Gustav Albeck's presentation in *Politiken's* literary history and in the two volumes dealing with the 19th century in the eight-volume *History of the Danish Church*. In the more detailed research into Grundtvig's work and in the essay debate on him literary scholars, theologians, educationalists and writers from other fields of study have also taken part. The works mentioned here can in no way be said to give even a survey and it is impossible to do justice to the many deeply-researched and detailed analyses that are often the product of many years intensive study of Grundtvig. Instead our approach must be to look at some examples which in flashes can give an impression of the expanse and the horizon of the work on Grundtvig – and which indirectly should point back to the vast range of Grundtvig himself.

In Grundtvig research this century two stages stand out, bounded by the Second World War. It was not until after the war that a more detailed Grundtvig research gathered momentum, not least under the influence of the national sentiment that was aroused by the German occupation of Denmark from 1940-45. Thus Steen Johansen published his distinguished Grundtvig bibliography in 4 volumes between 1948-54. But interest in Grundtvig has often been linked to general history and to intellectual developments in Denmark. In the period of German rule we can see this interest reflected in the Danish church historian, Hal Koch, who played a crucial role in the Danish cultural debate during and after the occupation. In 1940 at Copenhagen University he gave a series of lectures on Grundtvig which were published in 1944; the book has gone through several editions since and remains an important introduction to Grundtvig. At the same time Hal Koch's book on Grundtvig marks the transition to the second period. It is a continuation of the line of largely biographical portrayals of Grundtvig but simultaneously it points forward to a new, more specialised Grundtvig research. The difference between the two stages can also be seen in the fact that in 1939 in an article on Grundtvig criticism Hal Koch could make a distinction between Grundtvig writers who belonged within the grundtvigian movement and those outside it; such a distinction has no longer any real substance in the light of the vast number of books and articles that began to appear after the occupation.

The biographical approach to Grundtvig was heralded in earnest by Frederik Rønning's 4-volume work, *N. F. S. Grundtvig, A Contribution to the Portrayal of Danish Intellectual Thought in the 19th Century,* published in 1907-14. The book is a wide-ranging account of Grundtvig's life and works written in the style and language of 19th century biography and intellectual history, but it is the result of a comprehensive study and is still the broadest overall picture of Grundtvig. It was in these years before the reunion of North Schleswig with Denmark in 1920 that the plan of erecting a large monument to Grundtvig was conceived; around the same time Holger Begtrup published his 10-volume edition of Grundtvig's selected writings supplemented by a series of shorter studies on, amongst others, Grundtvig's view of the Church.

It used to be said that there was a Grundtvig renaissance in the 1930's, the decade in which the architecturally interesting Grundtvig Church at Bispebjerg on the north-east edge of Copenhagen was built. This 'renaissance' probably had only a minor influence on Danish church life, but the renewed interest in Grundtvig left a significant mark on Danish literature. In 1929-31 the 3-volume work *Handbook on Grundtvig's Writings* was published, in which a series of key passages for an understanding of Grundtvig's conceptual world are selected for the ordinary reader who because of Grundtvig's incredible range may have difficulty in finding the most significant passages himself. This situation had already been touched on by Jakob Knudsen, the Danish novelist of grundtvigian persuasion whose deep psychological works contributed greatly to making some of the grundtvigian ways of presenting problems familiar to a wider reading public.

The interest in Grundtvig in the 1930's found its most comprehensive expression in Anders Nørgaard's 3-volume work *Grundtvigianism* (1935-38), the most distinctive Grundtvig work before the war. Anders Nørgaard attempts to combine a historical account with what he regards as the true grundtvigian view and make it accessible for his time: "I am convinced that the grundtvigian view of the Word and the Church, of freedom and of the people and their culture has never had a greater message for any age than for our time, which amid confusion and disintegration battles to win a deeper understanding of the word, of freedom, of the people and their culture ... I am also convinced that a particular line of development within grundtivigianism is close to its final point, its destination. The humanist philosophy of man is breaking down: so is the humanist interpretation of Grundtvig. The grundtvigianism that by its very nature should have been at cross-purposes with the 19th century's steadily increasing current but was dragged along and became merely a tint in its water is no longer needed now."

The framework of Nørgaard's three volumes shows clearly where he locates the central point in Grundtvig. The first volume deals with the period from 1825-1872, the second with the period after Grundtvig's death, and the third is an exposition of Grundtvig's view of the human and the Christian. Thus grundtvigianism begins, according to Nørgaard, in the year when Grundtvig's view of the Church made its impact; what belongs to Grundtvig's life before that time is not included. Discussion on Grundtvig as a rallying point has many a time since concerned itself with the problem of where the central point in Grundtvig's life lies; in a discussion in the 1960's Kaj Thaning went so far as to say, "Tell me which year you focus on when you interpret Grundtvig and I will tell you who you are." Nørgaard's tremendous effort was not really followed up. Political events and the influence of Barth's theology within the Church raised other questions, with the result that Nørgaard's book has been underestimated as a source of inspiration for theological thought – for example on the still somewhat unclarified relationship between a grundt-vigian view of Christianity and the evangelical-Lutheran tradition of the Danish Church. As Nørgaard says, "Protestantism may have eradicated the false Roman tradition but it did not bring the true one into the light. It settled for the traditionless biblical theology, and was therefore totally unhistorical. Such unhistorical figures as the consistently logical prote-stant, Søren Kierkegaard, could appear ... Nobody realized that Christia-nity not only *was* history in the fullness of time but equally *is* the history of the resurrected Word, of the covenant, of the Christian people through the ages."

III

Before the Second World War a number of books had already been published on specific areas in Grundtvig, primarily biographical – for example, a book on Grundtvig and England and another on Grundtvig's mental illness. After the war single, complex problems in the enormous amount of material began to receive serious treatment.

1947 saw the formation of the Grundtvig Society, which has had a decisive influence on research into Grundtvig partly through its year book, *Grundtvig Studies,* consisting of articles, reviews and bibliographical information, and partly through its publication of a series of works on Grundtvig. The very first volumes in this series are books that one constantly returns to – Henning Høirup's work on the principle of contradiction in Grundtvig, and Helge Toldberg's book on Grundtvig's symbolism. Høirup demonstrates how the principle of contradiction plays a crucial role in the development of Grundtvig's thought, particularly in his view of the Church. In his presentation of the position of this logical-formal concept in the grundtvigian universe and its basis in the history of philosophy Høirup has greatly contributed to an understanding of the special balance between the subjective and the objective in Grundtvig. Theology and logic, or more explicitly Johannine dualism and the principle of contradiction that Grundtvig had learned previously in his university studies, are linked in a context that is unique, says Høirup. And he proves convincingly that when Grundtvig's symbolism "moves so freely as never before or since in the history of Christian hymnwriting", it is because as a correlate he has had "a cognition centre which he found expressed in the Creed with its large, simple, firm lines".

Toldberg's literary examination of Grundtvig's symbolism anticipates later structuralist literary research. He has set out to read Grundtvig's works from 1815 to 1872 as a single book, and here we find central explanations of key concepts such as "mirror", "mystery", "view" etc. in Grundtvig's poetical world. The book's method has been criticized but there is general agreement as to its significance. Several ideas are formulated which point forward to the use of the myth concept in later literature, for example, when in the relationship between history, Christianity and mythology he can write, "The association of Christianity and mythology in Grundtvig's symbolism explains how having relinquished Scandinavian mythology as an existential, religious substraction he could return to it as a favourite structure into which, through mirroring its images, he could infuse a content that would have been foreign to its old interpreters but which gave it a symbolic value that made it cherished and servicable for a later generation."

Høirup's and Toldberg's books are mentioned here as examples of a special genre in Grundtvig research which has proved to be particularly fruitful: a single and delineated theme or field in Grundtvig is selected for a rigorous investigation which can simultaneously illuminate the whole of Grundtvig's work. Such an approach lies behind William Michelsen's two books on Grundtvig's view of history and its assumptions; the Norwegian Sigurd Aarnes' treatment of the same subject in the early historical works; Villiam Grønbæk's book on psychological ideas and theories in Grundtvig; the Swede Harry Aronson's studies on the Christian and the human in Grundtvig's theology; and C. I. Scharling's examination of the relationship between Grundtvig and Schelling. In addition, in the series published by the Grundtvig Society there are a number of essays on Grundtvig's hymns by the hymnologist, Magnus Stevns.

K. E. Bugge's work on Grundtvig's ideas, *The School for Life*, is the first comprehensive treatment of Grundtvig's development in the field that he is perhaps best known for, education. Bugge relates Grundtvig's ideas to past and present theories of education and one notices in particular his emphasis on the present – in the grundtvigian category of "living interaction". As he says, "The practical and ethical value of two-way communication, which in our day is often presented as a brand-new discovery, was clearly recognized over 100 years ago by Grundtvig."

IV

Bugge's book appeared in 1965, two years after the publication of the work on Grundtvig that has been the most discussed since, and whose views still form part of the debate, namely Kaj Thaning's 3-volume work *First a Man – Grundtvig's Battle with Himself*. Thaning's book rests on an incredibly comprehensive study of the manuscripts, and from the day it was presented as a doctorate it has been criticised on a number of scores. But Thaning's insistence on 1832 as a new point of departure for Grundtvig and his development of this idea have been an inspiration far beyond the circle of Grundtvig scholars. It has thus been linked to the creation theology associated with K. E. Løgstrup, but the background for which is already created in the 1930's. At that time a number of clergy and high school people turned their backs on an exclusive, grundtvigian, Church Christianity; and partly under the influence of the theology of Danish Barthianism, *Tidehverv* (= "new era"), they pointed to Grundtvig's emphasis on a realistic view of human life. It has been said that the inspiration for this came to some extent from the Danish cultural philosopher Vilhelm Grønbech, who in 1930 had published a very distinctive view of Grundtvig and who later polemically coined the words "pilgrim's myth" for the Christianity that regards the earthly existence solely as a prelude to the hereafter, an expression that had a significant meaning in the post-war theological debate into which Kaj Thaning's interpretation of Grundtvig entered. Nor is Grønbech the only historian of comparative religion to feel challenged to write a book about Grundtvig. It is also true of Edward Lehmann before the Second World War and Søren Holm after the war, whose book bears the characteristic title, *Myth and Cult in Grundtvig's Hymnwriting.*

The thesis in Kaj Thaning's book is that in 1832 as a result of the England trips Grundtvig's life and thought makes a decisive break with the past – a conversion as it were, to human life. Thaning regards the crisis in 1810 as a kind of return to the orthodox Lutheran Christianity that Grundtvig had known in his childhood home. He views the subsequent course, including the new turn in his thinking on the Church in 1825, as a development of this, and as an effort to see human life and its expressions as something that derives its value only from being sanctified by Christianity. Not until 1832, according to Thaning, does Grundtvig solve the problem that is crucial for his whole life – the relationship between the Christian and the human – with the result that "he came to see temporal life as a heathen – a human life that could be lived without a care for eternity – in the battle for the living against the dead". Before 1832 Grundtvig was marked by what Thaning calls "penitential Christianity"; after 1832 the separation of the Christian from the human is completed, a separation emphasized so strongly that Thaning can speak of Grundtvig as the spokesman for the secularization that is a consequence of Christianity.

Criticism of Thaning has attacked partly his conceptual constructs, such as the use of the words "penitential Christianity", and partly his methodical approach to Grundtvig as expressed, for example, in the preface; "It may well be the task of the living to seek to understand the dead better than they themselves did." Behind every discussion lies the problem of continuity and/or breakthrough in Grundtvig. Perhaps Thaning has formulated his view on this most concisely in one of his pithy retorts to a critic during the subsequent wide-ranging debate: there is a "difference between the growth of recognition which quite naturally makes progress along with the changing struggle against time and problems which Grundtvig wages throughout his life – and the new philosophy in mid-life which was never seen as a new departure by Grundtvig himself but which his readers can testify to. He never forgot 1810, when he changed course in his life and returned home; nor 1825, when he made the discovery of a lifetime. This was something tangible. But that was not the case in 1832 – for then life took control of his very self, so that he had to revise all his old views. Now he professes to the life that is greater than himself, but in this connection he does not have a lot to say about himself and the significance of the new date. He sticks to the point ..."

V

How *different* the interpretation of Grundtvig can be – not just in choice
of subject but in approach and presentation – will become apparent if we
move from the largely theological debate on Thaning's view of Grundtvig
to the work being done in literary research under the influence of Aage
Henriksen's literary criticism. In his lengthy dissertation on Grundtvig
and the Danish poet, Jens Baggesen, as in the work of Poul Behrendt and
Jørgen Elbek, Grundtvig is placed within a broad, largely humanist context, the horizons of which are limited by a number of significant figures
in the history of literature, in particular Goethe. In addition, the
interpretations by Henriksen, Elbek and Behrendt are so intrinsically
different that it is difficult to gather them into one. Common to them all,
however, is a method of approach in which the Grundtvig texts, in particular the poetic and those from Grundtvig's early period until the poem
New Year's Morn in 1824, which are located as focal points by all three
critics, are subjected to a close reading in order to penetrate the personal
expanding consciousness and maturation process that Grundtvig under-
goes. The treatment moves along the border between art and science,
and an appeal is made above all to the reader to invest in the book with
his own world of experience while reading. The aim is not so much to
produce results in Grundtvig research as to penetrate the deep layers in
Grundtvig's person that can call upon still unrecognized possibilities in
the reader. Here research into Grundtvig is regarded as a process of ap-
propriation, where no fixed border exists between the researcher and the
object researched, because the tools for recognition that Grundtvig
employed in order to understand himself and his situation lie beyond the
traditional, not to mention positivist, concepts of research. Aage Henriksen can write, for example, that Grundtvig's "familiarity with life and
death" gives him "his weightless nowness between the past and the present, between memory and fantasy", and Poul Behrendt writes of the
quality of Grundtvig's comprehension after the breakthrough with *New
Year's Morn*. It is not a question of establishing from the start a distinction between the private subjective and the objective communal, thus
excluding half of the world from coming into existence. On the contrary,
it is a question of insisting on the private as "underground gold which must
be raised to consciousness. If *New Year's Morn* is directed outwards as a
tremendous redemption of the people's common heritage, then that
redemption was achieved because the work was a result of a suppressed

effort to christianize and illuminate the ancient atavistic element in Grundtvig's own being". Common to the three interpretations is the decisive emphasis they place upon a Grundtvig memorandum from 1810 first brought to light by William Michelsen in 1956, in which history is regarded on the basis of the letter to the seven churches in Revelation – a historical Christian view that was finally formulated in the poem *The Pleiades of Christendom,* from 1860 (1855). The continuity thus revealed over a very long period in Grundtvig's development forms amongst other things the background for Jørgen Elbek's summarising of his view as follows: "If one is willing to see his life as a writer as a gradual flowering of his inner self, it will become apparent that in his view of history he saw nothing that was not within himself."

VI

In 1972 – the centenary of Grundtvig's death and the year the Danish people voted to join the European Community – the Danish reading public were surprised by a new book with the title – *Frederik, A Folk-book on Grundtvig's Life and Times.* The author was Ebbe Kløvedal Reich, known as a politically-engaged, left-wing commentator, connected with the student uprisings and new religiosity. The book was sharply attacked by some reviewers, highly praised by others – with theologians and literati on both sides. It takes the form of a free composition on Grundtvig's life, and of all the books on Grundtvig it is probably the most widely read, and as far as can be gathered, read aloud too. The book is constructed on the apocalyptic number seven, which Grundtvig himself used, and contains amongst other things a symbolism for the days of the week and the planets; it is also furnished with many pictures and topical comments – as is clearly anounced in the preface. Its purpose is simply to bring Grundtvig back to life. Two passages from the preface explain which direction the book will take. Writing on Grundtvig's struggle with himself Ebbe Reich says, "I believe that what the enemies of Grundtvig and of faith call "madness" were the crucial moments in the battle, and I believe that they contain a message for us of an inner revolution, of an experience which we can use to carry his work forward: the struggle against divisions and boundaries". The connection between political consciousness and working on Grundtvig is stressed in the final paragraphs under the heading *Faith:* "But the last and the real reason I am writing about Grundtvig, is because he was firm in his faith in a way that both stirs me and attracts me. To believe, to praise, to long for, to sacrifice is the lot of the oppressed. But what is the free man's lot? Is it to reject faith, praise, longing, prayer and sacrifice? Only God can know whether the society we live in is alien to Him. But it does not require much perception to see that God is alien to society. Society has no idea who God is. It is far too busy with this, that and the other, all of which looks as if it is going to hell. Grundtvig's voice came to me like the voice of one crying in the wilderness. It made me listen, wonder, doubt, believe and sense. As life is when it proves to be greater than we suspected."

Through Ebbe Kløvedal Reich's book Grundtvig became linked to the change of mentality and the change in the approach to problems which had left their mark on Danish cultural life after 1968, and in this connection it is possible to speak of a kind of Grundtvig renaissance. It also found expression in Ejvind Larsen's book *Grundtvig – and Something on Marx,* which, via Marx and Grundtvig, concludes in a vision of a dialogic society: "There is no other alternative to outer subjugation and inner self-contempt than talking together." The book is characterized by a political engagement but is constructed as a traditional investigation and it is this approach above all that has ensured that the many and widely-varying opinions on Grundtvig in the Danish debate in recent years have never quite lost touch with each other. The book does owe something to Ebbe Reich, but such differing Grundtvig scholars as Kaj Thaning, Jørgen Elbek and K. E. Bugge have felt challenged to formulate their position on the view it presents. Ejvind Larsen and Ebbe Reich have written a play together on Grundtvig: *To Battle Against Kill-joys* (*Til kamp mod dødbideriet*), and it is also typical of the little but not insignificant Grundtvig renaissance in the context of approaches to problems raised by the youth rebellion that new guitar-tunes have been composed to a number of Grundtvig songs in regular use in schools and high schools.

VII

In the area of Grundtvig research over the past few years two projects stand out. One of these is Grundtvig's sermons. Whereas previous scholarship has seen Grundtvig as a poet, theologian, educationalist or historian, it has not been clearly pointed out that the genre Grundtvig employed most throughout his life is the sermon. When the research that Christian Thodberg is currently at work on is finally published as 12 volumes of Grundtvig's sermons, this genre will be raised to the high status it deserves.

Thodberg's approach is to examine the connection between the language and the content of the hymns and sermons. Already in a major article in 1972 he presented results that threw light on the complicated relationship between prose and poetic expression in Grundtvig. Writing of the sermons and Grundtvig's contemporary hymns he says, "Prose is unsettled, sometimes complex, unclear and elaborately argued, whereas the hymns as a rule breathe clarity and calm. The sermons that lead up to a hymn are a peculiar exception. In such cases clarity and inspiration, sometimes even the firm nature of the handwriting, reveal that perhaps a hymn is on the way, and the path from brief lapidary words in the sermon to the lines of verse in the hymns is now and then not so long ..."

In the same paper Thodberg writes of Grundtvig's development seen in the light of the sermons: "Thus if one reads the sermons one after the other, what is characteristic is not the great breakthrough or the well-known years 1810-11, 1824-25 or 1832. Even though Grundtvig acknowledges these dates he nevertheless reveals a more varied picture in the sermons. Nothing happens in Grundtvig that is not well-prepared. What is fixed at a particular time or as a rule at a later time as being a great breakthrough lies in embryonic form far earlier". Thodberg's research has resulted in a very fruitful working group at Aarhus University, where he and a number of students have presented the results of their various investigation of the hymns and the sermons in the volume *For the Sake of Continuity.*

The other major work in recent years is Flemming Lundgreen-Nielsen's massively constructed and incredibly detailed two-volume work *The Operative Word,* where, in a continuation of a previous book on Grundtvig's early romantic poetry he offers a unified account of Grundtvig's poetry, literary criticism and poetics from 1798 to 1819 – the years in which according to Lundgreen-Nielsen Grundtvig can be said in earnest to have had a position in the context of literary history. Lundgreen-Nielsen is the first to sort through the complete printed texts and complete manuscripts of a particular period, all of which are noted in the *Register of Grundtvig's Papers* drawn up in 1957-64. In contrast to Thodberg's structuralist interpretation of the symbolism, Flemming Lundgreen-Nielsen presents the material in the light of literary history and text analysis. He describes his approach thus: "The material is read, analysed and described in a strict, direct, mechanical, chronological order. Through his handwritten and printed texts Grundtvig is followed week by week, often day by day ... The point of this is that Grundtvig's own stocktaking – the years 1805, 1810, 1815, 1824, and 1832 give a clue to its nature ... denote the final result of a particular historical period in his life, but they can in no way be said to pass muster as realistic historical descriptions and summaries of his various stages." The exposition "attempts to seat itself at Grundtvig's writing-desk to go over his reading, follow his pen through the manuscripts and see things from the outside world capturing his attention – all this in an attempt to reconstruct his writing chronology in a series of historical "nows" from 1798 to January 1819". Lundgreen-Nielsen keeps his promise in the 1,000-page dissertation, which marks a major step forward in Grundtvig research and which will prove to be of incalculable value for anyone working on Grundtvig. Mention should also be made of Lundgreen-Nielsen's emphasis on Grundtvig's employment of a method of reading in his own critical practice during this period which reminds one "astonishingly" of the close-reading techniques of new criticism. As a literary historian Lundgreen-Nielsen also makes much of the peculiar fact that even though Grundtvig is a classic in Danish literature, in contrast to all the other contemporary Danish poets he has not left behind him a single classic work.

VIII

Many articles, accounts and even penetrating examinations of Grundtvig have had to be passed over here, but what has been dealt with will hopefully give some impression of the multiplicity of methods and results in Grundtvig literature – a multiplicity that points to the richness of Grundtvig himself but which is so extraordinary that at times one wonders whether it is the same person who is being discussed in the various treatments. In particular it seems as if there is still a need for a closer dialogue between literary critics and theologians. On the other hand it remains true of Grundtvig research that it is very rarely boring to read, which again has much to do with the subject under discussion. Otherwise the problems of Grundtvig literature are due to amongst other things the difficulty of saying who or what Grundtvig actually was. Early on, in 1810, he speaks of his historical nature as being characteristic of him, later in the *Literary Testament* from 1827 he speaks of himself as "half bookworm, half bard". But he was poet, hymnwriter, theologian, national educationalist, preacher, historian and – as he himself suggests and Flemming Lundgreen-Nielsen's research clearly proves – a bookworm.

The most original of Grundtvig's theological disciples in the 19th century, Otto Møller, himself both a clergyman and a theologian, wrote that one must not forget that Grundtvig was above all a poet. Møller never therefore wrote about Grundtvig but *out* of Grundtvig. Many others have sooner or later done the same, and part of the overall picture of Grundtvig literature is the number of quite brief, intuitively conceived comments on Grundtvig which can also be an inspiration in the work on Grundtvig's manuscripts. One meets them, for example, in Jakob Knudsen, and again in the Danish poet Martin A. Hansen, who in 1952 formulated what perhaps has been the inspiration to many Grundtvig researchers: "The path of personality is just as strictly defined in Grundtvig as in Kierkegaard. But in Grundtvig one has a stronger feeling that this path is quite different from that of individualism – is in fact its opposite. In Grundtvig the personal cannot develop without immediately being transmitted and united with the personal in others. Grundtvig has the effect of an originator after the three others, Luther, Kant and Kierkegaard. The last is the Protestant consummator. Grundtvig belongs to the future, he transcends protestantism and in him a culture seems to be in embryo."

BIBLIOGRAPHY

There is no complete bibliography available of Grundtvig literature, but there are reviews and up-to-date bibliographical information in *Grundtvig Studies*, the annual journal of the Grundtvig Society, from 1947 onwards. On the literary debate on Grundtvig readers are advised to consult the bibliography in Flemming Lundgreen-Nielsen's work mentioned below.

Books and articles in the order in which they appear in the text; numbers in brackets refer to direct quotations:

Anders Pontoppidan Thyssen: Den Nygrundtvigske Bevægelse, 1870-1887, København 1958. (*The Neo-grundtvigian Movement, 1870-1887. Copenhagen 1958*).

P. G. Lindhardt: Morten Pontoppidan, I-II, Aarhus 1950-53. (*Morten Pontoppidan, I-II. Aarhus 1950-53*).

Regin Prenter: Skabelse og Genløsning. Dogmatik 3. udg. 1962. (*Creation and Redemption. Dogmatics 3rd ed. Copenhagen 1962*).

P. G. Lindhardt: Konfrontation. Grundtvigs prædikener i Kirkeåret 1854-55 på baggrund af Kierkegaards Angreb på den danske og den 'officielle' kristendom, København 1974. (*Confrontation. Grundtvig's Sermons in the Church Year 1854-55 in the light of Kierkegaard's attack on the Danish Church and 'Official' Christianity. Copenhagen 1974*).

Poul Borum: Grundtvig i "Forfatternes forfatterhistorie". Red. Per Stig Møller, København 1980, (s. 57-58). (*Grundtvig in "The Writers' Literary History". Ed. Per Stig Møller. Copenhagen 1980, (pp. 57-58)*).

Carl S. Pedersen og Vilhelm Andersen: Illustreret Dansk litteraturhistorie, III-IV, København 1934. (*Illustrated Danish Literary History, III-IV. Copenhagen 1934*).

F. J. Billeskov Jansen: Danmarks digtekunst, 3, s. udg., København 1964. (*History of Danish Literature 3, latest edition, Copenhagen 1964.*) Dansk Litteratur Historie 2, København, Politikens Forlag 1965. (*Danish Literary History 2. Copenhagen, Politikens Publishers 1965*).

Den danske Kirkes historie, VI og VII (ved Hal Koch og P. G. Lindhardt), København 1954 og 1958. (*History of the Danish Church, VI and VII by Hal Koch and P. G. Lindhardt. Copenhagen 1954 and 1958*).

Steen Johansen: Bibliografi over N. F. S. Grundtvigs skrifter I-IV, København 1948-54.

(*Bibliography of the Writings of N. F. S. Grundtvig, I-IV. Copenhagen 1948-54*).

Hal Koch: Grundtvig, København 1944 og senere udgaver. (*Grundtvig. Copenhagen 1944 and later editions*).

Hal Koch: Grundtvig-litteratur, Dansk Teologisk Tidsskrift 1939. (*Literature on Grundtvig. Danish Theological Periodical 1939*).

F. Rønning: N. F. S. Grundtvig. Et bidrag til skildring af dansk åndsliv i det 19. århundrede I-IV, København 1907-14. (*N. F. S. Grundtvig. A Contribution to the Portrayal of Danish Intellectual Thought in the 19th Century, I-IV. Copenhagen 1907-14*).

Holger Begtrup: N. F. S. Grundtvigs Kirkelige Syn 1825. En historisk Indledning. København 1901. (*N. F. S. Grundtvig's View of the Church 1825. A Historical Introduction. Copenhagen 1901*).

E. J. Borup og *F. S. Schrøder (ed.):* Håndbog i Grundtvigs Skrifter, København 1929-31. (*Handbook on Grundtvig's Writings. Copenhagen 1929-31*).

Jakob Knudsen: Om Grundtvig, 1908, optrykt i Jakob Knudsen: At være sig selv, København 1965. (*On Grundtvig, 1908, reprinted in Jakob Knudsen: Being Oneself. Copenhagen 1965*).

Anders Nørgaard: Grundtvigianismen I-III, København 1935-38 (I, s. 8; III, s. 160). (*Grundtvigianism I-III. Copenhagen 1935-38 I, p. 8; III, p. 160*).

J. P. Bang: Grundtvig og England, Studier over Grundtvig, København 1932. (*Grundtvig and England, Studies in Grundtvig. Copenhagen 1932*).

Hjalmar Helweg: N. F. S. Grundtvigs sindssygdom, 2. opl. København 1932. (*N. F. S. Grundtvig's Mental Illness, 2nd printing. Copenhagen 1932*).

Henning Høirup: Grundtvigs Syn på Tro og Erkendelse. Modsigelsens grundsætning som teologisk aksiom hos Grundtvig, København 1949 (s. 400-401). (*Grundtvig's View of Faith and Realization. The Thesis of Contradiction as Theological Axiom in Grundtvig. Copenhagen 1949, p. 400-401*).

Helge Toldberg: Grundtvigs Symbolverden, København 1950 (s. 218). (*Grundtvig's Symbolism. Copenhagen 1950, p. 218*).

William Michelsen: Tilblivelsen af Grundtvigs historiesyn, København 1954. (*The Origin of Grundtvig's View of History. Copenhagen 1954*).

William Michelsen: Den sælsomme forvandling i N. F. S. Grundtvigs Liv. København 1956. (*The Strange Metamorphosis in the Life of N. F. S. Grundtvig. Copenhagen 1956*).

Sigurd Aa. Aarnes: Historieskrivning og livssyn hos Grundtvig. Oslo 1962. (*The Writing of History and the View of Life in Grundtvig. Oslo 1962*).

Villiam Grønbæk: Psykologiske tanker og teorier hos Grundtvig, København 1951. (*Psychological Thoughts and Theories in Grundtvig. Copenhagen 1951.*)

Harry Aronson: Mänskligt og Kristet. En studie in N. F. S. Grundtvigs teologi, København 1960. (*Human and Christian. A Study in the Theology of N. F. S. Grundtvig. Copenhagen 1960*).

C. J. Scharling: Grundtvig og romantikken belyst ved Grundtvigs forhold til Schelling, København 1947. (*Grundtvig and Romanticism seen in the light of Grundtvig's relationship with Schelling. Copenhagen 1947*).

Magnus Stevns: Fra Grundtvigs Salmeværksted, udgivet af Henning Høirup og Steen Johansen, København 1950. (*From Grundtvig's Hymn Workshop, ed. Henning Høirup and Steen Johansen. Copenhagen 1950*).

Knud Eyvin Bugge: Skolen for Livet. Studier over N. F. S. Grundtvigs pædagogiske tanker, København 1965 (s. 350). (*The School for Life. Studies in N. F. S. Grundtvig's Educational Ideas. Copenhagen 1965, p. 350*).

Kaj Thaning: Menneske først – Grundtvigs opgør med sig selv, I-III, København 1963, (s.

410

7, samt hertil indlæg i Præsteforeningens Blad 54. årgang, s. 435). (*First a Man –* *Grundtvig's Battle with Himself, I-III. Copenhagen 1963, p. 7, and additional contributions in The Periodical of the Clergymen's Association, vol. 54, p. 435.*)

Vilhelm Grønbech: Kampen om Mennesket, København-Oslo 1930. (*The Battle for Man. Copenhagen-Oslo 1930*).

Edvard Lehmann: Grundtvig, København-Oslo 1929. (*Grundtvig. Copenhagen-Oslo 1929*).

Søren Holm: Mythe og Kult i Grundtvigs Salmedigtning, København 1955. (*Myth and Cult in Grundtvig's Hymnwriting. Copenhagen 1955*).

Aage Henriksen: Grundtvig og Baggesen i bogen Gotisk tid. Fire litterære afhandlinger, København 1971 (s. 171). (*Grundtvig and Baggesen in the book Gothic Time. Four literary essays. Copenhagen 1971, p. 171*)

Poul Behrendt: Viljens Former. Augustin-Goethe-Grundtvig, København 1974, p. 192, (optegnelser udgivet af Michelsen i Grundtvig-Studier, 1956.) (*The Forms of the Will. Augustine-Goethe-Grundtvig. Copenhagen 1974, p. 192, notes edited by Michelsen in Grundtvig-Studies 1956*).

Jørgen Elbek: Grundtvig og Syvstjernen. København 1981. (s. 53). (*Grundtvig and the Pleiades. Copenhagen 1981, p. 53*).

Ebbe Kløvedal Reich: Frederik. En folkebog om Grundtvigs tid og liv. København 1972. (s. 10, 12). (*Frederik, A Folkbook on Grundtvig's Life and Times. Copenhagen 1972, p. 10, 12*).

Eyvind Larsen: Grundtvig – og noget om Marx. København 1974. (særudgave af tidsskriftet Studenterkredsen) (s. 79). (*Grundtvig – and Something on Marx. Copenhagen 1974. Special edition of the periodical The Student Circle, p. 79*).

Christian Thodberg: Prædiken og Salme hos Grundtvig. Dansk Kirkesangs Årsskrift 1971-72 (s. 123, s. 126). (*Sermon and Hymn in Grundtvig. The Yearbook of Danish Hymn Singing 1971-72, p. 123, 126*).

Christian Thodberg: For sammenhængens skyld. Ord og motiver i Grundtvigs salmer og prædikener. Grundtvig-studier 1977-78. (*For the Sake of Continuity. Words and Motifs in Grundtvig's Hymns and Sermons. Grundtvig Studies 1977-78*).

Flemming Lundgreen-Nielsen: Det handlende ord. N. F. S. Grundtvigs digtning, litteraturkritik og poetik 1798-1819, København 1980 (s. 26-27, s. 17). (*The Operative Word, N. F. S. Grundtvig's Literary Works, Literary Criticism and Poetics 1798-1819. Copenhagen 1980. p. 26-27, p. 17*).

Registrant over N. F. S. Grundtvigs papirer I-XXX, København 1957-64. Udarbejdet af G. Albeck, K. E. Bugge, Uffe Hansen, H. Høirup, Steen Johansen, Niels Kofoed, William Michelsen, Kaj Thaning, Helge Toldberg og Albert Fabritius. (*Register of N. F. S. Grundtvig's Papers I-XXX. Copenhagen 1957-64, ed. by G. Albeck, K. E. Bugge, Uffe Hansen, H. Høirup, Steen Johansen, Niels Kofoed, William Michelsen, Kaj Thaning, Helge Toldberg, and Albert Fabritius*).

Gustav Albeck's many essays are listed in Flemming Lundgreen-Nielsen's bibliography.

Martin A. Hansen: Leviathan. København 1950. (s. 89-90). (*Leviathan. Copenhagen 1950, p. 89-90*).

A Grundtvig Bibliography

Grundtvig Writings and Manuscripts

A complete catalogue of Grundtvig's writings is to be found in Steen Johansen's *Bibliography* of N.F.S. Grundtvig's Writings I-IV, Copenhagen 1948-54. The manuscripts are listed in *Register* of N.F.S. Grundtvig's Papers I-XXX, 1957-64. A complete edition of the collected works of Grundtvig does not exist, and the most important editions are:

Poetic Writings (*Poetiske Skrifter*) ed. Svend Grundtvig, 1880ff.
Selected Writings (*Udvalgte Skrifter*) ed. Holger Begtrup I-X, 1904ff.
Letters by and to Grundtvig I-II (*Breve fra og til Grundtvig*) ed. Georg
   Christensen and Stener Grundtvig, 1924-26.
Selected Works (*Værker i Udvalg*) ed. Georg Christensen og Hal Koch I-
   X, 1940ff.
Grundtvig's Song-works (*Grundtvigs Sangværk*) I-V, 1944 repr. 1983.
Diaries and Notebooks (*Dag- og Udtogsbøger*) ed. Gustav Albeck I-II,
   1979.
Grundtvig's Sermons (*Grundtvigs Prædikener*) ed. Christian Thodberg,
   I-XII, 1983ff.

The following is a chronological list of the texts cited in this book with an English title:

   1802 – The Private Schoolmasters (*Skoleholderne*)
   1803 – Ulfhild, a Historical Tale (*Ulfhild, en historisk Fortælling*)
   1806 – Brief Comment on the Songs of the Edda (*Lidt om Sangene i
          Edda*)
   1807 – On Norse Mythology (*Om Asalæren*)
        – On Schiller and The Bride from Messina (*Om Schiller og Bru-
          den fra Messina*)
        – On Religion and Liturgy (*Om Religion og Liturgi*)
        – On Scholarship and its Encouragement, with Particular Re-
          gard to the Fatherland (*Om Videnskabelighed og dens Frem-
          me, især med Hensyn til Fædrelandet*)
        – Journey in the Summer of 1807 (*Rejsen i Sommeren 1807*)

1808 – Gunderslev Forest (*Gunderslev Skov*)
   The Masked Ball in Denmark (*Maskeradeballet i Danmark*)
   – Willemoes (*Villemoes*)
   – On Oehlenschläger's Balder the Good (*Om Oehlenschlägers Baldur hin Gode*)
   – Freyr's Love (*Freis Kærlighed*)
   . Textbook in World History (*Lærebog i Verdenshistorien*)
   – Norse Mythology (*Nordens Mythologi*)
1809 – In Praise of Freyja (*Freias Pris*)
   – Scenes from the Decline of Heroic Life in the North (*Optrin af Kæmpelivets Undergang i Norden*)
1810 – Why has the Word of the Lord Disappeared from His House. Probationary Sermon. (*Hvi er Herrens Ord forsvundet af Hans Hus. Dimisprædiken*).
   – Idun. A New Year's Gift (*Idunna. En Nytaarsgave*)
   – Come Hither, Little Girls! (*Komme hid I Piger Smaa*)
   – New Year's Eve, or a Brief Glance at Christianity and History (*Nytaarsnat eller Blik paa Kristendom og Historie*)
   – Odin and Saga (*Odin og Saga*)
1811 – Scenes from the Battle of Norns and Aesir (*Optrin af Norners og Asers Kamp*)
   – The Hill by the Sea at Egeløkke (*Strandbakken ved Egeløkke*)
   – Saga (*Saga*)
   – Udby Garden (*Udby Have*)
1812 – Brief View of World Chronicle in Context (*Kort Begreb af Verdens Krønike i Sammenhæng*)
   – Why are we called Lutherans? (*Hvorfor kaldes vi Lutheraner?*)
1813 – The Chronicle's Retort (*Krønikens Gienmæle*)
   – On the Conditions of Man (*Om Menneskets Vilkaar*)
   – To the Fatherland (*Til Fædrelandet*)
1814 – Roskilde Rhyme (*Roskilde-Riim*)
   – Roskilde Saga (*Roskilde-Saga*)
   – Brief View of World Chronicle Considered in its Context (*Kort Begreb af Verdens Krønike betragtet i Sammenhæng*)
   – A Little Bible Chronicle for Children and the General Reader (*En liden Bibelkrønike for Børn og Menigmand*)
   – A Strange Prophecy (*En mærkelig Spaadom*)
   – On the Prospects for Christ's Church (*Om Udsigterne for Christi Kirke*)
   – On Polemics and Tolerance (*Om Polemik og Tolerance*)

1815 – Against the Little Accuser (*Imod den lille Anklager*)
   – Commemorative Song at the Ancestors' Grave (*Mindesang paa Fædres Gravhøi*)
   – Specimens from the Chronicles of Snorri and Saxo (*Prøver af Snorres og Saxos Krøniker*)
   – Latest Pictures of Copenhagen (*Nyeste Skilderier af Kjøbenhavn*)
   – Little Songs (*Kvædlinger*)
   – Heimdall (*Heimdall*)
   – Europe, France and Napoleon (*Europa, Frankrig og Napoleon*)
1816-19 – Danevirke (*Danne-Virke*)
1816 – The Evaluation in the 'Literary Times' of my Specimen Translations of Saxo and Snorri (*Litteraturtidendes Skudsmaal i Henseende til Prøverne af Saxo og Snorre*)
   – Biblical Sermons (*Bibelske Prædikener*)
1817 – On Revelation, Art and Knowledge (*Om Aabenbaring, Kunst og Videnskab*)
   – Ragnarok (*Ragna-Roke*)
   – The Easter Lily (*Paaske-Lilien*)
   – Prospect of World Chronicle Especially in the Age of Luther (*Udsigt over Verdens-Krøniken fornemmelig i det Lutherske Tidsrum*)
1818-22 – Saxo's Chronicle of Denmark (*Saxos Danmarks Krønike*)
   – Snorri's Chronicle of the Kings of Norway (*Snorres Norges Konge-Krønike*)
1820 – Beowulf (*Bjowulfs Drape*)
1824 – New Year's Morn (*Nyaars-Morgen*)
   – The Land of the Living (*De Levendes Land*)
   – The Dane Shield (*Danne-Skjolds-Drape*)
   – Exchange of Letters (*Brevvexling*)
1825 – The 18th Century Enlightenment in the Service of Salvation (*Det attende Aarhundredes Oplysning i Saligheds-Sag*)
   – The Church's Retort (*Kirkens Gienmæle*)
   – Rome and Jerusalem (*Rom og Jerusalem*)
   – On the Christian Struggle (*Om den Christelige Kamp*)
   – On War and Peace (*Om Krig og Fred*)
1826 – Important Questions for Denmark's Jurists (*Vigtige Spørgsmaal til Danmarks Lovkyndige*)
   – What is Christianity in Denmark (*Hvad er Christendom i Danmark*)

414

1826-27 – On True Christianity and on the Truth of Christianity (*Om den Sande Christendom og om Christendommens Sandhed*)

1827 – The Literary Testament of the Writer N.F.S. Grundtvig (*Skribenten N.F.S. Grundtvigs literaire Testamente*)

– On Freedom of Religion (*Om Religions-Frihed*)

1827-31 – Christian Sermons or The Sunday Book I-III (*Christelige Prædikener eller Søndags-Bog I-III*)

1828 – The Christian Faith (*Den kristne Tro*)

1829 – Chronicle in Rhyme for Living School Usage (*Krønike-Rim til levende Skole-Brug*)

– The River of Time or Outline of Universal History (*Tidens Strøm eller universalhistorisk Omrids*)

– Chronicle in Rhyme for Childhood Teaching (*Krønike-Riim til Børne-Lærdom*)

– Historical Teachings for Children (*Historisk Børne-Lærdom*)

1831 – On the Clausen Libel Case (*Om den Clausenske Injurie-Sag*)

– Political Considerations (*Politiske Betragtninger*)

1830-31 – Should the Lutheran Reformation Really Continue? (*Skulle den Lutherske Reformation virkelig fortsætte?*)

– Books and Ideas on Naturalism in the North, Past and Present (*Bøger og Ideer om Naturalisme i Norden før og nu*)

1832 – Norse Mythology or The Language of Myth (*Nordens Mythologi eller Sindbilled-Sprog*)

– Hagens Hymnbook (*Hagens Salmebog*)

1833-43 – Handbook on World History. According to the Best Sources. An Attempt by N.F.S. Grundtvig. I-III (*Haandbog i Verdens-Historien. Efter de bedste Kilder. Et Forsøg af N.F.S. Grundtvig, I-III*)

1834 – An Impartial View of the Danish State Church (*Den danske Stats-Kirke upartisk betragtet*)

– The Spirit of the Age (*Tids-Aanden*)

– Norse Gold (*Nordens Guld*)

– Education for State Affairs (*Statsmæssig Oplysning*)

1835 – The Golden Mean (*Den gyldne Middelvej*)

1836 – The Danish Four-Leaf Clover (*Den danske Fiir-Kløver*)

1836-37 – Song-Work for the Danish Church (*Sang-Værk til den danske Kirke*)

1837 – Last Night a Knock came at the Portals of Hell (*I Kvæld blev der banket paa Helvedesport*)

– First a Man – then a Christian (*Menneske først og Kristen saa*)

1838 – The School for Life (*Skolen for Livet*)

Grundtvig Literature in English

a) *Texts Written by Grundtvig in English*

Bibliotheca Anglo-Saxonica. Prospectus and Proposals of a subscription, for the publication of most valuable anglo-saxon manuscripts, illustrative of the early poetry and literature of our language. Most of which have never been printed. London 1830. 15 p. 2nd Ed. 1831.

Review of 'History of the Northmen, or Danes and Normans, from the Earliest Times to the Conquest of England by William of Normandy'. By Henry Wheaton. 1831. The Westminster Review. Vol XV, 442-457.

To Professor Whewell at Cambridge. (Lines in books, or lines in hand ...), *Poetiske Skrifter* V. 500-501.

Melrose Abbey and Abbotsford. (The dirge of Scotland in a word ...), *Poetiske Skrifter* VI. 470.

b) *Grundtvig Texts Translated into English* *(in chronological order)*

William and Mary Howitt: The Literature and Romance of Northern Europe. 2 vols. London 1852. II, 164ff.

The Hymns of Denmark. Tr. by Gilbert Tait (pseud.). London 1868. 153-155, 183-186, 207, 213ff.

Charlotte Sidgwick: The Story of Denmark. London 1890. 303ff.

John Volk: Songs and Poems in Danish and English. New York 1903.

The Easter-Lily. By Bishop N.F.S. Grundtvig. Tr. by Alexander Marlowe Blair. Nebraska 1919.

Hymns of the North. Tr. by S.D. Rodholm. 1919.

I. Buntzen: The American-Scandinavian Review 1920. p. 112.

A Book of Danish Verse, New York 1922. pp. 50-57.

Hymnal for Church and Home, 1924. Songbook for Danish Churches in America, containing 52 Grundtvig songs. Reprinted several times.

Christian Science Hymnal, Boston 1932.

The American Scandinavian Review III. 1942. p. 228.

A Sheaf of Song. Tr. by S.D. Rodholm. 1945.

J.S. Aaberg: Hymns and Hymnwriters in Denmark, 1945.

A Second Book of Danish Verse. Tr. by Charles Wharton Stork. With a foreword by Johannes V. Jensen. Princeton 1947. pp. 6-9.

In Denmark I was born ... A Little Book of Danish Verse. Ed. R.P. Keigwin, Copenhagen 1948. 2nd Ed. 1950. pp. 37-41.

The Land of the Living. Tr. by Jan Jepson Egglishaw. The Norseman 10. 1952, pp. 124-25.

A Harvest of Song: Translations and Original Lyrics. By S.D. Rodholm. With a biographical sketch by Enok Mortensen. Des Moines 1953. 193 pp.

Selections from »Shall the Lutheran Reformation really be continued?« Translated by Valdemar S. Jensen, ed. by Einar Anderson. 13 pp. New York 1957.

A Book of Danish Ballads. Selected and introd. by Axel Olrik. (1939). Repr. New York 1968. 337 pp.

Anthology of Danish Literature. Ed. P.M. Mitchell and F.J. Billeskov-Jansen, Carbondale 1972. 606 pp.

Mortensen, Enok: Den danske salme i Amerika. The Danish Hymn in America, Grundtvig Studies 1974, pp. 54-75 with English translation of Grundtvig Songs.

Selected Writings of N.F.S. Grundtvig, ed. with an Introduction by Johannes Knudsen, Philadelphia 1976. 184 pp.

A Heritage in Song. Ed. Johannes Knudsen. Askov, Minnesota 1978.

»The Danish High Mass« and a Selection of Hymns from »The Danish Hymn-Book«. Copenhagen, no date. 40 pp.

A Grundtvig Anthology. Selected by The Grundtvig Society. Tr. by Edward Broadbridge and Niels Lyhne Jensen. Centrums Forlag/Darton, Longman & Todd (1983).

c) *Monographs on Grundtvig*

Allen, Edgar L.: Bishop Grundtvig: A prophet of the North. London 1949. 94 pp.

Davies, Noëlle: Education for life. A Danish pioneer. London 1931. 207 pp.

Davies, Noëlle: Grundtvig of Denmark. A guide to small nations. Liverpool 1944. 56 pp.

Knudsen, Johannes: Danish Rebel. The Life of N.F.S. Grundtvig. Philadelphia 1955. XIII, 242 pp.

Koch, Hal: Grundtvig. Tr. from the Danish with introduction and notes by Llewellyn Jones. Yellow Springs, Ohio 1952. 231 pp.

Larson, Paul Merville: A Rhetorical Study of Bishop Nicholas Frederik Severin Grundtvig. Diss., Evanston, Illinois 1942, c. 365 pp.

Lindhardt, P.G.: Grundtvig. An Introduction. London 1951. 141 pp. Review.: Orbis Litterarum IX, 1954, 247-49 (Helge Toldberg).

Marais, J.I.: Bishop Grundtvig and the people's high school in Denmark. Pretoria 1911. 38 pp.

Nauman, St. Elmo H. (Jr.): The Social Philosophy of Søren Kierkegaard and Nikolai Frederik Severin Grundtvig. Ph. D. thesis. Boston University Graduate School. 1969. 224 pp. cf. Dissertation Abstracts XXX A, 208lf.

Nielsen, Ernest D.: N.F.S. Grundtvig: An American Study. Rock Island 1955. XII, 173 pp.

Sneen, Donald Juel: The Hermeneutics of N.F.S. Grundtvig. Diss. Princeton. N.J., 1968. 336 pp.

Thaning, Kaj: N.F.S. Grundtvig. Engl. Tr. by David Hohnen. Det danske Selskab, Copenhagen 1972. 180 pp.

d) *Articles in Journals and Collected Works*
Treatment of Grundtvig in other Works

Aaberg, J.S.: Danish Hymns and Hymn-Writers. Des Moines: The Committee of Publications of the Danish Evangelical Lutheran Church of America 1945.

Allchin, A.M.: Grundtvig's Translation from the Greek. The Eastern Churches Quarterly XIV, 1961-62, pp. 28-44.

Allchin, A.M.: The Hymns of N.F.S. Grundtvig. The Eastern Churches Quarterly XIII, 1959, pp. 129-43.

Allen, E.L.: Grundtvig and Kierkegaard. Congregational Quarterly ·XXIV, London 1946, pp. 205-12.

Andersen, J.O.: Survey of the History of the Church in Denmark. Copenhagen 1930.

Begtrup, H., Lund, H., Manniche, P.: The Folk High Schools of Denmark and the Development of a Farming Community. London 1948. 163 pp.

Belding, Robert E.: One European High School – Lesson for New Nations? Journal of Secondary Education XLIII, 1967-68, pp. 7-38.

Bjerre, Sv. Erik: Grundtvig. The Danish Folk High School and the Developing Countries. Grundtvig Studies 1973, pp. 160-171.

Boje, Andreas, D.J. Borup & H. Rützenbeck: Education in Denmark. The intellectual basis of a democratic commonwealth. London & Copenhagen 1932. 291 pp.

Bredsdorff, Elias: Danish Literature in English Translation. Orbis Litterarum V, 1947, pp. 187-257 (p. 216f. on Grundtvig). Reprint Westport, 1973. 178 pp.

Bredsdorff, Elias: Danish Literature in English Translation. A bibliography. Copenhagen 1950. p. 60-61 on Grundtvig.

Bredsdorff, Elias et al.: An Introduction to Scandinavian Literature from the Earliest Time to our Day. Copenhagen and Cambridge 1951. pp. 84-86.

Bredsdorff, Elias: Grundtvig in Cambridge. The Norseman. March-April

1952. pp. 114-123.

Campbell, Olive Dame: The Danish Folk School. New York 1928. 359 pp.

Christmas Møller, J. and Watson, Katherine: Education in democracy. The Folk high schools of Denmark. London 1944. 160 pp.

Cooley, E.G.: Bishop Grundtvig and people's high schools. Educational Review, New York, XLVIII, 1915, 452. pp.

Cooley, Franklin: Grundtvig's first translation from Beowulf. Scand. Studies and Notes XVI, 1940, pp. 234-38.

Desmond, Shaw: The Soul of Denmark. London 1918. 277 pp.

Dixon, Willis: Education in Denmark. Copenhagen 1958.

Driffield-Hawkin, T.: When Grundtvig worked at Exeter. »Denmark«. London, Aug. 1948.

Egglishaw, Jan Jepson: »The Land of the Living«. The Norseman. March-April 1952, 124ff.

Ehnevid, Tord: The Dominant Peoples in History according to Grundtvig and Hegel. Grundtvig Studies 1973, pp. 101-114.

Fain, E.F.: Nationalist Origins of the Folk High School: The Romantic Visions of N.F.S. Grundtvig. British Journal of Educational Studies XIX, 1971, pp. 70-90.

Foght, H.W.: The Danish folk high schools. Washington 1914. 93 pp.

Goodhope, Nana: Christen Kold. The Little Schoolmaster Who Helped Revive a Nation. Blair, Nebraska, 1956, 120 pp.

Gosse, Edmund: Two Visits to Denmark 1872, 1874. London 1911. pp. 78-87 on Grundtvig.

Gosse, Edm. W.: Four Danish Poets (i.e. Grundtvig, Bødtcher, H.C. Andersen and Fr. Paludan Müller). In Edm. W. Gosse: Studies in the Literature of Northern Europe. London 1879. Reprinted 1883.

Grattan, Hartley: The Meaning of Grundtvig: Skill plus Culture. Antioch Review XVIII, 1958, pp.78-86.

Haarder, Andreas: Beowulf. The appeal of a poem. Doctorate. Copenhagen 1975. 350 pp.

Harbsmeier, Götz: Grundtvig and Germany. Grundtvig Studies 1973. pp. 128-138.

Harjunpaa, Toivo: Grundtvig and his incomparable discovery. Lutheran Quarterly XXV, 1973, 54-70.

Hart, Joseph K.: Light from the North. The Danish folk high schools. Their meanings for America. New York 1927, 159 pp.

The Danish People's High School. Publ. by »The Association of People's High Schools and Agricultural Schools«. Tr. by Shaw Desmond. Copenhagen 1918. 169 pp.

Høirup, Henning: Grundtvig and Kierkegaard, their views on the church. Theology today XII, 1955. pp. 328-342. Repr. in: Grundtvig Studies 1956. pp. 7-20.

Janson, Kristoffer: Grundtvig and the Peasant High School. Scandinavia. Chicago 1884.

Jones, Llewellyn: Kierkegaard or Grundtvig? Christ. Century LXIX. 1952, n. 20, pp. 588-89. cf. ibid. n. 23, pp. 674-75.

Jones, Llewellyn: Grundtvig as a Scandinavian Precursor of Humanism. Humanist XIII, 1953, pp. 34-36.

Jones, W. Glyn: Denmark. London 1970, pp. 68-70 on Grundtvig.

Knudsen, Johannes: Grundtvig Research. The Lutheran Quarterly V, 1953, pp. 167-174.

Knudsen, Johannes: Grundtvig and Mythology. The Lutheran Quarterly VI, 1954, pp. 299-309.

Knudsen, Johannes: Grundtvig and American Theology Today. Lutheran World I, 1954/5, pp. 277-287.

Knudsen, Johannes: Notes about Grundtvig. Summer Issue of The Chicago Lutheran Theological Seminary Record (July 1955).

Knudsen, Johannes: Revelation and Man According to N.F.S. Grundtvig. Lutheran Quarterly X. 1958, pp. 217-225.

Knudsen, Johannes: One hundred Years later. The Grundtvigian Heritage. Lutheran Quarterly 25. 1983, pp. 71-77.

Larsen, Ejvind: A Natural philosopher after Grundtvig's heart, summary by Shirley Larsen. Grundtvig Studies 1973, pp. 225-232.

Lindhardt, P.G.: Grundtvig and England. Journal of Ecclesiastical History I, 1950. pp. 207-224.

Lund, Ragnar (ed.): Scandinavian Adult Education. Editor in chief: Ragnar Lund. First Edition 1949, Second Edition 1952. 297 pp.

Mac Kaye, David L.: Grundtvig and Kold. The American-Scandinavian Review III, 1942, pp. 229-239.

Malone, Kemp: Grundtvig's philosophy of history. Journal of the Hist. of Ideas I, 1940, pp. 281-298.

Malone, Kemp: Grundtvig on Paradise Lost. Renaissance Studies in Honor of Hardin Craig. 1941, pp. 320-323.

Malone, Kemp: Grundtvig as Beowulf Critic. The Review of English Studies XVII, 1941, pp. 129-138.

Manniche, Peter: Living Democracy in Denmark. Rev. ed. of »Denmark, a social laboratory«. Copenhagen 1952. 240 pp.

Manniche, Peter: The International People's College at Elsinore. Grundtvig Studies 1973, pp. 152-159.

Michelsen, William: A Century after Grundtvig. Grundtvig Studies 1973, p. 67.

Mitchell, P.M.: A History of Danish Literature, 2nd Ed. New York 1971. pp. 126-34.

Nielsen, Ernest D.: N.F.S. Grundtvig on Luther. Interpretations of Luther. Essays in Honor of Wilhelm Pauck. Ed. by Jaroslav Pelican, Philadelphia 1968, pp. 159-186.

Nielsen, Ernest D.: »Thomas Chalmers«. A study of selected writings of Chalmers to determine whether Grundtvig was influenced by Thomas Chalmers. Lutheran Tidings. VIII, 5. Dec. 1930 and 20. Dec. 1930.

Prenter, Regin: Grundtvig's Challenge to Modern Theology. Summary by Shirley Larsen, Grundtvig Studies 1973, pp. 219-225.

Rørdam, Thomas: The Danish Folk High Schools. Det danske Selskab, Copenhagen 1980. 196 pp.

Rohde, Sten: The Legacy of Grundtvig. Scandinavian Churches, ed. L.S. Hunter, London 1965, pp. 145-48.

Rosenberg, P.A.: Grundtvig. American-Scandinavian Review XXI, 1933, pp. 482-91.

Rush, F. Aubrey: Letters from England: Grundtvig Writes Home. The Norseman XI, pp. 263-270.

Savage, David J.: Grundtvig: A Stimulus to Old English Scholarship. Philologica: The Malone Anniversary Studies. Ed. by Thomas A. Kirby and Henry Bosley Woolf. Baltimore 1949, pp. 269-280.

Schroeder, Carol L.: A Bibliography of Danish Literature in English Translation 1950-1980. Det danske Selskab, Copenhagen 1982, pp. 66-70.

Simon, Erica: The Grundtvigian »Folkelighed« and Leopold Senghor's Négritude. Grundtvig Studies 1973. pp. 139-151.

Skarsten, Trygve R.: The Rise and Fall of Grundtvigianism in Norway. Lutheran Quarterly XVII. 1965, pp. 122-42.

Skovmand, Roar: The Rise and Growth of the Danish Folk High School. Grundtvig Studies 1973. pp. 85-100.

Skrubbeltrang, Fr.: The Danish folk high schools (Danish Information Handbooks). 2nd ed. Revised by Roar Skovmand, 1952. 88 pp.

Sneen, D.J.: Hermeneutics of N.F.S. Grundtvig. Interpretation XXVI. 1972. pp. 42-61.

Thaning, Kaj: »Man first«. Danish Foreign Office Journal, nr. 48, 1964. pp. 29-33.

Thaning, Kaj: Grundtvig, an Introduction. Grundtvig Studies 1973. pp. 68-84.

Toftdahl, Hellmut: Grundtvig and Søren Kierkegaard, Summary by Shirley Larsen, Grundtvig Studies 1973, pp. 225-232.

Toldberg, Helge: Zur Holsteinischen Reimchronik, Philologica: The Malone Anniversary Studies. Ed. by Thomas A. Kirby and Henry Bosley Woolf. Baltimore 1949, pp. 275-280, reprinted in the Festschrift Magen. Berlin 1958, pp. 392-405.

Tolderlund-Hansen, G.: Grundtvig's view of Christianity, in: The Danish Church, ed. Poul Hartling. Det danske Selskab, Copenhagen, no date, pp. 62-68.

Winkel-Horn, Frederik: History of the Literature of the Scandinavian North from the Most Ancient Times to the Present. Translated by Rasmus B. Anderson. Chicago 1884, IX 3 507 pp. (pp. 242-248 on Grundtvig).

e) *Summaries in English*

Aronson, Harry: Mänskligt och Kristent. Stockholm 1960. Summary: Man and Christian: pp. 294-301.

Bugge, Knud Eyvin: Skolen for livet. Copenhagen 1965. Summary by Noëlle Davies: The School for Life: pp. 361-369.

Grundtvig Studies. Copenhagen 1948ff. English Summaries in each volume.

Lundgreen-Nielsen, Flemming: Det handlende ord: N.F.S. Grundtvigs digtning, litteraturkritik og poetik 1798-1819. Copenhagen 1981. I+II. English Summary in vol. II.: The Active World: pp. 930-942.

Michelsen, William: Den sælsomme forvandling i N.F.S. Grundtvigs Liv. Copenhagen 1956. Summary: The Strange Metamorphosis in N.F.S. Grundtvig's Life: pp. 278-283.

Michelsen, William: Tilblivelsen af Grundtvigs Historiesyn. Copenhagen 1954. Summary: The Genesis of Grundtvig's View of History: pp. 349-362.

NOTE

This bibliography is based on "Bibliographie über Grundtvigliteratur in nichtskandinavischen Sprachen" by Eberhard Harbsmeier (*Grundtvig Studies* 1976, pp. 52-64, and, with supplements, *N.F.S. Grundtvig – Tradition und Erneuerung*. Copenhagen 1983 [the German edition of this book]).

List of Authors

* denotes published in English

SIGURD AAGE AARNES
b. 1924, M.A. Oslo University 1950, Grammar school teacher 1951-58 and 1960-62. Research grant from Science Research Council of Norway 1958-60. Associate Professor in Norwegian Literature at the Scandinavian Institute, University of Bergen since 1962. Ph.D. at University of Bergen 1962 with the dissertation *Grundtvig's Historiography and View of Life. An Examination of the Dual World Motif in the World Chronicles*, 1961.

Other Publications include *'Aesthetic Lutherans' and Other Studies in Norwegian Late Romanticism*, 1968 and *Test Borings in Norwegian Literature: A Literary History Guidebook*, 1983. Editor of four anthologies, mainly of Norwegian literature, and fifty or so articles.

K.E. BUGGE
b. 1928, B.D. 1954, D.D. 1965, Assistant Professor at Copenhagen University 1957, Associate Professor at the Royal Academy for Educational Studies 1964 and Professor there since 1981. Visiting Professor at Bangalore University 1970-71, 1974 and 1980.

Publications: *A Historical View of Theology and Education*, 1961; *The School for Life. Studies in Grundvig's Educational Ideas*, 1965; *Grundtvig's Educational World in Texts and Drafts, I-II*, 1968; *Basic Educational Ideas*, 3rd ed. 1981; *Ronald Goldman's Theory of Religious Education*, 1970; *Moral Education in Bangalore Schools, (Bangalore)* 1973.*

ANDREAS HAARDER
b. 1934, Gold Medal Winner at Aarhus University 1962, M.A. Aarhus 1964, University Scholarship at Aarhus 1964-69, Associate Professor at Aarhus 1969-75, Ph.D. 1975, Professor of English Literature at Odense University 1975, Committee Member of the Centre for the Study of Vernacular Literature in the Middle Ages, Odense University, (Chairman 1976-82).

Publications include *Beowulf. The Appeal of a Poem*, 1975* (doctorate), *The Epic Life,* 1979, and various articles for journals. Co-editor of *Medieval Scandinavia.** Public lecturer. *Funen's County Times* Research Prize, 1982.

JØRGEN I. JENSEN
b.1944, B.D., Associate Professor at the Institute of Church History at Copenhagen University since 1972.

Has published a number of essays on subjects in Church history, especially in the arts and Christianity, including Augustine's view of music; the grundtvigian theologian, Otto Møller; the modern Danish composer, Per Nørgård; the literary historian, Northrop Frye; and the relationship between the 12-tone composer, Josef Matthias Hauer and the dialogic philosopher, Ferdinand Ebner. Co-editor of the theological journal, *Phoenix.*

FLEMMING LUNDGREEN-NIELSEN
b.1937, studied in USA 1955-56, M.A. (Danish, German) 1965. University Scholarship at Copenhagen University 1965-68, Associate Professor in Danish Literature at Copenhagen since 1968. Ph.D. 1980.

Has published articles and reviews in various journals, newspapers and memorial volumes, and the books: *Studies in the Norse-Romantic Drama of Grundtvig,* 1965; *The Norse Narrative in the 18th Century. Contributions to the History of a Danish Genre,* 1968; *The Operative Word. The Poetry, Literary Criticism and Poetics of N.F.S. Grundtvig 1798-1819,* 1980.

WILLIAM MICHELSEN
b.1913, M.A. Copenhagen University 1939, Ph.D. 1954 with the dissertation *The Origin of Grundtvig's View of History* 1954. Associate Professor in Danish Language and Literature at Uppsala University 1942-50, Grammar School Teacher at Roskilde Cathedral School 1950-67, Associate Professor at the Institute of Scandinavian Studies, Aarhus University since 1968. Has also spent a year teaching at the Teachers Training College in Greenland and as Associate Professor at Gothenburg University.

Founder member of the Grundtvig Society in 1947, chairman 1972-79, co-editor of the society's yearbook *Grundtvig Studies* since 1968.

ROAR SKOVMAND
b.1908, pupil at Rødding and Askov Folk High Schools 1926-28. Studied

history and archaeology and took part in the Trelleborg excavations. M.A. 1935, Ph.D. 1944. Teacher of History at Askov Folk High School 1937-46, and at Krogerup Folk High School 1946-56. Government adviser on youth and adult education 1956-64. Professor of History at the Royal Academy for Educational Studies, Director of the Institute for the History of Danish Schools 1965-75.

Publications include: *Silver Hoards from the Viking Age,* 1942; *The Folk High School in Denmark 1841-92,* 1944 (doctorate); *Light Over the Land (on worker's education),* 1949, *The Popular Movements in Denmark,* 1951; *The Birth of Democracy 1830-70 (Politiken's History of Denmark vol.XI)* 1964.

CHRISTIAN THODBERG

b. 1929, pupil at Krogerup Folk High School 1948-49, B.D. 1955, Associate Professor of Philosophy at Copenhagen University 1960-64, Ph.D. 1966, Professor of Theology (specialising in Practical Theology) at Aarhus University since 1973. Canon at Aarhus Cathedral since 1973, Chaplain to the Royal Family since 1975. Committee Member of the Grundtvig Society, Chairman since 1979. Secretary of the Liturgy Commission under the Ministry of Church Affairs.

Has published among others: *The Tonal System of the Kontakarium. Studies in the Byzantine Psalticon Style** (Hist.Filos.Medd.Dan.Vid. Selsk. vol. 37, no.1); *The Neglected Service,* 1969, and editor/contributor to reports by the Liturgy Commission: no. 625 *Provisional Changes in the Service;* no. 750 *Bible Readings;* no. 848 *Episcopal Acts,* no. 973 (1983) *Proposals on the Baptism and Marriage Rituals.*

Grundtvig Publications: *A Forgotten Dimension in Grundtvig's Hymns. The Link with the Baptismal Ritual,* 1969; *Grundtvig's Sermons and Hymns, vols.* I-III in *Dansk Kirkesangs Årsskrift,* 1974ff; *For the Sake of Continuity, Words and Motifs in Grundtvig's Hymns and Sermons,* 1977; *N.F.S. Grundtvig's Sermons 1822-26 and 1832-39, vols I-XII (texts with detailed instructions).*

NIELS THOMSEN

b. 1938, B.D. Copenhagen University 1963, prize essay on Irenaeus 1960. Studied in Rome and Paris 1965-66 researching the theology and liturgy of the Early Church. Lecturer at Copenhagen University 1966-69. Rector of Ryslinge Free Church since 1969.

Publications include *The Strong-in-Faith Jutlanders and the Haugians,* 1961; *Gustav Brøndsted: History and Gospel,* 1965: and articles and essays for various periodicals. Has been active in the grundtvigian free school movement.

ANDERS PONTOPPIDAN THYSSEN

BIRGITTE THYSSEN
b. 1947, studied in the USA 1966-68, M.A. (History and Christian Studies) Aarhus University 1976, Teacher at Sixth Form College in Aarhus 1976-78, Research Fellowship at Institute for Church History, Aarhus 1978-80. Rector of Sahl and Gullev, Bjerringbro, since 1981. Various honorary offices.

Has written a lengthy dissertation on Grundtvig, the people and the grundtvigian movement.

ANDERS PONTOPPIDAN THYSSEN
b.1921, B.D. Copenhagen University 1947, D.D. Aarhus University 1958, Lecturer at Aarhus University since 1948, now Professor of Church History.

Research and Publications include: *Valdemar Brücker*, 1951; *Orthodox Grundtvigianism I-II*, 1954 and 1958; *The Neo-grundtvigian Movement*, 1958.

Led research project (1955-60) on popular religious movements and edited *The Breakthrough of Revivalism in Denmark 1800-1850 I-VII* with following contributions among others: *The Moravian Brethren*, vol.IV, 1967; *The Later Revivalism in Jutland*, vol. V, 1970; *Revivalism, Church Renaissance and the Nationality Struggle in South Jutland*, vol. VII, 1977. Editor/contributor to *Revivalism, and the Church in a Nordic Perspective*, 1969; *Cultural, Political and Religious Movements in the 19th Century (with H.P. Clausen and Poul Meyer)*, 1973; *The Structure of the Danish Folk Church*, 1979; *Secularization and New Religiosity (with Hans Iversen and Ole Riis)*, 1980; co-editor/contributor to *The Grundtvigian Peasant Environment (with Jørgen Holmgaard)*, 1981, and *The Church, the Crisis and the War (with I. Montgomery)*, 1982; publisher from 1977 of *History of Haderslev Diocese*. Articles in English include *The Rise of Nationalism in the Danish Monarchy* in *The Roots of Nationalism*, 1980.*

Translator

EDWARD BROADBRIDGE
b. 1944. Cert. Ed. London 1966, B.A. London 1967, M.A. Aarhus 1971. Teacher of English and Religious Studies at Randers County Sixth Form College 1967-79 and at Paderup County Sixth Form College since 1979.

Assistant Lecturer at Aarhus University 1971-76. Contributor to Arts Council New Poetry 1975 and Dictionary of Literary Biography (forthcoming). Editor of numerous EFL anthologies since 1974 and freelance co-producer for Radio Denmark since 1976. Translator for The Grundtvig Society since 1975, including English Summaries and, together with Niels Lyhne Jensen, A Grundtvig Anthology.

What can we learn from one another?

Aim and work of the Danish Institute

Det danske Selskab, The Danish Institute is an independent nonprofit institution for cultural exchange between Denmark and other countries. Abroad its aim is to inform other countries about life and culture in Denmark, particularly in the field of education, welfare services and other branches of sociology; at home to help spread knowledge of cultural affairs in other countries. Its work of information is thus based on the idea of mutuality and treated as a comparative study of cultural development at home and abroad by raising the question: What can we learn from one another? The work of the Danish Institute is done mainly in three ways:

1) By branches of the Danish Institute abroad – in Great Britain (Edinburgh) the Benelux countries (Brussels), France (Rouen), Switzerland (Zurich), Italy (Milan), West Germany (Dortmund) and its contacts in the USA and other countries. Lectures, reference work, the teaching of Danish, exhibitions, concerts, film shows, radio and television programmes as well as study tours and summer schools are an important part of the work of representatives of the Institutes that have been established abroad.

2) Summer seminars and study tours both in Denmark and abroad. Participants come from Denmark and other countries. The study tours bring foreign experts to Denmark and take Danish experts abroad. Teachers, librarians, architects and persons engaged in social welfare and local government make up a large part.

3) Publication of books and reference papers in foreign languages. Primary and Folk High Schools in Denmark, the library system, welfare services, cooperative movement, handicrafts, architecture, literature, art and music, life and work of prominent Danes are among the main subjects.

The author Martin A. Hansen called the Danish Institute a Folk High School beyond the borders: "In fact the work of the Danish Institute abroad has its roots in our finest traditions of popular education, which go right back to Grundtvig and Kold. The means and methods used are modern, the materials the very best and the approach to the work is cultural in the truest meaning of the word."

BOOKS ABOUT DENMARK

published by DET DANSKE SELSKAB (The Danish Institute) available from

Head Office in Denmark
DET DANSKE SELSKAB
Kultorvet 2
DK-1175 Copenhagen K.

Branch Office in Great Britain
THE DANISH INSTITUTE
3 Doune Terrace
Edinburgh EH3 6DY

U.S. Distribution
NORDIC BOOKS
P.O. Box 1941, Philadelphia, Pa. 19105

DANISH INFORMATION HANDBOOKS
Schools and Education in Denmark – The Danish Folk High Schools – Special Education in Denmark – Public Libraries in Denmark – Social Welfare in Denmark – Local Government in Denmark – The Danish Cooperative Movement

DENMARK IN PRINT AND PICTURES
The Danish Church – Danish Architecture – Danish Painting and Sculpture – Danish Design – Industrial Life in Denmark – The Story of Danish Film – Sport in Denmark – Garden Colonies in Denmark – Copenhagen, Capital of a Democracy – Aarhus, Meeting Place of Tradition and Progress – The Limfjord, its Towns and People – Funen, the Heart of Denmark – Women in Denmark

DANES OF THE PRESENT AND PAST
Danish Literature – Contemporary Danish Composers – Arne Jacobsen, by P.E. Skriver – Søren Kierkegaard, by Frithiof Brandt – N.F.S. Grundtvig, by Kaj Thaning – A Bibliography of Danish Literature in English Translation

DANISH REFERENCE PAPERS
Employers and Workers – The Ombudsman – Care of the Aged in Denmark

PERIODICALS
Contact with Denmark. Published annually in English, French, German, Italian, Netherlandish.
Musical Denmark, nos. 1-34. Published annually in English.

Nordic Democracy. *Ideas, Issues, and Institutions in Politics, Economy, Education, Social and Cultural Affairs of Denmark, Finland, Iceland, Norway, and Sweden.*
(Agent: Munksgaard, Copenhagen).